KENYA INTO THE 21ST CENTURY

Joseph Owino

Pen Press Publishers Ltd

KENYA INTO THE 21ST CENTURY
Copyright © Joseph Owino

ISBN 1-904018-67-X

First Published 2003 by
Pen Press Publishers Limited
39-41 North Road
London N7 9DP

Printed in Great Britain for Pen Press

KENYA INTO THE
21ST CENTURY

This book is dedicated to personal friends and to the everlasting memory of Kenya's heroes, the victims of Kenyan politics and corrupt practices, and the over 6,000 victims of Nairobi's Islamic Terrorist bomb: the late T J Mboya, M.P.; the late J M Karioki, M.P.; the late Kitili Mwendwa; First Kenya Chief Justice the late Dr Robert Ouko M.P.; the late Mrs Rose Wanjiku, mother and widow.

ABOUT THE AUTHOR

I have been a Kenyan refugee since April 1981, with refugee status to remain in Britain under the United Nations Convention Relating to the Status of Refugees of 28 July 1951 and its protocol of 4 October 1967. I am deeply grateful to Lord Eric Avebury, formerly of the British Refugee Council and chairman of the UK Parliamentary Human Rights Groups, Amnesty International and many friends, especially Mr and Mrs Anthony and Miranda Cordel, Rev. Emeritus John Stott of All Souls Church, Langham Place, Professor Emeritus James Huston of Regent College, Vancouver, Canada, and many others in Britain and Canada for their kindness and the help they have generously given me during the difficult part of my life as a refugee. I was released on 12 December 1980 on medical grounds, after more than ten years of imprisonment by the Kenyan authorities, suffering from heart and kidney failure and severely malnourished. I was allowed to come to Britain for medical treatment and arrived in Britain on 1 April 1981. I owe much, including my life, to many friends in Britain, who knew Kenya well and anxiously advised me and supported my application for political asylum. I now realise that, had I returned to Kenya at the time, I would certainly have been killed by the Kenyan authorities during the confusion which followed the 1982 coup attempt. The foiled attempt gave the government a pretext to eliminate all the known potential opponents and created maximum fear in the country. In prison, it was, perhaps, my will to survive, faith in Christ Jesus and prayers that enabled me to endure brutal physical and mental torture and a very poor diet. I was arrested in Dar es Salaam (Tanzania) on 27 March 1971, was refused a lawyer and returned to Kenya despite my plea to the Tanzanian government to protect me under the UN Convention. In Kenya I was charged with the offence shown below:

The reasons for your detention are as follows:

'You have conspired with others to overthrow by armed revolution the lawful Government of Kenya and to effect this have sought the assistance of a foreign Government'.

Duplicate Order served on the detainee personally by Mr Timothy M Mumbo S P and his signature obtained here below:

Signature
Date 30 April 1971
Time 16.35 hrs

THE PUBLIC SECURITY (DETAINED AND RESTRICTED PERSONS) REGULATIONS, 1966.

DETENTION ORDER

IN EXERCISE of the powers conferred by regulation 6(1) of the public Security (Detained and Restricted Persons) Regulations 1966, the Minister of Home Affairs, being satisfied that it is necessary for the preservation of public security to exercise control, beyond that afforded by a restricted order, over

JOSEPH DANIEL OWINO

(hereinafter referred to as the detained person), HEREBY ORDERS that the detained person shall be detained.

Dated this   day of

(D T arap Moi) MINISTER FOR HOME AFFAIRS.

Duplicate Order served on the detainee personally by Mr Timothy M. Mumbo S P and his signature obtained here below:

Signature
Date 30 April 1971
Time 16.35 hrs

THE PUBLIC SECURITY (DETAINED AND RESTRICTED PERSONS) REGULATION 1966 (L.N. 212 of 1966)

STATEMENT TO BE DELIVERED TO DETAINED PERSON WITH A COPY OF THE DETENTION ORDER (REG. 10(1))

(to be delivered as soon as reasonably practicable and in any case not more than five days after commencement of detention)

JOSEPH DANIEL OWINO

To a detained person by virtue of a Detention Order dated 30 April 1971.

This statement is written in the language, which you have stated you understand. The detailed grounds on which you are detained are:

Duplicate Order served on the

detainee personally by Mr Timothy M Mumbo and his signature obtained here below:

Signature
Date 30 April 1971
Time 16.35 hrs

The Provision of section 27(2) and (3) of the Constitution of Kenya concerning your case are as follows:

27, (2) Where a person is detained by virtue of such a law as is referred to in subsection (1) of this section the following provisions shall apply, that is to say:

(a) he shall, as soon as reasonably practicable and in any case not more than five days after the commencement of his detention, be furnished with a statement in writing in a language that he understands specifying in detail the grounds upon which he is detained;

(b) not more than fourteen days after commencement of his detention, a notification shall be published in the Kenya Gazette stating that he has been detained and given particulars of the provision of law under which his detention is authorised,

(c) not more than one month after the commencement of his detention and thereafter during his detention at intervals of not more than six months, his case shall be reviewed by an independent and impartial tribunal established by the Chief Justice from persons qualified to be appointed as a judge of the Supreme Court,

(d) he shall be afforded reasonable facilities to consult a legal representative of his own choice who shall be permitted to make representations to the tribunal appointed for the review of the case of the detained person; and

(e) as the hearing of his case by tribunal appointed for the review of his case he shall be permitted to appear in person or by a legal representative of his own choice,

(3) on any review by a tribunal in pursuance of this section of the case of a detained person, the tribunal may make recommendations concerning the necessity or expediency of continuing his detention to this authority by which it was ordered, unless it is otherwise provided by law, that authority shall not be obliged to act in accordance with any such recommendations.

Signature MINISTER FOR HOME AFFAIRS Date 30 April 1971 Time 16.35 hrs.

Duplicate Order served on the detainee personally by Mr Timothy M Mumbo S P and the signature obtained here below:

Without professional input, developing reliable contacts and support, it would not have been possible for me to write this book. As a mature research PhD student, I learnt a lot in preparing and maintaining a personal database and collecting data, which I started doing in 1988. Most of my work has been through desk research, newspapers, magazines, phone, fax, e-mail and travelling to many European countries and North America. However, I am indebted and owe much to the late Dr Robert Ouko, Minister for Foreign Affairs, for his encouragement and assistance which were invaluable and I felt deep sorrow over his untimely death. I thank several fellow Kenyans who, at a risk to themselves, their families and jobs, have helped me with my research, especially those at the University of Nairobi, members of the Institute of Development Studies, friends working with the Kenya Government, members of Parliament, those in KANU and those in Opposition Parties, Kenya Council of Churches, the Anglican church in Kenya, especially members of the Protestant Churches' Medical Association (PCMA), overseas NGOs and Charities working in Kenya. My many thanks and debts of gratitude to them is best given privately.

Secondly, I owe much help to the following organisations:

Chr Michelsen Institute, Department of Social Sciences and Development, Bergen, Norway, University of Stockholm, Department of Social Anthropology, Sweden and Dag Hammarskjold's Institute; FAO – UN-Food and Agricultural Organisation in Rome, ILO - International Labour Organisation in Geneva; United Nations Development Programme (UNDP) and the UN-World Food Programme (WFP) in New York; Food Production and Rural Development Division, Commonwealth Secretariat, Marlborough House, London SW1Y 5HX; Institute of Development Studies at the University of Sussex, Brighton BN1 9RE, England; The World Bank, The IBRD–International Development Association, 1818 High Street N W, Washington D.C. 20433, USA, and the European Union, General Secretariat of the ACP Countries' Group of States, Avenue George Henri 451, 1200 Brussels, Belgium.

Not to be overlooked is the help of several persons who gave generously of their time and thought. Many were called upon more than once, and some read portions of the manuscript. Since I cannot cite them all individually, I take this opportunity to thank them in general. While I profited greatly from all those who aided me, the responsibility for the final product is, of course, mine.

PREFACE

From the beginning of the 1990s, and now we have entered the twenty-first century, the economic development of the Third World has once again emerged as a fashionable subject. In the first year of the last decade, and at the close of the last millennium, we saw the fury over the Third World debt crisis. As the Prosecutor, People's Tribunal, Berlin, IFDA 1990, put it in an article entitled: 'Learning how to put people first':

> I am aware that even if we solve the present crisis, the world will experience the next one soon if we don't reform the international monetary system. Indeed, a new Bretton Woods is needed. Children are starving today because of the present crisis. It is a question of survival. Human development is at stake. And I sometimes think, when I read IMF reports dealing with economic performance criteria, this doctor might be able to conclude that an operation succeeded, but the patient died. The jury might consider to condemn the IMF and World Bank staff to live for one month in a Nairobi/Bombay slum, or in any country in the Third World as an educating experience in order to learn how to put people first.

The Bible teaches, 'It is useless to sew a new patch on an old garment. The worn-out fabric has no strength to support good cloth', and adds, 'it is of no profit to pour active wine into an old, dried, inflexible wine-skin'. (Jesus was referring to old systems of thought, old laws, old beliefs and the old life of an institution.) When looking at the reasons for the Third World's development failure, it is hard not to reach the conclusion that yesterday's solutions have caused some of today's problems. The time for piecemeal remedies or patchwork adjustment is long past. The world debt crisis, for example, is at such a pitch it is obvious that:

> ...economic development in much of the southern world is now not possible until the debt burden is cleared... There is little prospect of a return to sustainable growth in the North until southern purchasing power is renewed. That is a mutuality of interlocking interests that ought to prove irresistible. (M Meacher, 1994)

What is worth retaining from the Meacher analysis is that the crisis is of gridlock dimensions, and that the rationale for a solution is now inescapable. Whether it would be wise, as the quote suggests, to go on gunning for pre-crisis prescriptions, as if nothing had happened, is a moot point:

> ...the very concept of sustainable development, which in practice means sustainable growth, is a contradiction in terms. Northern income growth cannot be the solution to Southern poverty: a limitless expanding economic subsystem cannot go on growing indefinitely, eventually growing bigger than the necessarily limited ecosystem within which it developed. (Goodland and Daly, 1993)

Frances Moore Lappe challenges the basis of purely economic criteria: the mainstream, cure-all, supply–demand panacea and structural adjustment programme; according to her, famine is not caused by the scarcity of food but by scarcity of democracy and vested interests. She does not have in mind just any democracy, as the Republican or the so-called Christian right-wing North American democracy is capable of producing mortality rates twice as high as in Bangladesh: 'it is when the powerful consume the food of the weak and the weak have no means of preventing it, that a crisis situation ensues' (Lappe, 1993). The question of food (and lack of it) goes to the very root of economic and political malfunctioning. We live, in other words, in a world which, being either overdeveloped or underdeveloped, is fundamentally flawed. Landless Third World peasants work on fertile (virgin) land only to produce crops that are of no direct benefit to themselves. The price of one tea sachet will cover the wages of the female tea picker in Sri Lanka/Kenya/India for a whole week.

In 1980, the Independent Commission on International Development issues, led by the late former German Chancellor

Willy Brandt, submitted its report in the first year of the decade. A flurry of international gatherings drew the world's attention to the Third World predicament and, later in the same year, a Special Session of the United Nations launched the third Development Decade. The following year witnessed two development-related international conferences – on new and renewable energies and on the specific problems of the thirty-one 'least developed countries' – and one world 'premiere' when twenty-two ministers and heads of state met to discuss the main issues of poverty and development. As a result, this summit in 1983 saw the start of 'Global Negotiations', a planetary bargaining session covering all aspects of North-South economic relations.

It might, however, be safer not to have any illusions about the duration and outcome of this new spurt of interest in the 'Third World debt crisis, poverty and famine'. Perhaps the present excitement is only the latest manifestation of a cyclical phenomenon that, every ten years or so, compels the international community to express a sudden concern about the Third World's situation – before it rapidly returns to more important matters. Thus, the Pearson report, published at the end of the 1960s, was soon forgotten, and the development strategy adopted for the previous decade was neglected after a few years; as for the world conferences and summits of the North-South dialogue on environment/development, they have thus far yielded so few concrete results that we may be justified in doubting that the attention the 'Third World debt crisis, poverty and famine' still receives will last for long.

What is important is the realisation that what has been done by men can be undone by women/men working together. All that is needed is space to breathe, to be oneself, in order to make culture and write history. Making culture and writing history are what makes we humans specifically human. People are only too aware what their problems and their sufferings are: they live them, breathe them, bear them everyday. Their culture of silence is not the silence of those who cannot talk or cannot act. If they are silent, it is because they have been made silent, not by acts of God, but by acts of man. Development is not what happens around people or what is done for people or in the name of people.

People cannot be developed, they can only develop themselves.

It is therefore demeaning, dehumanising and eminently anti-development to define people by what they are not: ignorant, illiterate, poor, powerless. Most orthodox development starts out precisely from this point: an analysis of poverty, a definition of powerlessness, an ascription of the disease of ignorance, illiteracy, disability and invisibility. By contrast, I believe that development starts from the other end: from the power in the powerlessness, from the literacy in the illiteracy, from the ability in disability, from the formal in what the owners of development refer to as non-formal and informal. In other words, it sets out from where people are.

While certain failures of growth have now become evident, the very possibility of its continuation appears doubtful today. The shocks of the last two decades have shaken the optimism of the late 1960s and the prospects for 2000 have considerably darkened. The period of rapid economic expansion that the world experienced after World War II is probably over; in addition, there is cause to fear that the problems we have been unable or unwilling to solve during the previous decades: those, for instance, of environment, energy, unemployment, poverty and hunger, will take on added urgency in the year 2000 and beyond.

The need for change in development strategies is clearly felt today; the possible alternatives have so far been less precisely formulated. Ideas and proposals have not been lacking, but they have rarely gone beyond the level of objectives or even slogans. Basic needs, self-sufficiency, collective self-reliance: so many battle cries that, as yet, have had more political or emotional appeal than operational and concrete import.

This book is about Kenya's development programmes and proposes an alternative development strategy – (1) satisfaction of human needs and (2) a re-conceptualisation of the nature and value of work – the two pillars of the new economic framework that must now replace our simplistic and increasingly counter-productive reliance on 'more output' as the means to greater welfare. A third pillar, which comprises a major break with conventional economic thinking, is commitment to economic self-reliance.

(1) I strongly feel that Kenya must become a modern African state that remains as far as possible in harmony with the intrinsically African ideas and social values of the extended family system.

(2) I also believe that the theory of class struggle found in many advanced Western societies has no concrete historical relevance to Kenya or Africa. The traditional African values worthy of preservation in the new context are 'mutual social responsibility' and 'political democracy', for these would help to sustain organic society, preserve human dignity, maintain equality of opportunity, and prevent the emergence of 'antagonistic classes' as economic development proceeds in the twenty-first century.

(3) It is ironic how the Nairobi Islamic Terrorist bomb that killed 250 Kenyans and permanently wounded over 6,000 Kenyans, was a blessing in disguise; it brought back certain traditional values that we had lost in Kenya due to chronic poverty, tribalism and rapid westernisation; these are: African deep rooted communalism and egalitarianism, mutual social responsibility, the need for political democracy, the African universal charity, and the shared ownership of (as well as socio-religious attachment to) the land, that governs African societies. In an 'organic' sense, it showed that African society is a network of inter-dependencies marked by equality of sacrifice, contribution according to ability and returns according to need. It showed that African society in its own way is an exceedingly 'rational' society governed by values. These values in quite large measure have survived 'poverty', 'corruption' and 'unstable' democratic political structures since independence. The terrorist bomb showed Kenyans that our country remains rich with meaning to Kenyan people, even those caught up in the modern monetary economy. Without question, they have made part of the value synthesis that would underlie the coming development effort in the twenty-first century. If new democratic institutions and practices were made to reflect these social organic values, then everyone in Kenya would share both in 'poverty' and in 'prosperity' and there would be 'production by everyone' with

security for all.

The book is divided into nine chapters. It deals principally with the challenges of policy and strategic issues in development such as culture, social, economic and political development facing Kenya today as we enter the twenty-first century. It reviews the current Foreign Aid policy, strategy, management and its impact on development programmes retrospectively with focus on the past thirty years since independence and suggests alterations and reorientations based on new experience and changing circumstances.

CONTENTS

LIST OF TABLES AND
FIGURESTABLES

GLOSSARY

Baraza	Public meeting
Bwana mkubwa	Big man; used to denote people of authority or wealth.
Chai	Literally means 'tea'; used synonymously with bribe.
Harambee	'Let us pull together' derived from collective community labour; today used to denote any form of joint effort for development; Kenyatta's motto; and also inscribed in the Kenya coat of arms.
Jua Kali	Informal sector artisan
Magendo	Corruption; black marketeering
Majimboism	Administrative districts; decentralisation
Matunda ya uhuru	Fruits of Independence
Mpatanishi Arbiter!	Reconciler; Kiswahili word equivalent to Kikuyu Central Association (KCA) publication 'Muigwithania'.
Mwakenya	Contraction of 'Munugano wa Wasalendo kuikomboa Kenya' which may translate into 'Kenya Patriot' Redemption Union.
Mzalendo	Patriot
Nyayo	Literally means 'footprints/footsteps'; coined and used as a motto by Moi when he succeeded Kenyatta to denote that he would follow the path of his predecessor. The term has gradually acquired the meaning that Kenyans should follow in the footsteps of Moi.
Pambana	Struggle

Posho	Maize Meal
Shamba	Plot of land, farm, garden
Shifta Bandit	Applied in the 1960s by the Kenya Ethiopia governments to ethnic Somali dissidents who sought secession of parts of north-eastern Province from Kenya to join Somalia
Wanainchi	Literally means children of the soil; in common usage today, it means the citizen, the people, the common man and woman.

ACRONYMS AND ABBREVIATIONS

ACP	African, Caribbean and Pacific (Members States of the ACP-EU Convention of Lome)
ADEC	African Development & Economic Consultants
AfDB	African Development Bank
AfDF	African Development Fund
AI	Artificial Insemination
AIA	Appropriations-in-Aid
AIDS	Acquired Immune Deficiency Syndrome
AIE	Authority to Incur Expenditure
AMREF	African Medical Research foundation
APDK	Association for the Physically disabled of Kenya
ASAL	Arid and Semi-Arid Lands
BER	Business and Economic Research Company Ltd
BRP	Budget Rationalisation Programme
CAIS	Central Artificial Insemination Service
CBA	Cost-Benefit Analysis
CBK	Cooperative Bank of Kenya
CBS	Central Bureau of Statistics
CDR	Crude Death Rate
CID	Criminal Investigation Department
CIDA	Canadian International Development Agency
CIDIE	Commission for International Development Institutions on Environment
CIS	Cooperative Insurance Service
CLSMB	Cotton Lint and Seed Marketing Board
COTU	Central Organisation of Trade Unions

CMI	Chr. Michelsen Institute
CPS	Contraceptive Prevalence Survey 1984
CWSK	Child Welfare Society of Kenya
DAC	Development Assistance Committee
DANIDA	Danish International Development Agency
DC	District Commissioner
DDC	District Development Committee
DDF	District Development Fund
DDO	District Development Officer
DEC	District Executive Committee
DFP	District Focus Policy
DKK	Danish kroner
DLCOEA	Desert Locust Control Organisation for Eastern Africa
DSDO	District Social Development Officer
DTM	December Twelve Movement
EAC	East African Community
EADB	East African Development Bank
ESAMI	Eastern and Southern African Management Institute
EU	European Community
EIA	Environmental Impact Assessment
EIU	Economic Intelligence Unit
EMRG	Economic Management for Renewed Growth
EPU	European Payment Union
FAO	Food and Agricultural Organisation
FINIDA	Finnish International Development Agency
FIM	Finnish Marks
FLE	Family Life Education Programme
FPIA	Family Planning International Assistance
FPAK	Family Planning Association of Kenya

FUA	Fund Unit of Account (AfDF)
GMB	Green Belt Movement
GDP	Gross Domestic Product
GEMA	Gikuyu, Embu, Meru Association
GSU	General Service Unit
HIV	Human Immuno-deficiency Virus
IBRD	International Bank for Reconstruction and Development (World Bank)
ICDC	Industrial and Commercial Development Corporation
ICIPE	International Centre for Insect Physiology and Ecology
IIED	International Institute for Environment and Development
ILO	International Labour Organisation
IMF	International Monetary Fund
IMR	Infant Mortality Rate
IPA	Industrial Promotion Area
IPF	Indicative Planning Figure
ICOR	International Capital-Output Ratio
IDA	International Development Association
IDB	Industrial Development Bank
IFC	International Finance Corporation.
IFDA	International Foundation for Development Alternative
IGADD	Inter-Governmental Authority on Drought and development
IPFF	International Planned Parenthood Federation
IRH/FPP	Integrated Rural Health/Family Planning Programme
IRS	Integrated Rural Survey
ISM	Independent School Movement

JASPA	Jobs and Skills Programme for Africa
JKF	Jomo Kenyatta Foundation
KADU	Kenya African Democratic Union
KAF	Kenya Air Force
KANU	Kenya African National Union
KCA	Kikuyu Central Association
KCS	Kenya Catholic Secretariat
KGGCU	Kenya Grain Growers' Cooperative Union
KEMRI	Kenya Medical Research Institute
KENGO	Kenya Non-Governmental Energy Organisation
KETA	Kenya External Trade Authority
KFS	Kenya Fertility Survey 1978-1979
KIA	Kenya Institute of Administration
KIE	Kenya Industrial Estates
KIE	Kenya Institute of Education
KNAIS	Kenya National Artificial Insemination Service
KNCSS	Kenya National Council for Social Service
KNFC	Kenya National Federation of Cooperatives
KPLC	Kenya Power & Lighting Company
KPU	Kenya People's Union
KWDP	Kenya Woodfuels Development Project
LCB	Local Contract Bids
LPO	Local Purchase Order
LSK	Law Society of Kenya
MALD	Ministry of Agriculture and Livestock Development
MCSS	Ministry of Culture and Social Services
MCH/FP	Mother and Child Health/Family Planning
MDC	Ministry of Development Cooperative (Norway)
MEPD	Ministry of Economic Planning and

	Development
MEST	Ministry of Education, Science and Technology
MFP	Ministry of Finance and Planning.
MIDP	Machakos Integrated Development Programme.
MLD	Ministry of Livestock Development
MOCD	Ministry of Cooperative Development
MOF	Ministry of Finance
MOH	Ministry of Health
MOL	Ministry of Labour
MOTC	Ministry of Transport and Communication
MOW	Ministry of Works
MOWD	Ministry of Water Development
MP	Member of Parliament
MRP	Minor Road Programme
MUSWP	Minor Urban Water Supply Programme
MYWO	Maendeleo ya Wanawake Organisation
NCCK	National Council of Churches of Kenya
NCPB	National Cereals and Produce Board
NCPD	National Council for Population and Development
NCWK	National Council of Women of Kenya
NEHSS	National Environment and Human Settlement Secretariat
NFP	Natural Family Planning
NGO	Non-Governmental Organisation
NOK	Norwegian kroner
NORAID	Norwegian Agency for International Development
NSSF	National Social Security Fund
OAU	Organisation of African Unity
ODI	Overseas Development Institute

OECD	Organisation for Economic Cooperation and Development
OP	Office of the President
OPEC	Organisation of oil-exporting countries
PAL	Project annotated Listing
PCMA	Protestant Churches' Medical Association
PPCSCA	Permanent Presidential Commission for Soil Conservation and Afforestation
PTA	Preferential Trade Area for Eastern and Southern Africa
RARP	Rural Access Roads Programme
RDF	Rural Development Fund
RIDC	Rural Industrial Development Centre
SA	Salvation Army
SAS	Scandinavian Airline System
SADCC	Southern African Development Coordination Conference
SIDA	Swedish International Development Authority
SITC	Standard International Trade Classification
SRDP	Special Rural Development Programme
TAA	Technical Assistance Account (AfDF)
TARDA	Tan-Athi Rivers Development Authority
TFR	Total Fertility Rate
TRF	Tea Research Foundation
TRDP	Turkana Rural Development Programme
TSC	Technical Service Centre
UA	Unit Account (AfDB)
UK/MOD	United Kingdom/Ministry for Overseas Development
UN	United Nations
UNDP	United Nations Development Programme
UNECA	United Nations Economic Commission for

	Africa
UNEP	United Nations Environment Programme
UNFPA	United Nations Fund for Population Activities
UNICEF	United Nations Children's Fund
USAID	United States Agency for International Development
VADA	Voluntary Agencies Development Assistance
WFP	World Food Programme
WHO	World Health Organisation
WPGE	Working Party on Government Expenditure.

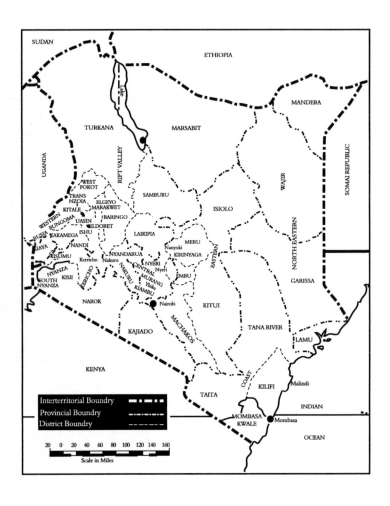

KEY FIGURES AND INDICATORS

Area:	582,644 km^2 (including inland lakes)
Total Population:	33.7 million Survey – University of Nairobi (mid 1997)
Annual Rate of growth:	3.6 per cent, 1995.
Density:	42.2 per km^2 (survey – University of Nairobi, 1992)

EDUCATION AND LITERACY:

Adult literacy Rate:	63% (1986)
Primary School Enrolment Rate:	104 per cent (1980)

HEALTH

Population per Physician:	10,000 (1989)
Population per Hospital Bed:	600 (1992)
Life expectancy:	men: 48; Women: 52 (1992)

MACROECONOMICS INDICATOR

Gross Domestic Product:	K.shs.95.26 (US$ 5.8) billion, Provisional 1985.
Gross Domestic Product per capita:	K.shs.4,792 (US$ 295)
Debt Service Ratio	(as a percentage of export of goods and Services): 26.2 per cent estimates 1988.

TRADE

Principal Exports (1989)	Coffee
	Tea
	Other agricultural produce
	Petroleum Product (re-export)

Principal Trading Partners: (1985).

	Export (per cent)	Imports (per cent)
Great Britain	18	14
Federal Rep. of Germany	13	9
Uganda	9	2.6
USA	5	5.5
Netherlands	6.8	
France	1.4	
EU	44.8	36.4
Saudi Arabia		18.6
Japan	1	10.2
Middle East		30.9
Tanzania	19.2	1.7
OPEC	3	29

SOURCE

Central Bank of Kenya, World Bank, African Review 1996
University of Nairobi and Economic Intelligence Unit, 1985.

Chapter I
CHANGING DIRECTION IN AFRICA

1.1   Introduction

Disappointments Of Independence

I plead sickness
I am an orphan
I am diseased with
All the giant
Disease of society
Crippled by the cancer
Of Uhuru
Far worse than
The yaws of
Colonialism,
The walls of hopelessness
Surround me completely
There are no windows
To let in the air
Of 'hope' for life!

Songs of a Prisoner
P.50 (1968)
Okot p'Bitek

Democracy, prosperity and self-rule, these were the vision and hopes of Africans at independence. But, today, few Africans express satisfaction with the fruits of 'freedom' (Uhuru). Those heady days of anti-colonial mobilisation, demonstrations and demands, though only three or four decades old, seem like an optical illusion, especially that which causes travellers in a desert to imagine they see an expanse of water, or it is like a dream from which one has awakened to another historical epoch. What went wrong?

Africa inherited handicaps from its colonial era. All colonial regimes, including apartheid South Africa, seemed to suffer from a peculiar form of political myopia - an inability to recognise when they had reached a terminal condition. In consequence, they never made provision for the proper continuation of the day to day tasks of governing the societies they were about to leave in the lurch. In practice this amounted to a failure to recruit and train an adequate number of civil servants. Partly, this arose from the culture of racial supremacy and arrogance clearly identified in an unquestioning belief among the colonial governors in the incapacity (assumed to be genetic) of those under their tutelage to perform any but the most humdrum and routine clerical chores. Educational systems therefore remained limited to the imparting of elementary literacy – and that in a foreign language – and, in the case of mission schools, an alien belief system. Since the very basis of 'modernisation and the much needed reform' (in the political sense of having clearly differentiated institutions to carry out allocative responsibilities) is the development of rational legal skills and secular values in decision-makers, it is clear that colonial education was woefully inadequate. As a result many of the successor regimes in Africa have been staffed by individuals who had only rudimentary and often contradictory ideas of how to approach often complex tasks of government. It can hardly be regarded as heinous then, that in many cases in sub-Saharan Africa, such ill-equipped individuals were forced to fall back on ill-considered and over-simplified authoritarian solutions doomed to failure from the start. 'Literally it has been for most African States a case of the blind leading the blind.' Notwithstanding lip-service ritually paid to democracy, this made it almost certain that this liberal Western political system was the first casualty in the new regimes. The blame for this must rest therefore in substantial part on the now departed colonial administration.

In mild mitigation, it must be said that the British in their last years, and even in the immediate post-colonial period, did attempt to make some amends by providing scholarships and military training for promising students to pursue higher studies in Britain. A cynic may dismiss this as paltry conscience payment for a major default, but the intention seemed to have been genuinely well meant. Unfortunately, like many well meaning actions, the scholarships scheme proved to have some serious dysfunctions. The most apparent one was the failure of the more highly educated indigent to return to his/her native land, there to employ his/her newly acquired talents in the tasks of development.

Since colonialism was undeniably an extractive enterprise, it should hardly be a matter of surprise that industries were seldom allowed to develop beyond an elementary level, and in consequence most of the successor African states were left with no resources other than primary produce (usually mono-cultural) to paddle on unpredictably fluctuating world markets. Hence, lack of administrative, management and professional experience was added to the technological handicap of having little capacity to diversify economic activity that would generate funds to support other non-profit-making developmental tasks. The result has been economic, social and political disaster!

Today, there is a realisation that a modern economy's most important capital resource is not money, raw materials or equipment but the human brain. The technological and cultural future of a nation depends on the way in which it develops, utilises and retains its talents and skills. 'The requirements of our science and technological based industries are outstripping our capacity to produce them' (President John F Kennedy). The term 'Brain Drain' is a fairly recent coinage but the process which it describes is as old as Western civilisation itself. Its causes for centuries, have been various, its effects upon the countries that were its beneficiaries were highly salubrious. Some brain drain eras were protracted but calm and peaceful; some were brief, stormy and spectacular.

The first recorded brain drain in Western civilisation took place during the reign of Ptolemy Soter in Alexandria when great numbers of intellectuals emigrated from Athens to the attractive atmosphere of the Ptolemaic Court with its incredible library. The conditions in both the losing and receiving states were characteristic: Athens had outlived its Golden Age and was falling into decay; Alexandria became a burgeoning culture and actively recruited Athenian intellectuals. Athens never recovered from its brain drain.

One of the most spectacular episodes in intellectual history resulted from the fall of the Byzantine Empire and the capture and sacking of Constantinople (Istanbul). First by the army of the Fourth Crusade (1204), then by Sultan Mohammed II (1453).

The artistic, literary and scientific wealth of the city-state before the disaster was almost inconceivable. The mass migration of intellectuals from Constantinople to Europe was directly responsible for (1) the cultural revival of Europe; (2) the end of the Dark Ages; (3) humanism; (4) the Renaissance. The emigrants established the great centres of learning, first at Padua, followed by Oxford, Prague, Heidleberg and many others. Without the brain drain from Constantinople, it is hard to imagine what the later history of Europe might have been. It need hardly be added that Constantinople though soon rebuilt by the Turks, never recovered its scientific leadership and cultural supremacy.

The United States of America (USA), profited from several minor but significant brain drains in the nineteenth century. The first of these began when Robert Owen, a Scots industrialist with socialistic ideas, arrived with his 'ship load of knowledge', to establish in 1825 the town of New Harmony and the beginnings of manufacturing industry on the lower Ohio River. Much more important in numbers and significance was the emigration of several thousand German intellectuals after the ill-fated demo-cratic revolution in Prussia in 1848. One of the chief beneficiaries of that movement was the American elementary and secondary public school system. Many schools to this day still carry the name of Carl Schurz, one of the leading figures in the emigration of 1848.

In our own troubled and unstable twentieth century, the greatest mass exodus of scientists, scholars, writers and artists mostly from Europe to America was set in motion by the rise of Adolf Hitler and his National Socialism. It began as a trickle in 1930, grew to a stream by 1934 and rose to a flood after 1938. Its effects on Europe as well as America are incalculable. The very outcome of World War II was to a great extent determined by this brain drain. Germany's failure to develop atomic weapons resulted largely from the loss of the best scientific brains. America's efforts, on the other hand, were vastly strengthened by the brilliant emigrants – Albert Einstein and Enrico Fermi to mention only two.

The long-term economic and social prosperity of a country depends on the knowledge available to it. Progress and development is based on knowledge - and knowledge is used by brains and increased by brains. 'Brains are like hearts – they go where they are appreciated' (Robert McNamara, President of the World Bank). Books are often thought to be the most significant embodiments of knowledge, but they are merely passive repositories. Human brain, talent and skill are the most vital.

The most precious wealth of any nation is its people and it is investment in those people that can turn around the economic destiny of any nation. Of course you need natural resources, but these are secondary. The notion that human brains, talent and skill are the most vital form of industrial capital may seem self-evident and trivial, but it is nevertheless true that an awareness that progress and development can be seriously impeded by lack of talent and skill has only developed during the last few years. People now realise that departure of talented, trained and experienced people from a country is at least as serious in the long run as an outflow of money. The slowness of this realisation has largely been due to the determination over the last hundred years by the economists who regarded men/women in general as a source of labour rather than wisdom. But modern industry and technology is based on man/woman's science, not his/her physical effort, and science depends on (indeed, is) knowledge.

Leading industrial analysts and economic planners contend that in the years ahead, the contribution of education to economic growth will exceed that of physical capital. And they contend that the 'return on invested capital' in science and formal knowledge will probably account for more than one fifth of a nation's growth. They are probably right, for the contribution of the knowledge revolution to economic growth has so far more than measured up to expectations. Knowledge has become a major national resource as important to a country as its land and mineral wealth. High technology is now the most dynamic and leading global industry; computer systems and software, semiconductors, advanced communications, aerospace and space commercialisation, bio-technology and pharmaceutical, medical technology, new materials and chemicals, electronic equipment - all these fields are changing our lives in dramatic ways and creating advances vital to economic growth and productivity in all industries.

But knowledge by itself is not enough; there must be the management and administration which knows how to put that knowledge to work. It was a characteristic of the Industrial Revolution that nations kept an anxious eye on the flow of goods and raw material, and maintained accurate accounts of their balances of trade. It is a symptom of the Knowledge Revolution that nations are becoming equally sensitive to the 'balance of ability'.

Alexandria was the first state to enjoy an organised brain gain. With the USA, the lure is the accumulation and development of scientific knowledge. In Alexandria it was Ptolemy's library. This storehouse of knowledge was conceived on a tremendous scale, and historians say that whenever a stranger brought an unknown book to Egypt, he had to have it copied for the library. For the purpose of dissemination, a considerable staff of copyists were engaged continually in making duplicates of all the more popular and necessary works, and in time Alexandria's library became the book-selling business that we know today.

Callimachus, the head of the library during the time of Ptolemy II and III, saw to the systematic arrangement and cataloguing of the voluminous accumulation of knowledge that attracted scholars from all over the known world (though mostly from Athens). Ptolemy II ingeniously offered these learned men twice the salary earned in their country of origin to stay and work in Alexandria, and Alexandria's heyday had begun. Today's situation contains striking parallels; for developing nations that have suffered a serious brain drain, the future does not look rosy. The responsibility lies with those reactionaries in the 'brain drain' countries who cannot or will not adapt as society requires. The problem is that the knowledge revolution has introduced change with such bewildering speed that the average human being cannot adapt to it. When a man/woman is uncertain of his/her direction he/she stands still.

History is repeating itself. As was the case with the decaying world of ancient Greece, the discovery of the extent of the 'brain drain' from the former Soviet Union, Lebanon, Yugoslavia, Iraq, Uganda, Somalia, South Africa, Hong Kong, Iran, Liberia and Rwanda, has stunned Development Agencies (UN, IMF, IBRD, OECD etc.), governments and industrial leaders, and presented them with the complex questions for which nothing in their past experience has prepared the answers. How much do we care about emigration of our scientists, scholars, writers and artists? At what point does this emigration become a drain? How is the drain going to affect industry and the economy at large? Does the brain drain, in the long term, constitute a service or a disservice to humanity at large? Is the brain drain only symptomatic of a much larger international problem?

As regards developing countries, it is estimated that out of a total of over three million scientists at present working in the USA, Britain, Canada, Australia, France, Germany, 45,000 to 50,000 are from India. At the end of 1989 there were 4,745 doctors with Indian qualifications employed in the National Health Service in the UK. One wonders whether the relative contribution of these medical doctors to the British health services is less than, equal to, or greater than, the contribution they might have made within the complex system of the Indian health service?

A senior government official in Malawi told me, 'the illiterate mass of people have no understanding or appreciation of the efforts of scientists or technologists. High intellectual activity is often considered as a "luxury" in a country where the mass of people do not have enough to eat, have a very poor health service system, poor housing and water supply. The high salaries seem inexcusable. Furthermore, political instability does not encourage people to follow any sustained work programme'. This simply adds to a maxim that 'Just as ignorance breeds poverty, poverty breeds ignorance in the next generations.'

The lack of facilities for higher education compels young men/women from developing countries to venture abroad for their higher studies, and they become exposed to the temptations of life in a sophisticated society before they have learned a sense of responsibility to their society. Many of the students sent abroad for study do not come back and those who do not return are usually the best ones. Those who come back do not find the proper environment in which to develop. The private sector (the multinationals) absorb the best of the returning graduates, denying government the manpower on which to base its long-term plans. Jealousies arise between departments over those few returning graduates in government service. Such returning graduates joining government service are, on many occasions, exposed to the vagaries of periodic political upheaval and instability.

1.2 Development Aid and Self-Reliance

The concept of development has probably existed for centuries in rudimentary form, but it was only after World War II and the initiation of decolonisation that social scientists were impelled towards defining, articulating and analysing the concept, indeed, it was the interdisciplinary nature of this task that many social scientists found particularly attractive. Nevertheless, it was the economic aspect of the definition that has come to dominate the so-called science of development. In common parlance, development has come to mean a high level of productivity, income and consumption. Conversely, underdevelopment means low levels of all these three. However, closely associated with under-development is the value judgement that the conditions are undesirable, need to be changed and can be changed.

It is here that sociologists, economists and political scientists come into their own, postulating the allied concept of modernisation. This refers to the process by which an under-developed society transforms itself into a developed one in economic terms and, in doing so, undergoes a metamorphosis, not only in the means and scale of the production of goods, but also in the social organisation and value system of the society undergoing the process. Unfortunately, the concept has a strong ethnocentric aspect, since it assumes that the institutional differentiation and political norms (the separation of powers for instance) that characterise 'developed' western societies are *ipso facto* superior to those of societies that have found it quite possible in the past to function without them. Clearly this is a matter of cultural perspectives, in which many societies may be patronisingly designated as developing or even underdeveloped; where the acquisitiveness of western individuals is more highly valued in development than the person who is in serene harmony with the environment, at the cost of material progress.

The word 'development' has cast its shadows over the landscape of international relations. Development can justifiably be called the surrogate religion of the second half of the twentieth century. One of the more revealing findings of contemporary anthropology is that all societies and civilisations, whatever their nature – and this includes Western civilisation – are underpinned by beliefs and myths. Myths are the products of a long evolution in humanity's creative imagination. While they are unreal (false) when measured against tangible reality, they nevertheless ring true inside the social imagination in which they originally took shape. In other words, the benchmark of the 'truth' of a mythical narrative is the extent of its social efficacy (Traore, 1990). Uniquely in human history though, modern Western myths stood out by the tangible demonstration they gave of the fact that it was possible to attempt the impossible, namely to step outside the realm of the imaginary and give actual shape in 'true' reality. It is this power to achieve against all the odds what has been held to be impossible that, more than anything else, accounts for the fact that Western myths were able to break the hold of their more traditional and ancient rivals and, eventually, to supplant them. Greek–Roman antiquity can be said to have been ruled by cosmology, the Dark and Middle Ages by theology, and the modern age by enlightenment, which is premised on the assumption that anthropos has broken free at long last and inaugurated the era of self-rule. This modern religion boasts its own deities, its own creed, its own values, ethos, rites and rules. The supreme rule, no doubt, is an unswerving allegiance and obedience to the invisible hand of the forces of market, 'as if they were laws laid down by a new universal god, a religion without atheists' (Galeano, 1992). Throughout history, civilisations have come and gone, each in turn making its impact on environment. In the end, however, they were always re-absorbed into nature.

What distinguishes Western modernity from all preceding civilisations is that it persistently and systematically sets out to separate rather than combine. It replaces harmony with conquest, holism with hierarchy, recognition with alienation, quality with greater value attached to what is tangible and measurable. Competition is given preference over cooperation, consumerism overrides welfare, and harmonious people's development surrenders to economic growth. Whereas the unifying strength of all previous civilisations had been the art of achieving harmony and balance, now a sense of impending doom and mortal threat prevails: the threat to environment, by-product of the age of conquest, has turned into a threat to humanity itself, bringing the realisation that conquest carries in it the seeds of terminal ruin and defeat. On the threshold of the third millennium we have witnessed the death of socialism, the death of radical ideologies (except of the far right) and triumph of market capitalism and liberal democracy, at the same time as an unprecedented impoverishment of the living environment. According to US State Department analyst Francis Fukuyama, this end of the history of ideas, consolidated by the de facto hegemonic reign of capitalism, inaugurates the 'era of the last man', in which we are condemned to become, again, bestial 'first men' (Fukuyama, 1992). We are asked to believe that history itself has come to an end, the fusion of liberal democracy and industrial capitalism now representing 'the only viable base for modern human society' (Fukuyama, 1989).

This is now the outcome, three centuries after Leibnitz's vision of unlimited progress. Those axiomatic questions that have beset the human mind for so long – about the meaning of society and how it ought to be organised, about human rights and duties, the meaning of human freedom and creativity, and how all these relate to environment – appear now to have been finally settled with the balance tipping heavily in favour of the West and its own criteria about what is valuable and good. While the West remains obsessed with material accumulation, with masculinity and conquest, Hinduism's five thousand-year-old tradition sees civilised life quite differently: it insists on 'non-violence', on renunciation, on the inner life and on 'the female' as pillars of society. It firmly holds to the principle that human life cannot be measured by material possession and that the goal of life cannot possibly lie in mindless conspicuous consumption.

Throughout the disasters of colonialism that beset India, and the triumphs that uplifted her throughout her long history, India has steadfastly allowed herself to be directed by the same lodestar: the identification of humanity with the whole of creation, a unity in diversity. Indians may look very poor to rich Westerners, Mark Twain once remarked, but in matters of spirit, 'it is the Westerners who are the paupers and the Indians are the millionaires'. Gandhi could shrug his shoulders at the paraphernalia of modern life: the good life and happiness cannot possibly be built on cold glorified pieces of paper and metal (money) which must of necessity conflict with Swaraj, the calm freedom to follow the personal truth. Nehru and the Hindu Nationalists, begging to disagree, signed up the entire sub-continent for modernisation, elsewhere described as 'westernisation in depth' (Latouche, 1983). The West's obsession with the senses, with material wealth pursued for its own sake, is for divine Krishna the very ruin of reason and destroyer of humanity, the cause of war, violence and terrorism.

Similar emphases and cultural overtones can be found in other non-Western civilisations and religions: the civilisation of the ancient Americas, those of Mesopotamia (now Iraq), the birth place of the written word, of the ancient kingdoms of Egypt and of Kush, the land of the 'Pharaoh', and the other ancient civilisations and empires of Africa, the 'cradle of humanity'. Chinese civilisation revolves around the search for a moral order on earth, sustained by virtue, ritual and reverence for the ancestors. The millennial wisdom about the elemental balance – between Yin and Yang, water and fire, sun and moon, female and male, darkness and light, white and black - underlies all Chinese thought, be it in matters of science, medicine, food or philosophy.

These truly ancient values have survived all aspects of Chinese life through the ages, including the upheavals of the 1949 communist revolution and the crushing of the democracy movement on Tiananmen Square in 1989.

Non-Western cultures are based on the idea of the godhead as immanent; their traditions and history are embedded in oracy and are therefore in a constant state of flux. In stark contrast, the Western God is transcendent, monotheistic, distant, and a literally supernatural God. The West's religion can be characterised as 'the religion of the Bible' (book), with a transcendent truth that is frozen, on record, safe, fixed and immune to human tampering. It seems not to matter that the book itself originated in the living and imaginative oral traditions of a small, pastoral, semi-nomadic group of people, whose terms of reference, vocabulary and precepts in the twentieth and twenty-first centuries is outdated and hardly fits a drastically changed urbanised world and its industrial complex.

Last but not least, the Western God is a male God, and its priesthood has always been a male priesthood, an institution which fits even less well the drastically changed and emerging gender equality perceptions of our present secularised age. According to Gerald Bartholomew (1990), in the last resort all civilisations make the culturally charged choice between equality and freedom: equality translates into internal mechanisms geared to the inhibition of the production of surpluses, while freedom translates into a valorisation of the production of surpluses which is typical of the spirit of capitalism. For the former, surplus is the 'cursed part'. The latter (Promethean) societies elevate the art of extracting surplus to a supreme virtue, even to the extent of reducing people themselves to the status of surplus (justifying slavery/labour) at the service of the maximisation of profits.

All of this is part of a carefully cultivated mystification which allows the developed countries to indulge in superiority delusion, while the 'underdeveloped' interiorise the myth that they are indeed incapable, incompetent and are 'the problem'. A decolonising of the mind on the part of the 'under-developed' and 'developed' alike is overdue.

Development starts in people's minds, in their attitudes, value systems and judgements. Julius Nyerere's now quite familiar dictum is truer than ever: 'people cannot be developed, they can only develop themselves'.

The root of the 'Alternative Development' philosophy can now be traced back to the Cocoyoc Declaration on Self-reliance, adopted by thirty-two social and natural scientists gathered at Mexico City in 1974, which included the statement that development growth processes that do not lead to fulfilment, here and now, of people's basic human needs, are devoid of meaningful content. Self-reliance as an alternative development model, asks fundamental questions about the what, the how, the why, the 'for whom' of development. It was popularised by the late Dag Hammarskjold Foundation at the University of Uppsala, Sweden.

Self-reliance is a basic pillar of Alternative Development. However, the concept is often misunderstood. It does not mean autonomy or self-sufficiency, although either of these states may occasionally develop from it. It suggests a regeneration or revitalisation through one's own efforts, capabilities and resources. Strategically it means that what can be produced (or what can be solved) at local level should be produced (or should be solved) at local levels. The same principle holds for regional and national levels.

Self-reliance changes the way in which people are enabled to perceive their own potentials and capabilities, which have often been, or still are, self-depreciated as a consequence of the dominant centre–periphery relations. The reduction of economic dependency, one of the aims of self-reliant development, is not intended to be a substitute for trade and exchange *per se*. There are always goods or services that cannot be generated or provided locally, regionally or nationally. Hence, self-reliance must necessarily achieve a collective nature. It must turn into a process of interdependence among equal partners as a means for solidarity over blind competition.

As opposed to the traditional paradigm, mainly concerned with the generation of material satisfiers (without much equity in the distribution), self-reliant development allows for a more complete and harmonious satisfaction of the entire system of fundamental human needs. It does not generate satisfiers only for the needs of having, but for the needs of being as well. Through the reduction of economic dependency, subsistence is better protected, in as much as economic fluctuations (recessions, depressions, etc.) do more harm where the structure of centre-periphery relations prevails. It enhances, furthermore, participation and creativity. It stimulates and reinforces cultural identity by increasing self-confidence. A better understanding of productive processes and technologies is also achieved when communities manage themselves.

Third World, as a politically weighted concept, becomes, as compared with First, a synonym for powerlessness, non-possession, non-access and non-entitlement. It is also synonymous with invisibility, displacement, exclusion and a culture of silence. Thus understood, the notion of the Third World escapes and transcends, for example, the North-South framework of the Brandt Report (Brandt, 1980). The unequal character of capitalist expansion, that cannot be overcome within the framework of capitalism, objectively requires that the world be remade on the basis of an alternative social system; and the peoples of the periphery are obliged to be aware of this and insist upon it, if they want to avoid the worst, that is, reaching the point of genocide, the real danger of which is amply shown by the history of capitalist expansion:

> The Third World: a political concept from my experience of the Third World in the First World such as the ghettos in the United States... Discovering the Third World in the First, I also became aware of the presence of the First World in the Third World... Third World is basically a political concept. The so-called 'First World' has within, its own Third World: the Third World has its First World represented by its ideology of domination, of power of the ruling classes. The Third World is, in the last analysis, the world of silence, of oppression, of dependence, of exploitation, of violence exercised by the ruling classes on the oppressed. (Freire, 1983)

Capitalism proposes to save the life of a few at the expense of the death of the many. This is, ultimately, an option for death. The

only valid alternative is life for all. Failing this would be tantamount to accepting the death of many, which, in the end, can
only spell death for all (Richard, 1993). Chomsky describes the
freedom claimed by the West as the 'freedom to exploit'. In
essence, the message of the New World Order is: 'we are the
masters, and you shine our shoes... The weak shall inherit
nothing' (Chomsky, 1991). In Africa, the combination of the
Cold War and apartheid created a hell on earth for millions. 'Who
knows', asks Mwalimu Nyerere, 'what lies ahead in the future
while the law of the jungle continues?' (Nyerere, 1992).

There has been a great deal of debate in the North–South
negotiations between Developing, and the Developed Countries
about a new international economic order. The debate has
covered a wide range of issues, such as: more aid to developing
countries, freer access to developed countries markets for
developing countries' exports of primary products and
manufactures, measures to stabilise the foreign trade of
developing countries, regulation of the transfer of technology, a
code of conduct for transnational corporations, and more control
of international economic agencies by developing countries.
These proposals were included in the report of the Independent
Commission on International Development Issues (1980),
commonly known as the Brandt report. Most of them, however,
did not go to the heart of the problems arising from the old
international economic order (Lewis, 1978a). These are essentially
the problems arising from what has been defined as the low level
of development of some developing countries. In order to deal
with them, the developing countries need much greater access to
long-term aid aimed primarily at promoting such development
and some of the ways in which aid can promote the development
objectives.

The fundamental problem, which development aid was designed to mitigate, was the impact of industrial society on the rest
of the world. The economic imbalances which exist between rich
and poor countries go back to the industrial revolution, which
began in Britain almost three centuries ago. This meant that
Third World countries have very large un-met basic human needs
– in food production, nutrition and agriculture, health services

including demographic conditions, education including literacy, shelter and clothing, energy, transport and communications, conditions of work and employment, recreation and entertainment, aggregate consumption, social security, human freedom, and environment protection etc., these stemmed from the consequences of colonialism. What, then, should be the role of development aid? If the underlying problems are so vast and aid so relatively small, is it worth giving aid at all? Part of the answer lies in its catalytic effects. Aid as a catalyst for change, applied in the right and innovative way, to real problems and situations, can have results out of all proportion to the resources devoted to it. Aid is supposed to be essentially neutral. It can do good, and it can also do harm. But, development aid makes up only a very small proportion of the total resources that flow from industrial countries to developing countries: loans, investment and trade account for far more.

1.2.1 PURPOSE OF AID

International aid has been given for a variety of motives. One important motive has been to use aid as an instrument of Foreign Policy, to win or at least keep friends among the recipient countries, to make them politically stable and bring them closer to the ideology of the donor countries. Hence national development aid agencies are mostly located in the ministries of foreign affairs of donor countries and their decisions influenced by career diplomats. It was under the influence of this motive that the volume of aid increased during the cold war between East and West. But aid as such has not been very effective in winning friends. It was perhaps the disappointment with its actual results that led to the stagnation of aid since then. When aid is primarily an instrument of foreign policy, the principal actors are governments trying to influence one another. Recipient countries tend to be treated as equal units represented by their governments, irrespective of their poverty or need for aid. The result is that the aid given to each country is less influenced by the need, as determined by population or poverty. Thus, the amount of aid per head of population in recipient countries tends to vary universally with population. Another consequence of the foreign policy interest in aid is that much of it is given on a bilateral basis, involving costly aid administration and duplicating work among themselves and *vis-a-vis* the multilateral institutions.

Another motive behind development aid has been to promote the exports of donors to recipient. One effect has been the prevalence of tied aid. This practice reduces the real value of aid as recipients have to pay higher prices when restricted to purchasing from a particular country. For example, in a pioneering study, Haq (1965) estimated that the excess costs of the tying of aid received by Pakistan was at least 14 per cent of total aid; similar estimates were found in later studies of other countries (UNCTAD, 1967)

The most important motive for aid giving, however, is the humanitarian one born out of the perceived moral obligation of the rich to help the poor. The humanitarian motive has been the basis of charitable assistance to relieve immediate distress in the case of famine and natural disasters at all times, within and between nations. When Clare Short, the International Development Secretary, criticised the Sudan appeal as unnecessary and misleading, stressing that the cause of the famine in South Sudan was war and not drought, she was howled down by outraged MPs and bewildered aid agencies. Who could possibly question something that is so obvious, so incontestably right? Who could deny a hungry child?

The major charities are the last sacred totem of late twentieth-century Britain, and have been largely immune from public scrutiny and public criticism. But the history of recent disaster emergencies such as Somalia, Rwanda and now Sudan prove that the aid world's simplistic mantras are very far from the truth. 'High-profile interventions from outside obviously have a role to play in relieving immediate human suffering, but they also contain a very large possibility of prolonging the conflict' says Rakiya Omaar, of African Rights, an agency that has been severely critical of the work of charities. 'They can end up giving a helping hand to one or other of the combatants. This is an issue that non-governmental organisations (NGOs) are not willing to address, and that is because it is a matter of institutional survival. They need a presence on the ground to raise money and justify their existence. But they rarely ask themselves: "Are we making a bad situation worse? Are we prolonging the war?"'

This is not a rhetorical issue, but a very real one that has been painfully learned, though insufficiently addressed, in the debacle of George Bush's Operation Restore Hope in Somalia in 1993, in the feeding of the Hutu army of genocide in the refugee camps in Zaire and Tanzania in 1994 and in the Serb siege of Sarajevo. 'I see this as the central issue of this decade,' says Roy Williams, head of the foreign disasters office in USAID, the largest governmental development agency, with a budget of billions of dollars. 'In the past, we have acted on a simple sense of moral outrage, as if that was the only reality you had to operate in. But, as in Rwanda and Bosnia, we found that there are others all too willing to take advantage. We have got to help, but how can we be sure that we are doing the right thing, rather than acting just on a sense of outrage? We are still working at it.'

Williams's words point to the hidden contradiction that underpins the famine business. It is the contradiction between the simplistic, emotive messages about starving children, promulgated by the media and the messy, confused political reality of the Sudan. That reality is what the aid agencies euphemistically term 'complex emergencies', and includes disasters induced by war. No one can explain the complexities of Sudanese politics in a book mainly dealing with Kenya. But everyone can relate to starving and dying babies in their mothers' arms. It is in the institutional interests of NGOs to repeat this simple message and raise funds from a deeply concerned public or from a pressured government. But those funds then have to be spent in the confused political minefield of Sudan, where real-life warlords and a diabolical Islamic and tyrannical government is in power; and where there is no escape from the politics of war, regardless of how kind or generous or humanitarian your intentions are.

For understandable reasons, no one from the aid agencies wants to talk in public about the diversion of food aid to fighters, the manipulation of aid workers by combatants and the reinforcement of the authority of the nasty government/warlords by agencies working in their territory. Such issues would only confuse the public at home and compromise that vital but naive humanitarian desire to help by handing over cash.

The war is normally explained as a struggle between northern Muslim Arabs versus southern African Christians: the Islamic government in Khartoum wanting to forcibly convert and politically enslave or exterminate the southern population. The reality is more complicated because of the oil in the Sudanese south: in the past ten years, the southern opposition who are fighting for survival has splintered and fragmented along tribal lines, or even into warring factions within the same tribal group, such as the Dinka or the Nuer.

The emergence of large-scale international aid to the developing countries is basically due to a humanitarian motive, although other motives have influenced the ways aid has been distributed and administered. The case for more aid and more effective use of aid rests ultimately on an appeal to the humanitarian motive and in demonstrating that aid can indeed relieve poverty. But while acute distress due to the causes of famine, drought and conflict occurs only occasionally and is amenable to assistance over relatively short periods, the developing countries suffer from a chronic condition of mass poverty. Therefore what distinguishes international aid in its present form is that aid is now addressed to helping developing countries, not just to relieving present poverty, but to remedy the underlying causes of such poverty. The problem of achieving these objectives as rapidly as possible is the main challenge facing development aid policy.

Aid alone cannot solve the problems of mass poverty in the developing countries. First, the concept of development will have to change in order to satisfy the urge of the people in developing countries to participate in the events and processes that shape their lives. Secondly, the governments in the developing countries must decentralise and bring aid closer to the people. Aid can only take the form of resources transferred from one set of countries to another, therefore a large part of it consists of transfers between governments; 'the participants in the charitable transfer are not individuals, but nation-states jealous of their sovereignty'. Now people are no longer prepared to bow to the dictates of a far-off centre. One is seeing increasing ethnic disruption and political violence and, at the end of it, what people are saying is that, they want political and economic power to be shared with them. So effective decentralisation of power becomes a condition for development. Unfortunately, many governments in developing countries have not understood the message. On the other hand, international development aid suffers by its very nature, from two limitations mentioned above in meeting this challenge. The root causes of mass poverty cannot be overcome by donor governments simply handing sums of money to recipient governments. To be successful, the transfer of resources must be based on an analysis of the causes of mass poverty.

In the 1950s/1960s the theory that inspired international aid relationships was that, mass poverty was due to the low levels of national incomes in developing countries, due in turn to the absence of some 'missing components'. The search for these missing components identified a number of candidates including: shortage of capital, shortage of foreign exchange, low level of education, poor health and nutrition, rapid population growth and weakness of the agricultural sector, etc. The role of international aid was, therefore, seen as remedying each of these factors, the fashions in opinion changing briskly at every annual conference on the subject. In practice, however, much of the flow of aid was used to expand the modern sector, especially the industrial sector in urban areas. For example, most of the development aid from Britain to India went to major industrial projects, especially power, including coal, and provided the infrastructure for that purpose because this is what the recipient government wanted to do anyway (and not what the people wanted). Most of the poor Indians, however, were in the traditional sectors and in the rural area. Therefore, although national income increased in some cases quite rapidly, not necessarily due to aid, there was little impact on mass poverty.

But, since the late 1970s there has been a change of emphasis especially with international NGOs. Nowadays, the emphasis is on providing development aid so that it directly reaches the poor. More can certainly be done in this way. For example, in the proposal for the third UN Development Decade for the 1980s to provide drinking water supply to all people in the developing countries, it has been argued that:

> Linking aid to projects with a predominantly social rather than economic content might generate more warmth and a broader based appreciation of the benefits of aid. When one builds houses and clears slums rather than set up industries, the points of conflict on the issue of economic policy are minimised, and the dialogue on overall performance gets automatically divorced from particular acts of assistance. (Patel, 1971)

But there is a limit to the extent to which mass poverty can be relieved by the public provision of such consumption services. Beyond that, measures are needed to increase the incomes earned by the poor by raising their productive capacity.

The most successfully based development models have come from Japan. These were the first examples that enabled President Clinton to initiate something similar in the United States by investing in people or, as he calls it, 'putting people first'. President Clinton did this, by retraining workers investing in technology, and providing scholarships for education. His programme was very much aimed at duplicating the Japanese successes. The issue of investing in people is the central theme in Human Resource Development. Disregarding the current crisis in the banks and the government, Japan has been very careful to invest in people and training. They have prepared workers for the next generation of industries, carefully retraining them for structural change so that they can move into new industries in a systematic fashion. The situation has been very different in the USA and Europe, where there has been tremendous resistance to change, because people in older industries are fearful of losing their jobs.

1.2.2 CONDITIONS OF AID

Once the purpose of aid is established, the next problem is to ensure that aid is used for that purpose. This is the function of performance conditions for aid. When the purpose of aid is seen primarily as supplementing domestic savings to promote growth, these performance conditions revolve around the savings rate of recipients. The key concept is that of matching aid with self-help.

> ...A marginal rate which is higher than the average rate of savings is the main lever of a development programme and should be the principal condition of aid to underdeveloped countries. (Rosenstein-Rodan, 1961)

> ...Economic growth depends on a great many institutional and psychological factors, but in terms of finance, which is the chief province of foreign aid, it depends on adequate expenditures on public services and on capital formation. Taken together, and ex-cluding defence, public expenditure and gross capital formation together should absorb at least 30 percent of gross domestic product (GDP), leaving 70 percent for personal consumption. In less developed economies public expenditure and capital formation absorb nearer 20 percent, and consumption takes 80 percent. The financial condition for self-sustaining growth can therefore be put starkly, if not precisely, by saying that the share of consumption must fall from 80 percent to 70 percent of gross domestic product. When you allow for the increased consumption taken up by population growth, and the per capita increase as well, I judge that the ratio of consumption should not fall by more than one-half-of-one percent per year, so that a fall from 80 percent to 70 percent should take twenty years. The essence of my proposal is that the amount of foreign aid should be tied to success in achieving this objective. (Lewis, 1964a)

A number of performance conditions were proposed along these lines. Apart from the assumption that savings are the main constraint on growth, the weakness of these criteria is that they are based on past performance and that the result is to use development aid to reward success which may be due to a variety of factors not necessarily connected with conscious policy effort on the part of the recipient. If the main object is to ensure the efficient use of development aid:

> It should be made clear to any country for which a (consultative) group is being set up that the group's concern with recipients performance is not confined to a review of progress, but extends also to consideration of future policy. Since future policy is likely

to be the principal determinant to the level of future requirements, and since the level of development aid available is itself likely to affect the future policy, the group clearly cannot be debarred from effectual discussion of policy by, for instance, considerations of national sovereignty. The time for the group to discuss a five-year development plan – to take the most conspicuous example – is not after it has been published but while it is still under consideration. (J White, 1967)

When it appeared in the mid-1960s that the volume of development aid was unlikely to increase significantly, attention shifted to elaborate country reviews of economic performance to improve the allocation and effective use of development aid. These reviews covered all aspects of government policies, not only the use of aid funds, but also of domestic resources. But aid is essentially a transaction between the people of rich countries and those of the poor, and governments are only the intermediaries in this transaction. The aid-giving process is not particularly well served by broad-ranging reviews of all government policies:

Such a recipe for international intervention or even involvement on an extensive scale cannot suit the realities of the approaching twenty-first century. The strident style of performance-oriented development aid diplomacy smacks of neo-colonialism to many in the developing world. There is something awkward about punishing ordinary people for the temporary aberrations of their leaders. Performance for society can only be judged over the long pull no society can be free from upsets and stresses and strains from time to time. The style that is most likely to suit the next decade of the 21st century is not one of intervention or even involvement but duty done without too much fuss or subsequent bother. And it is doubtful if most of the voters in the developed countries have an appetite for detailed reviews and judgement about distant countries, the inner logic of whose development they neither comprehend nor wish to comprehend. (Patel, 1998)

What is needed, therefore, is a specific agreement between donor and recipient about future policy regarding the use of development aid. This is the rationale behind project development aid as distinct from programme aid.

The only requirement imposed by the specific project provision of the articles is that, before a loan is made, there shall be a clear agreement both on how the proceeds of the loan are to be expended and on what the loan is expected to accomplish. (World Bank, 1969)

Also, as the UN Expert Group recommended (United Nations, 1951)

...We do not suggest that development aid should be given unconditionally to developing countries. This would not be wise. Each grant should be linked to a specific function, and there should be international verification that the funds are used only for the purpose for which they have been granted.

Project aid has been criticised because it has often suffered from a fallacy of misplaced concreteness, i.e. it has been mostly for physical constructions and also to cover only the foreign exchange costs of projects. Recipient countries have therefore been demanding more aid in the form of programme aid. But, in principle, project aid is a way of ensuring that the purpose of aid is examined carefully beforehand by donor and recipient alike and that aid is used for agreed purposes. The principle of project aid is essentially that of supervised credit, which has been successful and widely accepted in the case of agricultural loans.

However, a difficulty arises even with project aid, from the fungibility of financial resources; that the actual purpose for which aid is used may not be the ostensible purpose for which it is given.

If the project to which development aid is ostensibly tied is a 'high priority project', which would in any case have been part of the recipient's plan, and which he/she would otherwise have undertaken with his/her own money, then obviously the aid given enables the recipient to release his/her own money from project A (which is now aid financed), to continue with project B, C and D, which he/she financed with his/her own money, the utilised his/her money now released from project A in order to add a new project E to his/her original development plan or expenditure schedule. This could mean that the donor of aid ties his aid to project A, studies it minutely and satisfies him/herself that it is technically sound and economically right, while in reality – as distinct from appearance his/her aid may go into project E, which he/she may know nothing about, which he/she did not study, and which may be neither technically sound or economically right, nor generally the kind of thing that the aid would want to support. (Singer, 1965)

There is certainly this limitation of project aid in principle; it is, however, a limitation which is inherent in international development aid. Any method of avoiding such diversion of funds would require such extensive international intervention in domestic policies of recipients as to be totally unacceptable. Further, the diversion of funds is likely to be relatively small in practice, if aid is more deliberately tied to the kind of development measures such as education, infrastructure and economic institutions. It is precisely because such measures have not been vigorously pursued in the developing countries in the past three decades. It is only by spelling out these measures in, and getting a consensus for, a list of specific projects as particularly aid-worthy, and allocating aid to these projects, that faster progress can be achieved in meeting the challenge of aid policy more successfully in the future.

1.2.3 VOLUME AND DISTRIBUTION OF AID

The conditions for development aid have important implications for the volume of and allocation of aid. In the current negotiations between the developed and developing countries, the target for development aid has been laid down primarily in terms of principle of ability to pay, for example, total transfers at 1 per cent of the GDP of donors and official aid as 0.7 per cent, rather than according to need for, and utilisation of, aid by recipients. Further, the allocation of aid has been mainly on the basis of political, especially foreign policy, considerations leading to a very inequitable distribution among recipients.

But once it is agreed that aid should be given for specific development projects as defined above, there is a better alternative for determining the volume and allocation of aid. The volume of aid would be determined by the amount that each recipient country is willing and able to use according to these conditions. Much therefore depends on the recipient country. As the influential Indian journal *Economic and Political Weekly* observed editorially on 5 July 1980:

> ...The inflow of external assistance, in both gross and net terms, has shown a noticeable decline since 1975-76. The principal reason for the slowing down of the inflow of aid is the slow progress of the development projects for which the aid has been meant, because of lack of domestic financial and real resources and administrative failings. So instead of aid being the constraint on development, it is utilisation of available aid which has been limited by the insufficiency of the development effort.

The above proposal implies that the amount of aid that is given for a particular project should not be limited to its foreign exchange component but to whatever amount is needed to permit the recipient government, given its circumstances, to implement it. The result would be that the progress of development in the developing countries would be relieved of the financial constraints, as far as this can be done by international aid. The allocation of development aid among recipients would depend primarily on the recipients, rather than on the political preferences of the donors. In particular, it would have the effect of increasing the flow of aid to the least developed among the developing countries. The targets for aid should be based, not simply on the capacity of donors or the needs of recipients, but on the extent to which the aid promotes development.

Although aid on this proposal is primarily oriented towards the development objective, it is possible to reconcile it with the other motives behind aid. A large proportion of the aid of individual donors is given bilaterally for foreign aid policy considerations, because if given through the multilateral institutions, their contribution to particular recipients becomes anonymous when merged with other funds. But it may be possible to combine the political advantage of liberal aid with the economic advantages of aid administration by the multilateral institutions, if individual donors use the multilateral institutions as 'executive agents' for the aid given to particular recipients. One of the problems arising from the foreign aid policy interest is the inequitable allocation of aid among recipients. Therefore, there should be greater international coordination of development aid flows among recipients as there now is for the distribution among donors. Similarly, the balance of payments concerns of donors has led to extensive tying of aid. When an individual donor unties its aid, it may suffer some balance of payments effects, but these effects are likely to be less if all donors do so together. (Sundrum, 1983)

1.2.4 TERMS OF AID

The financial resources the Third World countries get from the World Bank and a considerable part of the bilateral aid and grants from individual donors are in the form of loans. If developing countries increase the pace of their development, this loan component is usually increased. Therefore, we must consider the extent to which the development of the Third World can be financed by borrowing.

Commercial banks usually measure the credit-worthiness of their clients by their income or wealth; this approach has also been extended to the cases of loans to governments, whose credit-worthiness is measured by the amount of outstanding debt to total income, or more usually by the proportion of annual debt-service payments to export receipts, known as the debt-service ratio. In the case of private borrowers, this measure of credit-worthiness is really a rough indicator of willingness to repay. In the case of government borrowers, the willingness to repay loans depends so much on political factors that it is a matter for political judgement. From an economic point of view, the main consideration in lending to government is their ability to amortise the loan on agreed terms.

Sometimes the case for soft loans or grants to a country is made on the grounds that it is not 'credit-worthy' for commercial loans, i.e., it will not be able to honour the interest and capital repayments. This argument seems to imply that there are no viable projects in these countries, and that the country is not 'developable'. It is clearly preferable to base an argument for soft loans simply on the fact that a country is poor, rather than introduce spurious notions of credit-worthiness. In principle, any loan is justified if the returns from investing in it are sufficient to repay the loan on the terms on which it is borrowed; this depends on how the proceeds of the loans are used. But in the case of foreign loans borrowed by governments, there are some other problems:

> The volume of debt is of no significance if the loans have been invested economically. By 'invested economically', I mean that the loan must add more to national income than it costs. But I also assume that the economy is able to translate extra income into foreign exchange: to convert it into revenue if the loan is for a public purpose, and to convert these revenues into foreign exchange. I also assume that enough of this extra income accrues within the lifetime of the loan, i.e., that one is not borrowing on short-term to finance long-term investment. Given these conditions, a loan is not a burden but a blessing; the larger the debt burden, the better the country will be. (Lewis, 1987a)

Given the share of the increase of national income that governments can mobilise to meet service, there is a limit to the rate of interest at which it can borrow, known as the critical rate of interest (Hayes *et al.*, 1964). Most of the discussions about the debt-service burden has been concerned with the ability of borrowing countries to convert their savings into foreign exchange. Therefore, the ratio of debt or debt-service changes to exports has generally been used to limit lending. This approach is unsatisfactory for a number of reasons. First, this ratio has not been very high in developing countries compared with the historical experience of borrowing relative to exports undertaken by Latin America, Australia and Canada. Second, this approach discriminates against countries whose exports are small and are expanding slowly.

> ...Such an approach is unfair to the larger countries, which, because of their geographical diversity, import very little. For example, the Chinese Peoples' Republic or India, need to import only about 5 percent or less of national income, and on any such rule of thumb is permitted a maximum debt charge of 1.7 percent of national income. The error in this approach is that it assumes

that a country with relatively small imports must also have relatively small exports. But, if China's or India's debt charges came to 5 percent of national income, why should she meet her obligations by importing 5 percent and exporting 10 percent of her national product? If debt limitations are to be imposed, they should be in terms of national income and not trade. (Lewis, 1987a)

Third, this approach relates the amount that a country can borrow to the amount of its exports in a relatively short period. If funds are borrowed for development purposes, they will help the country to repay only in the long run. Therefore, such loans must be made for a sufficiently long period. If, for any reason, this amount cannot be done, there must be arrangements for rolling over loans by incurring new debt to pay off old debts. The World debt crisis, for example, is at such a pitch that it has become obvious that: currently there is no more serious consideration linking the Third World to the First World than the Third World's debt. Nothing is locking Third World countries into the international market so securely as their burden of debt repayment. If debtor countries seek to repay their debt in full which they can only do with great hardship to their people and repeated rescheduling, they will remain utterly dependent on the North for the unforeseeable future. Yet as William Clark projected in 'cataclysm' (Clark, 1994), a purposeful default on the part of debtor countries which led to economic sanctions from the North, would cause even more hardship to Third World people, unless the Third World countries developed self-reliance strategies, in order to dispense with the debt burden. But it cannot develop such self-reliance while it is shouldering this burden. The vicious circle can be broken only through the cooperation and solidarity of the developing countries, who believe that the transfer of resources from poor to rich countries cannot and must not continue indefinitely.

The IMF sees its primary role as lying in the preservation of the integrity and functioning of the International Financial System. Bretton Woods itself did not emerge from a vacuum: under the subtitle 'The congenital inability of the IMF to deal with development problems. The original sin of the IMF', Ismail

Abdalla alleges that the Bretton Woods Conference was essentially a conference about monetary and financial problems of industrialised capitalist countries. In the official name of the institution which has come to be called the 'World Bank', or the International Bank for Reconstruction and Development (IBRD), 'the word "reconstruction" precedes "development". The priorities of Bretton Woods were obvious' (Abdalla, 1980). Helping international banks recover bad loans from Third World countries, regardless of what effects these have on local populations, falls entirely within the IMF's logic and remit. The World Bank was originally sponsored by the USA to regulate the 'Marshall Plan's' post-war West European economies under its direction, although at present it mainly issues loans to Third World countries, principally for development purposes (or for what passes for development in the World Bank's eyes).

The IMF and the World Bank are creations of the 1944 Bretton Woods Conference of international economies and bankers – John Maynard Keynes represented the UK (Hancock, 1989). Their main terms of reference were very much those of the dominant state in what was then a 44-member organisation, they are still:

> ...At the World Bank... votes are entirely based on the size of the financial commitment that each member state has made. There is no pretence of equality – the economic superpowers run the show. (Hancock, 1989)

The IMF and the World Bank, over the years, have increasingly operated in tandem, with the World Bank lending a substantial part of its funds to assist in the implementation of its sister organisation's structural adjustment programmes. Under strong North American pressure, the World Bank in recent years has again been persuaded to lend more to the private sector and to privatisation schemes, and less to governments. Cernea's 1985 anthology, published under the auspices of the World Bank, may carry the 'Putting People First' motto proudly in its title. The reality of the book is somewhat different: the subtitles 'Putting Cost–Benefit Analysis First', and 'Cost–Effectiveness: Fairly Quick And Fairly Clean' figure prominently (Chambers, 1985).

Elsewhere in the same text it is stated that the challenge is 'to find more cost-effective ways for outsiders to learn about rural conditions' – ways that lead closer to optimal trade-off between cost of collection and learning, and the relevance, time and actual beneficial use of the information and understanding that is gained. Rapid Rural Appraisal, subsidised by cost-free collaboration of the peasants, is no doubt 'cheap, efficient and quick': a far cheaper, more efficient and quicker mode of knowledge extraction than the 'long and dirty' high-tech approach of the old professionalism.

'We must enable the rural poor to demand and control more of the benefits of development' (Chambers, 1983). This looks and sounds generously democratic and progressive, until probing questions are asked about who is represented in the 'we' and who gave 'us' the (sacred?) mandate which ordains that 'we' 'must'/'must not'? And what secret powers of understanding equip 'us' with the knowledge and skills to 'enable' others? And what is the nature of the development that is being promoted, if indeed it is so separated and separable from the humans involved, that it has to be brought to them before its true 'benefits' can be appreciated and enjoyed? This norm operates even when, more often than not, as Nyoni points out, those agencies which:

> ...try to help others change, do not themselves change. They aim at creating awareness among people, yet they themselves are not aware of their negative impact on those they claim to serve. They claim to 'help' people change their situation through participation, democracy and self-help, yet they themselves are non-participatory, non-democratic and dependent on outside help for survival. (Nyoni, 1992)

Structural adjustment programmes (SAP), in parallel with income generating activities, fail to take account of women's reproductive roles and are based on the assumption that women's time is elastic (Elson, 1991). Recent research has shown that, far from having an elastic schedule, in at least one-third of all cases the woman is the breadwinner (Diepeveen, 1993). Her income, even at the best of times, is rarely 'extra'. Included in the SAP packages are 'stabilisation' policies which include devaluation of the local currency, decontrolling of wages and prices, a reduction of government expenditure on social services, particularly health, and the removal of subsidies from parastatals such as marketing boards. All of these are measures which hit women (and children) especially hard (their death warrant to starve). The moment the target growth rate has been achieved, cost in human terms notwithstanding, repayment of national debt (to the World Bank, IMF and other international bankers) is once again possible. That is the hidden agenda of SAPs. Or that is what, in theory, ought to happen. In practice, a sudden glut of raw materials and processed commodities can only result in a fall in world prices, which Third World producers can only make up by yet more production and yet more exploitation and devastation of the natural resource base. As an added bonus, the affected countries are even further integrated into the global economy in the process. All this is good news for the First World consumers. But SAPs do not just free the market. They also enslave countries. The process almost invariably starts by throwing millions of people out of their jobs. 'How indeed is it,' asks Shiva, 'that a process that is based on freedom needs to create so much lack of freedom?' (Shiva, 1992). There is no freedom or democracy in starving man or woman.

For Third class citizens – according to IFDA, the crisis has reached alarming proportion: 565 million women are living in poverty. Poverty for rural men has risen by 3 per cent over the last 20 years; for women the increase has been 48 per cent. In 10 African countries women and children constitute 77 per cent of the population. But they have a legal right to own property in only 10 per cent of the households in those 10 countries… women and men cannot see any advantage in having smaller families. On the contrary, when children are the only future means of support, control of the (size) of the family is seen as a source of poverty, not of wealth (G. Kinnock, 1992).

1.3   Conclusion

The Western tradition, however, is not entirely monochromatic:

John Stuart Mill (1806–1873) and Thomas Malthus (1766–1834) before him, stood for what we would identify now as the alternative, sustainable tradition of western scientific thought. Unfortunately, for all practical purposes, the conviction among economists and scientists has not been supported, that it was possible to rely on human ingenuity, technological innovation and the Promethean spirit to overcome obstacles to the path of progress such as escalating population growth.

Only in the late twentieth century, with the publication of the club of Rome's 'Limits to Growth' (1972), was this Panglossian confidence seriously shaken for the first time. The launch of the development era, signalled by Truman's 1949 Inauguration Speech, preceded this dawning of realism. Under its reign, economic well-being or, more appropriately 'well-having', became the universal goal to be pursued by all peoples of the globe and sustained, as a moral duty, by the Western nation states with financial help, technological transfer, and competent expertise in those (mainly Southern) regions which are now designated as 'underdeveloped' zones.

Labelled 'underdeveloped', these were deemed – and recipro-cally declared themselves – to stand in need of development aid. This was provided as a matter of course by the 'developed' countries: 'noblesse oblige' 'Development' became the catchword, and 'aid' its practice (van Nieuwehuijze, 1985).

Developed countries NGOs became interventionism bases, their self-appointed mission of modernisation, extension, innovation, management, technology transfer and development aid grafted on ethnocentric perceptions of what is wrong (with 'them') and what is right (with 'us'). What makes the interventionist project possible is, beyond doubt, the power of money. But, deeper moral questions on what this right to intervene is based have remained unanswered.

In truth, the West did not just happen upon the so-called under-developed countries: it was the West that had created them in the first place and then run away leaving the problem (Griffin, 1968). Development was perceived as the process by which peoples move from underdevelopment towards the universal destiny of economic well-being and few searching questions about its ecological, cultural, social and ethical implications were asked in the past: 'World Development is like apple pie: nobody can be against it' (Sachs, 1992a).

Education, like development, is either domesticating or humanising and liberating. Critical consciousness is as much at the core of education as it is at the core of development:

> ...the development process is in fact educational process, or rather it should unfailingly be viewed as such. We cannot conceive of development in the absence of education any more than education is the absence of development. (Faundez, 1986)

Development, education, communication and humanisation are all part of the same process. Process means progression, creation, moving upwards and towards what is desirable and 'better' (more human). 'Product' and 'outcome' are part of the epistemological universe gravitating around the obsession with growth which, once reached, can only mean decomposition and death in its final 'outcome'. Most development projects, not least because they are so commonly and approvingly perceived as 'a basic instrument for intervention' are not even owned and controlled by people themselves: there is an internal contradiction between 'intervention', on the one hand, and 'development', education and humanisation, on the other. Alternatively, if intervention is going to be the main guiding principle of all development policy, it should at the very least operate both ways – in a dialogical, constructive and creative manner, without exhibiting the monopolising one-sidedness which always has been and still is the mark, in particular, of mega-projects.

Education as critical consciousness and, therefore, the source of a constant process of innovation and creation is lacking in most organisations, including some that claim to offer precisely this 'input'. What commonly goes under the name of 'development' can and should be designated by what it is all about, namely economic growth, or whatever target has been ordained by the high priests of the 'new colonialism' (Shiva).

Rather than advocating 'alternative' development – a totally self-defeating exercise at the best of times, because it implicitly recognises the dominant mode's claim to ownership of development – or 'alternative to development' (Sen, Crown, 1988), both the reality and the term 'development' itself need to be captured and reclaimed.

The word 'development' should then be reserved for what it was coined for in the first place: to indicate growth, yes, but also and above all to invoke creation, culture, education, ownership and control, the satisfaction of fundamental human needs and everything involving autonomous human agency. There cannot be any 'self' if the centre of gravity is made up of 'intervention', if there is no ownership and control or, at least, an intentionality and movement towards autonomy. Autonomy does not exclude sharing and participation: ownership and control, on the contrary, are an absolute condition for genuine participation. There is a place and a space for organic integration, for articulation (between the macro and micro, government and people) for Gramsci's (internal/external) 'organic intellectuals'.

Chapter II
KENYA IN THE POLITICAL CONTEXT

2.1 Constitution

> The idea of progress could not have become part of general
> thought until men/women see that, in one respect or another,
> they were improving their lot.
>
> (Julian Huxley)

Kenya became a republic on 12 December 1964. Having had a federal (so-called majimbo) constitution, with the Queen as the formal head of state, for only one year following independence, a new constitution was then adopted based on a unitary state, and as from 1966 on a unicameral National Assembly. Kenya's form of government was partly founded on the so-called Westminster model. Its constitutional arrangements were also influenced by the American system, and provided for an executive president and a division of powers between a National Assembly, an Executive and a Judicature (Constitution of Kenya, 1969).

The National Assembly (or Parliament) had 158 elected Members, 12 nominated Members, and Attorney-General, sitting as an ex-officio non-voting member. Parliament holds general legislative powers. Parliamentary and presidential elections are normally held every five years, but the President may at any time prorogue or dissolve Parliament (Constitution of Kenya, 1969, section 30, 33, 36, 42, 59).

The powers of the Executive are vested in the elected president, who from 1964 to 1992 has stood unopposed for direct election by the national suffrage. The President appoints

Ministers to form his cabinet from among the Members of Parliament. The Cabinet is collectively responsible to the National Assembly, which means that Parliament may declare (which it has not) that it has no confidence in the cabinet, in which case the President and his cabinet would have to resign. The President appoints an Attorney-General, who acts as the principal legal adviser to the Government (Constitution of Kenya, 1969, sections 4, 17, 26, 59, Ghai & McAuslan, 1970).

The Judicature consists of the High Court presided over by the Chief Justice, who is appointed by the President, and the subordinate courts including the Kadhi Courts, which deal with matters of family and succession in accordance with the Muslim religion, and which determine whether or not legislation passed by Parliament is constitutional. Rulings by the High Court may subsequently be taken to the Court of Appeal. The judiciary has a reputation of being insulated from political influence, although use of criminal proceedings for political ends has been reported (Constitution of Kenya, 1969, sections 60, 61, 64, 67).

Chapter V of the Constitution contains a Bill of Rights (violated since independence) setting out the fundamental individual human rights and framework of Kenyan citizenship (Constitution of Kenya, 1969, sections 70–86).

On 9 June 1982 a constitutional amendment was passed by Parliament, Kenya became a *de jure* one-party state, (Africa Contemporary Record 1982–1983, 1984). This action was taken despite earlier statements by the KANU Government in 1965 opposing a one-party state constitution, on the grounds that such an act would be in contravention of the freedom of assembly and association enshrined in the Constitution (Gertzel *et al.*, 1969). Thus, except for the one-party constitutional amendment of 1982, the form of Kenya Constitutional arrangements closely resembles those of many western states!

2.1.1 POLITICAL CULTURE AND PARTY STRUCTURE

In the closing of the twentieth century, Kenya's Presidential and parliamentary elections were held at the end of December 1997 and resulted in the re-election of President Moi to a fifth and, he claimed, a final term of office. His ruling Kenya African National

Union (KANU) party achieved a slim overall majority in an expanded legislature. A number of former cabinet ministers lost their seats. Despite reports of electoral irregularities and poor weather which extended the voting period, the elections passed off relatively peacefully and were given qualified endorsement by independent observers. The president's candidacy was helped by the failure of very weak opposition to unite behind a single candidate and by tribal splits and divisions among the opposition parties. Early in January 1998 a new administration was appointed and was notable for the appointment of a new finance minister.

The Moi administration was under considerable pressure in 1996–1997 to enact constitutional and legal reforms ahead of the general election. These demands were pressed by a coalition of interested groups, including all the opposition parties and the churches under the umbrella body, the National Convention Assembly (NCA). A series of political protests, orchestrated by the NCA's executive council (NCEC), took place mid-year 1997 in Nairobi and elsewhere and resulted in clashes with the security forces that heightened the political atmosphere in which many people were killed by Moi's organised thugs.

However, in a sudden volte-face in July 1997, the President responded to strong international pressure by acknowledging the need for reform, and in September, working through an Inter-Parties Parliamentary Group, KANU and some opposition legislators reached a broad consensus on a minor package of reforms which were enacted in November. The reforms, which included repealing some laws dating back to the colonial era, helped to defuse the political situation and avert a mass boycott of the elections which had been threatened by the NCEC.

(A)

HEAD OF STATE   President Daniel arap Moi

GOVERNMENT   The Kenya African National Union (KANU) party

DATE OF NEXT ELECTION   December, 2002

POLITICAL STRUCTURE   In November 1997 a number of constitutional changes were made which included the repeal of laws dating back to the colonial period and allowed for the formation of a coalition government and a review of the constitution by an independent commission. Executive power is vested in the President, vice-President and Cabinet; both the vice-president and cabinet are appointed by the president.

VOTING PATTERN   In presidential elections, the winning candidate must receive no less than 25% of the votes in at least five of Kenya's eight provinces.

POLITICAL INSTITUTIONS   Legislative power is held by the National Assembly.

(B)

LAST GENERAL ELECTION RESULTS
29–30 DECEMBER 1997

I: Presidential Elections (p)

	Party	Votes Cast	% of Poll
Daniel arap Moi	KANU	2,445,801	40.1
Mwai Kibaki	Democratic Party	1,895,527	31.1
Raila Odinga	National Development Party	665,725	10.9

There were twelve other candidates

II: Legislative Elections

Major Parties	Seats
KANU	107
Democratic Party	39
National Development Party	21

Ford-Kenya	17
Social Democratic Party	15
Others	11
Overall Total	210

In addition to the 210 directly elected seats, a further 12 members are appointed by the President from nominations submitted pro rata for their parliamentary representation.
(p) Provisional

Beyond the institutions and procedures formally prescribed in the constitution itself, subsidiary legislation and political practices have over the years served, in some degree, to modify constitutional customs. During Kenyatta's presidency (1963–1978) there was a considerable strengthening of the Executive powers following the assassination of his arch-rival Tom Mboya, at the expense of parliamentary and cabinet responsibilities. The result was the emergence of personal rule based chiefly upon personal loyalty to the President, patron–client linkages and coercion. Secondly, the President became constitutionally above the law of the land. The trend has been carried further during Moi's Presidency. A political culture has emerged, in which the authority of the President is unquestionable, constitutionally and politically.

Furthermore, there has been a practice of enlarging the administration to the extent that the majority of Members of the Parliament are Ministers, Assistant Ministers and Members holding positions in the Parastatal boards. This has rendered virtually ineffectual the constitutional provision that Parliament may cause the Government to resign if a vote of no confidence is carried in the National Assembly.

Whatever genuine political debate previously existed in the Kenyan Parliament was replaced by a personalised style of leadership and rule, by virtue of which Presidential directives and orders are issued, and whose constitutional basis is not always fully evident. Criticisms of the President and his Government (as distinct from individual Ministers or civil servants), however constructive and well grounded in fact, have tended to be dismissed out of hand, branded as 'anti-Nyayo', or 'an act of treason'. Parliamentary immunity has been flouted. Members have often been arrested inside the Parliament buildings for things they have said in a Parliamentary debate.

The increasing authority of the President in recent years has affected the role of the bureaucracy and its technocrats in decision-making. It was long an axiom that the Kenyan bureaucracy dominated the policy-making process. Some political commentators went as far as to say that the bureaucrats constituted a separate social class (Hyden, 1984). If these tenets were ever true, they will have to be re-examined here. Major policy announcements are being made almost daily, often in vague, ambiguous, and sometimes self-contradictory terms. Their wider implications are not always carefully considered, as a result of which subsequent 'clarifications' have become necessary. Suffice it to mention one such case here.

In 1984 a group of prominent Kenyan women of the National Council of Women of Kenya (NCWK), reportedly demanded greater representation for women in senior decision-making positions in the country. The President reacted strongly against these demands by saying that for women to demand equality with men was tantamount to suggesting that the Bible was wrong, when it states that the man is head of the family. Less than two years later, the President announced that women leaders were to be appointed heads of the twenty Kenyan parastatals by the end of 1986. (*Weekly Review*, 24 January 1986)

The cult of personality of President Moi's leadership even incorporated an identification with Kenya's recent history and Jomo Kenyatta, the 'wise/heroic/magnanimous' deeds and decisions of the leader and 'Father of the Nation' (Baba wa Taifa) which were generally disseminated through the radio, television, schools and the ruling party. The strongman (Moi) needs and demands veneration and obedience. Moi constantly surrounds himself with followers who constantly reaffirm their faith in his exceptional leadership, wisdom and generosity. All or the bulk of strategic positions in the political, bureaucratic, police and military hierarchies are filled with people loyal to the President. These include relatives, especially close ones such as brothers, sons, and cousins, friends and classmates, kinsmen and tribesmen. For these and other followers, the expectation of sharing in the spoils of office reinforces the personal link to the chief. For many Kenyans opposed to President Moi's leadership and personal rule the essence of his system was captured in a mocking description which followed the government's organised murder of Dr Robert Ouko the Foreign Affairs Minister: 'All power emanates from the centre of the system, from our imperial (mtukufu),' Baba wa Taifa, President Daniel arap Moi. Political success and personal enrichment depend on the position held by different planets as they circulate around the sun-king. Since President Moi, through his control of the state apparatus, bestows access to our country's increasingly scarce resources, the closer the politician-planet to the centre, the more power he can trap and reflect on down to his own satellites and flunkey. As our politicians orbit endlessly around the President, they compete with each other to sing his praise loudly and attract his favour. Obsequious loyalty brings its own reward.

Due to the style of Moi's government, which became associated with a centralisation of decision-making in the Office of the President, the Ministers and senior civil servants of the economic department, particularly in Finance, Planning and National Development, experienced certain changes in their roles as economic advisers and decision-makers (*Africa Confidential*, 9 April 1986). The Chief Secretary in the Office of the President played a key part in this shift in political and administrative competence. He did not merely head the entire civil service, he had acquired a political role as well, linked to the authority of the President. He acted on behalf of the President's office in the day-to-day running of the line ministries, and attended KANU Parliamentary group meetings. While this style of government had certain positive effects, notably in the field of economic policy, it was also felt to have given rise to some degree of bureaucratic reaction and possibly inertia. In particular areas, delays and backlog resulted. While the quality of the Kenyan civil service, one of the best, inherited from Britain and recognised throughout Africa as the 'best', this development affected its efficiency.

In assessing the recent performance of the Kenyan administration, distinctions should be drawn between its different
constituent parts, and also among its various levels of activity.
There can be no doubt that the overall quality of the civil service
has improved in terms of its members' personal technical and
professional qualifications. Two crucial factors can be singled out,
as affecting the output and performance of these now better
qualified civil servants. Firstly, the serious lack of adequate
recurrent resources to put qualifications to effective use.
Secondly, the interconnection between political and
administrative processes of decision-making. The operating
ministries feel the effects of both. On the other hand, the
Provincial Administration, which comes directly under the
President's Office has been strengthened in most respects.

There is also a considerable variation in the level of competence and efficiency between the top layer of civil servants and the
middle cadres. The latter are still lagging behind, partly as a result
of competition from the private sector.

After a brief period of two-party politics immediately
following independence, with the Kenya African National Union
(KANU) and Kenya Democratic Union (KADU) as the principal
actors, the latter was eventually dissolved, with most of its
remaining leaders crossing the parliamentary floor to join KANU.
KADU's constituency had been drawn from the smaller tribes or
ethnic groups, such as the Kalenjin, Masai, Mijikenda etc, and the
party had professed a federal constitution (Majimboism), as a
safeguard against a perceived political threat from the numerically
dominant Kikuyu and Luo ethnic groups. A considerable section
of the present KANU leadership of Kenya were in fact former
members of KADU. However, in the early years of Kenyan
independence, the influence of the Kikuyu and Luo peoples
predominated within KANU. The colonial administration for its
part had favoured a Majimbo constitution, which was initially
introduced on 1 June (Madaraka Day) 1963, to protect the smaller
tribes, white settlers, the Arabs and the Asian minority, when self-
rule was first accorded to Kenya. Full independence was achieved
on 12 December of the same year.

It was not until 1966 that a new party emerged headed by the late Kenyan first vice-President Jaramogi Oginga Odinga, the Kenya People's Union (KPU), with a populist orientation with Luo predominance, albeit also including prominent Kikuyu leaders, such as Bildad Kaggia, who had shared prison and detention with Jomo Kenyatta during the Mau Mau Emergency period, and who became KPU vice-President. Its formation followed the defection from KANU by the then vice-President Oginga Odinga, and 29 other Members of Parliament. Having left the KANU party, on whose ticket they had originally been elected, the defectors to the new Party were compelled, as a result of a series of legislative manipulations on the part of the incumbent KANU government, to stand for re-election in their individual constituencies. In this 'Little General Election', a majority of the KPU group lost their seats, largely as a result of administrative rigging, harassment, beatings and detention of supporters by the state apparatus which, in effect, intervened in favour of one of the contesting parties, namely, KANU (Mueller, 1984). Three years later, in 1969, Tom Mboya was assassinated which was followed by the deliberate massacre of innocent citizens at the new Kisumu hospital by presidential security guards and the Kenyan police, during the opening ceremony by President Kenyatta. The leaders were detained without trial and the party was proscribed and its assets taken over by the government. A prominent Kikuyu, J M Karioki, MP, who protested against the massacre of innocent people and the banning of the opposition party was himself murdered on the orders of Jomo Kenyatta. Already, during that period, the blurring of distinction between the administrative machinery of the incumbent political party and of the state apparatus had become evident.

From 1969 until June 1982, Kenya remained a *de facto*, if not *de jure* one party state. During this period KANU ceased to function as a party between elections, which were conducted approximately every five years. The moribund nature of KANU was repeatedly deplored by prominent members. In the mid-1970s, Martin Sikuku, MP, claimed in Parliament that KANU was dead. When asked by other members of the House to substantiate this claim, the Deputy Speaker, Jean-Marie Seroney,

MP, and a lawyer, ruled that it was not necessary to substantiate the obvious. Shortly afterwards, they were both detained without trial. This happened because President Jomo Kenyatta was constitutionally above the law of the land and held the power of life and death!

Since Moi's peaceful take-over of the Presidency in 1978, and particularly with the introduction of the one-party system in 1982, steps were taken to overhaul the party machinery, and to revitalise KANU. For the first time since KANU's formation, a financial statement and balance sheet were presented by the national treasurer to the Annual Delegates Conference in August 1986 (*Weekly Review*, 22 August 1986). Regular elections for party offices were held, and a KANU Manifesto and a new KANU code of Disciplines and conduct were adopted (*Daily Nation* and *Standards*, 9 April 1986). However, the requirements for clearance from the party in order to stand for election, whether at the local or national level, were retained. The current practice of using the clearance system as a mechanism for barring candidates, has as such no basis in the KANU constitution. In a *de jure* one party state, this system has far-reaching implications for the entire process, and can be questionable in terms of the country's electoral laws.

Most importantly, a party membership campaign was carried out in 1984, and a new one launched in July 1986, to turn KANU into a mass party with a political claim to be truly representative of the Kenyan people. A target of six million members was set (*Daily Nation*, 2 September 1986). The methods applied in the recruitment campaign were in a number of cases tantamount to outright coercion (*Weekly Review*, 5 September 1986). Compulsory KANU membership was introduced for all public employees, including the parastatals, from the top down to clerks and messengers (*Ndumbu*, 1985). Various forms of pressure have since been applied. One case in particular was reported by the media from Nanyuki, where administrative police, acting on the orders of the district commissioner, barred government employees and heads of department from entering their offices, unless they could produce valid KANU membership cards. The President later castigated over-zealous civil servants for going too far and reiterated that KANU membership was voluntary, despite previous directives to the contrary (*Kenya Times, Daily Nation, Standards*, 1 September 1986).

Numerous cases of Provincial Administration staff being used for recruitment purposes were reported, although it is the responsibility solely of KANU branches at various levels to conduct the campaign (*Daily Nation*, 9 September 1986). Government vehicles are also released by department heads and parastatals for party recruitment purposes (*Standards*, 19 September 1986). One cabinet minister even directed district officers to step up recruitment activities (*Daily Nation*, 22 September 1986). State and party organs seemed indeed to be merging into a one-party regime.

2.1.2 STATE APPARATUS AND LEGAL INSTRUMENTS

Independent Kenya inherited a centralised system of government from the colonial period, based on an administration controlled by provincial and district commissioners and, below them, cadres of district officers, chiefs and assistant chiefs, who together represented the extended arm of the Executive (Wallis, 1982; Mueller, 1984). This structure, which is referred to as Provincial Administration, was principally geared towards maintaining law and order and, as such was, and today is, ill equipped to perform the difficult task of preparing and implementing national or regional development programmes.

Nevertheless, since independence the work and responsibilities of government at the provincial and district levels have greatly expanded in a developmental sense, but the pivotal role of the Provincial Administration staff under the Office of President has not changed and seems to many experts and observers to be in need of radical and drastic reform or total abolition.

Coupled with a strong institutional framework, Kenya inherited at independence a host of draconian legal instruments of control and repression from the colonial era (Mueller, 1984; MacWilliam, 1985). Much of the state of emergency legislation of the Mau Mau period (1952–1956) was retained intact, with some amendments to meet new circumstances; while new laws with colonial antecedents were approved by Parliament. One particular representative antecedent was the legislation to issue or deny licences for holding public meetings (freedom of association). The Preservation of Public Security Act predating independence, was re-enacted in 1966, under the provision of which detention without trial remains legal. The Societies Act, requiring all societies and associations to register as such, has its counterpart in a colonial ordinance. Likewise, the Chief's Authority Act is a colonial creation conferring extensive powers on the chiefs (a civil servant), who form part of the Provincial Administration.

The centralised state apparatus was charged with administering these laws, and its collaboration with police, Special Branch and Criminal Investigation Department (CID) officers, to function as a security network as well. Security committees were established at national, provincial, district and division levels whose duties are to gather intelligence through police, chiefs, assistant chiefs, headmen and informer networks within the local community, to diffuse and control tense situations, and to prevent the fruition of new and competing political associations.

Consequences of the congestion of channels of expression and legitimate dissent include the widespread circulation of so-called 'seditious' publications, the proliferation of clandestine activities, and the concomitant formation of movements to organise and direct them. Prior to the August 1982 coup attempt, a clandestine group known as the December Twelve Movement (DTM) had been formed, and was in the process of publishing a newspaper under the title *Pambana* (*Race & Class*, Vol. XXIV, no.3, 1983). Following the collapse of the coup, scores of oppositional elements were arrested: many including university students were shot on sight, some tortured and detained, and some charged and convicted under legislation other than the Preservation of Public Security Act. By no means all belonged to the rebellious Kenya Air Force (KAF), although the majority were from the KAF service. The attempted coup was used as pretext for a general clamp-down on all forms of opposition to create the maximum fear.

For a couple of years after the attempted coup, the situation seemed relatively calm, and apparently under control by the regime. But in early 1986, a new clandestine movement surfaced under the name of Mwakenya (*Weekly Review*, 11 April 1986). It issued a series of leaflets entitled Mpatanishi, which were consecutively numbered (*Weekly Review*, 13 June 1986). Initially, the Mwakenya group was dismissed as a tribalistic body (*Standards*, 16 April 1986), composed of a few disgruntled elements (*Kenya Times*, 15 April 1986), of the educated elite, serving foreign masters (*Sunday Nation*, 13 April 1986), and who had escaped the security network following the August 1982 disturbances (*Kenya Times*, 19 April 1986). The regime reacted by arresting a great number of people suspected of belonging to the group, and of possessing 'seditious' publications (*EIU Kenya Country Report* no.4. 1986). Severe physical torture and sentences were meted out on three Mwakenya members for the sabotage of railway lines and telephone wires (*Weekly Review*, 11 July, 1986). Judging from the pattern of arrests, it became clear that the group had a broader base than previously thought, extending beyond intellectuals, and that it was not ethnically homogeneous (Godfrey, 1986). The swift response by the regime suggested that it was determined to nip such movements in the bud, before they were able to mobilise popular support.

The ultimate guarantors of the regime are, of course, the armed forces and the security establishment. The Ministry of Defence was abolished shortly after Jomo Kenyatta's death. All matters of defence and internal security have now been brought directly under the authority of the Office of the President (Nelson, 1983). Following the abortive coup of August 1982, the rebellious air force was disbanded, and has now been rebuilt to a strength of 1200–1500 persons. Its reconstruction was supervised by Brigadier Mohamoud Mohamed, who was appointed Chief of the General Staff, after the retirement of General Mulinge.

After the attempted coup had been quelled, the army was rewarded with a fifteen per cent pay rise for privates, and up to thirty per cent for officers, in an attempt to ensure the service's loyalty. New army barracks costing nearly seven million Kenya pounds was authorised (*Africa Contemporary Record* 1982–1983, 1984). Army officers in Kenya are a law unto themselves and are allowed to engage in magendo (corruption), without being reprimanded or charged in any court of law. With a series of transfers and new appointments in the top echelons, including the promotion to the most senior military post of an ethnic Somali with no apparent political ambition, President Moi seems to have secured the support of the armed forces for the time being.

The national security establishment comprised the police with its various constituent parts, including the Criminal Investigation Department (CID), the Special Branch and the paramilitary General Service Unit (GSU). The total regular police force consists of about 20,000 persons. The CID is responsible for criminal investigation and the maintenance of all criminal files. It also works in close liaison with the Special Branch, whose tasks are internal intelligence and the investigation of subversive criminal activity. The GSU is an elite and highly mobile internal security unit, formed in 1953, during the Mau Mau state of emergency period, to be deployed for the purpose of restoring law and order in civil disturbances, riots and crime waves. It consists of about 3,500–4,000 persons trained by Britain, Israel and (before Mandela's ANC government) by South African specialist instructors (Nelson, 1983).

An adjunct to the police force is the so-called administrative (formerly 'native/home-guard') police, under the control of the Provincial Administration. These are used mainly by chiefs and Assistant Chiefs in the execution of their responsibilities for law and order (harassment for tax avoidance and political opponents of KANU, minor policing, for brewing unlicensed liquor etc). The National Youth Service and KANU youth wingers are, to certain extent, also employed in quasi-police duties.

2.1.3 CORRUPT PRACTICES AND CONSEQUENCES

Corruption (magendo is the Kiswahili term in common usage in East Africa) may be defined as the misuse of power and public office for private profit, preferment or prestige, or in the interest of a particular group or class, in a way that constitutes a breach of the law or accepted standards of conduct. (Kameir & Kursany, 1985)

The Berlin-based Transparency International, which campaigns against corruption publishes an annual corruption index, based on the perceptions of businessmen and a wide ranging database. It comes as no surprise that Nigeria was, until recent 'adjusted' figures, at the top of the 52-country league table, with Bolivia, Colombia, Russia, Pakistan, Indonesia, India, Egypt. Kenya, following on South Africa came in 32 and Malaysia at 33. Britain was at the bottom of this league.

It is all, of course, frightfully secret and the evidence only occasionally spills out into the open. Such a scandal famously exploded in the Congress with the US Senate hearings into 'kick-backs' paid around the world by the big aerospace companies, Lockheed and Northrop etc. The result was the 1977 Foreign Corrupt Practices Act.

Doing business in most developing countries involves bribery and corruption. Commission payments to officials or rulers can run as high as thirty per cent. The cash, disguised by over-invoicing, finds its way into the secretive bank accounts of the Caribbean, the Channel Islands and Switzerland. Everyone concerned with exporting – in board rooms, banks and in authority knows and condones the practice. In authoritarian, military-run or endemically corrupt countries, it is the only way to proceed. One way to prevent corruption is to ensure that bribery to secure business contracts becomes a criminal offence everywhere and is properly enforced (Clinton Davis, 1997).

There are many problems in conceptualising corruption or graft. The most difficult is the answer to the question: whose law and whose standard? Legislation, norms and standards are themselves social products, the outcome of political processes. Laws are codified and formalised norms, the breach of which is punishable in courts of law. Professional and ethical standards may be more or less formalised, but are usually not accorded the status of law (Scott, 1972).

In 1971 the Public Service Structure and Remuneration Commission (Ndegwa Commission) conceded that incidents of corruption do occur in Kenya Public Services. Nevertheless, the Commission had no objection to civil servants owning and operating private businesses, provided strict codes of conduct were adhered to (Kenya Government, 1971). This situation is unlikely to cover all situations involving conflicting interests, which civil servants may encounter. When almost a decade later the Civil Service Review Committee (Waruhi Committee) reported on the state of civil service, it went further than the Ndegwa Commission by stating that: '...there has been gross neglect of public duty and misuse of official position and official information in furtherance of civil servants' personal interest' (Kenya Government, 1980). It also elaborated on the conflict of interest, arising from civil servants' engagement in private business stating that it had '...received overwhelming evidence from members of the public, to the effect that some public servants utilise Government facilities in order to benefit them-selves.' Despite these findings, the Waruhi Committee endorsed the Ndegwa Commission's recommendation that civil servants be allowed to hold private business interests, although it emphasised more strongly specific aspects of the ethical code to be observed, recommending, *inter alia*, that civil servants should declare their private interests. It also proposed that a committee should be set up to oversee these matters. No action was taken on these recommendations.

Why is the phenomenon of corruption particularly rife in the so-called developing countries like Kenya? Much of the explanation can be found in the size of the public sector relative to the private sector. As part of the colonial legacy, on independence, the state apparatuses in most developing countries are the only developed industry. The state handles a disproportionately large share of the national resources of a country and, above all, it intervenes in and administers the multitude of rules and regulations, import/export schedules and licensing systems which, taken together, constitute the policy environment in which private business operates. As a result, access to the administrative system, directly by way of office or informally through a proxy, becomes a primary objective for ambitious people in business and politics.

In this general context, it might be useful to distinguish between: two different types of corruption: (a) petty corruption and (b) grand corruption. They are fundamentally different, as far as the scale and causes are concerned, as well as in their conse-quences. Corruption in developing countries is often explained by reference to the lingering on of traditional value systems, which are particularistic in orientation and based on exchange of gifts and services between kinsfolk. When people brought up in a system like that enter a modern bureaucratic structure where universal rules apply, they are placed immediately in a personal dilemma. Should they abide by the rules of their new place of work, or remain loyal to the traditional value system, which forms an integral part of their social background? A young bureaucrat, whose education has been paid for through collections among relatives, clansmen/women and the local community, is under very severe obligation to reciprocate by helping his/her kinsfolk and to provide them with jobs and services, which he/she may be able to procure by virtue of his/her position. The incidence of corrupt practices like nepotism, is thus explained in terms of traditional loyalty taking precedence over modern standards of conduct within a bureaucracy.

Another cause of petty corruption in recent years in Kenya can be found in the deteriorating economic conditions since the culmination of the coffee/tea boom. Real wages have declined substantially since the late 1970s and early 1980s and following the implementation of structural adjustment programmes (SAP), particularly for the low and lower middle-income groups both in private and public sectors (*Statistical Abstract*, 1984). To cope with their personal economic problems, wage earners are compelled to try and find supplementary sources of income, either legally or illegally to survive. In this type of situation, deteriorating living standards for low income groups come to represent a major driving force behind the increasing petty corruption, which may be observed in Kenya.

Neither of these explanations goes very far to account for what has been termed grand corruption. Whereas petty corruption of the traditional kind is based on some sort of reciprocity, or alternatively on a personal predicament, resulting from a sudden decline of real wages/salary, there is little evidence of reciprocity or dire need in the various forms of grand corruption. For the classes and social strata engaging in grand corruption, the motive force is the get rich quick (the Robert Maxwell style) appropriation of economic surplus on a substantial scale. The groundnut scheme in Tanzania in the 1950s may be a classic of the genre and one from which countless lessons might have been learned. For these groups, corruption is essentially another form of surplus appropriation and capital accumulation. Whether that is illegal, is immaterial. Although it is exceedingly difficult to disclose grand corruption by way of systematic investigation, there is sufficient available evidence in Kenya and elsewhere in Africa to suggest that its volume has remained more or less constant, or has been rising alarmingly in post-independence Kenya. Annual Reports of the Auditor-General constitute an important source of evidence. The relative distribution of spoils among various factions in Kenya may have changed slightly following the relations with international donors concerned and the murder of Dr Robert Ouko, Kenyan Foreign Affairs Minister by his fellow ministers with the consent of President Moi, but the total volume of corruption has probably remained the same or even increased.

Events surrounding the murder of the Kenyan Foreign Affairs Minister, Dr Robert Ouko, is complex but became clearer after the evidence to the judicial commission of inquiry in Kisumu from the retired Scotland Yard detective, John Troon, who investigated the killing. According to Mr Troon, Dr Ouko was probably murdered because of his allegations of high corruption, coupled with a personal dispute between him and the then energy minister, Mr Nicholas Biwott (London, *Observer* Sunday, 27 October 1991).

A Swiss-based group of consultants, BAK, had been in close contact with Dr Ouko since 1987, when Ouko was trying to rehabilitate the failed Kisumu molasses plant. In letters to Dr Ouko a BAK director, Marianne Briner-Mattern, confirmed that certain members of the Kenyan government including the vice-President and Minister of Finance, George Saitote, had been demanding 10–15 per cent commission in return for the awarding of contracts, as a consequence Kisumu has remained a ghost and run-down town in Kenya (London, *Observer* Sunday, 27 October 1991).

A similar story, one of far too many corrupt acts in Africa, relates to a scheme by the Anglo American Company in the early seventies, so the claim was made, to offer a bribe to turn a single large grain growing scheme near Lusaka (Zambia) into the granary of Southern Africa. Vast areas of bush were cleared, ploughed, nitrified and planted. Within a few years this multi-million scheme was abandoned. There was no capacity on such a scale to combat disease from excessive rainfall or the effects of drought, or the labour troubles which arose. Zambia has since been importing maize from Malawi, once regarded as a poor cousin.

In the past, the media have reported a number of corruption scandals, involving civil servants and costing the country a fortune. More recent press reports suggest that this type of corruption has certainly not abated. That corruption is rampant in the police is common knowledge. Also in a series of well-researched articles in the *Kenya Times*, a number of corrupt deals and smuggling rackets involving private businessmen and civil servants working in collusion, were disclosed. Furthermore, in 1986 it was announced that a major contract worth K.shs. 4 billion had been awarded to a French consortium of banks and the contractor Spie Batignolles for the construction of the Turkwel Gorge hydro-electric scheme (*Sunday Times*, 26 January 1986). It was later claimed that the contract cost Kenya twice the amount it would otherwise have cost, had international tendering procedures been followed (*Africa Confidential*, 9 April 1986). The allegation was that ministers had taken bribes from the French consortium to conclude the deal without proper tendering procedures having been observed. Repeated statements were made by politicians and senior civil servants, including the former chief Secretary, deploring the prevalence of corrupt practices in the civil service (*Daily Nation*, 20 September 1986). The Public Accounts Committee of Parliament regularly discussed the Annual Report of the Auditor-General, which usually contains sharp criticism of corrupt practices by public servants. Corruption has also been the subject of many editorial comments.

Whether corruption can be characterised as endemic to the politico-economic system of Kenya is perhaps open to question, but the evidence clearly points in that direction. And so it is claimed by Kenyans themselves. In mitigation, one might add that it now seems to have become common business practice on the part of transnational companies to offer chai (tea) to sweeten their tenders. If politicians and civil servants also solicit bribes, the collusion would appear perfect.

Why is grand corruption so bad, if it leads to financial accumulation? Above all, it is a parasitic phenomenon, because grand corruption has become a major (some would say predominant) means of income generation and capital accumulation, for certain groups and social strata, in place of productive investment. As such, it only marginally contributes to creating wealth; it redistributes only what has already been produced. A fair proportion of capital accumulated by corrupt means tends to leave the country legally or illegally. The illegal nature of most such outflows makes it well nigh impossible to estimate their magnitude. However, the recorded legal private outflow of investment income has risen sharply since the late 1970s, both in absolute terms and relative to capital inflow (Godfrey, 1986). There is no reason to believe that illegal outflows have behaved differently. To the extent that capital accumulated illicitly remains in Kenya, it is unlikely to be invested to its full productive potential. Secondly, it introduces a sense of arbitrariness into tendering and procurement procedures, which is highly detrimental to fostering a sound business climate. Thirdly, it further exacerbates the unequal distribution of income and wealth, which, in turn, undermines a bureaucratic culture, purportedly based on universal principles involving equal treatment by public institutions of 'wanainchi', regardless of position, ethnic background, race or status. The process feeds on itself and is thus being perpetuated.

The adverse consequences of corruption are as follows: (a) Corruption leads to inefficiency in public administration. Strong exception must be taken to the view that corrupt practices perform a practical function by oiling the state machinery. The total capacity of the public sector is not enhanced through bribery. It may prove expedient for an individual or a firm to offer bribes so as to acquire some advantages or to have a particular service performed, but it makes no rational sense for the system as such in its totality, not least because engagement in corrupt practices will always be time consuming and wasteful. Corruption merely changes the distribution of access to public goods and service. All Kenyans must therefore see corruption as the development of the worst aspect of our national social life that must be eliminated at all costs. (b) It creates inequalities in the distribution of *matunda ya Uhuru* (the fruits of independence), i.e. goods and services, because only those who are capable of paying are served, or served first. (c) It diverts attention away from long-term productive investment and related economic activities, in preference for quick profit and immediate satisfaction. (d) Giving *chai* adds to the cost of investments and development activities and represents a form of overhead charge, to which the investor always adds on the price of the product.

2.1.4 ETHNICITY AND PATRONAGE – ROOTS OF CONTEMPORARY CRISIS

Some of Kenya's current problems are rooted in the colonial experience. Colonial administration failed in various ways to erect a sturdy base for responsive and effective post-colonial administration in Kenya.

Modern Kenya was artificially created as a state in 1895. First, colonial administration lumped together heterogeneous Kenyan people in common territory. It also, albeit unintentionally, sharpened ethnic consciousness by a 'divide and rule policy'. Kenya had a variety of traditional political structures which contained several traditional societies, each with its own political, economic and social values, its own cultural values, myths and symbols. But colonial administration created its own artificial administrative boundaries and local government on cultural-linguistic lines which did foster ethnic consciousness. A divisive sense of separateness was promoted by the formation of local Native Authorities to administer land rights and certain taxes. The colonial assumption was that Africans lived in tribes, and that these should therefore, constitute the basis for administration, became a self-fulfilling perception.

The second important factor was the uneven regional impact of modernisation introduced by colonial rule in Kenya. Some regions developed cash crops and prospered, others did not. Kenya/Uganda Railway construction spurred agricultural development in areas where the line traversed. Towns and hence urban employment, emerged in the homelands of certain groups, thus favouring their economic advance. The establishment of mission schools in certain regions of Kenya, usually near the railway lines, gave local ethnic groups an enviable head-start with Western education. Consequently, some people benefited from these opportunities for upward mobility, whereas others were regarded as backward. Uneven development thereby stimulated ethnic consciousness: those holding the advantages strove to retain it, whereas others clamoured for their fair share of the pie.

As independence approached, this dichotomous 'we' and 'they' mentality was underscored by a new fear – the suspicion on the part of the disadvantaged and/or peripheral people that the well-to-do tribes would consolidate their position by controlling the post-colonial state structures. Few ignorant, semi-educated politicians could resist the temptation to capitalise on these mutual anxieties to bolster their personal following. Some Kenyan politicians with implicit support of the departing colonial administrators exploited, and thus magnified, ethnic consciousness by manipulating tribally oriented cultural symbols and rhetoric which evoked tribal unity in the face of a common enemy. Aspiring leaders goaded their audience: 'we must organise and help one another or else we shall lose out to "them".' Thus emerged a symbiotic relationship between leaders who aimed to promote personal political ambitions and their followers who craved the rewards that political power entailed; jobs, education and public investment were the prizes.

Tribes and tribalism in Kenya are in one sense a thoroughly modern creation by the British colonial administration. The sense of shared identity and interest that define a tribe was often absent in the pre-colonial period in East Africa. Nor were modern antagonists necessarily historical enemies. The current bitter rivalry between the Kenyan Kikuyu and Luo is a twentieth-century neo-colonial phenomenon and a colonial creation. Indeed, prior to colonial manipulation, neither Kikuyu or Luo constituted a distinct ethnic group. There were, instead, acephalous, localised agricultural communities in central Kenya who spoke a mutually intelligible Bantu language and shared cultural beliefs and practices such as female and male circumcision. The Nyeri, Muranga and Kiambu segments of the Kikuyu were often at war with each other and sometimes one of these groups would enlist Masai allies. Around Lake Victoria, a similar situation prevailed among the Luo-speaking communities. The three conditions which were fulfilled during the colonial rule which fostered the tribal consciousness of the Kikuyu and Luo peoples were: (a) the cultural-linguistic grid of district administration, (b) uneven development and (c) Kenyans' political competition for land ownership in the colony in the post-war era. Even today the boundaries dividing these groups remain flexible, membership depending upon the arena of competition.

The point is that, what is usually labelled ethnicity or tribalism is really the same thing as nationalism. The rivalries engaging the Kikuyu and Luo in Kenya are essentially part of the same parcel as the divisions between the Flemings and the Walloons in Belgium, the French and English in Canada or the Scots and the English in the UK. A sense of cultural uniqueness and a determination to guard ethnic interests is the essence of both nationalism and ethnicity. A necessary condition for both is the tangible manifestation of cultural distinctiveness – generally language, and sometimes religion and customs as well. But these traits only become politically salient when aggravated by uneven development, political competition, the self-serving tactics of ambitious politicians and foreign interference. Hence, colonialism was the incubator of Western-style conflict in Kenya to be sure, but more significantly, of a multi-national or poly-ethnic state.

Ethnic formation was one key aspect of social change in Kenya during the colonial era; class formation (discussed later) was another. The significance of this latter process lies in the weak articulation of modern capitalist classes – bourgeoisie and proletariat – and a correspondingly widespread peasantisation. This laid the social foundation for a form of patriarchal rule in Kenya and in the sub-Saharan African countries.

In a society like Kenya, characterised by sharp class, and tribal contradictions and a materially vulnerable citizenry, whose social consciousness has not yet crystallised into a class consciousness of its own (i.e. capable of acting collectively as a class force), patronage (or clientelism) tends to play a significant role in politics (Clapham, 1985). Patronage is basically a relationship of unequal exchange, in which a superior patron provides a form of security or benefit for an inferior client, who in turn lends support in elections or in some other ways to his patron. In Kenya, where the state is a major provider of goods and services, access by the patrons to the state system, including its posts and positions, becomes crucial, so that they can have resources at their disposal for distribution to clients. By the same token, patrons also need political support from their clients in order to reach those positions. Patronage in Kenya operates at all levels of society, linking the top positions to the lower echelons through a complex chain of patron–client relationships, which may be very difficult for outsiders to disentangle.

A patronage system fosters a highly personalised and particularistic style of politics and leadership which we see in Kenya. In this situation, class contradictions and other bases for political mobilisation cutting across clientelist systems, tend to be discontinued and pushed into the background. The vulnerability of clients militates against a break with patronage networks. Clients are inclined to prefer the relatively limited short-term security offered by the patrons, to the insecurity of fundamental class-based upheavals, whose outcome may be altogether uncertain.

Clientelist politics do not preclude factionalism and shifting alliances across occupational and other group boundaries as circumstances change. On the contrary, networks of patron–client relationships, as a form of participation and control, have to respond to the contending networks on an ad hoc basis, and to realign themselves, as the situation may require. In short, factionalism is a hallmark of Kenyan politics (Bienen, 1974), and was the main reason for the failure of the opposition parties in Kenya's general elections of 1992 and 1997 to unite behind a single candidate and when splits and division among the opposition enabled Moi to remain in power.

Appeal to kinship and ethnic identity, is a typical expression of clientelist relations. In common parlance, it is called 'tribalism'. The scope of tribalism is considerable in Kenya with its multi-national/tribal state formation. Ethnic identity naturally pre-dates colonialism. But cultural expression of the various tribes/nationalities, including language, tradition, dress and music have persisted, and today represent a significant asset in their contribution to the cultural richness and ethnic diversity of Kenya as a country. 'Tribalism', as an ideological phenomenon, on the other hand, is essentially a colonial creation, forming part of a 'divide-and-rule' strategy, which colonialism sought to perpetuate through a Majimbo constitution. But, despite the discarding of Majimboism as a form of institutionalised ethnic sentiment and the adoption of a new constitution based on a unitary state, ethnic thinking is still sufficiently entrenched in Kenya to play a role in politics even after independence. The relative success of the Kikuyu in the post-independence period in business and politics, was, for instance, perceived by other Kenyans as ethnic favouritism by President Kenyatta (himself a Kikuyu) to the detriment of other tribes who received a lesser share of government spending (Leys, 1975).

Notwithstanding the pervasiveness of 'tribalism' as the ideo-logical basis of patronage networks, it is officially denounced as divisive by politicians from all quarters. Instead, the Kenyan ideology of 'African Socialism', 'national-building', and populism is being propagated, epitomised by the national slogan of 'harambee' under Jomo Kenyatta and that of 'Nyayo' since Moi took office. Populism, as an ideology, glosses over conflicts of social interest, and emphasises the common 'national' interest in development for Kenyans, regardless of ethnic affiliation, class origin or religion. Conversely, all 'foreign ideologies' like capitalism and scientific socialism, are vehemently denounced as anathema to Kenyan traditions and ways of thinking (*Kenya Times*, 6 March 1985).

The perverted version of the original concept of 'harambee' or self-help, has become a significant tool in clientelist politics (Barkan & Holmquist, 1986). Politicians exploit the harambee institution for their own political purposes, by 'buying' support and votes from the peasantry through generous contributions to projects or to put the matter differently, by bribing the electorate. In turn, the peasants take advantage of harambee projects to extract (or repossess) some surplus from the politicians. Examples of misuse of 'harambee' have become so numerous that the very idea is being brought into disrepute. This applies not to political misuse as such, from which even the peasant contributors benefit in some measure. The growing disenchantment with harambee projects stems from the many reported incidents of cheques being offered as a contribution by a *bwana mkubwa* patron, and subsequently not being honoured by the banks. The elements of reciprocity standing at the heart of the patron–client relationship is thus betrayed – the patron gets the publicity of having contributed lavishly 'from himself and friends' while the clients in actual fact get nothing. Furthermore, many cases of mismanagement or outright embezzlement and theft of collected funds have been reported on many occasions without anybody being prosecuted (*Daily Nation*, 8 March 1985).

With the onset of economic recession in 1982, following the culmination of the 'coffee boom', the scope of 'harambee' narrowed to the peasantry using it as a mechanism to extract surplus from politicians and the state. Instead, harambee has degenerated into a form of illegal taxation. Originally conceived as a voluntary institution, harambee is increasingly becoming compulsory in character (Holmquist, 1984). This development has bred further disaffection from self-help programmes.

Finally, cutting across class distinctions, are a number of ethnic associations, e.g. the Luo Union, the New Akamba Union, the Gikuyu, Embu, Meru Association (GEMA). These bodies were active in matters not defined as politics; welfare, cultural, social and economic affairs. In the post-independence period, some of these associations, especially GEMA, gradually assumed a political posture, performing the functions of a quasi-party. In 1980, all these associations were disbanded by the Moi's government order (Nelson, 1983).

2.1.5 FOREIGN RELATIONS

Kenya is a member of various international organisations, foremost among which are the United Nations (UN) and the Organisation of African Unity (OAU). Kenya is also an ACP signatory to the ACP/EU Convention of Lome, and a member of the Commonwealth and the Non-Aligned Movement. Of particular regional significance in recent years has been Kenya's membership of the Preferential Trade Area for Eastern and Southern Africa (PTA), which may prove instrumental in promoting Kenyan exports to other African countries.

After the so-called Shifta war of the mid-1960s which originated in territorial claims by Somalia to parts of North-Eastern Kenya, relations between the two countries were normalised when Somalia officially renounced any territorial claims it may have previously held over parts of Kenya. The North-Eastern Province of Kenya remains an area of continuing unrest. Kenya and Ethiopia maintain cordial relations, which were formalised in a treaty of friendship and cooperation concluded between the two countries in 1979.

Of the major powers, the closest relationship has been maintained with the former colonial master, Great Britain, and more recently with the United States of America. Both had during the Cold War period and now a strong geo-political and defence interest in the political and economic stability of Kenya. The entire state apparatus of Kenya is modelled on the British system and British traditions that have left an imprint in most spheres of life. Economic and commercial relations are strong, and Britain is Kenya's main trading partner, as well as a major source of Development Aid. In the military field, Britain has long been the principal supplier of arms, equipment and instructors as outlined in the 1964 military agreement between the two countries (Nelson, 1983).

The United States since the early 1980s assumed a more prominent role as an ally and an excellent friend of Kenya. The USA is a major provider of Development Aid, a source of foreign investment funds and an important trading partner. Since the 1980s when facilities for Access Agreement were concluded, the United States gained access to naval facilities in Mombasa and to air facilities in Nanyuki and Nairobi (Nelson, 1983). From a geo-political point of view, Kenya is regarded by the USA as a geographic element in the USA's rapid deployment force strategy in the Indian Ocean. The USA has now surpassed the UK as the principal supplier of arms and military equipment to Kenya. In

1986 the USA was scheduled to significantly step up security assistance to Kenya.

Severely hit by drought in 1983-1984, Kenya in late 1984 became a founder member of the regionally based Intergovernmental authority on Drought and Development (IGADD) which in addition to Kenya, comprises Djibouti, Ethiopia, Somalia, Sudan and Uganda. It objectives and programmes include improvement of early warning systems for impending drought, boosting the development of drought resistant crops, and soil erosion. IGADD therefore offers the prospect of developing useful regional links in new fields of cooperation (*EIU Somalia/Djibouti Country Report*, no. 3, 1986). Kenya is also a member of the Desert Locust Control Organisation for Eastern Africa (DLCOEA) based in Nairobi. Outbreaks of migratory locust swarms occur periodically and can involve widespread destruction of crops in many parts of Eastern and Southern Africa if not checked by concerted regional action at an early stage.

As a central point for international communications in Africa, Kenya became a popular and much used venue for large international conferences. Kenya also hosted the UN Environment Programme (UNEP), now moved to Spain, and the UN Centre on Human Settlement (Habitat), the only two headquarters of UN organisations located in Third World Countries.

2.2   Human Rights

2.2.1   DEFINITION OF HUMAN RIGHTS

Human rights could be generally defined as those rights which are inherent in our nature and without which we cannot live as human beings. Human rights and fundamental freedoms allow us to fully develop and use our human qualities, our intelligence, our talents and our conscience and to satisfy our spiritual and other needs. They are based on mankind's increasing demand for a life in which the inherent dignity and worth of each human being will receive respect and protection.

The denial of human rights and fundamental freedom is not

only an individual and personal tragedy, but also creates conditions of social and political unrest, sowing the seeds of violence and conflict within and between societies and nations. As the first sentence of the Universal Declaration of Human Rights states, respect of human rights and human dignity 'is the foundation of freedom, justice and peace in the world'.

For centuries, there has been a persistent and widespread conviction that some 'human rights' are so essential to the fulfilment of the individual's personality, that they can be called 'natural rights'. They are held to be 'natural', in the sense that their recognition is implicit in the facts of social organisation. Hobhouse says, 'A true moral right, is one which is demonstrably justified by its relation to the common good, whether it is actually recognised or not'.

The second aspect is a distinction between theoretical and enforceable rights. It is important to note the form in which rights are granted. The statement in a constitution, that certain specified rights are guaranteed will remain totally worthless if there is no way by which citizens can see that the government does, in actual fact, guarantee his/her enjoyment of them. Governments sometimes use such paper guarantees as a device by which to evade obligations which public opinion wants to compel them to assume. Rights are accorded on paper, but the necessary steps to implement them are never taken, or texts are framed in such a way as to defeat the expressed intention.

The modern citizen today is much more dependent on the state, not only for essentials of civilised life, but for much of what goes to make up his/her standard of living, and the problem of the relation of rights to duties has become much more complex. The two changes are inevitably closely related. As the minimum standard rises, as the citizen comes to demand more and more from the state, obligations increase commensurately with rights. But the increase is not merely quantitative. It is also qualitative. Our conceptions of what men/women require from the state in order to lead a full life have moved from the purely physical plane to include the intellectual, the emotional and the psychological. The problems of translating these requirements into practical policies are such that it is becoming less and less possible to find solutions for them in terms of hard and fast rules. At one time, the citizen's rights amounted to little more than the right to be protected from physical assault and from starvation. Today, the right to be protected from starvation has been extended to include the right to food which is adequate in quality as well as quantity etc.

The fundamental civil and political rights of individual Kenyan citizens are enshrined in Chapter V of the Constitution of Kenya. Kenya has also ratified the International Covenant on Civil and Political Rights (Skalnes & Egeland, 1986)

2.2.2 TRADE UNIONISM

Trade Union activities in Kenya are generally regulated by two Acts of Parliament – the Trade Disputes Act and the Trade Union Act. This legal framework provides an elaborate machinery for handling industrial relations including an industrial Court, as stipulated in the former Act (Cockar, 1981). In terms of the later act, the Registrar of Trade Unions has wide powers to register and deregister unions, and to inspect their accounts, membership registers and other documents. In addition, a tripartite Industrial Relations Charter between government, employers and unions has been in force since 1962, with subsequent amendments in 1980 (Cockar, 1981). This charter binds the parties to keep industrial peace as long as industrial agreements are in force. The constitution of the Central Organisation of Trade Unions (COTU), established in 1965, grants the President of the Republic powers to revoke the appointment or election of senior union officials, and gives the government the right to representation in the organisation's governing council, executive board and finance committee. (*Financial Review*, 22 September 1986)

The terms and conditions of work are regulated within the legal framework of the employment Act of 1975 and other statutory provisions, such as the Regulation of Wage (General Amendment) Order 1982. In 1973, the government issued Wages Guidelines, as part of a general income policy, which were subsequently amended in 1982.

In 1984, Kenya had 31 registered trade unions of which 28

were affiliates of COTU. The unions' activities are circumscribed not only by the constraints of the established legal and bureaucratised machinery, within which they have to operate. Their bargaining power has in recent years also been severely weakened by the recession and the highest rate of unemployment in the country.

Roughly 400,000 employees were unionised in 1985 (Kenya Government, 1985), out of a total labour force of approximately 1.1 million (Statistical Abstract, 1985), i.e. about 36 per cent. The public sector accounts for more than half of wage employment, but in 1980 the Kenya Civil Servants Union was de-registered. In 1984, of the unionised wage workers in 18 unions, about 22 per cent were women (Kenya/Ministry of Labour, 1985a), which roughly corresponds to their share in the total wage labour force (Statistical Abstract,1985).

The Industrial Court in 1984 registered 306 collective agreements, but only 244 of them, covering a total of 120,202 employees, submitted forms with the required data, which has been used here to represent the general picture as to conditions of employment. With these qualifications, the 1984 information shows that on a countrywide basis the average minimum basic wage rate for the lower income groups negotiated between employers and unions, was K.shs. 613 per month. The statutory minimum wage as from 1 May 1985 was K.shs. 576 per month for the lowest income groups in Nairobi and Mombasa, and K.shs. 530 per month in other towns (*Ely Quarterly Economic Report*, no.3, 1985). A housing allowance, equivalent to a minimum of 15 per cent of basic monthly wage, is payable to all employees, and may also be provided in kind. The average working week was 44.3 hours. On the first of May 1986, the President directed that a five-day working week be introduced for the private sector as well as the public sector, which had received a similar award on Labour Day, 1983 (*Kenya Times*, 2 May 1986). The average negotiated annual leave entitlement in 1984 was 24.8 working days with full pay, which is higher than the statutory minimum of 21 days. Annual leave allowance amounted to K.shs. 244 on average. The average annual sick leave entitlement was 37 days with full pay. The statutory entitlement is 30 days with full pay, and thereafter a maximum of 15 days with half pay in each period of twelve days consecutive service. In cases of redundancy, the average negotiated severance pay was 15.8 days for each year of completed service (Kenya Ministry of Labour, 1985). In terms of the Employment Act of 1976 (section 7(2)) a woman employee is entitled to two months maternity leave with full pay, provided she forfeits her annual leave in that year (Cockar, 1981).

A compulsory public pension scheme exists for all in wage employment. It does not apply to self-employed workers, such as peasants. Employees and employers each pay 5 per cent of the employees' gross monthly emoluments into the National Social Security Fund (NSSF). On retirement, employees receive a lump sum equivalent to the accumulated amount plus interest (National Social Security Fund Act, 1965). For employees earning more than K.shs. 1000 per month, membership of the National Hospital Insurance Fund is compulsory, for which a monthly contribution of K.shs. 20 is collected. Employees earning less than K.shs. 1000 per month may become members on a voluntary basis. A member is entitled to free hospitalisation (National Hospital Insurance Act, 1966).

The size of the labour force capable of unionisation is admittedly small relative to Kenya's total labour force. Nonetheless, because of the importance of the trade union movement for a large proportion of Kenya's urban population in negotiating better terms and conditions of employment, it has constituted a significant political arena since early development during the colonial period. Aspiring politicians have used unions as their platform to gain political office. Cases in point include the first Secretary General of COTU, the late Tom Mboya MP, Juma Boy, MP and Denis Akumu, MP; all have been a Member of Parliament (Goldsworthy, 1982).

2.2.3 PRISON CONDITIONS AND CAPITAL PUNISHMENT

The prison population of Kenya, numbering about 41,000, are held in quarters intended for 14,000 (*Weekly Review*, 1994).

This serious overcrowding has led to deplorable conditions for the inmates. Due to very poor hygiene and the low nutritional standard of food, many prisoners contract new diseases or develop more acute or advanced forms of the illnesses from which they were suffering on entry to prison. Medical treatment is grossly inadequate. Physical torture, death by beatings and other maltreatment occur systematically, albeit primarily in police cells prior to conviction and imprisonment. Generally political prisoners are regarded as 'enemies of state' and get the worst treatment, prisoners' death in police custody or in prison is frequent and cannot be reported, because it destroys Kenya's image with aid donors and overseas. Lack or delay of medical treatment however, has torturous effects and many prisoners die painfully.

A special prison problem concerns the 4,000 or so children who every year accompany their convicted mothers to jail. According to a prison report, in the last 22 years more than 75,000 children have spent time in prison under totally inhuman, unacceptable, and degrading conditions with their single mothers, who were serving sentences for petty crimes like theft, illegal hawking and brewing because no one else was available to take care of their children (*Africa Now*, 1995). The vice-President of Kenya, Mr Saitote, admitted that a solution has yet to be found to the problem of children accompanying their mothers to prison.

Certain serious crimes are punishable by death in Kenya, e.g. murders, robbery with violence etc. In the trials which followed the August 1982 coup attempt, a number of death sentences were pronounced over those found guilty of high treason. Those sentenced were hanged at Kamiti maximum security prison in 1985 (*Africa Confidential*, 1985). Many former KAF personnel have since been granted amnesty, although a certain number still remain in custody.

By the end of 1995, Amnesty International reported that over 250 prisoners were held under sentence of death. Having exhausted the various possibilities for appeal within the court system, they could only hope for an act of Presidential clemency, for which the Constitution makes provision. Of late, an unknown number of regular criminals, notably murderers and robbers, have been executed.

2.2.4 PREVENTIVE DETENTION AND DEPRIVATION OF CITIZENSHIP

Section 85 of the Constitution empowers the President, in terms of the Preservation of Public Security Act to detain any person without trial for an unspecified period of time, and subject to announcement in the Kenya Gazette, any person who is considered a threat to public security. Such acts of preventive detention are also exempted from legal action under other constitutional provisions. Thus, section 83 states that any steps taken under the Public Security Act shall not be held to be inconsistent with, or in contravention of, any part of the Constitution i.e. the Bill of Rights in Chapter V. These constitutional and legal provisions have been invoked on a number of occasions in the post-independence era. The practice of preventive detention without trial in Kenya, has rarely been questioned in public debate on grounds of principles, this is because of intimidation (including one's family members), threats and even murders by the security agents. One exception, was in 1982, when the former editor-in-chief of the *Standards* newspaper, Mr George Githii, in an editorial comment, spoke out against preventive detention, as a method of silencing political opponents of the government. The owner of the Newspaper Lonrho, was warned by the Office of the President that the *Standards* newspaper would be closed down, unless Mr Githii was immediately dismissed (Nelson, 1983). Shortly thereafter he was relieved of his post by the owners of the newspaper.

The number of detainees officially gazetted is no more than a dozen, but the number of people actually held, without having been brought before a court under section 85 (2) and (3) of the Constitution in accordance with the habeas corpus principle, is much higher. Detention without trial is a sensitive issue in Kenya, because the Kenya Government relies heavily on Western Development Aid which is conditional on Kenya's 'human rights record'. The government and its security apparatus prefers the ethnic cleansing method to eliminate known trouble makers (opponents) rather than detain them unless they are public figures (policy: 'remove the bad apples by their roots').

The countrywide security network is used to identify and locate oppositional elements (trouble makers), who are considered a threat to the established order and the powers to be. In this context, the security service employs a large number of grassroots paid informers, who frequent bars and other places where people congregate and exchange views in order to pick up information. Anything of a suspicious nature is then reported back to appropriate authorities for action, which is then taken immediately.

Section 94, subsection (1) (a) of the Constitution, states that a Kenyan Citizen may be deprived of his citizenship, if that citizen has shown himself by act or speech to be disloyal or disaffected towards Kenya. In an unprecedented and deeply disturbing case, this section was invoked against Mohamed Salim Lone, who was deprived of his citizenship by announcement in the Kenya Gazette of 28 August 1986 (*Daily Nation*, 5 September 1986).

2.2.5 POLITICS OF JUSTICE AND FREEDOM OF EXPRESSION

The Kenya judiciary has long been considered absolutely independent and insulated from political influence. Politics were generally conducted within a framework of constitutionalism and legality. Individual rights were actually expanded in the 1960s and 1970s (MacWilliam, 1985).

This widely established view is now critically challenged. The process of the Kenyan legal system which is supposed to protect all Kenyans is now open to misuse and abuse. The Kenyan judiciary is being utilised to maintain existing power relations and to bolster a regime which has a very narrow political constituency. Apart from the constitutional powers being used to detain innocent citizens without trial and to deprive individual Kenyans of their birth-rights and citizenship, fraudulent criminal proceedings, ethnic cleansing and murders are increasingly being used by the government to displace troublesome opposition elements in Kenya. (*Race & Class*, Vol. XXIV no.3, pp.245-258)

The discussions on the 'Party Structure and Political Culture' above and on the political climate for open debate are issues crucial to the development of individual freedom in Kenya. It indicates that freedom of expression has its definite limits in Kenya. However, there is no formal censorship. Although some debate does occur, there is a cloud of real fear and the limits beyond which political commentators should not venture, lest risking intimidation, victimisation, detention without trial and possibly mysterious death, are only vaguely defined. Some good investigative reporting is being undertaken and excesses disclosed, but for the most part such reporting is inconsequential and completely ineffective. Frequently vivid public criticism of the civil service in general for its inefficiency, and of some specific individuals for corruption or mismanagement is regarded as a legitimate form of expression. In particular, the delivery and subsequent publication of church sermons are increasingly viewed as an effective means of giving voice to public discontent over a range of social ills and malpractice, but these also carry grave risks to the individuals (Jutterstrom, 1986).

Allegations of misconduct, however, may also represent a form of disguised political attack. Thus, sharp criticism is tolerated as long as the addressee is not specified, or easily identifiable, such as one of the President's protégés or the President himself. Constitutionally, the Kenyan President is above the law of the land and therefore above all criticism!

As a result, the art of writing between the lines for a readership thoroughly familiar with the context and historical circumstances of events, has been assiduously cultivated by certain reporters. Often oblique reference and allusions to recognised phenomena and political actors, may be as effective as overt criticism. But it requires a conscious audience; for the unwary and uninitiated it may be difficult to follow. For the many who do not master the technique of reading between the lines, self-censorship may represent the only logical response. Articles then tend to focus on themes which are unlikely to cause any offence or controversy. If not, the author may be branded, in the name of nation-building and consensual politics, as an 'anti-nyayo' radical, or as a purveyor of foreign ideologies, or as a disloyal rumour-monger.

The printed news media consist of three English-language dailies, *Kenya Times/Sunday Times* (since April 1983), *Daily Nation/Sunday Nation* and *Standards/Sunday Standards*. The two former have also Kiswahili editions, *Kenya Leo/Kenya Weekly* and *Taifa Leo/Taifa Weekly*.

The nation group of papers is owned by Nation Printers and Publishers Ltd, a public company with nearly 3,000 shares, of which the Aga Khan holds a controlling 60 per cent (Ekirapa, 1986). The Standard belongs to Lonrho, two of the dailies are thus owned by foreign interests. The *Kenya Times* is owned by KANU and is its organ, and consequently reflects government opinion. This paper reported that the KANU treasurer, the late Justus ole Tipis, was in financial difficulties, but declined to disclose the size of debt which the *Kenya Times* group had incurred (*Weekly Review*, 22 August 1986).

There are a number of weeklies and monthlies covering a whole spectrum of interests, although mostly concerned with entertainment and social affairs. Three notable exceptions are the *Weekly Review* and its sister publication of the *Financial Review* which sold close to 17,000 copies in the first half of 1986. A few local newspapers exist in the area outside Nairobi.

The electronic media are the exclusive domain of the government controlled Voice of Kenya, which broadcasts and telecasts in both English and Kiswahili. The Kenya News Agency is also controlled by the government and reporters are trained at the School of Journalism at the University of Nairobi.

2.2.6 FREEDOM OF MOVEMENT, ASSEMBLY AND ASSOCIATION

Kenya is a comparatively mobile society. Its relatively extensive communications infrastructure and service network have facilitated the movement of people within the country. The prevalence of labour migration is but one feature of this mobility. Generally, there is no hindrance to the movement of individuals for economic or other reasons. However, police road blocks may be frequently encountered, whose main purpose is crime prevention, but which also are misused and abused from time to time in controlling the movement of political opponents (trouble-makers) of the government. Administrative police, under the supervision of chiefs and assistant chiefs, monitor the movements of political opponents, the coming and going of people identified as not belonging to a particular village or locality, what they say and their purpose in the area, they can be arrested and detained on any pretext.

No formal restrictions exist on emigration, but individuals who are known as trouble makers (political opponents), are sometimes restricted from leaving the country for emigration or other purposes outside Kenya, and if their passport have been impounded by the immigration authorities, they cannot leave the country without Presidential permission.

Under the Public Order Act, section 5, the holding of every public meeting and procession, requires a license from the relevant authorities, which is issued on the basis of an application stating the purpose of the meeting, time and venue, agenda, list of speakers. The provincial administration officer/the district commissioner may grant or refuse at his/her discretion. There is no appeal. The commonest pretext for refusal is that a meeting is judged likely to cause a breach of the peace. There are numerous cases of applications being turned down to mention only one. But, perhaps the most blatant example of political misuse and abuse of power of this legal position, was the total refusal in 1966–1967 of all KPU meeting applications before the 'little general election', while KANU was granted 804 permits to hold their meetings (Mueller, 1984).

The Societies Act requires every society to be registered. The Registrar of Societies may refuse registration on the grounds that the society submitting an application, is pursuing an unlawful purpose. The registrar holds wide discretionary powers to determine which society shall be considered unlawful, and repugnant or otherwise undesirable.

2.2.7 POLITICAL PARTICIPATION

The perceived unsuitability of KANU as a vehicle for channelling demands upward from its rank-and-file membership, as a basis for subsequent policy formulation, coupled with coercive forms of recruitment of new members, resulted in the estrangement from the electoral process of large sections of the electorate in Kenya. In the 1974 general election, the turn-out was 78.4 per cent of the registered voters. In 1979, the corresponding figure was 60 per cent, plummeting to only 41.6 per cent in the 1983 general election (Source: Supervisor of Elections). The proportion of eligible voters who actually register is, however, hardly one hundred per cent. At the time of the census in 1979, the total population of Kenya was 15.3 million. Given the youthful age structure of the population, it may be justifiably assumed that about 55 per cent were at that time below voting age (18 years), i.e. 8.4 million people were not eligible to vote (Kenya Central Bureau of Statistics, 1981b), leaving approximately 6.9 million Kenyans eligible to vote. Of these, as many as 6.2 million registered as voters. In 1979 general election, however, only 3.2 million did in fact vote. This was only 51.6 per cent of the eligible voters, as compared with 60 per cent of the registered voters. For the 1983 elections the assumption may arguably hold true that a corresponding 8–9 per cent reduction may be made in the ratio of participation to registered voters, in order to arrive at a ratio of votes cast to the number of eligible voters. Following this analysis, the effective electoral participation rate in 1983 would have been about 38 per cent.

In April 1986, it was announced that KANU would introduce a new polling system for preliminary election of candidates for Parliamentary seats. Voters would queue up behind the candidates of their choice. The justification for introducing preliminary elections was the proliferation of candidates for one-person constituencies, to the extent that the elected candidate might have only a minority of the votes cast, the remainder being spread over a large number of other contestants. A further justification was the elimination of rigging by the introduction of an 'open system'. The mechanisms and modalities of instituting the system were to be worked out later, but well ahead of the General Election (*Daily Nation*, 10 April 1986; *Weekly Review*, 11 April 1986). In the late August of the same year, the KANU Annual Delegates' Meeting unanimously adopted the new electoral procedures (*Weekly Review*, 29 August 1986).

It soon transpired that the new polling system had initially met considerable opposition from the churches. At a NCCK conference (consisting of predominantly Protestant denominations) on 21 August 1986 in Nairobi, in which 1,200 pastors took part, a statement was adopted expressing strong reservations as to the new regulation: 'If the procedure to line up behind the candidates is followed and if many church leaders or other Christians refrain from taking part in the elections, they will have been denied their human and constitutional rights.' (*Beyond*, September 1986). In a well argued article in the NCCK magazine, it was asserted that the line-up system would have a divisive effect on church congregations and that the system would '...antagonise rather than foster peace, love and unity...' A strong case was made for the use of secret ballot, which was seen as the only effective safeguard against intimidation and blackmail before elections and victimisation afterwards. As to the filing of petitions of complaint, a queuing system would render such actions meaningless, as *ex post facto* verification of results would no longer be possible (*Beyond*, September 1986). With the introduction of a queuing system in preliminary elections, voters' alienation from the electoral process could well be accelerated.

The Law Society of Kenya (LSK) issued a statement calling for a public debate on the proposed changes in the polling system, and reminded the government of LSK's duty under the Law Society of Kenya Act to assist the public in matters touching upon, ancillary and incidental to the law (*Weekly Review*, 5 September 1986). In response to persistent opposition, the President in the end succumbed to public pressure, and made exemptions for church leaders, senior military and police officers. Persons in these categories were now to vote by proxy (*Daily Nation*; *Standards*; *Kenya Times*, 6 September 1986). The issuing of exemptions immediately gave rise to new problems, relating to the discrimination and definition of exempted persons as well as the fate of the exempted persons' proxies. These problems remained unresolved. This action, nevertheless, appeased some of the clergy, who thanked the President for his decision to exempt them from queuing (*Daily Nation*, 8 September 1986).

Other church leaders persisted in their criticism of the government even to the point of opposing the one-party system (*Daily Nation*, 22 September 1986). It seems as if the churches became the 'voice of the voiceless', as the normal channels of expressing discontent appear to be effectively closed. Of late, the churches have drawn public attention to further issues of concern, such as corruption and misuse of the 'harambee' tradition for political purposes (*Beyond*, 1987) But, the NCCK's victory seemed not to have been without a price, their spokesman and leader opposing vehemently the new voting system, the Anglican Bishop Alexander Kipsang Muge was mysteriously killed in a road accident near Eldoret! The critical posture of the churches extended far beyond the debate on the queuing system. It probably stemmed from their involvement in work at the grass-roots level, where abject poverty stands in stark contrast to the extreme wealth and conspicuous consumption of the upper classes. The fact that the Bible is often invoked, when justifying their involvement in 'political issues', pointed to their inspiration from South African church leaders like Bishop Desmond Tutu and variants of liberation theology. The strength of the churches as an oppositional force lies in the deep-rooted religious tradition in Kenya and the class affiliation of the majority of churchgoers. Many church leaders in Kenya are highly respected persons and enjoy more widespread popular support than the politicians. Any move against the church leaders by a corrupt and degenerate secular leader like President Moi and his corrupt henchmen, would be seen as an attack on the very foundation of society and the church.

2.2.8 MINORITIES AND REFUGES

In terms of political influence and access to the fruits of independence, some national minorities have been effectively marginalised. This applies particularly to the nomadic pastoralists, who, for a variety of reasons, have an elusive attitude to their relations with the modern state. Their nomadic way of life makes them difficult to administer. For this and other reasons, the approach of officialdom has been largely negative, and shown itself in this form. Official attitudes, for example, touch less than helpfully on the allocation of state development resources to the areas inhabited by the nomadic pastoralists, and on the encroachment into their traditional grazing territories by national parks, hydro-electric schemes and agricultural projects.

Occasionally, very serious atrocities have been committed on minorities by the Kenya police and the armed forces including the most recent one in 1998. For example, in February 1984, an incident occurred in Wajir, a typically pastoral area. The gravity of this incident was belatedly understood by the international mass media which reported it extensively. The government was reluctant, however, to admit to anything until MPs from the district raised the issues in Parliament, demanding a commission of inquiry. Thirteen diplomatic missions protested jointly to the government (*Amnesty International Newsletter*, vol. XIV, no.6, 1984 and *Africa Confidential*, vol. 5, 1984).

It transpired from the reports that a large number (between 1,000 and 4,000) of ethnic Somalis had been rounded up, and made to lie down on an airstrip outside Wajir town, after having been stripped naked. They were kept there during daytime in the hot blazing sun for 3–4 days without water. When the group tried to escape they were shot by the guards. The number killed has never been accurately ascertained, but it is estimated that between 300 to 1,300 people were killed in this massacre. The Minister of State in the Office of the President responsible for defence and internal security matters, conceded in Parliament that fifty-nine people had been killed when resisting an order to surrender their firearms. Some government officers were simply transferred following this incident and nobody was charged with or punished for this wicked and abominable crime.

There is solid ground to believe that many of the atrocities that have been committed by security forces in different parts of Kenya have been on the direct order of the President, ministers or senior government officials. But, in the Wajir incident, it would appear that the incident was likely to have been the tragic result of persistently harsh official rhetoric over an extended period of time, extremely inept and aggressive administration in a sensitive border area with many firearms in circulation, combined with gross indiscipline on the part of police, GSU and units of the Kenya armed forces.

On a totally different plane, the Asian community in Kenya perceive their position to be that of an insecure minority. Their important role in trade, construction and manufacturing, might seem to indicate the opposite. However, the government's policy of Kenyanisation has in some measure resulted in economic discrimination against the Asians; this needs to be corrected. Popular sentiments with racialist overtones are sometimes exploited by politicians. The looting of Asian-owned shops in Nairobi in the aftermath of the 1982 coup attempt was unfortunate, but it was an evident expression of popular resentment against their role in the economy (*Viva*, August 1982).

Kenya has not been immune from the civil conflict in the region. The country shares common borders with both the Sudan and Somalia and is burdened by the large number of refugees fleeing civil conflict. The authorities have repeatedly requested help from the United Nations to repatriate the country's refugee population.

Kenya has ratified the Convention regulating the status of refugees (Skalen & Egeland, 1986), and cooperates with the UN High Commissioner for Refugees, who has an office in Nairobi. Over the years Kenya has generously provided sanctuary for a large number of refugees, despite its own economic problems. Their number is currently 21,000, mainly from Somalia, Rwanda, Sudan, Ethiopia, and Burundi.

The refugees' right not to be repatriated against their will to the country from whence they fled, has generally been respected. Two flagrant exceptions were in 1971 and the exchange in 1984 of political refugees ('the refugee was later hanged by the Kenya Government') between the former EAC partners – Kenya, Tanzania and Uganda – as goodwill gestures amongst themselves, after finally reaching accord over the distribution of the assets and liabilities of the dissolved EAC. The Nordic governments and Amnesty International made a joint protest to the three governments on the grounds that the exchange of refugees was in gross violation of the refugee convention they had all ratified.

2.3   Conclusion

The discrepancy between, on the one hand the laudable constitutional guarantees of individual rights and freedoms, and the ratification by Kenya of certain international conventions of the same nature, and the actual practice of the Kenya

Government, is a source of grave concern. The continued invocation of certain legal instruments seriously undermine guarantees contained in the Kenya Constitution, and serves effectively to curtail democratic freedom of expression, assembly and association.

Chapter III

ADMINISTRATIVE STRUCTURE AND AID MANAGEMENT

3.1 Administrative System (Provincial and District Administration)

The new empires are the empires of the mind.

Winston Churchill

Kenya is administratively divided into eight provinces, encompassing forty-two districts, excluding the extra-provincial area of Nairobi. The administrative system is now structurally uniform throughout the country. The districts are further subdivided into divisions, locations and sub-locations. A district also contains a system of local administration, that is to say of local authorities in the form of a county council, whose boundaries usually coincide with those of the district and frequently of one or more town councils.

The so-called Provincial Administration forms the backbone of this administration system, through a hierarchy of provincial and district commissioners, district officers (at the divisional level), chiefs (at the location) and assistant chiefs (at the sub-location). The Provincial Administration is the main executive arm of the central government, operating under the direct supervision and authority of the Office of the President.

The other ministries are usually represented by their own officers in the various territorial units, although the extent of this representation down to the level of the sub-location, varies quite considerably between the ministries and between the districts. In the densely populated agricultural areas, for instance, the Ministry of Agriculture usually has its own officers at the sub-location, while other ministries have representatives only at the district or even provincial level. In their particular fields of competence, the various ministerial representatives are responsible through their respective hierarchies to their ministry headquarters.

The boundaries and the structure of Kenya's present Provincial Administration was taken over virtually unchanged from the colonial period. During the Mau Mau state of emergency in 1952, which was a struggle to end colonial rule, the colonial administrators devised a draconian system of Law and Order, to control and defeat the Mau Mau freedom fighters. The measures included a subtle manipulation of the provincial boundaries, which favoured the minority tribes that supported them during the struggle. The system ensured disproportionate representation of the small tribes, *vis-a-vis* the majority tribes. When the new government under KANU came to power in (1963), the system was virtually left unchanged, but was still charged with many of the same old functions. The Provincial Administration was established primarily for the purpose of maintaining law and order, but was also expected to supervise and coordinate the development projects that were initiated during that period. Such projects demanded technically competent staff. The conflict between a horizontal integration of staff in the district and the vertical integration implicit in the functional responsibilities of the various ministries, was already evident during the colonial period. This has since been the subject of both administrative tensions and policy review. The Ndegwa Commission of 1971, for instance, said:

...As we have seen, the relations between the Provincial Administration and the Technical Ministries in the field are an area of weakness inherited from the colonial past... The Provincial Administration claim they have responsibility without power, as regards the actual implementation of local programmes and projects, directly controlling neither the staff involved nor their budgets. The Technical Ministries have power, but have no responsibility for overall policy, only for their particular specialised programmes... the system of field administration was never designed around the concept of planned development and project management. (Kenya Government, 1971)

One of the main issues examined by the Ndegwa Commission, was the challenge of transforming the old colonial emergency 'law and order' system of administration which had ruled Kenyans by a complicated policy of 'divide and rule' that ensured control and domination by a small group of colonial administrators, white settlers, members of the native security personnel and regular police. Independent Kenya required a type of open democratic and development-oriented system of administration. While the Ndegwa Commission was obviously aware of the need for such changes and saw serious problems and weaknesses facing the administrative framework for district development, the Commission nevertheless, was reluctant to recommend major overhauls of the established arrangements.

3.1.1 BACKGROUND TO DISTRICT FOCUS POLICY

The district development committees (DDC) were in existence at the time of the Ndegwa Commission, but were characterised as 'not an efficient body either for plan making or for coordinated plan implementation'. Although the main thrust of the Commission's recommendations was not directed towards the district administration, but towards the need for 'greater rationality in the machinery of rural administration', the Commission considered the Provincial Administration to be the crucial factor in realising further improvements. In view of the demands that were placed on the Provincial Administration, the Commission wished 'to build up a more specialised, professional staff structure to enable it to perform the specialised tasks for Development Administration'. It did this by creating the new post of district development officer (DDO). The Commission also suggested the establishment of a post of district planning officer (DPO), but of the two categories, only the DDO posts were instituted, and this after some hesitation. This delay was partly caused by a disagreement between the Office of the President and the then Ministry of Finance and Planning, as to departmental responsibility for the DDO staff. Finally, it was decided that the DDOs should belong to the establishment of the Office of the

President.

The Ndegwa Commission went into considerable detail as to what it expected from the appointment of the DDOs including the professional qualities required in the new cadre, with its responsibility for the developmental activities of the Provincial Administration. Despite the original precision of the Commission's approach, the relationship between the DDO and the district commissioner (DC) (a duplication of responsibilities), has remained somewhat vague and undefined, reflecting a certain reluctance on the part of DCs to exclude development activities from their overall responsibilities, as the principal representative of government in the districts. More significantly, however, the appointment of DDOs did not resolve the main problems of coordination at the district level in either planning or implementation, since the Ndegwa Commission gave neither the DDO, nor the District Development Committee (DDC), explicit authority over the staff and resources of the various implementing ministries. On the planning side, there were no clear mechanisms available to translate the district plans and priorities, where these were in fact formulated, into the ministerial work programmes and budgets at the central government level.

Under the Ndegwa Commission's recommendations, the DDC was expanded to include some measure of popular representation in the committee, such as the local Members of Parliament, KANU office bearers and members of the local county council. Prior to this change, the DDC had been composed entirely of civil servants, with elected representatives forming part of another body, the district development advisory committee (DDAC).

The fundamental traits of the Kenyan development administrative system, namely strong centralisation and vertical integration, persisted throughout the 1970s. The Ndegwa Commission clearly did not go far enough in its attempt to create 'an effective focus for rural development' at the district level. In reviewing the situation in 1982, the Working Party on Government Expenditure stated:

> From the point of view of any district level officer, coordination of district activities and indeed identification with the needs of the people becomes secondary to satisfying his/her superiors in Nairobi on whom his/her promotion depends. There is a lack of a sharp, carefully coordinated focus on rural development at district level.

The weaknesses in the rural development programme, implicit in the strongly centralised system of administration, was inherited by the Kenyan government at independence. The system was reinforced and consolidated in the period following independence and has been generally recognised as unworkable, wasteful of resources and unresponsive to the needs and aspirations of independent Kenya. This has been repeatedly and strongly emphasised as previously indicated, it was one of the issues with which the Ndegwa Commission was specifically commissioned to examine as it did, and the commission was required to recommend several alternative approaches, including a far-reaching devolution process:

> ...it has been very persuasively argued before us that, to bring about a fully rational approach to rural development, there should be a single unified District Budget, covering all the various Ministry programmes in the District, and administered by a District Manager (DM) or District Chief Executive Officer (DCEO) with a large measure of independent power and authority over all field officers. We believe that a basic change of this nature while sound in theory, would be premature. (Ndegwa Commission Report, 1971)

As stated above, the Ndegwa Commission restricted itself to fairly modest proposals, aimed primarily at the Provincial Administration, without attacking the main structural problem, namely the conflict between the vertical integration of the ministries and the horizontal integration desired in the district. When the 1982 Working Party discussed the issues of district involvement, they were sharply critical of what they found, which was described as including 'many instances of mismanagement, corruption, inefficient organisational procedures, failures to follow established procedures, a lack of public accountability and very poor implementation of programmes.' The conclusions and recommendations of the Working Party were later translated into the District Focus for Rural Development policy, which was officially introduced in July 1983 (Kenya Office of the President, 1984).

3.1.2 DISTRICT FOCUS POLICY

In 1983 the District Focus Policy for Rural Development was officially launched, as a major administrative restructuring of the government system (Kenya Office of the President, 1984). Essentially, it represented a policy for the decentralisation of development planning and implementation to the district, as the basic operational unit in the rural development process. As an exercise in administrative restructuring, this decentralisation policy makes sense in terms of rationalising civil service functions and of increasing efficiency in the public services (Rondinelli & Nellis, 1986). But, there are however, a number of problems of a political nature, which relate to the earlier discussions of Kenyan politics. In particular, it is still difficult in 1998, to see how in principle a political system, based in the final analysis on patronage, personal rule and rapidly shifting factional alliances, can provide an entirely adequate foundation for decentralised system of authority which presupposes rational decision-making, grounded on universalistic principles of administrative management, which can implement economic reforms, modernisation and abolition or restructuring of Provincial Administration.

Furthermore, as long as the budget ceiling is determined centrally, the DFP does not in itself ensure that some districts are not favoured at the expense of others. In 1998 it is not difficult to substantiate that the DFP in political terms bears a close resemblance to a centralisation measure. In an economic sense, the districts were in fact not accorded any significant autonomy, as long as resources were centrally controlled. Moreover, the district commissioner (DC), whose pivotal role in policy implementation was reinforced, is answerable ultimately to the Office of President. The DFP might therefore be described as a decentralisation of control, rather than a devolution of power from the centre. By implication, the same political forces as currently operate at the central level would be involved through their district proxies in determining the inter- and intra-district allocation of funds under the DFP arrangements. To put it slightly differently, the DFP could be interpreted as a resurgence of KADU policies. However, there is a historical difference, in that the DFP bear the resemblance of providing a genuine measure of decentralisation and democratisation of the state apparatus, designed to redress previously created regional development imbalances.

In the new District Focus Policy, particular emphasis is placed on: (a) district planning, (b) horizontal integration, (c) enlarged district responsibilities and (d) increased authority. In the main, these new developments involve stricter obligations on the ministries to base their programmes and budget on the district's own plans and priorities. Guaranteed by the ministries, the funding of district-specific projects within specified budget ceilings, requires desegregation of the ministerial budgets on a district-by-district basis; and the by-passing of previous bottle-necks at the provincial and/or central ministerial level by increasing the authority of the district in financial management, procurement and project implementation.

Under District Focus Policy, the supervisory and disciplinary authority of the DC over the other ministerial staff, has been increased, mostly by virtue of the enhanced authority of the Treasury, the District Tender Board, and the newly established District Executive Committee, all of which fall directly under the responsibility of the DC. Great emphasis has been placed on efficiency and financial discipline through the upgrading of the capabilities of the District Treasury. Better qualified district accountants are sent to the districts, as well as a newly created cadre of district internal auditors. The latter have special significance in the district structure, since in carrying out their financial control and audit duties, they are directly responsible to the Permanent Secretary to the Treasury, and not to the local DC or Office of the President.

The new District Executive Committee is of particular interest. In formal terms, it is a sub-committee of the DDC charged with 'the technical preparation of plans, management and implementation responsibilities of the DDC'. Its membership is restricted to civil servants, and thus resembles the composition of the DDC prior to the implementation of the Ndegwa Commission's recommendations.

The District Focus Policy depends heavily on several cycles of reiterative planning. In this context, it is envisaged that the office of the DDO should be strengthened through the creation of a District Planning Unit with an assistant DDO and a statistical officer. However, in most districts this planning unit consists only of the DDO, more than three years after the introduction of the District Focus Policy. The DDO is responsible for preparing the annual budget, and for overseeing the introduction of the district-specific projects. In addition, the DDO is secretary to the DDC and the DEC, and is required to participate in the Divisional Development Committee's meetings, and deputise for the DC at such meetings and in other committees.

Qualified staff for strengthening the DDO's office, and thus making it possible for the office to perform all these duties, would probably be available. What seems to be the major bottleneck, is lack of resources (money to pay staff salaries) office space, supporting personnel and staff houses. Recruiting expatriate staff (donors external assistance) to strengthen the proposed planning unit under DDO, would therefore hardly have represented a viable alternative solution. Moreover, such an initiative would require to be pursued within an administrative framework, where the main lines of responsibility run through the DC and the Provincial Administration to the Office of the President. The political nature of these arrangements could well have placed expatriate staff in the planning unit, in a politically sensitive situation.

3.1.3 IMPLICATIONS FOR DFP

The implementation of the District Focus Policy was clearly an attempt to solve one of the main structural problems, which has troubled the Kenyan Development administration since independence. It is, of course, an exercise of decentralisation, but one that implies an increased control by the centre over the periphery to the extent that the Office of the President and the Ministry of Finance, through their respective Provincial Administration and audit officials, control the operations of all sectoral ministries at the district level. The District Focus Policy does not give the districts greater autonomy, but has concentrated their administration by delegating authority within the administrative system, with the aim of improving efficiency in management. Little attention has been given to the devolutionary aspects of decentralisation (i.e. the delegation of specific decision-making powers to lower level authorities). Popular representation is restricted within the DDC, although it takes a slightly more comprehensive form at the lower divisional and locational levels.

The policy of District Focus for Rural Development, as launched in July 1983, was the start of a restructuring process, under which Kenya's forty-two districts were to become the main foci for rural development focus. District-based projects funded by sectoral ministries, non-governmental organisations or self-help schemes were in future to be selected, planned and implemented at district level, and as such were labelled district-specific projects. Under the District Focus policy, the provinces and their administrative structures and boundaries became redundant and were seen as a waste of scarce resources. The policy did not call for the introduction of a whole new institutional framework of government administration, but rather for a transfer of responsibilities for development implementation from ministerial headquarters and Provincial levels to the districts.

Furthermore, it was explicitly stated by the government that this reform did not imply the allocation of additional development resources to the district. Indeed at the present, and for the next few years to come, the central government saw its major task under the IMF's, SAP as trimming the ongoing development budget, by terminating projects with insufficient funding or with too heavy recurrent expenditure implications and not getting involved in the development of new projects. For many districts in Kenya, the development programmes are still at a standstill; the only possibility for starting up new schemes seems to relate to small projects, which fall within the Rural

Development Fund's field of activities or donor-aided development. For donor aid, the District Focus offers a prospect of enhanced efficiency at the district level. Bearing in mind, however, that this policy involved little additional autonomy for the districts, and that the budget rationalisation programme is centrally controlled, donors should be aware that they may not relate directly to the districts but must proceed through the responsible departments in the central administration.

Although the new District Focus Policy was introduced in mid-1983, it is not yet fully implemented or completely operational. There are still serious constraints and delays in deploying staff of operating ministries to the district level, some sluggishness in desegregating central ministry budgets by district, and in the issuing of authority to incur expenditures (AIEs) to the respective department heads at district level. Such constraints are only to be expected, however, in view of the magnitude of restructuring which the new policy entails. Furthermore, continuing training activities are required over a longer period of time to convert the new structure into a smoothly functioning system (Kenya/Office of the President, 1995).

In 1995, it is reliably understood that the former Chief Secretary undertook a comprehensive evaluation of the progress made thus far in implementing the District Focus Policy. The results according to this source is that the DFP is a complete failure. But, the results have not yet been made known to the public.

3.2   Foreign Aid Management

3.2.1   TECHNICAL ASSISTANCE PROGRAMMES

Advising African Development Aid Programmes and management has become a major industry with European and, North American consulting firms and experts charging as much as US$ NBS 180,000, a year of an expert's time. At any given moment sub-Saharan Africa has at least 90,000 to 100,000 expatriates working for public agencies under official aid pro-grammes. More than half of the 8–9 billion dollars spent yearly by donors goes to finance these people. Yet in the three decades since independence, Africa has plunged from food self-sufficiency in the 1960s to widespread and humiliating famines, starvation and deaths. The Sudanese Government, for example, with the help of Western Aid, World Bank, IMF loans and Arab investment, has put vast sugar and cotton plantations on its best land along the Nile. It has ignored rapidly falling yields for small-holder farming since the 1970s. The government seems not to have noticed that the land on which eight out of every ten Sudanese depend for their livelihoods is slowly perishing due to over-use and misuse. The government invested little in the Southern Sudan, or in dry-land regions, where people like the Hadendawa live. So when drought comes, these pastoralists and peasants have no irrigated settlements in which to take temporary refuge, no government agencies to buy their livestock, no sources of drought-resistant sorghum seeds ready for planting when the rain resumes. Neither has the government's investments in cash crops produced money to pay the nation's way through the drought. The result is mass starvation and death on a grand scale with huge foreign debt services around the government's neck: the Sudan's external debt in 1995 was estimated at US$ NBS 15–17 billion. The Hedendawa and Southern Sudanese tribes are facing virtual extinction.

In Kenya relations with the international donor community have been strained following the lapse of the IMF's ESAF arrangement in July, 1997. Donors interviewed, remain concerned over the standard of good governance and in December, 1997 the government established an Anti-Corruption Authority to address these concerns.

While the question of expatriates in general, and more specifically of technical assistance personnel (TAP) as part of aid packages, has received much attention over the years, this problem has very recently become a particularly sensitive issue as far as donors are concerned in Kenya. A policy of Kenyanisation has been pursued since independence, and has gradually led to a diminution in the need for foreign expertise. Recent pronouncements indicate that government is now determined to look afresh at this issue, and make further and more determined efforts to reduce the number of expatriates and consultants working in Kenya. The prospect of graduate unemployment, coupled with the continued presence of thousands of expatriates, has created popular pressure on government to devote greater attention to this problem.

In 1985 there were reported 9,039 expatriates in Kenya, of whom 6,967 worked in the private sector, 1,225 under Teachers Service Commission, 451 in the Civil Service, and 200 elsewhere in public institutions. This represented a decline from 18,000 in 1977 and 12,000 in 1982 (*Weekly Review*, 1985). Between 1981 and 1986, 23,160 foreign nationals were issued with work permits in Kenya (*Africa Economic Digest*, 1986). In January 1985, Parliament revoked a section of the Immigration Act, exempting certain categories of expatriates, such as doctors, lawyers, engineers, accountants and agriculturalists from applying for work permits (*Weekly Review*, 1985). The fact that clearance of TAP was transferred to the Directorate of Personnel Management in the Office of the President, further underscores the seriousness of the government's approach to this question.

No comprehensive survey of Kenya's manpower situation exists to assess accurately the need for foreign expertise. The government has indicated, however, that such a study will be considered soon. The Kenya educational system has produced a large number of graduates who with the addition to Kenyans returning from training overseas, are ready to take over and fill the gaps previously occupied on a temporary basis by expatriates. However, the supply of Kenyan professionals and skilled labour remains uneven. There appears to be an oversupply of general administrators, graduates in liberal arts and social sciences, statisticians and mathematicians, but there is nearly a serious shortfall in trained teachers, technicians, scientists and engineers.

Although the great majority of expatriates are to be found in the private sector, the excessive use of technical assistance personnel connected with aid projects is increasingly being questioned. Directly linked with their numbers is the cost of TAP. Including all overheads and administrative expenses, an expert could according to a Kenyan official, cost up to K.shs. NBS 2 million per year, although in many other cases this figure could be lower. Some donors add the cost of TAP to their regular financial allocation under Kenya's aid programme. This figure does not include the cost of technical backstopping by professional staff at their home headquarters. Some donors add the cost of their regular financial assistance flows to the annual allocation under the country programme. This arrangement thrust the opportunity costs of TAP into sharp focus. In aggregate terms, it has been estimated by the experts that expatriate advice and supervision consumes more or about forty per cent of all external assistance to Kenya. (*Africa Report*, September/October, 1986).

In addition to their number and cost, the role of TAP is being increasingly scrutinised. In this regard, a series of substantive and well grounded observations have been put forward by Kenya officials. Transfer of technical know-how to Kenyan counterparts and colleagues remains unsatisfactory; training is seriously neglected. The appreciation of, and sensitivity to, the social environment in which TAP work, leaves much to be desired; cases are cited of condescending and rude manners, which are unduly domineering *vis-a-vis* Kenyan colleagues to the extent of marginalising them, instead of stimulating and working with them. The technical component of TAP job descriptions and activities has gradually been reduced to management, coordination and control on behalf of the donor. Donors' insistence on TAP as direct controller of projects, is perceived by Kenyans to border on the insulting.

Although, the Kenyan government recognises that it will still need expatriates for many years to come, it reserves the right to be more selective than before. On the basis of a careful assessment of expatriate personnel needs by professional category, specific requests will be submitted which are likely to be for a different type of personnel. Emphasis will be on more senior TAP with long experience, not only in their own respective professions, but also from working in an environment resembling that of Kenya. Secondly, Kenya would prefer longer contracts. Two-year stints are barely sufficient to become acquainted with developmental problems, let alone make a noteworthy contribution to solving them.

On the question of the TAP at district level and below from the DFP perspective, the general attitude is reserved, but not dismissive. However, a closer examination of personality (*vis-a-vis* professional qualifications) would be required in clearance procedures. Postings at local levels are likely to be more demanding on TAP, in terms of ability to adapt and relate to the social milieu, where expatriates would be more exposed and conspicuous than in a larger town or city.

In addition to experts, most aid programmes include another category of TAP, namely the volunteers. Most donor agencies have a volunteer service, of which the UK-VSOs was started at independence in 1963. At present there are many VSOs in Kenya spread all over the country, but somewhat concentrated in Western, Nyanza, Central, Rift Valley and Coast provinces. The bulk of the volunteers work as teachers, in harambee secondary schools, as instructors in youth polytechnics, or as social workers, e.g. with the child Welfare Society of Kenya etc.

A volunteer costs in the vicinity of K.shs. NBS 800,000 per year, including overheads and administrative outlays. These funds-in-aid have tended to change, somewhat, the role of the volunteer from being one of technical assistant to being in addition a provider of financial assistance. Kenyan institutions requesting volunteers appear less and less to require a technically qualified person, but rather the resource that come with him/her, i.e. vehicles and funds-in-aid. Administrative arrangements demand, however, that volunteers as providers of development resources also perform a third role, namely that of financial controller. These three roles tend to be in conflict, causing problems for individual volunteers in the daily discharge of their duties.

3.2.2 POLICY ISSUES ON AID MANAGEMENT

While Kenya's economy encountered significant problems in the second quarter of the 1970s, the experience and legacy of these earlier years helped to shape development aid policies in Kenya over a much longer period, and in particular, to focus continuing government and donor attention on funding the capital and technical assistance content of development projects. Amid the early growth and optimism which continued into the 1970s, necessary consideration was perhaps not always given to wider policy implications, notably to recurrent expenditure, maintenance outlays, distribution of services, user charges, staff development requirements and foreign exchange constraints.

A further feature of the earlier period was a relatively open and liberal approach to the use of technical assistance personnel, which the administration saw partly as a prerequisite for the attraction of foreign development aid, and the donors used in part to help and supervise the implementation of the particular projects they were funding. The early Kenyan position on the subject was carefully set out in the Second Development Plan (1970-1974), Kenya Government, (1969).

> Kenya acquires technical assistance from foreign government and international organisations in order to remove short-term manpower constraints and thus enable Government to plan and execute the Development Plan Programmes. More specifically, the need for technical assistance is established by shortfalls in the numbers of qualified citizens who are required for the high and middle level manpower posts in the public sector. These shortfalls are not simply problems of inadequate numbers of individuals with appropriate formal education and training. Almost all high and middle level manpower posts required the possession of significant experience on the part of persons occupying these posts. Technical assistance is therefore also required in order to provide young professionals with opportunities to work with seasoned professionals in their own fields, enabling them to acquire the practical experience which is prerequisite for assuming major responsibilities.

Apart from the particular economics surrounding the first decade of Kenya's independence, there were at that time two major developments, which were to have an important influence on the approach of Scandinavian countries to development aid questions in Kenya. The first was the publication in 1972 of a major ILO report on 'Employment Incomes and Equality - A Strategy for Increasing Productive Employment in Kenya' (ILO, 1972). The second was the effect of the 1973 oil crisis and related developments on the Kenyan economy.

Development Aid and management, including Kenya as a case study, was the subject of detailed investigation by the task force on concessional flows, set up by the Joint Ministerial Committee of the Board of Governors of the World Bank and the IMF (Cassen *et al,* 1986). In reviewing the development aid programmes and their management in Kenya, this study assessed the policies pursued by the donors and the Kenyan authorities, and the effectiveness of institutional arrangements in various areas. Here, it is immediately apparent that there was no aid programme as such, to Kenya, if by that term it is implied the provision of resources, guided and managed by a clearly identifiable and coherent set of policies and objectives. Development aid flows to programmes in Kenya were diverse in their origins, objectives, and in the management procedures involved in the transfer of resources. This diversity sprang in significant measure from the extensive number of agencies involved. In 1983, for example, apart from the NGOs, there were some 48 bilateral and multilateral organisations with active development aid commitments in Kenya. The great majority of these were in principle operating within guidelines for development aid management formulated by the OECD, who are closely associated with policy and management approaches pursued by the World Bank and the IMF, and were formally pledged to the economic development of the country.

Beyond these general obligations are found to be a diverse range of objectives and motives, where development aid was only one of several instruments contributing to a long-term relationship with Kenya, whether in a commercial direction, in a geopolitical/military or ideological context, in a developmental or humanitarian sense, or even in the handling of bureaucratic and political pressures (NORAD, Aid Review, 1987).

This evident diversity of donor origins and objectives had important implications for development aid processes within Kenya. On the one hand, it may have brought a certain stimulus and richness to technology and organisational forms, which may be seen to best advantage in the rural access roads programmes (RARF), in rural development focus (RDF) activities and in the rural focus approach. However, the multiplicity of donors also added greatly to the complexity of administrative problems facing the government departments, and to a proliferation of different types of equipment and supplies.

This situation in turn gave rise to acknowledged difficulties in areas such as staff training, and in the effective provision of maintenance services and spare parts. Further competition among donors reduced the quality of assistance, notably through the tying of capital aid to the trade and products of particular countries. Most bilateral donors in Kenya tended to bind their aid in this way, although there were also general provisions for certain local purchases, and for waiver arrangements in particular instances. At the same time, there is a certain recognition that aid-tying arrangements can, on occasion, make bilateral assistance programmes politically acceptable to donor countries themselves.

Within the implementing ministries, the involvement of a large number of donors in a particular sector can create serious administrative and management problems for the departments concerned. In this context, branches of government may be required to devote quite disproportionate attention to necessary dealings with donors, with adverse consequences for the effective conduct of their own primary responsibilities. Nor is the presence within government departments of a range of expatriate advisers, each concerned with the supervision or monitoring of a particular bilateral programme, necessarily conducive to the best interests of Kenya's public service. The wish to minimise disadvantages of this kind, is said by the administration to be a major reason for its predilection for sectoral specialisation by donors.

The multiplicity of donor objectives also has significant implication for the development of aid policy and management, and this clearly influenced perceptions of the aid process within the Kenyan administration. In sectors such as energy, where major procurement interests are involved, the government tends to take the view that bilateral development aid is part and parcel of a commercial transaction and, in such areas, finds it frequently inappropriate to embark on development policy discussions regarding the sector concerned. Even more significantly, the proliferation of donors and donor objectives can divert their attention, and that of the administration, from fundamental priorities, such as the establishment of a self-reliant Kenyan public service staffed by qualified Kenyans, and geared to the provision of effective and efficient local services. Instead, disproportionate time and energy is devoted to the negotiation and implementation of a disparate range of inadequately planned and under-funded projects.

Administrators play a key role in the process of development aid implementation, but their respective capabilities in Kenya obviously varies quite significantly. Therefore, it is not uncommon for the same programme, planned and designed along similar lines, to be perceived in differing ways in different districts. It may, for example, be suggested here that the relative success of the UNICEF-sponsored primary Health Care Programme of the Ministry of Health varied greatly among the different districts in which development aid was implemented. Whether at a district level the programme proved a success or failure seems to have been closely related to the efficiency and competence of the implementation team. Embu is mentioned as one district where the programme worked successfully.

The District Health Management Team (DHMT), according to UNICEF is composed of eight officers, drawn from the operating ministry and from health institutions in the district. The team, however, liaises with officers of other ministries. This includes when possible an officer, for example from the DSDOs office and one from the DAOs as permanent officers in the DHMT. This enhances the capacity of the team to identify and define health problems in its area of operation.

Within the District Development Committee (DDC), there is also a special sub-committee on health. In order to promote more coherent planning and implementation practices in health programmes, the activities of this sub-committee should be co-oriented profitably with those of the sub-committee on women's issues. Such a liaison could help to highlight the role of women, as the principal providers and managers of the family's health, and thus ensure a broader perspective in overseeing the local health management system.

One possible way of directing development aid resources more efficiently and more effectively, could be to identify, encourage and strengthen such a district-based team and com-mittee, and assist their emergence as viable instruments of development implementation. In accordance with this approach, the selected team could be allocated sufficient material and management resources to carry out their tasks. Implementing teams, drawn from local cadres, are usually constituted for specific development purposes, and their relative success and very survival may frequently depend on the availability of relevant development resources.

In Kenya, targeted development aid is a prerequisite for development assistance. Targeting is above all a strategy which calls for both careful planning and implementation. The identification of appropriate implementing channels therefore comes to assume a crucial significance. The relevant 'sector' team could represent one such channel to be mobilised in the development field.

The District Focus with the DDC and its sub-committee, is now drawing attention to the leading role of the district, as an implementing unit in the development process. Being closer to the field, the officers at the district level are generally more in touch with the realities of the target groups than are officials at headquarters. This may be an advantage as far as poverty-orientated aid is concerned.

The District Focus Policy, made the district a crucial planning and implementation unit, and held certain promises for future greater attention to local priorities, self-reliance and participation in development in the rural areas by local communities, than had hitherto been the case. Among other things, the district focus strategy presumably makes it easier to plan and implement inter-sectoral development programmes or projects at the local level. With respect to targeted aid, integrated multi-sectoral planning is in many ways preferable to a single-sector approach.

Poverty is a state of material and social deprivation, and its causes and consequences are multiple. Poverty-orientated development aid should aim at building up a self-reliance capability among the poor, and using local resources available in the area to help the poor to move out of the humiliating situation which poverty represents. Development inputs, which are orientated towards alleviating poverty, should be concentrated on both wealth and income-generating activities, as well as on social welfare programmes for deprived families at the village level. Ideally, this task demands inputs from several sector services simultaneously: agriculture, pastoralism, health, education, and social services. Integration and coordination of multi-sectoral activities at the district level, should be facilitated by the restructuring of the administrative system, and by the proximity of local administrators to the field and the 'problems'.

An integrated development approach in Kenya, however, has not always been practically feasible without a heavy input of expatriate management resources, as demonstrated in the Turkana Rural Development Programme. In certain circumstances, such a method may even become counter-productive in the long run by making the recipient country psychologically more dependent on aid. This would, in fact, be contrary to several donors objectives. Due to their remoteness, Turkana, along with other districts in the arid and semi-arid lands (ASAL) zone, constitute special cases in many ways. The lack of administrative resources, evident in these districts, may not necessarily hold true in other instances, for example, in Bungoma District. Thus, an integrated approach to Bungoma did not have the same adverse effects with respect to local capacity-building, as it had to some extent in Turkana. Inter-sectoral programming has many advantages, nevertheless, in the context of targeted aid, and as an option for donors development assistance, this approach should not be rejected outright on the basis of experience drawn exclusively from Turkana.

In order to reach targeted groups, a sectoral approach may provide an alternative to an integrated multi-sectoral approach. To draw a sharp line however, between the two ways of channelling aid, seems to be altogether quibbling. What is defined as sectoral assistance at the central level, may very well draw near to inter-sectoral at the local level. Furthermore, the distinction between the two is very often a matter of scale. While integrated development assistance tends to be area-based, sectoral programmes normally cover a larger geographical area. Both approaches nevertheless require greater care in the selection of areas for development assistance. 'Programme selection' may be undertaken according to both regional and sectoral criteria, where the selection of marginal areas, such as Turkana, Samburu or

Masai, represents one line of regional approach. Regional selection, however, does not necessarily preclude the application of sectoral criteria, and there is a strong case for combining the two criteria.

Examples of sectors, which have chances of benefiting donor-defined target groups in Kenya, are health care, water supplies and vocational training. Large-scale development programmes within these sectors, are an option for donors' support. Development assistance to Kenya has not had significant equalising effects on the distribution of resources among the population, in a situation where class and regional differences, as well as gender inequality, have increased over the years. This situation makes it essential to select areas of assistance carefully.

Experiences gained from previous development aid activities in Kenya should be constructively applied in the process of defining new areas of development assistance. The constitution and practical use of an institutional memory system, could provide a most efficient and purposeful instrument in strengthening planning processes. Norway, for example, had more than twenty years experience of development assistance to Kenya - Turkana and Bungoma, these accumulated resources constitute a formidable capital of knowledge, yet to be exploited.

3.2.3 PRIORITIES IN AID COORDINATION

Since the 1960s, the individual project has in effect represented the basic unit of development administration and aid management in Kenya. Sectoral frameworks have generally been uncertain in character, while budgetary procedures have rarely been strong enough to ensure an effective ranking of programme priorities. In most cases, projects are discussed and prepared between donors and operating ministries, without the finance and planning departments having the necessary instruments to ensure that the further demands on manpower and recurrent revenues, generated by these projects, are kept within manageable limits. Until the early 1980s, there was little restraint on the tendency of donors and implementing ministries to over-extend commitments, or to accord greater preference to the formulation of new projects, than to the proper implementation of existing schemes. 'As when a hunter notches up kills in the stock of his rifle, a new project initiated gives rise to the sense of a job well done' (Duncan and Mosley, 1985).

While the pressures against improved sectoral coordination are deep seated, increasingly in the 1970s there was a sense of unease, both in the administration and the donor agencies, over the unsatisfactory nature of existing practices. The Kenyan government itself was understandably cautious, since a coordinated approach by donors, could be seen as limiting the administration's field of choice, as to the particular conditions of donor involvement. But, within government, there was a certain conflict of interest between planning and finance ministries, which are concerned with programming and expenditure control, and the operational ministries, whose principal preoccupation is with the expansion of their respective functional programmes. Among donors, there was often an inclination never fully restrained, to pursue particular interests for commercial or other considerations.

Despite these various difficulties, there was a continuous effort in Kenya to strengthen practical forms of coordination at a sectoral level through improvement in ministry management and budgetary processes, and the development of government-led consultative arrangements, notably in the field of agriculture and rural development. In parallel, under its improved budgetary procedures, government prepared a forward budget and public investment programme, which incorporated donor-funded projects, as well as those of the major parastatals. If pursued over a period of years, and extended in scope, these sectoral consultations should help to overcome certain of the problems arising from the diversity of aid programme in Kenya, and make a practical contribution in major development fields.

Significant issues relating to Development Aid Policy, were raised by government in its 1986 sessional paper on Economic Management for Renewed Growth, which focused particularly on inter-connections between the development and recurrent budgets. The administrative measures used by the government to keep the increase in the budget within manageable limits, has been to establish ceilings for development and recurrent expenditure for each ministry. However, the ceilings set for recurrent expenditure seem more to constitute a residual afterthought, once the development allocation has been decided, than a function of operating expenditure requirements, generated by past and ongoing investment. The result is that many development projects have come to a standstill, or have been operated far below capacity, when the projects have been transferred from the development to the recurrent budget. The magnitude of the difficulties facing the government is illustrated by the fact that even the annual recurrent costs of grant-financed projects, have been estimated to average fifteen per cent of the investment cost.

Foreign aid contributed to this problem by almost exclusively reserving its funds for financing capital costs. Government's immediate problem of financing the deficit in the balance of payments, made it even more than difficult to turn down a grant for a development project, because of its implications for some future recurrent budget. Therefore, a major responsibility, for achieving a better balance between financial resources for development projects and those for operating and maintaining such projects, rests with the donors, if they are genuinely concerned about the impact of their aid on development. Only through a more liberal attitude towards financing recurrent costs, can a better balance be achieved between investment in, and operation of development projects. Even if this were to lead to a decrease in investment, this might, from a development point of view, be more than compensated through a better utilisation of existing structures.

The options left to Kenya, for creating a more effective balance between investment in new structures and operational costs, were very limited. Donors' as well as government's inclination to create such a balance by relying on 'harambee' and 'user fees', is basically a paper solution. Recent developments indicate that 'harambee', as an instrument for general taxation, has been rapidly reaching its upward limit. Introduction of user fees for services which the public associates with a government obligation was bound to create resistance. Harambee, as an instrument to cover recurrent costs, will only be a solution in special cases and circumstances.

Increased taxation, in whatever form, will therefore, provide only a partial solution to Kenya's budgetary problems. This will be particularly true in the case of donor supported projects and programmes directed towards the least developed and neglected regions such as Nyanza and North Eastern Provinces in Kenya, and the weakest sections of the population.

3.2.4 ADMINISTRATIVE POLICIES AND PROCEDURES

At least four developments within Kenya in the late 1980s would appear to have had a particular direct influence on the process of aid management:

1. the 1986 budget rationalisation programme;
2. growing official donors reservations over the use of expatriate staff and consultants;
3. the increasing significance accorded to rural focus initiative and,
4. the need for administrative restructuring within central government.

The combined weight and thrust of these developments suggests that donors wanted to give particular attention to new requirements related to these initiatives. In particular, they wanted to ensure that their respective aid programming and implementation arrangements with the Kenya Government, made most effective use of local resources, local procedures, local institutions and local capacities leading to self-reliant development. Detailed and specific features of such new direction are set out in Section 3.2.5 giving general considerations to the general aspects and implications of these developments.

Firstly, the damaging economic consequences to Kenya of freewheeling relations between donors and operational ministries, suggests that increasing attention should be required of aid agencies to maintain the closest working links with the government department concerned with finance and planning matters, and where appropriate, with the President's office. In the administrative structures of central government, the Office of the President appears not only to have been strengthening its responsibility for the particular tasks and functions, such as development coordination, rural focus, and personnel matters, but has also taken a decisive stand on a range of economic policy issues, to an extent which many aid agencies including leading international organisations, may not have quickly or fully recognised.

While frequent, and generally valid, criticism of the Kenyan administration's handling of the practical problems of development aid management are made by foreign officials serving with aid agencies in Nairobi, it is perhaps not always sufficiently appreciated, that, on the Kenyan side the aid dimension is only one element in the business of government and the development process and that in these wider perspectives, aid arrangements raise not only administrative and managerial problems, but also frequently touched on sensitive political issues. While the necessary internal resolution of such domestic problems may frequently impede the smooth flow of aid programmes and disbursement ratios, ultimately, a process of political decision-making is required, whether in SAP negotiations or in aid programming. Here the involvement of a leading department, such as the President's office, becomes an increasingly significant element in many discussions concerning development aid questions.

In the future, handling of development aid arrangements in Kenya and the budget rationalisation programme discussed below, will provide the main framework for management of decisions within the administration. This is a process, in which the World Bank and the IMF are closely involved, and where both domestic budgetary arrangements and external funding provisions, would be the subject of international monitoring. In this new situation, where future World Bank funding could well be linked to the effective implementation of the budget rationalisation programme, there may be increasing local and international pressure on donors, to ensure that the financial and accounting aspects of their aid programmes are fully integrated into Kenya Government's structures and procedures. If effectively applied both to donors and recipient ministries, such a monitoring process could perhaps help prevent the type of corruption incident, which occurred over Turkwel Gorge project. Leading aspects of the budget rationalisation process include a certain orientation of development expenditure towards the type of district-specific rural focus schemes supported by the RDF, and the determination of a more effective, relevant and productive balance between interconnected outlays in the development and recurrent budgets. Consequently, the policies successfully pursued by donors in the implementation of RDF programmes, could well become the subject of increased political and administrative attention both in a rural focus and a budgetary context. In addition donors may require to address themselves carefully to the new administrative and financial problems that will arise in the future funding of items within the recurrent budget, which will be managed under somewhat different administrative structures and procedures to those used in the development field.

Amid these new initiatives arrangements for the integration of formally agreed aid programmes, within the relevant provisions of the Kenyan budget, will certainly become more complex, more demanding, and more necessary to sustaining effective relationships in the cooperation field. In this context, it could well be that donor agencies may have a great deal to learn from each other, from the international bodies, and from the Kenyan administration. In such exchange of knowledge and experience, the World Bank's role could be of particular significance, not so much in terms of high policy dialogue, but in more mundane and practical fields. This would probably include sectoral consultations under Kenyan auspices on subjects such as industrial sector priorities or educational needs. More specifically, in the field of aid management, the World Bank itself pioneered the effective use of Kenyan accounting, auditing and tendering procedures, which enabled it to reduce its dependence in certain programme areas, on the use of expensive advisory staff. It is perhaps important here to stress the positive view, which the World Bank, UN agencies and certain other donors took of these arrangements, which are discussed further in Section 3.2.5.

As regards Kenyan accounting and auditing procedures, the World Bank is generally satisfied that the use of these tools can save time and effort, and facilitate reimbursement, reporting and auditing, at an acceptable level, and within a reasonable time period. In this regard, the World Bank attached particular importance to the close cooperation it has received from the Treasury and the Controller and Auditor General's Department, which enjoys an institutional status comparable to that of the judiciary, and a reputation for competence, efficiency and integrity. Its annual reports are submitted directly to the Public Accounts Committee of the National Assembly, and while immediate administrative action is seldom taken on its recommendations, its direct, detailed and pointed observations on the financial practices of government departments, are the subject of intense parliamentary scrutiny and discussions, and are widely reported in the national press and overseas. For example, the misuse of public funds to build a new redundant Eldoret Moi National Airport (*Daily Nation*, 12 April 1998).

The World Bank also makes extensive use of Kenyan procurement procedures for local contract bids, involving both the central and district tender boards. The bank is generally satisfied with these procedures, but has been reviewing with government particular practices, employed within these arrangements, in order to ensure that the procurement system yields the best feasible results. It felt that other donors should take an active interest in the specific improvements proposed by the bank.

In the field of financial management, the Nordic and Dutch agencies were particularly successful with the Kenyan planning services on the establishment of viable financial and administrative procedures for the implementation of RDF programmes, which could have a fuller relevance in the context of district focus priorities. Of particular significance, as confirmed by the World Bank's experience, is the role of the district internal auditors, who report directly to the Permanent Secretary to the Treasury, and not to the district administration, in relation to their specific responsibilities for controlling and auditing the entire range of financial transactions at the district level. Two points should be particularly stressed here, regarding the role of the district internal auditors. Firstly, these officials are concerned, not only with the *ex post* audit accounts, but also with the *ex ante* control of all payments, before they are finally authorised within the district administration. Secondly, they belong to a special service coming under the direct authority of the Treasury, which as indicated above, has a recognised reputation for professional competence and integrity.

In the supervision of projects, donors such as the UK-ODA Department of International Development and the EU have made increasing use of consultants or experts recruited locally on the basis of professional merit, and funded under their respective technical assistance arrangements.

In the payment fields, the EU experience in relation to its integrated rural development project at Machakos District, may be of particular relevance for donors concerned to move away from the direct payment system, and make maximum feasible use of Kenyan institutional arrangements in the implementation of programmes. Here, in order to overcome delays resulting from slow moving financial procedures and economic constraints affecting the administration, a cash-float system was introduced by agreement with the Kenya Treasury, on which the project officers could draw in the event of possible delays. This type of arrangement, together with the Lome Convention procedures accords the Permanent Secretary to the Treasury formal responsibility, as the EU Commission's national authorising officer for the control of ACP–EU programmes in Kenya. It ensures that the EU development aid funding is closely integrated into the Kenyan system, (and those of other ACP countries), with the minimum of practical difficulty under the direct payment system shown below.

In project programming procedures, the experience of the UK–(ODA/IDD) and to some degree the EU, may also be of relevance to the aid management discussion in Kenya. In the case of UK–(ODA/IDD), administrative arrangements for major projects have included the preparation of specific plans and time schedules, which detailed not only the technical and financial aspects of the particular scheme, but also itemised the various contractual obligations falling on the donor, the recipient and concerned third parties. Painting on a broader sectoral canvas, the EU's indicative programme with Kenya followed a similar pattern, listing and time-tabling a series of contractual engagements between the European bodies concerned and the Kenya Government.

The budget rationalisation programme, which addresses itself both to the administration and to donors, could well lead the Kenyan authorities to take a more direct interest in aid management problems, notably as these relate to the government departments most directly concerned, and perhaps especially to the external resources department of the Treasury. An indication of the government's approach to major issues in this field, was evident in a reassessment, undertaken in the mid-1980s by the administration, of the foreign aid programme in Kenya, which was particularly concerned with the problem of controlling donor funds. A desire to reduce the large portion of aid budgets devoted to expatriate staff and consultants costs, was a major preoccupation of this review. In this regard, the government estimated that expatriate and consultants advice and supervision costs consumed forty per cent of all foreign aid budgets (*Africa Report*, September 1986). There was also a revelation by the late Dr Robert Ouko, Kenyan Foreign Affairs Minister, that thirty per cent of all foreign aid budgets to Kenya ended up in corrupt practice (*Observer* (London), 27 October 1991). Another question, which was likely to occupy a prominent place in the discussions on aid management issues, was the government's own budgetary and balance of payments problems, and the emerging graduate unemployment. The problems of reducing this particular component of development aid, represented a subject, to which donors and recipients alike, were required to give increasing attention.

3.2.5 ADMINISTRATIVE INADEQUACIES

More than fifty per cent of all the Kenya Government's development budget is provided through the foreign aid programme. With few exceptions, aid activities aimed at extending and improving government services, and by the end of the 1980s were planned eventually to be taken over or controlled by the Kenya Government. The impact of aid is therefore largely an outcome of the fulfilment of donors conditions and future performance of the government. This section therefore summarises briefly the administrative inadequacies that exist in Kenya under the following seven headings:

1. The direct payment systems.
2. Inadequate financial control.
3. The Expenditure Review and New Budget Process.
4. Kenyan use of External Aid Assistance.
5. Kenyan Accounting and Auditing Procedures.
6. Kenya Government Procurement Procedures.
7. Kenyan recent Policies and Donor Responses.

It is now generally recognised that the level of inefficiency in the Kenyan public sector institutions started an irreversible decline at the beginning of the 1980s. The main reasons for this irreversible decline stemmed from the following factors:

(a) A disproportionately large share of recurrent public funds were being used to cover salaries and wages of public servants which are over-manned, inefficient and corrupt. The Kenya Government is the only major employer with a rapidly expanding population, while insufficient funds are available for other expenses such as transport, rural development, education, health service, housing, and other basic needs provisions, etc.

(b) Promotions are often made on the grounds of tribe, kinship and race, rather than on good performance, merit and ability. There is no equal opportunity policy in Kenya and the public service is rampantly corrupt and corruption has become part of national life at every level of administration.

(c) There is a growing lack of financial discipline in almost every sector of government including public utilities and parastatal bodies. In the report on the 1982 Working Party on Government Expenditure, chaired by the Governor of the Central Bank of Kenya, Mr Philip Ndegwa stated that:

> The collapse of financial discipline in project implementation seriously undermined the capacity of the Government to plan and use the scarce resources available in an efficient and effective

147

manner. The result is that Government facilities and structures are neglected and allowed to fall into disrepair. Government contracts are invariably more costly than need be and excessive cost escalations in Government programmes is almost taken for granted in certain instances, cases of gross misuse of Government resources are reported and often not punished. (Kenya Government, 1982a)

The government procurement procedures are relatively time consuming, partly because of controls against mismanagement, corruption and misuse. In 1982-1983, procurements were further delayed because of inadequate financial discipline and over-commitment of limited government funds. Donor funds, set aside for disbursement through the Treasury for specific projects, were often temporarily allocated to more pressing government needs, and were frequently not available for the relevant projects at the required time. This situation resulted in an unwillingness on the part of many local suppliers to accept Government Local Purchase Orders (LPOs), until the required funds had become available within the relevant branch of the administration. The result was a drastic slow-down in project implementation or abandonment of donor funded projects such as the Kisumu molasses plant. A Swiss-based group of Consultants BAK.

3.2.5.1 Direct Payment System
In order to overcome problems created by the division of funds and administrative delays, most bilateral donors came to assume an increasing responsibility for project implementation.

In the early 1980s, there was a significant increase in the volume of direct payments from donors for the provision of goods and services, including local supplies. Some donors also decided to cover counterpart contributions, originally agreed to be Kenyan government responsibility.

A further reason why direct payment was preferred was that the reimbursement process did not work satisfactorily. This was basically due to the operating ministries failing to provide the Treasury with evidence of expenditure eligible for reimbursement. The Treasury, for this reason, was not able to draw the amounts that had been committed by the donors. This was generally not a problem with all donors commitments, which usually took the form of advance payments.

The direct payment system provided a solution only in the short run. Even if speedier implementation was attained, financial constraints were likely to be felt at the operation and maintenance stage, when the project was taken over by the government. In the long run, direct payment arrangements undermined the Kenyan system, because they tended to reduce the authority and responsibility of Kenyan officials both in overall planning and coordination, as well as in sectoral implementation and control.

The direct payment system gave technical assistance personnel a very central and powerful position in Kenya, and perpetuated the need for foreign experts, even in situations where fully trained and qualified Kenyans could have taken over responsibilities. It led to a conflict of interests with donors' TAPs; and also led to duplication in administration and to poor coordination between donors and the Kenyan authorities both at central and district levels. This hampered both the Kenyan take-over and effective integration of external aid with indigenous development activities.

Foreign aid assistance, planned and implemented largely outside the Kenyan administrative system, was frequently not included in the government's annual estimate of revenue and expenditure. As a result, there was a tendency for donors and operating ministries to prepare and initiate new projects, without the Treasury ascertaining whether the resulting increased demands on Kenyan manpower and recurrent resources could be fully met and utilised. This led to a situation where the additional demands generated by the many new projects being implemented far outran the domestic resources available.

3.2.5.2 Improvement Towards Financial Control

Following the adoption of the 1982 Ndegwa report, there appeared to have been a marked improvement in the financial discipline of government ministries. In the early 1980s, there was a serious lack of control over the level of government expenditure, with the budgetary deficit rising to 8.7 per cent of GDP in 1981. This ratio was brought down to a forecast level of about 4 per cent in 1983, where it has since remained (World Bank, 1986a). The government's strategy to ensure budgetary equilibrium over the longer-term was set out in Sessional Paper no.1 of 1986, as well as in other official documents.

Firstly, it was foreseen that a higher budget priority should be accorded to immediate productive services, like agriculture and industry, with a reduction in the relative share of education, health and other basic human need services. Secondly, there was a recognition by government that in the past the available donor funds had been spread over too many projects, and that this caused delays in project completion, linked with an inability to meet recurrent outlay requirements.

A central objective of budget rationalisation was to identify projects with potentially high productivity, in order to advance their completion. Projects with low potential were postponed or cancelled, in order to release funds for those schemes with higher rate of return. At the same time, the government sought to improve utilisation of completed facilities by limiting the number of new projects, shifting resources towards operation and maintenance requirements, and ensuring improved utilisation of physical infrastructure capacity. Under the rationalisation programmes, it was also foreseen that the infrastructure and parastatal budgets should also be included in the forward budget processes of their respective parent ministries.

Government strategy further envisaged an increase in user fees for public services, as well as increased 'harambee' contributions, in order to augment revenue required to cover recurrent costs. In this regard, the government hoped to effect an annual growth rate of some fifteen per cent in such revenues, (which were classified in the Kenyan budgetary system under 'appropriations-in-aid').

Treasury circular No.7/86 stated that all externally aided projects and programmes must be included in the respective ministries' budget proposals under development ceilings determined by the government. Each ministry was required to ensure that the recurrent cost implications of aid projects, especially expenses for additional staff and for operation and maintenance, were taken into account and given the higher priority during the forward budget process. Furthermore, the ministries were required to assess whether each aid project was in conformity with the sector priorities and the selection criteria of the budget rationalisation programme.

For certain projects, there was to be further re-negotiations with donors to re-define existing commitments and where appropriate to shift resources to higher priority projects, or preferably to supporting sector programmes. It was foreseen that this enhanced flexibility should assist in improving the utilisation of existing capacity.

In addition to the criteria mentioned above, priority was to be given to projects which improved the conditions of small farmers, pastoralists, landless rural workers, urban poor and handicapped people. Another important selection criterion was the opportunity to earn or save foreign exchange by using local materials and equipment or extending the life of imported machinery and equipment by improved maintenance.

3.2.5.3 The Expenditure Review and New Budget Process

The government appointed a task force on budget rationalisation, which, *inter alia*, was charged with the responsibility of securing better coordination between the external resources and the budgetary supply departments of the Treasury. It was anticipated that this task force would initially be concerned with the establishment of broad sectoral priorities and criteria to determine the allocation of resources in the operating ministries.

In addition, criteria were established for reviewing and determining priorities in making allocations to the recurrent and development budgets. These criteria related especially to provisions that have major financial implications, such as subsidies, and programmes which required the introduction or further development of user fees.

In order to ensure that sector reviews were carried out and budgetary restraints were exercised the Treasury declared that the following requirements should take immediate effect under the 1986 budget rationalisation programme. (Kenya/Ministry of Finance, 1986)

(i) Programme/projects and items of expenditure, not included in the first year of the three year forward budget, were not to be included in the draft annual estimate for the normal budget year, immediately following the year in which the forward budget was approved.

(ii) Token provisions were to be deleted from the forward budget.

(iii) During the next three years (1986/1987–1988/1989), there were to be no supplementary estimates involving the inclusion of new projects or new items of expenditure during the revised estimates preparation.

(iv) When determining the individual departmental ceilings in the recurrent estimates, the Treasury was to indicate the levels of appropriations-in-aid (AIAs) to be collected, based on levels previously agreed, and if there was any decline from the agreed levels in the Ministry proposals, the gross expenditure limits were also to be reduced.

3.2.5.4 Kenyan use of External Aid Assistance

Under the 1986 budget rationalisation programme, the Kenya administration indicated that it would be endeavouring to integrate external development aid assistance under specific ceilings within its own budget estimates, along the following lines:

If realistic cost estimates for all selected projects exceeded the development budget ceilings for a Ministry, then projects would be identified which would either be delayed or postponed. Projects delayed would be those, that:

(i) could be postponed with nil or least damage to the project;

(ii) have the lowest stopping and recommencement cost;

(iii) have nil or the smallest proportion of foreign aid committed to them;

(iv) are partially financed by highest cost sources of foreign aid; have the highest proportion of locally financed foreign exchange cost;

(v) have the highest proportion of Kenya Government contribution since domestic funds were limited'. (Kenya Ministry of Finance, 1986)

The Government also indicated that under the budget

rationalisation process, the administration was not in a position readily to receive and utilise all grant commitments, far less all loan commitments. According to the projected budget out-turn for 1986/87 to 1988/89, the government could utilise only about 120 million Kenya pounds of grant commitments, leaving un-utilised grant commitments of some 60–80 million Kenya pounds per year. In this general context according to the World Bank sources, there was at the time estimated to be a pipeline of donor commitment aggregating some US$ NBS 1.2 billion.

Within the framework of the budget rationalisation pro-gramme, and to increase the utilisation rate of foreign aid assistance, the government requested donors to redirect certain low priority project commitments to sectoral programmes or to certain higher priority schemes. Over the next three years, there was in aggregate an expected budget deficit of 608 million Kenya pounds. This needed to be met by net borrowing, so the government also requested donors to provide budget support on soft terms to meet part of this balance; while also requesting donors permission to use 45 million Kenya pounds, at the time accumulated in counterpart funds under commodity assistance arrangements.

3.2.5.5 Kenyan Accounting and Auditing Procedures

During the 1980s, when most bilateral donors used direct payment arrangements, there was reduced interest in the dis-bursement and control performance of the Kenyan administration. In contrast, to most bilaterals, the World Bank, UN agencies and a few smaller donors concluded agreements or covenants with Kenyan authorities for utilising the existing accounting system. The World Bank was satisfied that these arrangements saved time and effort, and facilitated disbursements, reporting and auditing at an acceptable level of and within reasonable period of time.

For their national agricultural extension projects' programmes in Kenya, the World Bank was supplied with accounts, which were the Treasury computer printouts of payments appearing in the government ledger; the expenditure reports were prepared by a project accountant in the implementation unit of the Ministry of Agriculture on both a monthly and annual basis. The Audit was carried out under the Auditor General's regular programme for auditing government accounts.

The key to the arrangement lay in the allocation to the individual project of a separate budget line, in effect a separate budget sub-head, in a three digit budget, which contained up to 999 items. There was also formal provision on a project basis for the listing of individual accounts and disbursement categories, corresponding directly with expenditure 'items' in the government ledger. This covenant requirement, in turn, enabled both project accounts and disbursement categories to be prepared directly from the government ledger.

The formal agreement or covenant with the government provided the World Bank with the right to scrutinise the underlying vouchers and, if necessary, to have the statements audited separately. But since the expenditures were audited on a routine basis by the Auditor-General, the World Bank would normally exercise its right only in special cases.

The completion of the monthly project expenditure report was generally made available about thirty days after the end of the month. The Auditor-General's report was, according to the special covenant, available to the World Bank in its final form, and accepted by Parliament, about fifteen months after the conclusion of the budget year.

Within the project implementation unit of the Ministry responsible, the project accountant was expected to undertake normal budgetary duties, as well as producing monthly and annual expenditure reports. If other donors wanted to use the Kenyan system, with similar arrangements to those established for the World Bank, the system would be considered as a model. This would require, in some cases, specific recruitment of new project accountants, specified printouts at agreed intervals, and the right to separate audit in particular instances.

3.2.5.6 Kenyan Government Procurement Procedures

The Kenya Government's procurement procedures were described in the Supplies Manual of 1978. The bidding or tendering procedures were outlined in the manual, which covered preparation of specifications, invitations to bid, receipt and opening bids, as well as evaluation and final awards. The procedures were based on a competitive public tendering policy.

The World Bank relied on the procurement procedures for Local Contract Bids (LCB). A World Bank internal memorandum of 30 April 1986 stated that in cases where procurement problems occurred, these were mostly related to shortcomings in practice, and did not emanate from the procedure itself. The World Bank therefore, decided to review and ascertain that the following requirements were comprehensively covered in bidding documents:

(i) Foreign firms wishing to bid under LCB should be allowed to bid (although this was not excluded under Kenyan procedures);

(ii) pre-qualifications of bidders were specified;

(iii) evaluation and award criteria were specified (Kenya procedure to award to lowest bidders);

(iv) bid submission and opening procedures were specified;

(v) bidding document were completed.

The District Tender Board can deliberate and make final decision for open tender up to K.shs 60,000 for procurement of a single item within a particular financial year. Amounts above this limit have to be adjudicated by the Central Tender Board. In the tendering and bidding field, it is recommended that donors should consider following the type of procedures currently practised by the World Bank.

3.2.5.7 Kenyan Recent Policies and Donor Responses

At the consultative meeting in Paris in 1986, a number of donors expressed a genuine appreciation for the Kenya Government's efforts to restore and maintain a balanced economy. The need for budget rationalisation was understood by donors, although there were limits to the willingness of some donors to abandon or postpone their own project in the interest of high-priority projects. Points made by donors at the 1986 consultative meeting are summarised in the following paragraphs.

Budget rationalisation was seen to represent an unwelcome constraint, especially for the intended beneficiaries and the government, but also for donors. It seemed important that opportunities for delegation of authority and for takeover by local councils, NGOs and user associations, should be systematically considered before final cuts were made by central government. Another possibility, which had already been used to a great degree by some donors, was 100 per cent donor financing of development costs, as well as support with recurrent expenditure for an agreed number of years before Kenyan takeover.

At the 1986 consultative meeting, many donors also indicated their willingness to increase commodity and programme aid, but were still basically project-orientated, because there were doubts as to whether government policies were sufficiently addressing social welfare and income distribution priorities. Some donors questioned whether, as a result of outside pressure, Kenya had not been diverted from following its own budget rationalisation policies, and referred to the government's agreement with French interest over the Turkwel Gorge Project. Certain donors also felt that acceptance of Kenya's request for more general assistance could be considered only in the context of significant economic policy reforms, political changes and human rights record improvement.

Individual donors stressed a number of other points, which required further reflection on the part of the government. Firstly, it was felt that the criteria for selection of development priorities had not been elaborated in sufficient depth. Neither had the operational strategies for development in Kenya towards the year 2000, outlined in Sessional Paper no. 1 of 1986, been adequately clarified, particularly in relation to efforts to reduce the population growth rate. Several donors feared that the lower priority accorded to health services might also have a negative impact on efforts designed to contain rapid population growth (World Bank: Consultative Group for Kenya, 1986).

3.2.6   MONITORING AID EFFECTIVENESS

The question of aid effectiveness was under discussion in donor circles for some time in the 1980s/1990s. Political concern and the pressure of public opinion added to general preoccupation as to the proper use of development aid money, and the extent to which it reached intended beneficiaries. To answer the simple question about how effective is development aid, is no easy matter. Conceptual vagueness and lack of adequate methodologies makes it exceedingly difficult to come forward with clear-cut and authoritative answers.

An attempt has been made on a global basis, in a study commissioned by the joint World Bank/IMF Task Force on Concessional Flows (Cassen *et al.*, World Bank/IMF, 1986). This report stated that although much of development aid is never formally evaluated, a fair amount is in effect subjected to various types of assessment. The study claims, after reviewing hundreds of reports, that most development aid does work in terms of its own objectives to achieve a reasonable rate of return. That this is said to hold true, even in the difficult circumstances in which development aid operates, is particularly noteworthy. The crucial question then to ask is: What are those objectives?

Effectiveness can only be measured in terms of the specific objective set for a project or programme. If such an objective is unambiguous and quantifiable, such as building a road from A to B, to given standards, at a specified cost, and within a certain period of time, that task of measurement is straightforward. The problem arises when the objective eludes quantification, e.g. certain forms of socio-cultural enhancement, or institution-building programmes. Conceivably, it would be possible to arrive at some qualitative assessment of effectiveness even in such cases, but with a lesser degree of exactness and with more scope for subjective judgement.

The problem is further compounded by the existence of multiple objectives for the same project, with no stated scale of priority. In reality this is the case for most development aid projects. Not infrequently, an objective may even be internally self-contradictory. In assessing overall effectiveness, some kind of trade-off then becomes inevitable. This invariably involves normative, subjective and arbitrary judgements. What usually happens, in the interest of accuracy, is that the particular objectives, that can best be quantified and measured, take precedence over those that cannot. In effect, the degree of quantification of an objective becomes a proxy ranking of importance, and thus implicitly determines the hierarchy of project objectives. 'Softer' and less quantifiable objectives tend to recede to the background.

Inherent in any evaluation of social development, where aid is but one factor in the process of change, is the problem of isolating the effects that result specifically from development aid as an agent of change, as distinct from other economic and social developments. Development aid projects are not, and can never be, experimental, in the sense that results are compared to those in control groups, which have not been subjected to the effects of aid interventions.

The time dimension in development aid effectiveness assessments, is critical in determining the lasting impact of projects and programmes. It is a serious weakness in evaluation procedures that *ex post facto* evaluations are rarely undertaken. The overwhelming majority of evaluations are carried out at completion, or shortly thereafter. To make judgements concerning the post-completion long-term impact at that point in time, is impossible. Donors should change their evaluation practices, and attempt, however difficult the task may seem *ex post facto* assessment of social impact, some five to ten years after completion of major project or programmes. In Kenya, such studies might be undertaken on the Turkana road, and in some years on the rural access roads programme (RA.RP) as well.

Effectiveness in development aid is not an absolutist concept; projects are not simply successes or failures. It makes sense to speak of degrees of effectiveness. In turn, this raises the question as to how much below a theoretical optimum, can a project still be characterised as a relative success? At what level does it tip over into the category of development aid failures. This question is crucial to donors who presumably all accept a loss or write-off account, given the difficult circumstances in which aid operates. In the final analysis, it will have to be decided what the permissible size of that account should be, relative to total disbursements.

Notwithstanding the difficulties of measuring the effectiveness of development aid quantitatively, there is some intuitive, qualitative understanding of certain projects as failures, whatever the parameters by which they are judged. Cassen *et al.* (1986) distinguish between two categories of failures:

(1)   reprehensible failures;

(2)   less reprehensible or virtuous failures.

The former are inexcusable mistakes, due to inability to learn from past experience, poor or improper planning of technical or social aspects, or sheer incompetence in implementation. The latter have failed; it may be argued in mitigation, due to over-ambitious objectives on the part of the donor and/or recipient. Although it is quite laudable to be ambitious, a project might go wrong if one is trying to do too much too fast in difficult circumstances. Following this reasoning, it may be tempting for donors to engage in 'safe' projects, e.g. large infrastructural works, which within a narrow framework of evaluation, may be termed successful, rather than trying to design complex rural development programmes, where successful outcome would pose a much greater challenge. Such selectivity on the part of the donors may produce comfortable figures on the balance sheet of success and failure. But it will probably not help a recipient country like Kenya tackle intractable and very urgent problems, such as reaching the acute needs and development requirements of the very poor and destitute.

Blame for failures may be attributed to either the donor or the recipient, or to both. Donors tend to blame the recipient for policy frameworks not conducive to development, lack of absorptive capacity and inefficient administration. Recipients point to the administrative and coordination problems created by the donors' diversity of procedures, conditionalities, policies and methods of operation. For Kenya the bilateral and multilateral donors now approach fifty in number, without including the extensive range of International NGOs. The increasing commercialisation of aid, together with aid-tying arrangements, further complicate the picture. The adverse systemic effects of this multiplicity of donors and proliferation of projects are substantial, and probably not fully appreciated by the donor community as a whole, even less by individual donors, who tend to regard their own activities as more important than any other aspect of the country's development.

There are no easy solutions to these complex problems. In the course of patient discussion, it may be hoped that in future some progress can be made towards their resolution. It is suggested here that, in the future, negotiations on the Kenya/donor cooperation programme be conducted at a political level, and that *ad hoc* joint expert group meetings held on topics of mutual interest would go some way towards that end. On the issue of institution-building joint meetings involving, for example, Kenya Institute of Administration management experts and donor expertise on comparative institutional performance and efficiency, might be a concrete beginning. This might be done in conjunction with management training programmes for operation and maintenance staff of minor urban water supply programme (MUWSP) and road construction and maintenance (RCAM). On poverty issues, Kenya and donors' church organisations would appear to be natural partners in extended Kenya/donors consultations, beyond the confines of the countries' civil services. Academic institutions might likewise be suitable. The increased use of Kenyan consultancies might form part of the same policy orientation. Efforts in this direction might prove a sensible departure from paternalism inherent in much conventional policy dialogue. It should be recalled that Kenya has a comparatively sophisticated and well qualified civil service and other cadres, whose potential for participating in consultations of this nature are of a particularly high order.

A positive spin-off from broad-based discussions extending beyond civil servants, is likely also to be the enhancement of inter-personal relations, which could prove conducive to the more effective implementation of aid programmes at all levels. For the time being, it would be strongly advisable for donors to assume a self-critical attitude; to identify their weaknesses, before levelling harsh criticism against recipients who fail to comply with diverse, sometimes contradictory, conditionalities, which donors seek to impose on many developing countries.

3.3 Qualitative Assistance

3.3.1 TARGETING AID

In the 1960s, the ideal relationship between a donor and recipient country was based on the principle that international development aid should be extended on the terms of the recipient. With a growing recognition that there are inherent problems in such an approach, in terms of aid reaching wide sections of the population as beneficiaries, the philosophy was gradually modified. The trickle-down mechanism did not seem to work along the lines originally assumed, and new ways were sought to ensure that the poor, women, children, and other target groups really would benefit from development aid funds. The pendulum thus swung towards conditionality, with NGOs as channels of assistance circumventing the bureaucracies of recipient countries, and towards the view that aid projects should be designed in such a way as to reach specific target groups. The current preoccupation with targeting aid should be seen against these perspectives.

Poverty alleviation and promotion of equality are explicit aims of many donors' development aid assistance. The priority accorded to the poorest, as a target group, has been spelled out in several donors' policy statements. Consequently, current thinking suggests that projects and programmes should be designed and planned in such a way that the chances of reaching the poorest are maximised.

3.3.2 IDENTIFYING TARGET GROUPS

In Kenya the poor are: the peasants with only small holdings of land, pastoralists with herds below the survival minimum, landless ex-agriculturalists, destitute nomads, single mothers, farm labourers, unemployed in urban areas, people with various disabilities, and others. Taken together, these groups constitute a major part of the Kenyan population (Eglund, 1977).

In dry districts like Samburu, Turkana, Isiolo, Mandera, Wajir Masai for example, over 60 per cent of the pastoral population is estimated to exist below the poverty line, and in such circumstances are not self-reliant in terms of food production (Schwartz and Schwartz, 1985). This figure may even be higher in many districts in Kenya today, because by 1988 it was rising in several districts with the introduction of SAP.

The relative number of female-headed households and single mothers also appears to be growing in many parts of Kenya. It is currently estimated that 40 per cent of the smallholdings in Kenya are managed solely by women, who are all formal heads of households, and another 47 per cent are managed by women in the absence of their husbands (Kenya/Ministry of Culture and Social Services, 1986). Many of these small-scale holdings run by women are less than one hectare in size (SIDA, 1982). These women are particularly vulnerable, as their access to resources is limited, and a great number of them face acute problems in feeding their families.

For UN aid agencies and some bilateral donors, development assistance to Kenya aims at several target groups. The rural poor and women have been mentioned as specific beneficiaries of UN aid agencies and other donors' aid. However, these two groups represent quite broad elements in society, and need to be defined more narrowly in order to provide operationally useful categories.

When selecting women as a target group for a special project or programme a proper definition or characterisation of that group should be formulated on the basis of economic and social criteria and standards. The practice of referring to women in general as a target group, runs the risk of misdirecting funds. In the local context, elite women, for instance, have far more capacity and resources than other women to utilise external support. If this is not acknowledged, development assistance may very well contribute to perpetuating existing inequalities.

A proper target group analysis is important for two reasons: it facilitates monitoring and evaluation of the development inputs, and specifies the beneficiaries with greater precision, increasing the efficiency and benefits of the development aid provided.

The problems of defining target groups are many. In Kenya an analysis is facilitated, by a relatively good supply of relevant statistical and socio-economic material at both national and district levels. The major constraints affecting a clear-cut target group definition must be sought in the planning procedures and implementation process.

Firstly, the objective of targeted development aid as an issue is seldom given priority in the dialogue between the donors and the government. Secondly, the Kenyan administrative system is not designed to cater for targeted assistance. Hitherto its centralising orientation has tended to restrain local initiative and local participation in the development process.

Furthermore, the shortage of skilled manpower, especially at provincial and district levels, represents another constraint. Budget limitations, disbursement deadlines, and the overloading of work on capable administrators are also factors which in general militate against the effective implementation of development aid programmes.

These are some of the reasons why NGOs are frequently considered to be better suited to reaching the designed target groups than the often slow-working government machinery. Donors support to NGOs operating in Kenya has increased substantially over the years. Nevertheless, the great bulk of donors development aid funds in Kenya, is channelled through the government, and it is within this context, with all its constraints and possibilities, that ways of reaching the poor have to be identified.

3.3.3 KENYA'S FOREIGN DEBT

Kenya is one of the few sub-Saharan African countries to avoid a full rescheduling of external debt. Although a partial rescheduling was negotiated with the Paris Club of official creditors in January 1994 under standard terms, the rescheduling was limited to restructuring accumulated payments arrears. With debt-service payment currently running at around US$ NBS 600 million a year, debt commitments are considered manageable and the country is currently on its principal official debt-service obligations. Despite a debt burden of some US$ NBS 7.5 billion, of which around 70% is owed to official creditors, a high element of concession and a lengthy average maturity has meant that the debt-service ratio, estimated at 19% in 1997, is not particularly onerous. As such, the country is not a leading candidate for concessional debt relief.

At the end of July 1997, the IMF allowed the first year of a three-year ESAF loan to lapse with the second semi-annual loan under the arrangement undisturbed. The suspension of funds by the IMF was linked to concerns over allegations of corruption, poor governance, lack of accountability and public transparency. The freeze caused the World Bank to suspend the second tranche of its annual SAP credit and also led the African Development Bank to suspend its balance-of-payments support. Bilateral donors also suspended aid programmes and a meeting of the consultative donor group which had been postponed in mid-1997 remains on-hold.

Although the government is expected to press for an early resumption of IMF support in their exploratory talks, the IMF is likely to wait for progress on its major grievances before it will release funds. This was not expected to be forthcoming until the last quarter of 1998. External debt was expected to increase over the outlook period. A restoration of donor aid flows this year should enable the country to fulfil its debt-service obligations although there is official concern that a protracted donor freeze could give rise to temporary debt-service difficulties this year. The Kenyan authorities are likely to press ahead and make further inroads into clearing the backlog and interest arrears (see Table 3.3.1)

Table 3.3.1   External Financing

					(US$ millions)
	1993	1994	1995	1996(e)	1997(e)
External Debt	7118	7160	7382	7435	7485
of which					
Short-Term	903	678	636	600	670
Medium/Long-Term	6215	6482	6746	6835	6815
Debt/XGS (%)	306	268	248	244	229
Debt/GDP (%)	124	100	83	82	73
Debt Service /XGS (%)	27	33	26	23	19
Int. Payments /XGS (%)	11	12	9	9	8

Source: Barclays Bank International, Nairobi 1998

The country is not expected to press for a full Paris Club rescheduling over the outlook period.

3.4   Conclusion

As has been indicated above, the new budget rationalisation policies, based as they are on stabilisation and structural adjustment programmes, have important implications for donors, implications which may suggest possible lines of approach to be pursued in the adaptation of aid policies.

First, radical change in government policy on the recruitment of local staff, has consequences for the administration's approach to the use of expatriate personnel, particularly in regard to established posts. Technical assistance in most aid programmes has, hitherto, been made available for three main reasons: firstly, to provide specific technical expertise, which cannot be obtained locally; secondly, to assist with the professional training of local staff; and thirdly, to prepare and supervise specific programmes, which the aid organisation is concerned in funding through grant or loan finance. For many agencies, the third role has tended to assume a special significance, and here, there may be need to reflect, as the World Bank and other organisations have done, on ways in which this supervisory role could be most effectively handled by the use of local institutions, local personnel and local consultants.

As regards the expertise and training functions, there would again appear to be a case for looking more deliberately and systematically at the professional and technical training priorities for those cadres, with which donors are most closely associated, and explore with the Kenyan administration the possibilities for strengthening relevant in-service and other staff development programmes. Consequently, in the future choice of personnel for any continuing technical assistance, particular consideration should be given to candidates with a strong background in professional training activities, and in the interconnection between technical and financial programming, which has become an area of growing concern for the Kenyan administration, and indeed also for donors. A further preoccupation of government is to secure a more effective exchange of technical experience and knowledge in conditions of greater professional equality. This suggests the possibility of instituting special joint meetings of professional associations and bodies for in-depth discussions on subjects of mutual technical interest, connected with the implementation of specific development programmes.

As regards the inter-related development and recurrent budgetary problems, it is increasingly apparent that donor policies have, to some degree, contributed to present difficulties, largely because of their narrow focus on the funding of development projects and programmes *per se*, and their limited regard to recurrent expenditure implications. For a government facing significant balance of payment constraints like Kenya's, any offer of development aid support, making an initially positive contribution to the country's foreign exchange position, must always be difficult to resist, and frequently leads to a severe discounting of future recurrent expenditure implications. Thus, in the case of Kenya, externally supported development projects normally give rise to recurrent expenditures equivalent to some 10–15 per cent of the original project cost. The provision of development finance, therefore, has far-reaching budgetary implications, and it will clearly be necessary, in the future, for donors to ensure that their programmes are fully integrated into the Kenyan administration's planning and which Kenya has introduced with a view to rendering its import-substitution and export-orientated industries more competitive in both regional and international markets. Particular attention has been focused on market opportunities under the PTA system, which in the Kenyan view, and that of other governments in the region, represents a potentially useful mechanism for developing an increasing volume of trade in the Eastern, Central and Southern Africa and the Indian Ocean areas. While certain technical and administrative improvements have recently been made in the functioning of the Zimbabwe based PTA clearing house, serious foreign exchange shortages continue to represent a major constraint on the development of intra-regional transactions.

Again in the Kenyan view, and that of other governments in the region, the provision of convertible currency units to individual member states, to be used essentially for intra-region transactions, could help stimulate the expansion of trade among the Eastern, Central and Southern African and Indian Ocean countries. The provision of such support through some form of regional approach, would undoubtedly be warmly welcomed by the Kenyan administration, and, it would seem, also by other PTA members, who would be willing to enter into serious discussions with interested donors on this issue.

The strenuous efforts made by Kenya to increase the efficiency of its manufacturing and other industries are, of course, directed not only to the PTA but also to the wider international market. The question of securing improved access to Western European markets is, therefore, a matter of considerable interest to the Kenyan authorities, who believe that the various stabilisation and structural adjustment programmes, which they have implemented throughout the 1980s/1990s can fully succeed, only if they have increasing opportunities to export a growing range and volume of exports to trading partners in Europe and elsewhere in the industrial world.

Chapter IV
SOCIAL DEVELOPMENT

4.1 Poverty and Distribution of Income

> Unto every one that hath shall be given, and he shall have abundance: but from him that hath not shall be taken away even that which he hath.
>
> St Matthew 25.29

Poverty is a difficult concept to define. Most definitions are somewhat arbitrary and must necessarily be so. Once defined, poverty is an even more difficult subject to present in an operational sense, and to measure with a reasonable degree of accuracy. Poverty may be seen in absolute and relative terms. In an absolute measurement, a poverty line is calculated in terms of basic necessities, below which a person is considered poor.

Relative poverty, on the other hand, is concerned with inequality in the distribution of resources, whether they are means of production (land and other forms of property which can be used productively) or items of consumption, related to income levels. While relative poverty may be measured through statistical methods, such as the gini coefficient, in most developing countries the available data are generally inadequate, or not reliable enough, for the computation of such measurement. As a result, resort must often be made to somewhat cruder forms of measurement.

4.1.2 ABSOLUTE AND RELATIVE POVERTY

Greer and Thorbecke define absolute poverty in the following sense: 'A household is defined as poor if it is unable to provide its members with sufficient quantities of basic necessities such as food, clothing, shelter, health and education'. 'Sufficient quantities' are the 'amount necessary to maintain physical well-being'. (John and M C McHale, 1978). In their analysis, food is singled out as a key factor, and absolute poverty is equated with nutritional deprivation.

Their principal criterion is a recommended daily allowance of calorific intake per adult equivalent as set by WHO/FAO and modified to fit Kenyan conditions. Caloric consumption is crucial in food poverty assessment, as calories can be used as a good overall proxy indicator of a balanced diet.

Nutrition is admittedly only one of the variables included in the above definition of poverty. The focus on the food variable is, nevertheless, justified for at least two good reasons. Firstly, average smallholders in Kenya spend about 74 per cent of their total expenditure (including the imputed value of home-produced items) on food (Greer and Thorbecke, 1986). This reflects the very high priority accorded to food as a basic need, although some poor households may choose luxuries over necessities. Thus, it has been reported that the strong emphasis on high priced cash crops in certain areas, e.g. the sugar belt in Western Kenya, has led to a deterioration in food supplies and to ensuing very serious nutritional deficiencies. However, it can normally be assumed that if a household is poor in food, it is likely to be poor in all other relevant variables as well. Secondly, food poverty directly influences the other variables. Nutritional deprivation reduces physical growth, ability to learn and work (i.e. ability to earn an income), and increases susceptibility to diseases.

The calorific minimum requirement may, in turn, be converted to a monetary poverty line, which expresses the minimum level of income or expenditure necessary to meet the nutritional needs of a household. For policy formulation and evaluation, which centre around incomes, markets and prices, this is a more useful measurement than calorific minima. Generally, many sections of the Kenyan people experienced a considerable improvement in their welfare after independence, as a result of high economic growth rates, rising levels of real income, as well as extension of social services, such as education and health. This trend was followed by bouts of contraction in the economy which followed political instability brought on by such crises as Tom Mboya's assassination, the Kisumu massacre and the outlawing of the KPU. It re-emerged relatively buoyant with the exception of a temporary deterioration after the 1973 oil shock, until the culmination of the 'coffee boom' in 1978/1979. From that period, which roughly coincided with the transfer of power from Kenyatta to Moi, the economic situation has continued to deteriorate and levels of income have been declining. The effects of the dissolution of the EAC were beginning to be felt on the export side, and the import bill for oil therefore rose sharply to the second rise in crude oil prices. In 1983–1984, a severe drought further accentuated Kenya's economic problems. Taken together these factors had an adverse impact on general welfare levels and increased the incidence of poverty from which many Kenyans have not recovered. With decreases in tea and coffee prices on the world market, rural incomes have declined for the large proportion of smallholders producing these export crops.

In its degree of prevalence, absolute poverty is overwhelmingly a major rural problem in Kenya, where, because of land and population pressure and increasing landlessness, rural poverty appears to be rising in many areas of the country. The fact that the domestic terms of trade have been moving against the rural areas serves to underscore this trend (Sharpley, 1986a).

Price controls and subsidies on certain important foodstuffs, such as maize-meal (posho), have helped to improve food intake, but have had a stronger impact in the urban communities than in the rural areas. Nonetheless, actual urban food prices have tended to stay above the prescribed levels, particularly in times of shortage. In this context, market forces appear to have a momentum of their own, although price controls tend to exercise a dampening effect.

In 1977 a study found that 24 per cent of rural children aged 1–4 countrywide, were physically stunted, and by 1982 this proportion had reached 31 per cent (Vandemoortele, 1986). For Western and Nyanza Provinces, the increase from 1977 to 1982 was dramatic, from 16 to 33 per cent (Nordberg, 1986). The introduction of a free primary school milk programme in 1979 did probably ameliorate the children's nutritional situation somewhat.

A study, using IRS-l survey data (1974–1975), showed that about 40 per cent of smallholders were estimated to consume less than the recommended daily allowance of calories. The proportion ranged from 32 per cent in Eastern Province to almost 46 per cent in Western Province (Greer & Thorbecke, 1986). The greater part of all food-poor individuals (about 75 per cent) were found in Eastern, North-Eastern, Coast, Nyanza and Western Provinces. The severity of food deprivation was greater in the Coast and Nyanza Provinces. Increasingly, female-headed households, other factors being equal, allocate household income in such a way as to acquire more calories per adult equivalent, than do male-headed households.

The insensitivity of the IMF and the World Bank to the social consequences of its SAP's conditionality measures, the corrupt practices by the Kenyan authorities and the heartless exploitation of the peasantry by the 'bwana mkubwa' helped to increase the severity of rural poverty in Kenya. The IMF insistence on cuts in public expenditure tended to adversely affect social services such as health, education, water supplies and basic necessity - 'food supplies'. Likewise, its persistent animosity to food subsidies and price controls, have further contributed to widening and deepening levels of poverty and absolute deprivation in Kenya. The now accepted principle of cost-sharing, in conjunction with the provision of social services, is no doubt consonant with IMF thinking. Although the team accepts the validity of the cost-sharing approach, there is every reason to insist on mechanisms, e.g. graduated tariff structure, whereby the social welfare of vulnerable poor groups may be effectively protected.

Depending on the largely arbitrary level of the poverty line adopted, variations will arise in the proportion of the population, who are defined as suffering from poverty. Using an urban poverty line of K.shs. 5,422 per year, Crawford and Thorbecke, (1978) estimated that 25 per cent of urban households were poor in 1976. Collier and Lal (1980), on the other hand, using a poverty line of K.shs. 2,150, estimates that less than 5 per cent of households were poor in 1974. Vandemoortele (1982), using rural and urban poverty lines of K.shs. 2,269 and K.shs 3,935 per year respectively in 1976, arrives at a conclusion in between the above two, and estimates that 33.1 per cent of rural households and 15.3 per cent of urban households had income below their respective poverty lines.

Whatever reliable data exist on income distribution in Kenya, are now rather dated (ILO, 1972; Ng'ethe, 1976; Kaplinsky, 1978b; Vandemoortele, 1982). Using data from 1976, Vandemoortele estimated that the top decile of Kenyan households earn 46.82 per cent of the national income; the bottom decile a mere 0.87 per cent, and the lower half of the households only 13.85 per cent. The gini coefficient for income distribution was 0.5855 in 1976 i.e. very skewed distribution indeed (Vandemoortele, 1982)

4.1.3 INCOME DIFFERENTIALS

A common method of depicting relative poverty or inequality for wage or salaried employees, is to examine the state of income differentials. These offer an immediate and easily comprehensible picture of the phenomenon, without necessarily revealing the full complexity of the subject. Although statutory minimum wage levels in any country may fall below the absolute poverty line, as defined above, this is not always the case in the developed countries such as Britain. But, in Kenya, however, it is undoubtedly the position.

Here it is important to distinguish initially between, on the one hand, income earners whose remuneration derives basically from a single source of income, e.g. wages or salaries, without support from a supplementary origin and, on the other hand, people who have several sources of income.

The statutory minimum wage was intended to be a guarantee against sub-standard remuneration for those who are gainfully employed as wage earners. These wage rates are set for various levels of skills and categories of posts. There is also a differentiation by geographical area, as costs of living vary considerably from one locality to another. These levels are adjusted periodically, depending on the movements in consumer price indices.

On 1 May 1985, a 20 per cent increase in minimum wage was

announced in Kenya, albeit not applicable to the civil service. The minimum gross wage for the lowest rung of the ladder (i.e. general labourers, cleaners, sweepers, gardeners, ayah, domestic servants, day watchmen and messengers) was set at K.shs. 576 per month in Nairobi and Mombasa, and K.shs.530 for other towns. For agricultural labourers, the wage rate rose to K.shs. 270 per month (EIU Quarterly Economic Report no.3). In addition to the gross wage, all employees continued to be entitled by law to a housing allowance, equivalent to at least 15 per cent of the gross basic wage.

The employers' contribution to the obligatory National Social Security Fund (NSSF) - a public pension scheme - is 5 per cent of the employee's total gross emoluments (including overtime pay, if any). Some companies also offer fringe benefits, such as related purchase of commodities, free tea twice a day, free medical treatment, and travel allowance, etc.

The range of remuneration in the private sector is, of course, very wide. An unskilled general labourer in Nairobi may typically receive basic gross earnings of K.shs.576 per month, plus a 15 per cent mandatory housing allowance, bringing the total to K.shs. 662. After allowing for fringe benefits in kind, the labourer's total earnings may come to perhaps K.shs 700 in monetary terms.

At the other extreme, a Kenya citizen at the chief executive level in finance and insurance may earn an average basic gross salary of K.shs. 22,923 per month. The messenger to chief executive ratio would then be 40:1, if basic gross emoluments are compared. Adding fringe benefits, the ratio could rise to 80:1 (Price Waterhouse Associates, 1986). The corresponding ratios for an expatriate chief executive in a large manufacturing company to a messenger would be 112:1 and 150:1 respectively.[1]

---

[1] Urban and rural households are not discrete categories, strictly speaking. A number of urban-rural transfer mechanism are operative, e.g. remittances. Most industrial workers are, for instance, urban residents, but their families remain in the rural areas cultivating the shamba. Such households assume a 'straddling' position between sectors. (2) The gini co-efficient may vary between 0, expressing complete equality, and 1, which indicates total inequality.

Within the public sector, income differentials are not as marked as in the private sector, but the top to bottom ratio is still high. In October 1985, new salaries and conditions of service for civil servants were announced, as recommended by the Civil Service Review Committee. The annual salary for the lowest job group A ranged between a minimum of Kenya pounds 339 (equivalent K.shs. 565 per month), and a maximum of Kenya pounds 552 (equivalent K.shs. 929 per month). At the other end of the scale, the chief secretary and Chief Justice in the highest, newly created job group T, will earn an annual salary of between Kenya pounds 10,986 (K.shs 15,550 per month) and Kenya pounds 10,986 (K.shs. 18,310 per month). The ratio between the highest and the lowest in the civil service, would then be over 32:1 (ETU Quarterly Economic Report no.1, 1986). The same obligatory benefits will accrue to civil servants, as to those employed in the private sector, but the public sector is less likely than the private sector to offer benefits beyond the statutory requirement.

Nominal minimum wage rates have been eroded by high inflation rates over the past three decades. Between 1975–1985, the real minimum wage rate fell by 52.9 per cent and by 86.5 per cent between 1985 and 1995. This downward slide in real wages did not apply to the lower income groups only. The average real wage earnings for all types of employees in the private sectors, fell by 17.5 per cent in the 1980–1985 period; for the manufacturing sector alone the figure was 23 per cent for the same period (Godfrey, 1986). This has undoubtedly led to a deterioration in living conditions for large sections of urban dwellers in salaried employment. For the lowest income groups it has been a disaster. The basic income levels have fallen below the poverty line, so that the proportion of poor urban households has increased substantially since 1976.[2]

---

[2] The figure for executive emoluments and fringe benefits indicate the cost to the company, not the monetised benefits accruing to the employee in question. Account has not been taken of the equalising effect of the graduated person income tax. Nor is income from capital included.

4.1.4 DISTRIBUTION OF ASSETS

For employees in the so-called modern sector, whose principal source of income is their wage or salary, the differentials in personal emoluments from that source, may be a fairly reliable indicator of income inequality. However, many employees derive an income from capital as well. If the latter is taken into account, the income differentials tend to be higher than the wage/salary differentials would indicate. The estimates of income distribution by Vandemoortele (1982) above, are based on total national income data, including all sources of income, rather than personal emoluments alone. The effects of the unequal distribution of assets, particularly land, are therefore built into this form of calculation.

In this context, it is apparent that assets, which can be used for productive purposes, are a source of accumulation, and tend therefore, to reinforce and accelerate income inequality overtime. While intricate problems arise in making estimates of income distribution in Kenya, an even greater challenge comes in securing reliable updated statistics, on which to base estimates of wealth distribution. This issue is politically sensitive, particularly in regard to land ownership, which does not ease the difficulty of obtaining free access to relevant information.

One estimate of land ownership concentration, based on 1976 data, yields a gini coefficient of 0.8, which means in the Kenyan context that the top 10 per cent of Kenyan farmers own about 73 per cent of the fertile land, and the lowest 50 per cent of farmers only 5 per cent of the fertile land (Vandemoortele, 1982). However, these figures may overstate the current degree of inequality, because of the subdivision of large farms, which has taken place in recent years.

The proportion of households owning no land is increasing. In 1976, IRS-2 figures showed that 11.4 per cent of rural households were landless. They were not all poor, as many were in formal employment, or engaged in trade. More than 7 per cent of rural households without land, could be termed poor (World Bank, 1983). If one turns to the statistics of holding size, contained in the last three Integrated Rural Surveys (IRS) from 1976 to 1978, the proportion of households in the zero hectare

175

category went up sequentially from 13.7 per cent in 1976 (IRS-2) to 17.9 and 21.6 per cent in 1977 (IRS-3) and 1978 (IRS-4) (Kenya/Central Bureau of Statistics, 1981a). There is no reason to expect this trend to have slackened, given the rate of population growth, poverty and land availability.

The search for wage employment by the landless, or by marginalised peasants without adequate income from agriculture, has resulted in continuing rural/urban migration, which, in turn, contributes to the further growth of slum-like and squatter settlement areas on the fringe of the cities (Nairobi, Mombasa, Kisumu, Nakuru, etc) and minor urban centres. Many smaller towns now also have large slum quarters of poor and destitute people in Kenya.

People without either land or jobs are now Kenya's real destitute. The Kenyan labour force (available for work) is currently estimated to number 14.6 million people, and to be growing at a rate of 3.8 per cent annually. In absolute terms, this means that at least 800,000 (eight hundred thousand), additional jobs will need to be created every year to stabilise the employment situation (Economic Survey, 1995). Some of these may be absorbed in agriculture, but a majority are likely to migrate to urban centres to seek wage employment which does not exist. In 1984 to 1985, wage employment in the modern sector grew by 4.9 per cent, representing 54,700 new jobs, which was above the number targeted by the Fifth Development Plan. In the same years, the urban informal sector created 18,100 new jobs (Economic Survey, 1986). These combined figures fell short of employment needs at the time.[3]

---

[3] Conceptually, zero-holding refers to a holding on which no pieces of land are being cultivated, i.e. it is in the zero hectare category, and no cultivation is intended in the course of the survey period, although it may provide grazing for livestock. However, some of the households, which initially qualified as a zero-holding, ceased to be so, by virtue of acquiring or cultivating some land as the survey progressed.

4.1.5 THE POOREST GROUPS

Absolute poverty, or income too low and insufficient to meet basic human needs, results from a lack of income generating opportunities. The creation of such opportunities depends on: (a) availability of land; (b) location of wage employment; (c) distribution of infrastructure; (d) accessibility of service, (Kenya/Central Bureau of Statistics & UNICEF, 1984). Denied these opportunities, people will stay poor. And the degree to which such opportunities are denied, will determine the severity of people's poverty.

On the basis of the above discussion and analysis, it is possible to identify a number of particularly poor and vulnerable groups in Kenya. When considering the poor people as target groups, to be reached by development programmes, these are the groups to which particular reference is made. They include: (a) pastoralists; (b) marginal small-holders (men & women); (c) landless rural workers (men, women and young people); (d) jobless and poor urban people (men, women and young people); (e) handicapped people - physical, and those with psychological problems; (f) children.

Some clarification is necessary as to groups b. In current usage, any peasant with a holding of less than 20 hectares is a small-holder. In the Kenyan context, 20 hectares is a relatively large holding, which would normally yield a comfortable income. Hence, the poverty line, in terms of holding, should be set much lower, perhaps at 1 hectare only. In this context, it should be recalled that the mean holding size in 1978 was 1.2 hectares. For these reasons, reference, is made to 'marginal small-holders', as a relevant group of rural people. Moreover, cutting across all the above categories, is the high incidence of female-headed households. Thus, in any one of the above groups, households headed by women are particularly vulnerable.

4.1.6 EMPLOYMENT, INCOME AND EQUALITY

The 1972 ILO report, which represented a path-breaking contribution to that organisation's world employment programme, was intended to provide government with a technical analysis of its employment problems, and also to offer policy guidance, in the development aid and trade context, to international institutions and bilateral agencies, involved in Kenya's development. Many of its recommendations were subsequently incorporated in the country's third and fourth development plans, covering the period 1974–1983.

In essence, the ILO mission advocated a strategy of redistribution through growth, within the framework of a mixed economy. The overall objective was to direct a large proportion of resources to areas or groups, previously denied access to them, so that the benefits of growth would be more equally shared among the population than had hitherto been the case.

Of particular significance, was the attention which the ILO mission accorded to employment and development in Kenya's 'informal sector'. The existence of significant groups, engaged in unregistered 'informal activities' in poor countries, has long been acknowledged, activities characterised by ease of establishment and limited skill and capital requirements. What was new in the ILO analysis was the recognition that many informal sector activities represent a relevant economic adaptation to the factor endowment and income level of a country. Thus poor consumers cannot afford quality items where capital is scarce, and labour plentiful. A detailed pursuit of this analysis brought government and donors to recognise that the informal sector could provide a range of goods and services for poor people, which helped them as producers, broadened their purchasing choice as consumers, and raised their economic and social welfare beyond previous levels. It was perceived that there were ways in which the informal sector could be assisted to do all this more extensively and effectively. These possibilities were important in increasing the formulation of government and donor policies in the 1976–1986 period.

So far as development aid was concerned, the ILO mission noted that by 1972 donors had become much more concerned that their programme should not only accelerate economic growth, but also help achieve a better distribution of benefits. It was evident to the mission that donors were showing a preference for financing agricultural, rural development and other programmes designed to increase employment and benefits to the very poorest section of the community.

4.2 Gender Relations

4.2.1 POSITION OF WOMEN IN KENYA

Gender relations and the status of women in Kenyan society are moulded by a set of factors related to tradition, legislation and culture. Kenya is a country with a great deal of local variations and ethnic differences, and female–male relations are, therefore, likely to differ considerably from one area to another. Class and age are also factors which influence women's position in society.

Thus, Kenyan women are not a homogeneous group, and this fact should be taken into account when defining women as a target group in the context of a development programme. In general, women in Kenya have a subordinate position to men. This is particularly the case with reference to the marriage institution, where the power of the man in his role as husband and father is virtually indisputable (*Weekly Review*, 20 July 1979). The male prerogative within the family is regarded as a natural privilege, which Kenyan men of all categories are reluctant to relinquish voluntarily. This attitude is not least pronounced among the male elite.

The Parliamentary debate in 1979 on a revised Marriage Bill, represented a case in point. The heated debate, which this proposal aroused in Parliament, reflected the delicate and controversial nature of the matrimonial issue (*Weekly Review*, 20 July 1979). The new bill sought to liberalise outdated marriage and divorce laws, by consolidating into a single legislative act all the existing marriage laws in Kenya. The bill had a bias towards the western mode of marriage, although a provision was included to make polygamy legal (*Weekly Review*, 20 July 1979). Indirectly, the revision meant an improvement in the rights and position of women. Among other things, it gave the wife the right to decide if her husband should be allowed to take a second wife. The Marriage Bill of 1979, however, was rejected by Parliament, under the pretext that it was 'un-African'. (*Weekly Review*, 22 February 1985). An earlier version of the bill had been tabled in 1976, but it had met the same fate as the 1979 bill.

The situation of Kenyan women could be, and perhaps will be, improved considerably through legislation. Gender inequality in Kenya is partly founded on differences between legal rights for women and men and is wholly accepted as discriminatory and an abuse of women's human rights. Development aid donors can undoubtedly have a role to play in this context by raising the issue of women's legal position and human rights in their discussions with the present Kenyan authorities.

Women in Kenya have contributed and contribute substantially to the economy and political stability of the country. For instance, the proportion of females working in the agricultural sector, the backbone of the country's economy, exceeds the proportion of males. The female labour force in fact constitutes perhaps as much as two-thirds of the total labour force in agriculture. Besides being responsible for the cultivation of food crops, women shoulder a major part of the work load in cash crop production (Kenya Ministry of Culture and Social Services, 1985). The massive contribution, which women make by their labour in the productive sectors, is not matched by their legal rights and decision-making power in society. Women have limited inheritance and property rights to land, and female membership in agricultural cooperatives is very low (Kenya/ Ministry of Cooperative Development and DANIDAI 1985). In short, women as a group, are largely excluded from major areas of economic life and responsibility for our country.

Further, women are responsible for the rearing of children and stability of the homes. As many as 40 per cent of Kenyan households are thought to be headed by women (Kenya/Ministry of Culture and social services, 1985). Particularly among poor families, women hold key positions as breadwinners for the household.

It is a fundamental belief in some African traditions that, when a woman is healthy and respected as a person in her own right, all society stands to gain. A healthy woman is one who is physically sound, spiritually alive and psychologically strong. She is interested in contributing to the betterment of her home, village, tribe and society, and willing to learn how to do this. She chooses to have children when and if she has the resources and support to care for them responsibly. She spaces her pregnancies so that her own physical health remains intact, and she seeks appropriate health supervision during her pregnancies. A healthy woman is a person to be reckoned with when injustice, discrimination, racism/tribalism and apathy threaten her very existence. We need to contribute to the development of healthy African women with our science, our technology, our loving concern for all people. We all stand to gain from these efforts.

The incongruity between the social status of Kenyan women and their workload, has made it more and more apparent that something must be done soon to correct this situation. The development of the society has in many ways reinforced the skewed nature of this relationship (Talle, 1983). The comparatively high level of education among Kenyan women, has had a very limited impact in terms of vesting increased political power in women. Kenyan women constitute only about two per cent of local authority councillors, and Parliament has very few female members out of a total of 222. Only one or two of those women representatives are elected, the other two are nominated. Bearing in mind that women comprise 55–58 per cent of Kenya's total population and 60 per cent of the electorate, the limited involvement of women in Kenya's political leadership remains a puzzling question and cannot be ignored or brushed-off.

Female deprivation and exclusion from vital decision-making processes and responsibilities undoubtedly represent a serious constraint affecting the active participation of women in the development process. The fact that men hold a dominant position at almost all levels and areas of society, has led to a diversion of international aid resources towards meeting the needs of Kenyan women.

Female circumcision is another area of Kenya's social life which must be dealt with immediately. Female circumcision is still widely practised, and the extensive disfigurement of the vulva that results often leads to severe lacerations during childbirth. These circumcisions also can impede progress in the second stage of labour when the infant is being pushed through the lower vagina and perineum. The increased pushing effort required, combined with poor nutrition and exhaustion, result in a precariously thin recto-vaginal wall and subsequent tearing or fistula formation. Once a fistula forms, it results in constant leakage or urine mixed with faeces and an offensive odour. These women are then ostracised to the outskirts of the village and no man will touch them again. However, they may also have no food, no source of shelter and certainly no emotional comfort from friends. Recto-vaginal fistulas can only be corrected by surgery which is unavailable to most rural women, where this abominable custom is still practised. Therefore, these women, because of shame, become permanent outcasts of society, the untouchables. This is a poor reward for the woman who submitted to the will of men for circumcision and to have the children that were so important to her man, her village, her tribe and her own security. It does, of course lower the birth rate but there are much better ways to accomplish that goal.

4.2.2 GOVERNMENT POLICY ON WOMEN

Kenya Government has no declared policy on female participation in development programmes nor on specific issues relating to the improvement of women's situation in Kenya. Any development which bypasses women and their social and economic contribution to society is scarcely worthy of the name, since it ignores the 55–58 per cent of Kenya's population who are responsible for the bearing and early education of the nation's children and also have a crucial role in production and reproduction. All Kenya's development programmes should be examined to see how they will affect, or are affecting, the living standards of women and their families, women's opportunities to earn an income, and women's right to some say about their own lives including the number and spacing of their children. The status of women in Kenya is not only closely linked to national development but also women's fertility and Kenya's future.

Women are always seen as part of the family, and as such, they are regarded as contributors, as well as beneficiaries, on an equal footing with other family members, when it comes to participating in Kenya's economic development. The conceptualisation of women as an integral part of the family has created certain problems of communication in the consultations between the male-dominated Kenyan government and donors in the context of targeted development aid programmes. In such target group discussions pursued by donors, women are on occasion singled out as a specific category of beneficiaries. While this approach is justified as a development strategy to improve the plight of Kenyan women, it is not always perceived as such by Kenya's male society. Indeed, donors by their gender-specific approach, have sometimes unjustifiably been accused of creating antagonisms between men and women.

There were indications, however, that government was becoming aware that the question of women's treatment deserves a place in political debate at the national level and a change in governmental attitudes. Most importantly, in 1976 the Women's Bureau was established in the Ministry of Culture and Social Services, with overall responsibility for coordinating all women's programmes in the country. Since its inception, the major donors to the Bureau have been Denmark, Norway and Sweden.

Furthermore, the Fifth Development Plan (1984–1988) pointed to certain inequalities between men and women in the productive sectors. For instance, it acknowledged that men were favoured in comparison to women, in so far as employment practices in the modern sector were concerned, and that special measures to correct this imbalance were required. To point to gender inequalities in a national development plan was amazing in a Kenyan male dominated society; it signalled the beginning of a gradual change in attitudes. In the development plan, women are now referred to as special target categories in the case of agricultural and health care programmes. One such programme was the community Action for Disadvantaged Rural Women in the Ministry of Planning and National Development, which concentrated its efforts on the need of women in the arid and semi-arid areas of Kenya.

In July 1985, Kenya hosted the United Nations Decade for Women Conference. The Conference was, *inter alia*, a gigantic manifestation of the concern and interest that women all over the world, as well as in Kenya, took in issues related to women and their future. The Conference did not, however, precipitate a discussion on the role of women in Kenya, as was anticipated, and hoped for by many. The discussion on women's issues appeared to have reached a standstill, at least within government circles.

4.2.3 WOMEN'S ORGANISATIONS

Among other things, the role of the Women's Bureau is to promote the organisation of women on a countrywide basis, and particular encouragement is given to women to organise themselves into so-called women's groups. A typical group consists of 30–40 women, who are involved in some form of income-generating activity ranging from agricultural and livestock concerns, and house improvement activities, such as roofing and purchase of furniture and utilities, to small-scale businesses, environmental improvement and handicrafts. The groups are registered with District Social Development Officers (DCDOs). There are now approximately over 16,000 registered women's groups in the country, although many of these are dormant; the total membership is estimated at slightly over 630,000 (Kenya/Ministry of Culture and Social Services, 1985). A registered group may apply for financial assistance to initiate activities, but only about 10 per cent of the groups have actually received any funding from the Ministry, and the majority of groups generate their own resources through individual contributions from members.

Membership in a women's group seems to provide individual women with a certain feeling of social security, but appears to be of less importance to them in economic terms. Due to lack of sound management and stable financial resources, many of the groups are running their business enterprises unprofessionally, and with no significant financial returns. However, the 'success' of women's groups should perhaps not be measured in terms primarily of profitability, but in terms of the solidarity and network relationships they apparently create among women. It should be recalled that the women's groups in fact began as self-help groups, where women helped each other in times of need, and where group activities reflected mutually supportive relationships.

A majority of the groups are affiliated to the Maendeleo ya Wanawake Organisation (MYWO), which is the largest and most popular of the Women's organisations in Kenya. The MYWO is in principle an NGO, but liaises closely with the Women's Bureau, both at the central, district and local levels.

The MYWO has grown from a small organisation with a few hundred women's groups and a full-time staff of two persons only, into a giant national movement with almost 330,000 individual members and a permanent staff of 70 employees (*Weekly Review*, 2 February 1986). The headquarters of the organisation, Maendeleo House in Nairobi, is an impressive building, which cost K.shs. 14.5 million to build, with financing secured partly through contributions from women's groups throughout the country. Maendeleo House, which was officially opened by the President in 1980, is a rallying point for a range of women's activities. In particular, it provides a centre for seminars and courses where women leaders and MYWO field staff meet to discuss practical problems and issues relating to the progress and development of Kenyan Women.

The running of the MYWO has not been without its problems. There have been differences between leaders within the MYWO, as well as with women leaders outside the organisation. For instance, in 1981 the MYWO, together with some other organisations, withdrew from the National Council of Women of Kenya (NCWK), as a result of a certain difference of view between prominent leaders in the two organisations. Since then, however, the relationship between the MYWO and NCWK has been normalised, although the MYWO did not, in the event, return to the NCWK.

At the beginning of 1986, the chairperson of the MYWO and its executive officer were dismissed, allegedly because of financial mismanagement, organisational irregularities, favouritism and corruption (*Weekly Review*, 21 February 1986). Subsequently, an interim committee was appointed by the Government, with the tasks of setting up a new accounting system for the MYWO, and streamlining its organisational routines and practices. This direct intervention by the corrupt government in the affairs of the MYWO could endanger the organisation's future status as an independent NGO.

Women's groups offer the major organisational platform for

Kenyan women. In fact, at the government level, official consultations on women's issues very often resolve themselves in practice into a discussion concerning women's groups. This implicit confusion of women, as a social category and as an organisational structure based upon female recruitment, may have certain unfortunate consequences for the broader understanding of gender relations and women's position in the society. Male privileges and men's monopolisation of political and economic resources, will probably not be questioned, as long as the whole issue is confined to a discussion about women's groups. Neither the Women's Bureau nor the MYWO seems to be ready to raise publicly the issue of male dominance. On the contrary, the former MYWO chairperson stated that, MYWO's current ten-year programme to raise the standard of family life in rural areas, should not be viewed as posing a 'threat to men's traditional rights, as masters of the home' (*Weekly Review*, 25 April 1990). And indeed, cooperation, rather than confrontation with men, has been the course most frequently followed by women leaders in Kenya.

4.2.4 WOMEN AND DEVELOPMENT AID

The concept of women's groups has left its mark on development aid policy towards women in Kenya. The massive organisation of Kenyan women's groups, has been taken as a sign of progress, and the groups have been regarded as the perfect instrument for implementation of female-directed development assistance. Hence, a major part of the aid resources targeted towards women has been channelled through women's group structures. An inevitable limitation of such an approach has been that women, who are not organised into such groups, are in effect the majority of Kenya's poorest women, they tend to fall outside this part of the development aid programme. The hitherto widespread faith in the Kenya women's group, as the key vehicle for raising the standard of living of the poorest Kenyan women, has begun to be doubted.

Although women's groups definitely have a role to play in Kenyan society, any belief in the potential of these groups to nurture social and economic development among the very poorest women in Kenya should be regarded with caution. The composition and general orientation of the groups should be carefully scrutinised, before development aid assistance is allocated to them. Hence, it is recommended that support to women's groups should be provided on a selective basis, and should constitute only one among several channels for assisting Kenyan women.

For example, integrating women into ongoing projects/programmes may be held back, inter alia, by the lack of a coherent policy or strategy across the operating ministries on issues relating to women and development. Besides, the objectives of many development programme components are ill-defined, as far as targeting women is concerned. From a woman's point of view, integration into certain of these projects may not even be desirable. First and foremost, integration should benefit women, and help them improve their situation, and be a goal in itself.

Efforts should be invested in defining strategies, and finding practical ways of reaching women, and addressing their specific concerns. Projects and programmes should be designed in such a way that women, both in their role as producers and providers, would stand to benefit from such assistance. To a large extent the effectiveness of development aid assistance to Kenyan women should at present be a matter of careful programme identification and formulation.

4.3   Health Care System

4.3.1   KENYAN RURAL WOMEN – THEIR HEALTH AND THEIR FUTURE

As one approaches a rural Kenyan village at midday, the scene is quite similar to many parts of other African countries. Children, from those just able to walk to teenagers, are numerous and actively playing a variety of childhood games in the dusty courtyards. Girls aged 9 or 10 are half-carrying and dragging their toddler siblings along with their games. They occasionally call to the younger children under their supervision who might be wandering beyond acceptable bounds. Men are gathered under the closest tree, sitting on fallen trees or makeshift benches or on the ground. They are talking animatedly and more often than not, drinking local beer. A few may be heard to complain that their noon meal is late, but then quickly return to talk of politics, friends or agriculture. It is the hottest time of the day and, at first glance, the scene is one of relaxation and contentment.

A close look into a village, however, reveals the women of the village in their traditional role - that of worker. Women in their late teens through mid-forties provide the principal work force for the entire village. In fact, it is usual to see a barefooted young woman in a brightly coloured dress with a baby on her back, a baby in her belly, and the day's supply of firewood or water on her head as she returns from her 3–4 hour journey to collect this wood or water. Other women are similarly adorned with small children while weeding the family's maize, millet or small vegetable garden. Older women (though rarely more than 50 years old) without young children may be seen carrying a basket on their head and one in each hand with a day's purchase (if, indeed, any money is available for such purchases) from the market several kilometres away. These brief encounters with the Kenyan village women reveal much about their role and status within the family and tribe, in fact represent much about the role and status of women throughout much of sub-Saharan Africa.

This section describes a value orientation towards Kenya women's health and its impact on Kenyan society, women as persons who deserve respect, with the companion values of equality, justice, autonomy and love, accorded all who are 'persons'. The view of medical science and technology as adjuncts to improving the condition of all humanity will be applied to exploring how the health of Kenyan women can be improved, and what this improvement in women's health can mean for the whole village, Kenyan society, the African continent and the world at large.

Health can be defined or viewed in a variety of ways. For many, health is simply defined as the absence of disease. Millions of Africans (especially children) would certainly improve their state of health and avoid early death if diseases such as AIDS, malaria, measles, diarrhoeal infections were eliminated. Likewise, many physicians and nurses working in Africa would welcome fewer illnesses and improved diagnostic and treatment tools. With this definition, however, one is looking primarily at the physical aspect of living, the body. What about the mind and the spiritual dimensions of 'healthiness'? The body can be disease free, but if the mind and spirit are wanting, health is limited.

In our study, the definition of health (described elsewhere in this section) is much broader and based on a combination of the World Health Organisation's definition and that of Parsons. We repeat, because this is critically very important:

> Health is much more than the absence of disease. Health is the state of optimum capacity of an individual which allows her/him to effectively perform roles and tasks which have been accepted as appropriate life goals. Health involves the interaction of mind, body and spirit in achieving one's life goals, and optimum health cannot be achieved without positive performance from all three. (WHO, 1980)

Some friends think it inappropriate to discuss this idealistic view of health when talking about Kenya, Africa or any other developing nation, especially, since the absence of food and preventable infectious diseases are killing millions as I am writing now. Yet if we only concern ourselves with improving the food supply and immunisation programmes, we condemn even more healthy children and adults to death from overpopulation, crowding, environmental pollution and apathy. Kenyan women, who can barely maintain enough health to care for the many children they already have, will have the additional burden of more surviving children, more mouths to seek meagre food for, and even less time to develop into important members of society as women. With our modern health technology, knowledge of factors which contribute to total health, and a caring concern that all people have equal access to good health, we must share our vision of total health for all peoples.

Blum (1974) has postulated that medical and nursing care and the provision of health services are relatively minor inputs into one's state of health. We must look beyond the providers of health and illness services to other factors. He goes on to suggest that the greatest impact on whether one is healthy or not is the environment in which we live, including one's early foetal and current physical environment, followed by socio-cultural, educational and employment factors. Next in line for determining one's state of health is one's personal behaviour or lifestyle, followed by health services and then hereditary factors. If we accept this set of determinants of health for all, not just Western settings, then we can more fully understand why it is imperative to discuss a multi-science approach to improving health in Kenya and for that matter Africa. Health workers need to work closely with agricultural experts and environmental specialists, as well as those who are working on programmes of education and economic and political strategies which together will enhance the life of all Kenyan people.

T McKeon (1978) states that the main determinant of health is the way of life an individual chooses or is forced to follow. In today's Kenya, the emphasis is on a 'forced' lifestyle, especially for most women; culture, tradition and lack of knowledge of any alternatives keep the Kenyan rural woman barefoot, pregnant, and not asking any questions about their lot in life. This is the way it is for women. Should it be this way? How can health workers, who are predominantly women help to inculcate a different set of expectations for other women, a different set of values? Since lifestyle is influenced by one's environment, socio-economic status, culture and educational level as well as personal choices, it is strongly suggested that lifestyle is the most important variable in determining the health of an individual. Given this reasoning, it follows that an integrated approach to health and health care (mind, body and spirit) is indicated if we wish to alter the overall health of the women in Kenya and Africa. Without healthy women, there will be no healthy children, no healthy men and no further development of the continent.

Survival of the fittest has real meaning for Kenyan rural women and the African continent. With very high neonatal and infant mortality rates and overall life expectancies in the 40s, those women who survive to teen years and begin their families are usually among the healthiest of the tribe. With repeated closely spaced pregnancies, heavy work responsibilities and poor nutrition, however, the general health of women gradually deteriorates by their mid- to late-twenties. If the woman does not die in childbirth (a common occurrence even today), she faces threats to life from AIDS, malaria, malnutrition and accidents, etc.

Part of the poor health status of women can be ascribed to their lack of concern for themselves. It is very unusual to have a woman seek health supervision in a rural clinic or urban centre for herself. She makes every effort to walk to these dispensaries because one of her children needs attention. In some rural parts of Kenya, the only health supervision a woman receives is during pregnancy and childbirth, but these are very rare occasions, and this may be done by traditional birth attendants (TBA) with little preparation in overall health supervision for non-pregnancy related conditions.

Our study team questioned a sample of Kenyan rural women in the eight provinces about their state of health including those on the borders of Uganda, Tanzania, Somalia and Ethiopia. The answers gathered gave little information beyond, 'I am okay'. Generalised complaints of dizziness, bad stomach, or backache may have been shared, but these usually came from the older, non-childbearing women. From the physical examination of the women selected for medical tests, the doctors variously found severe anaemia, malnutrition, HIV positive and evidence of parasitic diseases, but it was, and continues to be, very rare that women complain about these or their symptoms until it is too late.

Some would suggest that a woman's lack of concern for her own health comes from ignorance, and that education is the answer. We think education and information-sharing about health and disease are vital if the individual is willing to learn and ready to learn. How does one convince a woman that she is important enough to need attention for herself so that she is motivated to learn how to protect herself from disease and to keep herself healthy? The key to this health dilemma centres on the woman's image of herself. All the medical technology in the world is rendered useless if the woman does not think she is important enough to avail herself of medical or health care. Importance in this context is defined as whether the needs of the woman are sufficient to take time to seek care for herself. Very often her time is given to her children's needs and those of her man.

Most Kenyan rural women do not spend time thinking about work outside the home, political activities or education. They accept that their lot is not to have these, and they do not waste time thinking about them. Even educated women in Kenya whom we interviewed, who are beginning to be politically conscious and seek employment outside the home, will often end such discussions of personal growth with an apathetic, 'Who will listen? Who cares? I do what I have to do, and try not to make waves'?

We think all Kenyan women need to think about fulfilling their own potential and becoming the healthiest they can be, for we believe that it is only through equal partnership in life and society that the whole Kenyan society will improve and develop. As someone once said, the slaver resides in the gutter just as much as the slave, because he has to stay there to keep the slave down. Likewise, Kenyan men will remain oppressed and stagnant as long as they keep women subservient. To progress, develop and grow is possible only when all are liberated, when all can develop their full potential as productive members of Kenyan society, Africa and the World.

One of the strategies we think will improve the health of rural women in general is to have all districts in Kenya and all rural health clinics or dispensaries institute a comprehensive health clinic model rather than segregated, illness or age specific clinic on a given day. In this way, women who have to travel several kilometres on foot with a sick child may also have the opportunity to have the pregnancy and their own health needs looked after on the same day. This model of primary health care services is predicated on the use of trained health workers who can spot symptoms of illness in all ages, and who are willing, when looking after a small child with dehydration from diarrhoea, to also look at the mother and her health status. It is also important for health workers to view the woman as worthy of attention, and to praise even her smallest effort in improving her own health and that of her family.

These primary health centres have been most successful else-where in integrating child spacing, teaching and services for the same reasons of availability. An additional advantage of having the child spacing clinics within the structure of a multi-purpose clinic is we found some women prefer that no one else knows of their decision to use contraception. Privacy of all services is vital to success, but particularly when it comes to child spacing activities newly introduced to areas with cultural and religious taboos.

An additional technological solution to women's surgical needs can be implemented through flying doctor squads, roving surgical teams and the like. This means surgical availability on a monthly or bi-monthly basis, but the surgery would be available and the women made acceptable once again to their village. All of these corrective activities are important. But we also need to pay attention to the reasons for and possible elimination of, female circumcision, the prevention of maternal malnutrition and prolonged pushing during labour.

However, we believe that, if women are simply objects to be treated in whatever way males choose, we will continue to focus our technological powers on treatment of problems instead of prevention. Kenyan society will stagnate, wars will increase and all will be destroyed in the name of science, power and dominance. A beginning step is to accord Kenyan women full personhood. Their ideas and efforts can be used as we work together for Kenyan development, progress, peace and prosperity where everyone is respected and loved. A basic respect for human dignity is required. The individual who comes for health or illness care is a 'person'. Human beings carry both the rights and responsibilities of living in society as adults.

Kenyan rural traditional cultures and growing urban societies and patterns of health and illness care, however, tend to discount the personhood of women. Women are often treated as objects to be used (or abused) for the training or experiments of others, for the pleasures of men, for the production of children, or as chattels. This view of woman as less than a person has significant bearing on the health and status of each woman. It is central to understanding the current health or lack of it among women in Kenya and in Africa.

Let us take a brief historical look at how this view of women came to be in an attempt to understand whether and how it might be changed in the future. We will set aside the debate on foetuses and children as persons, and concentrate our efforts on adult women and men.

The historical roots of unequal treatment of women go back to the dawn of time. Unequal laws and moral codes favouring males go back to the earliest writings of the ancient near eastern world. The history of mankind is very largely one of domination by men over women. Even the early religious writers held the view that women were less than men, less than persons. Thomas Aquinas (1225–1274) considered women misbegotten males and Martin Luther (1483–1546) viewed women's sole purpose as being to produce children. If she died in childbirth, so be it. This attitude is reflected in Freud's famous statement about anatomy as destiny, and in the idea that a woman is a uterus surrounded by a supportive mechanism.

Explanations for male dominance throughout history vary. One is that men went to war and were protectors of their families, including the accumulation of property and goods. They wanted sons as heirs, and they wanted to make sure their sons were biologically theirs so virginity became a property value to ensure inheritance. Another view was that women, because of their capacity to be pregnant and nurse infants, were unable to fight in wars to conquer new territories. The more powerful male (property owner and protector) achieved dominance. Others point to the generally greater physical power of males and claim male dominance is the natural order. Religion either sanctioned this view or was used to sanctify it, so that male dominance became the 'will of God' or 'the gods'.

We are concerned with a crucial issue here. In 1984 a group of prominent women of the National Council of Women of Kenya (NCWK) (see Chapter II), reportedly demanded greater representation for women in senior decision-making positions in the country. President Moi reacted very strongly against these demands by saying that for women to demand equality with men, was tantamount to suggesting that the Bible was wrong, when it stated clearly that the man was the head of the family.

If male dominance is natural or of divine origin, some may doubt that it should be changed. If it is simply a matter of 'might makes right', then women can reverse roles whenever they achieve power and political influence. We suggest that neither of these positions fit our modern and changing world. We believe the enhancement of society is a major reason for man-woman relationships and dominion by either is counterproductive. Equal partnership is the goal, and that requires women be seen and accepted as full and vital partners in development and in all sectors of the Kenyan economy and society.

We repeat that the objectification of women is unethical, wrong, discriminatory and sinful. The unethical treatment of women can be seen as a lack of sensitivity to the woman as a person. She is seen as an object to be cared for only if she produces the right number and sex of children at the right time, in addition to cooking, gardening, and other work to maintain the health and well being of the male members of the family unit. Some might even say a woman is a sex object to be played with, abused, and then discarded for another, younger model. What is missing is simple human decency. Immanuel Kant (1804), a Prussian philosopher, claimed that humans are ends in themselves and not a means for someone else's ends. For Kant, this is the basic ethical principle from which all others are derived. It means that even if one voluntarily sells one's labour to another, this does not abrogate the right or the responsibility to participate in deciding what is produced and how it is produced. Voluntary servitude is still servitude, and it violates the categorical imperative which, when applied to work, means that one cannot use another person as a tool for one's ends. Work must be performed in freedom, through voluntary cooperation.

People, women or men, are not to be used for the good of someone else. Kant's ideas say women are not breeding animals whose purpose is to provide troops for the nation's military or bodies for the factories or farms. Likewise, children are not to be produced as an insurance policy to provide retirement income and care in the parent's old age. Persons are people who are accepted for themselves - as ends in themselves and not a means to someone else's ends, even if that end is itself good.

The final suggestions for improving the health of Kenyan women and society as a whole, are embodied in the concept of responsible parenting. Who should reproduce, when, and how often are valid questions for our modern age. The raising of these questions, even if they hurt the powerful, implies that there is no such thing as a 'right' to bear children. Indeed, in our modern age it is time to recognise that there exist no 'rights' without corresponding responsibilities. Therefore, if one chooses to reproduce, it should be done responsibly. No one has a right to produce children. Rather, they have a responsibility not to procreate under certain circumstances.

What does responsible parenting imply? Responsible parenting begins before conception when those who are unable or unwilling to raise a child responsibly should never conceive. While many Kenyans claim that contraception and abortion are wrong, it is suggested here that the real immorality is irresponsible adults harming an innocent child through birth. To produce a child merely as a by-product of sexual activity hardly denotes respect for the child as a person. This idea is contrary to Kant's concept that persons are not ends in themselves, and not to be used for someone else's gain. It is immoral to use a child to accomplish the ends of adults, yet it happens frequently.

In some cultures, fathering many children is interpreted as 'macho' a symbol of maleness. Oddly enough, taking care of one's children is not seen as 'macho'. Some men make women pregnant without any intention or ability to care for the results of their maleness. In other cultures, many children are viewed as a sign of 'wealth', even if the children are starving or die from lack of care, food and shelter. No child should be born to parents who are unwilling or unable to care for it - starvation, malnutrition, lack of clothing and shelter, lack of education and a decent standard of living, lack of love and emotional support are all harmful to children. To put it positively, every child has the right to be wanted and to be cared for physically, emotionally and spiritually.

Unwanted children are harmful to parents as well. First of all many children closely spaced causes physical deterioration of the mother's body and her general state of health. Each pregnancy then represents an even greater risk of maternal death from anaemia, haemorrhage and general debility resulting in fatal infections postpartum. Unwanted children drain the financial and emotional reserves of the father, if he stays around and makes any attempt to care for them. They drain the emotional reserves of mothers as well.

Therefore, to produce children irresponsibly also violates a basic concept of justice, which goes beyond the good of the majority to a concern with all persons. Justice is also concerned with the allocation of resources, especially scarce resources. These resources in a developing Kenya include food, shelter, land, health supervision and medical care, to mention only a few.

4.3.2 HEALTH CARE STRUCTURE AND POLICY

Presently, the Kenya Ministry of Health accounts for 8 to 9 per cent of total recurrent government expenditure (Kenya Government, 1996). External donor commitment to the health sector, constituted 7.1 per cent of total grants and loans in 1984 (Kenya Ministry of Finance and Planning, 1985). A large proportion of external assistance is coordinated under the Integrated Rural Health and Family planning Programme (J7RH/FPP), which started in 1980.

The health structure of Kenya can be regarded as a pyramid, consisting of some five levels. On the top of the pyramid is the Kenyatta National Hospital, under which come the eight provincial centres, then hospitals in district centres, and lastly health centres and dispensaries in the rural areas. Missionary organisations provide about a third of all modern health care services. Of development expenditure on the health sector in the 1977–1982 period, 70.8 per cent was devoted to the national, provincial and district hospitals/mission hospitals (Ellefsen *et al.*, 1985).

The Fifth Development Plan (1984–1988) reiterated previous broad policy objectives for future health efforts, namely to: increase coverage and accessibility of health services in rural areas; to further consolidate urban, rural, curative and preventive and promotive services; to increase emphasis on MCH and family planning services in order to reduce morbidity, mortality and fertility; to strengthen the Ministry of Health's management capabilities with emphasis on the district level; to increase inter-ministerial coordination; to increase alternative financing mechanisms, particularly user fees. (Nordberg, 1986)

Kenya's health care system has an urban, curative bias, which means that the majority of the population receive unsatisfactory access to health services, and that preventive health care is relatively neglected. Furthermore, coordination is weak between health services and other activities impinging on health levels, such as agriculture, food, water development, education and social services. A reorientation is clearly needed towards environmental health programmes, such as improved water supplies, basic sanitation and control of disease vectors (mosquitoes etc.). Better organised health education, improved quality of family planning services and support to community-based health care, need to be emphasised. (Nordberg, 1986)

4.3.3 HEALTH STATUS OF THE POPULATION

The health status of the majority of the Kenyan population improved considerably during the 1960/70s and early 1980s. Since independence, life expectancy at birth has increased from 48 to 56 years. Infant mortality has decreased from 112 to 77 per 1000 live births over the period of 1960–1982 (World Bank, 1983a). But, the implementation of successive stabilisation and structural adjustment programmes since 1986 and the spread of AIDS has reduced Kenyans life expectancy at birth from 56 to 44 years. Infant mortality increased from 77 to 114 per 1000 live births over the period 1986–1997 (UNICEF/Kenya Medical Research Institute, Memo. 1997).

It is difficult to assess the relative importance of the various determining health factors. But, the insensitivity of the IMF to the social consequences of its conditionality measures may have helped to increase the severity of rural poverty in Kenya. Its insistence on cuts on public expenditure tends to adversely affect social services such as health, education and water supplies. Likewise, its persistent animosity to food subsidies and price controls, may have further contributed to widening and deepening levels of poverty and poor health in Kenya. Less effective control of some communicable diseases, poor hygienic conditions for the rural population, and lack of health care facilities for those living in rural areas are major factors.

The 'true' disease pattern in Kenya remains, to a large extent unknown, because most treatment is done at home with traditional methods or with drugs from the nearest shop. The uneven accessibility to, and variable quality of health facilities, still limits patients use of these services. The official morbidity and mortality figures indicate that Kenya's major health concerns can be grouped into three broad categories:

(1) Diseases of the respiratory system: these include pneumonia, tuberculosis (all forms), bronchitis and whooping cough, which are found mainly in high-altitude areas. This group of diseases accounted for 20 per cent of all outpatient cases treated by health services in the 1980s and 1990s.

(2) Parasitic and infectious diseases: the major disease in this group include malaria, which is widespread in the warm low-lands around Lake Victoria in south-western Kenya and in the coast region; schistosomiasis is found in irrigation scheme areas with other vector-borne diseases, such as sleeping sickness, filariasis, etc. These diseases are responsible for high morbidity and mortality rates in Kenya, accounting for over 18 per cent of all deaths reported in the 1980/90s.

(3) Diseases related to poor environmental sanitation: such diseases include amoebiasis, enteritis, the dysenteries and other intestinal parasitic diseases. Intestinal diarrhoeal diseases accounted for 10.9 per cent of out-patient morbidity in 1980/90s (Kenya/Central Bureau of Statistics & UNICEF, 1984).

Together these three groups of diseases accounted for nearly 70 per cent of all deaths reported in 1980/90s, and for over 60 per cent of the total reported morbidity. About 53 per cent of reported childhood deaths have malnutrition as a contributing factor, and approximately 20 per cent of reported deaths in children under five years are attributed to diseases which can be prevented by immunisation.

Major diseases of infants are pneumonia (26 per cent), enteritis and other diarrhoeal diseases (21 per cent) and malaria (6 per cent). For children under the age of five, the conditions accounting for the majority of admissions to health facilities are: measles (23 per cent) pneumonia (21 per cent), enteritis and other diarrhoeal diseases (10 per cent) and malaria (8 per cent) (UNICEF, 1990).

The AIDS (Acquired Immune Deficiency Syndrome) disease has hitherto been prevalent in Kenya as in neighbouring countries since 1985, despite official denials. However, the HIV (Human Immuno-deficiency Virus) virus has spread at an alarming rate. A study of Nairobi prostitutes, undertaken by the Kenya Medical Research Institute (KEMRI), revealed from blood tests in 1983 that no members of this group had anti-bodies against the HIV virus. By 1985, the seropositive proportion had reached 53 per cent, while by 1991–1992, it had risen to 80 per cent. Although most of the HIV carriers were likely to have acquired the virus by penetrative sexual intercourse, infection through blood transfusion cannot be ruled out. It was only in the early 1990s, when a national AIDS Committee was established, that the Kenyan health authorities began to address this problem seriously.

The nutritional situation in Kenya is far from satisfactory and is very poor in some regions. Admittedly, the average per capita availability of calories has been higher in some areas than the FAO/WHO minimum daily allowance of 2362 calories since the good days of 1960s, and was replaced at 2810 calories during 1976–1980. Maize, cassava and pulses are the main dietary sources of calories (and protein). Per capita protein availability (from maize, millet, beef, fish, pulses, etc.) was estimated at 79.3 grames per day in 1981, substantially above the FAQ/WHO allowance of 46.0 grames. However, these per capita figures mask large inequalities in consumption, as well as in the spatial and temporal distribution of food supplies. The incomes of approximately three quarters of Kenya's population are too low to provide adequate nutrition from the most basic diets, and the proportion rises from 83 to 91 per cent if calculations are based on food items typically used in each region (Kenya/Central Bureau of Statistics & UNICEF, 1996).

Under-nutrition and starvation is on the rapid increase. Stunting, which means low height in relation to age, is a sign of chronic under-nutrition, and commonly peaks at two to three years of age, while wasting, which means low weight to age, and reflects acute under-nutrition, is most prevalent, occurring mainly between one and two years of age. A prevalence of stunting has been increasing, from 24 per cent in 1977, 35 per cent in 1987, to 48.7 per cent among pre-school children in 1996. The deterioration has been dramatic in Western Nyanza, Coast, Eastern and North Eastern Provinces (Kenya/Central Bureau of Statistics & UNICEF, 1996).

High stunting prevalence appears to be associated with high morbidity, high population density, land fragmentation and low levels of education. Poverty is associated with many of these factors. Malnutrition is more pronounced in households with land holdings of less than 1.5 hectares, and the proportion of such households has grown alarmingly in Western, Nyanza and Central Provinces. Choice of crops is also important, while other factors, which can assist in preventing malnutrition, include education, water supply improvements, child spacing and a lower number of children.

4.3.4 PATTERNS OF DISEASE

The pattern of diseases in the rural areas of Kenya has arisen from three major sources - infection, malnutrition and accidents. Cutting concentrated on the infection aspect mainly amongst children and mothers. Accidents are probably important, but there are little numerical data about them in rural communities. Burns are a common and serious cause of disability and death among children.

Infection can be divided into:

(1) malaria, schistosomiasis, onchocerciasis, worm infestations, viral, e.g. measles, encephalitis, haemorrhagic fever.
(2) Bacterial, e.g. tuberculosis, leprosy, cholera, pneumonia, meningitis and sexually transmitted diseases.

Cutting illustrated how some of these infections are being controlled but some are spreading to new areas, e.g. cholera.

There is a close relation between malnutrition and infection in many diseases in Kenya (e.g. tuberculosis, measles and diarrhoea).

An undernourished child is more likely to be infected and more likely to succumb to infection than is a well-fed child. The poorer the nutrition of the mother, the smaller the child and the greater the risk of perinatal death.

The most serious and common diseases are related to poverty (limited resources), superstition (unscientific belief) and environmental dangers rather than to the tropical climate itself. The world's best medicines are better nutrition, hygiene and water supplies.

Vulnerability - the most vulnerable groups to infection in Kenya's climatic environment are the poor (especially those with no land), the young (children in the first month of life, the second half of the first year and toddlers) and women of child-bearing age (15–40). The rural poor communities in Kenya are characterised by high birth rates and high child mortality, comparatively short lives and a small proportion of old people. Women have lower mortality than men in all age groups in Kenya. Female mortality is higher in child-bearing ages and also among young girls where the birth interval is an important risk factor: the shorter the interval the greater the risk to the children and the greater the mortality. The food available is less when children are closely spaced and the older toddlers are neglected. Infant mortality is highest in the first, fifth and subsequent children.

The introduction of the westernised model of health care, including prestige hospitals like Kenyatta National Hospital, high-tech medicine and doctors trained in western medical schools, has made it even more obvious that the conventional health care cannot undertake the kind of activities needed to improve the health of the great majority of Kenyan people. It is widely recognised that the injection into Kenya of an expensive westernised socio-economy of health, no more enables health to trickle down to the people who need it most, than the injection of a capital intensive high-tech industrial sector enables wealth and well-being to trickle down.

For some years 'Another Development in Health', aimed at enabling people in their villages and towns to create better and healthier conditions for themselves, has been gaining momentum and there are encouraging signs that much can be achieved even in low-income countries. For example, Morley, Rhode and Williams 1983, cite a typical model - state of Kerala in India.

> Though one of the poorest states in India, Kerala has the highest levels of life expectancy, literacy and utilisation of health services, as well as the lowest infant and child mortality. Kerala demonstrates that equitable socio-economic and health policies are not necessarily incompatible with democratic government and that a high Gross Domestic Product is not essential for health: fair shares for the many are better than large share for the few.

Health is wealth, and this needs to be seen as an integral part of a comprehensive strategy for decentralised, participatory development, based on the recognition that the only real development in humans is traceable to personal, social and political as well as economic development and that, if it is to be effective, people must be enabled to do it for themselves.

When WHO was founded after the Second World War, it defined health as 'a state of complete physical, mental and social well-being, and not merely the absence of disease or infirmity' (WHO, 1946). Today many people regard health not just as a state of well-being but also as a process or a capacity to develop. But, whether one takes a static or a developmental view, health needs are virtually synonymous with basic human needs. An economy that promotes health will be an economy directed to meeting basic human needs. The following are, in fact among the basic needs recognised by WHO in the context of 'Health for All':

FOOD. Access to enough of the right kind of food. Elimination of hunger and malnutrition in Kenya.

EDUCATION. A basis for developing individual potential, participating in society, and for looking after personal family health.

WATER AND SANITATION. A continuous supply of safe drinking water and effective means of variation.

DECENT HOUSING CONDITIONS. These contribute to physical, mental and social well-being.

SECURE WORK AND A USEFUL ROLE IN SOCIETY. This is identified by WHO as a fundamental need.

Emery (1984) suggested six requirements for healthy work. Three are related to the intrinsic nature of the task:

1. The task that allows room for the individual to make decisions.
2. The task that allows the individual to learn (and the learning task that is challenging and creative).
3. The task that presents variety.

The other three requirements are related to the nature of the work interaction.

4. Mutual respect and support between peers and supervisors;
5. Work that is meaningful;
6. Work that is directed towards a desirable end.

Seeking to meet these requirements in Kenya obviously has the profoundest implications for all aspects of vision, mission, priorities, and economic activity, from the choice of technology to business goals and Kenyans' aspirations.

4.3.5 TRADITIONAL AND INTEGRATED VIEW OF HEALTH

Traditional medical systems received detailed attention in the 1970s and early 1980s both from anthropologists and doctors. This attention was given approval by WHO in their optimistic efforts to promote medical care for everyone by the year 2000 (which is impossible using only orthodox methods).

Modern medical practice is bound to remain in short supply in Kenya, concentrated in urban areas, and increasingly expensive, leaving the mass of rural people in Kenya dependent on traditional beliefs and treatment. Moreover, many patients utilise either modern or traditional medicine (or both) whichever they think to be more effective. It therefore behoves anyone working in tropical medicine to become acquainted with the nature of the indigenous system.

Medical care in Kenya may take many forms: (a) family remedies, (b) herbalists, using traditional herbal remedies, (c) users of symbolic medicine which work by suggestion, (d) Diviners and witch doctors of many different types, (e) Muslim healers (hakim), (f) Barbers doing simple surgery, (g) faith healers of apostolic churches (considerable success is claimed with mental illness), (h) quacks and charlatans, and (i) modern western medicine.

There are problems of correlating traditional systems with western medicine, both in urban and rural areas. The following considerations apply:

(a) Traditional practitioners jealously guard their secrets.

(b) Qualified doctors and nurses distrust and dislike the traditional practitioners.

(c) Traditional methods are sometimes dangerous, e.g. through lack of hygiene, use of strong purgatives etc.

(d) Traditional medicine depends on faith and trust rather than on scientific treatment.

(e) If traditional practitioners are incorporated in the official system, how are they to be paid?

Patients and practitioners usually operate at several different levels, depending on their assessment of the nature and seriousness of the affliction, e.g.

(1) Herbal remedies for commonplace symptoms (rarely recorded or tested)

(2) Concoctions dependent on symbolic rather than pharmacological components.

Many of these remedies involve an explicit element of sympathetic magic. While many simple ill-health conditions are attributed to natural causes, if the patient fails to respond, a whole range of supernatural or malevolent human agencies may be suspected. Patients ask, 'Why should this happen to me?' The practitioner (diviner-priest) looks for disturbances in the social or interpersonal relationship of the patient rather than for a physical causal agent. The practitioners perform rituals, give explanations for the disturbances and prescribe remedial action, which is often effective, as the patient has trust and faith in the practitioners.

Traditional medical systems can give lessons to western medicine particularly about the dependence of health on harmonious social functioning. Lifestyle is the most important variable in determining the health of an individual. Given this reasoning, it follows that an integrated approach to health and health care (mind, body and spirit) is indicated if we wish to alter the overall health pattern in Kenya. It is necessary to study traditional medicine more closely, to try out those practices which may be harmful. There is agreement on the value of traditional medical practice and the need to improve its effectiveness through training.

The dependency/self-reliance issue is related to the relative value given to the formal and informal sectors of the economy. The blindness of conventional economics to the value of the informal economy is an instance of the metaphysical assumption, derived originally from the philosophy of Descartes and now underlying current economic science, that only the material, tangible, measurable side of the material/non-material duality can be scientifically understood. In the sphere of health this finds expression in the idea that the human body is best understood as a machine, whose only essential characteristics and functions are those that can be quantitatively measured; that health consists of the proper functioning of this machine; and the way to improve its functioning is by intervention, for instance, by drugs, surgery, transplants, etc. – from outside.

This idea of health has encouraged people to feel dependent for their health on medical scientists and medical mechanics more knowledgeable than themselves. But awareness is now growing both of the importance of the informal economy and of the psychosomatic element in health. This can be seen as one aspect of an incipient swing, both in economics and in health, away from the old paradigm based on dominance/dependency towards a new paradigm based on self-reliance, i.e. 'an integrated view of health'.

This definition of 'an integrated view of health', is much broader and based on a combination of the WHO's definition and that of Parsons. Health is more than the absence of disease. The body can be disease free, but if the mind and spirit are wanting, health is limited. 'Health is a state of optimum capacity of an individual which allows her/himself to effectively perform roles and tasks which have been accepted as appropriate life goals'. Health involves the interaction of mind, body and spirit in achieving one's life goals, and optimum health cannot be achieved without positive performance of all three.

4.4 Kenya's Population

4.4.1 DEMOGRAPHIC SURVEY, NAIROBI UNIVERSITY

Kenya is classified by the World Bank as a severely indebted low-income country. It has a largely rural population, currently growing at around 3.5 per cent a year, which is imposing a major strain on the economy in terms of land, jobs and public expenditure. Although the rate of population growth has slowed since 1990, growth remains worrying and the authorities continue to strengthen family planning programmes. With some three quarters of the country classified as arid or semi-arid, the population is unevenly distributed and some 75 per cent of the population is confined to 10 per cent of the land area. The high population density is exerting pressure on land resource while the presence of a growing number of rural unemployed is a major long-term problem.

The current population of Kenya is estimated to be about 30.7 million people (Demographic Survey Nairobi University, 1997). According to the 1969 census, the country had a population of some 10 million people. Between this date and the next census in 1979, the country contained an average annual rate population increase of above 3.3 per cent. But, it was approaching 3.8 per cent, and was estimated to be approximately 4 per cent in 1989. The population policy statement shows that over 30 per cent of the national budget is consumed by education, with about 65 per cent of this amount going to primary education, hence the cost of its provision is likely to increase dramatically.

Today an 'average' Kenyan woman, whose history of childbearing replicates that of her contemporaries of all age groups, would give birth to almost eight children. This is known as the total fertility rate (TFR), and Kenya's birth rate is among the highest in the world. As Kenyan planners point out, were this fertility rate to remain constant into the year 2001, the country's population would grow by 4.3 per cent annually to reach 38 million by that year. If instead, Kenyan families were gradually to decide to have fewer children, that by the year 2000 the total fertility rate fell to only five or six children, the population would then be some 35 million. This latter figure is now the demographic basis for much of Kenya's strategic planning.

In response to the high annual population growth rate, and the adverse effect on national development goals, a number of measures were taken by the government, to manage population growth and keep it in harmony with resources available to sustain it. Among the most important of these measures was the establishment of the National Council of Population and Development (NCPD), and the formulation of Population Policy Guidelines, to act as a basis for coordinated action for population growth containment. Other significant measures included the adoption of revised economic guidelines (Kenya/Government, 1986). These measures make it explicit that population, like other sectors of the economy, must be planned and properly managed, if levels of economic development to sustain favourable standards of living for all Kenyans are to be maintained over the next 25 or 30 years.

In an effort to achieve a comprehensive understanding of the interrelationship between population growth and economic development, the government has in the last three decades undertaken a series of fertility surveys. These include the Kenya Fertility Survey of 1977/1978 and the 1984 Contraceptive Prevalence Survey (Kenya/Central Bureau of Statistics,1980/1984). These investigations were undertaken in addition to a number of demographic surveys and to the decennial census of 1979. Thus a considerable wealth of demographic data now exists on past population trends, the current situation and the likely scenario in Kenya beyond the year 2000. Among specific aspects covered by such data sets, is information on population dynamics, i.e. mortality, fertility and migration, fertility levels, nuptiality and contraception in Kenya.

In the following sections, a particular scenario is made:

(a) to highlight the possible consequences of the current rate of population increase for the Kenyan economy and society, with particular reference to health, education, employment and agriculture;

(b) to discuss briefly the country's population policy guidelines and the measures that need to be taken to implement the guidelines through coordinated action of the National Council for Population and Development (NCPD);

(c) to offer an explanation of fertility trends in Kenya over the last decade, and assess the possible conditions for fertility transition in the future;

(d) to discuss the nuptiality patterns and changes in the country, and assess the implications of these for fertility transition in Kenya.

(e) to review the current situation on contraception use in Kenya, and attitudes towards contraception, offering possible explanations for both existing attitude, current use level and possible areas for improvement.

4.4.2 THE NIGHTMARE SCENARIOS

In this section, reference is made to certain statistics relating to the demographic situation in Kenya. The consequences of the annual rates of population increase contained in these statistics on national economy and on social services, such as health, education, housing and employment, are not difficult to portray.

In the plan for Kenya's economy, as set out in Sessional Paper no.1 of 1986, the government was concerned with achieving a series of objectives: (1) it proposed to reduce expenditure on basic need services, such as education and health (IMF condition for SAP), particularly in view of the fact that these sectors are traditional consumers of large proportions of the national budget, and was claiming 42 per cent of the recurrent budget. (2) In order to finance national development, the government aimed at spurring agricultural production, targeted to achieve an annual economic growth rate of 5.6 per cent over the next 15 to 25 years.

Despite the fact that the above measures, appear largely economic in character, one of the main prerequisites for their achievement is sound population management. The government's objectives are based partly on the lesson of past experience, which demonstrates the effects that rapid annual rates of population growth can have on basic needs services, and on the national economy as a whole.

The adverse effects of rapid population increase were highlighted in the Population Guidelines of 1984 (Kenya/NCPD, 1984). According to this policy statement, land statistics suggests a scenario with 'increasing pressure on land, accompanied by fragmentation, land degradation through soil erosion and unplanned settlement in marginal lands, resulting in a slower growth of agricultural output.' The policy statement also points to the fact that only 33.3 per cent of Kenya's land area is arable, and contains population with densities in excess of 150 persons per square kilometre.

With respect to food production, population size is viewed as a major factor in determining the country's food policy. Food policy in Kenya has as its main aim, the production of sufficient food to satisfy the nutritional needs of the population, while at the same time providing surplus production for export. The relevance of this policy is confirmed by the need for frequent food imports to supplement local production, and by the persistence of nutrition-related deficiencies, especially among pregnant women, children, infants, disabled and the elderly.

The annual population increase of some 3.8 or 4 per cent exceeded the capacity for agricultural technology to make land more productive. It is estimated that more than one million families in Kenya are landless. This in turn leads to a situation where a majority of landless people have to cultivate marginal areas, thus posing considerable threats to the environment. With continuing high annual rates of population increase, various alternative outcomes could be envisaged in the agricultural sector.

In this context, alternative indications are given within 15 to 25 year perspectives as to the impact of variations in family size on key economic variables, such as: (a) net agricultural production per capita, (b) basic food requirements and (c) net cereal imports, which is directly related to the consequences for cultivation of marginal land, and for social and environmental conditions. Reference is also made to the implications of variations in the total fertility rate (TFR) for the educational and health sector's infrastructure, staffing and service needs, and for consequential incremental expenditure, which in these areas are already absorbing approximately half the government's recurrent budget. For example, in 1980 agricultural production in Kenya was worth about Kenya pounds 791 million. This figure gave an output per capita of Kenya pounds 55, on the assumption that the country maintains on average an 8.1 total fertility rate (TFR) per woman. If the country were to achieve a family size of four children per woman, this figure could rise to Kenya pounds 80 by the year 2000. (Future Group, 1984)

In the area of cereal production, maize as a major food crop in Kenya provides a relevant case for demonstrating what could happen to food production under current and future trends in population growth. For example, the country needed about 8.2 million tons of maize by the year 2001, assuming 8.1 children born on average per woman. With an average of 4 children per woman, requirements would drop to 5.2 million tons and only reach 7.6 million tons by year 2010. Based on 1976 maize output of 2.5 million tons, an annual growth rate of 3.5 per cent was predicted in maize production. Using this rate of increase, a maize deficit of some 2 million tons would be foreseen by the year 2010 (Future Group, 1984). Although Kenya's agriculture is in a better situation than that of many other African countries, it is still a classical example of agricultural production in Africa, where 'land distribution does not coincide with population distribution, traditional subsistence methods of farming are predominant and lack the technological and managerial foundation for a meaningful agricultural revolution' (World Bank Report, 1986).

In education, Kenya's history shows that at independence the country's primary education system enrolled approximately half the children of school age. This system now enrols more than 90 per cent of 5–12 year olds, reflecting government's aim to provide universal primary education. At the current high rates of population increase, enrolment would rise to more than 3.9 million to over 13 million in 2001. Lower fertility rates e.g. a four-child average per family, could reduce this requirement to only 6 million by the same year. Under the prevailing population growth rates, it was anticipated that 140 million Kenya pounds could be spent on primary education by the year 1997/1998, with the possibility of reaching 225 million Kenya pounds by the year 2010.

With respect to the teaching force, a teacher–pupil ratio of 1 to 38 was recorded in 1980. If this ratio is maintained and the fertility performance of the Kenyan population remains high, the country would require more than 337,000 teachers by the year 2001. These figures could stay within the manageable levels of 167,000 by the year 2000, should a TPR of 4 be achieved. The potential education expenditure implicit in the above statistics are altogether formidable. These figures clearly demonstrate that if the country is to achieve its stated economic goals with regard to education, then demographic measures would have to represent a significant element in any realistic strategy.

In a broader context, the analysis shows that there are important consequences of differing family size for the school-leaver problem, labour force growth, housing needs, and social dependency of the active and gainful employed work force. While many aspects of Kenya's demographic situation in the year 2010 are now largely predetermined, and current policy measures in the population field can, for the most part, affect only the longer term situation, the relevance of this demographic analysis lies in its very direct illumination of the fundamental political, economic and social problems confronting Kenya in 1999 and the years ahead. The government is currently facing political, economic and social instability and is lacking a policy guideline, a genuine and determined leadership. Nowhere is this more apparent than in the interconnected problems of unemployment, rural poverty, the health of the nation, radical land reform and the productive use of fertile land. Kenya's well-being as a nation will eventually depend on finding satisfactory solutions to these thorny problems, and defining realistic priority programmes for the future.

Population policy in Kenya seeks to address the problems of rapid population growth vis-a-vis availability of improved standards of living and decent housing for all. This particular issue is more critical in the urban than in the rural areas. The annual rate of population growth in the major cities such as Nairobi, Nakuru, and Mombasa is about 7 per cent. This has led to serious constraints in the provision of affordable housing and to inadequacies in provision of health, healthy urban environment, and sanitary services. As a result, slums and squatter settlement have mushroomed and the deterioration and pollution of the urban environment has intensified, grave fears of the public health hazard is real. It is evident that little can be achieved by improving the state of urban housing under the present high annual rates of urban population increase.

In response to the exceptionally high population growth rate and its adverse effects on the country's development objectives, various official initiatives have been taken in the population field. Alongside programmes sponsored by the Ministry of Health, the more significant of these has included the formation of the National Council for Population Development (NCPD), and the formulation of Population Policy Guidelines (Kenya/ NCPD, 1984a). The guidelines, which provide a basis for coordinated policy and action, embrace an extensive range of social and economic goals, including a reduction in the population growth rate, in fertility, and infant and child mortality, and the encouragement of Kenyans to have small families, and the increased availability of contraceptive services. But these objectives are being poorly implemented and ineffectively managed through a range of poor educational training, poor information and counselling.

The main implication of health in relation to population in Kenya, is that further improvement in public health beyond the current level is constrained by rapid population increase. Currently, government operates some 1,182 health institutions, in addition to running some 555 family planning delivery clinics. The institutions are still plagued by inadequate medical personnel, poor service delivery points and financial mismanagement and other limitations such as, ratios of one doctor to 10,000 persons and of one nurse for every 2,500 persons, reflect current levels of population and of medical staffing. These ratios have deteriorated in recent years, under prevailing rates of population increase. (Kenya/NCP, 1984)

Within the 1984 Population Policy Guidelines, basic 'strategies and priorities' include the documentation and evaluation of population programme activities, research in demography, fertility determinants and contraception, the provision of population education, and the improvement of family planning and health service delivery systems. While these areas are considered to be among the most deficient and needing support, there are also forgotten special cases needing urgent devotion and greater attention in health programmes, these include the very poor counselling role of the medical profession from doctors to traditional midwives dealing with routine pre-natal delivery and infant health problems.

Within these population policy perspectives, the improvement in the status of women through equal access and opportunities in higher education, training and remunerative employment, would appear to demand greater attention by government and development aid donors than it currently receives. This would seem to be particularly the case in both secondary scientific education and vocational training, where the facilities and quality of instruction available to girls, are normally at a much lower level than those to be found in boys' schools and classes. If the quality and availability of girls' education can be improved in these areas, then it should subsequently be feasible to address the problems of girls' primary education more effectively, bearing in mind current sociological advice that at least four years of formal education are necessary to make any noticeable impact on social attitudes and fertility levels. In this context, scientific education and relevant vocational training for girls, would seem to merit consideration by international development aid donors to Kenya.

The picture that the government's population policy presents with respect to labour force growth, is one of rapid increase in the working age of the population. It shows that the labour force is made up of some 85 per cent of the population aged between 15 and 59 years; this grew from about 3.3 million workers in 1960 to 6.1 million in 1979, with a projected level of 8.9 million in 1988 and 14 million in 1998. These figures have been realised in Kenya.

Faced with such stark realities, the modern Kenyan economy can only absorb 16 per cent of the labour force, with the rest having to find employment in the informal sector (Kenya/Central Bureau of Statistics, 1989a).

The labour force was growing at a much slower rate than that of the population at large. Between 1981 and 1983, it grew at an annual rate of about 3.5 per cent, as compared to a population increase of 4.0 per cent. At that rate of population growth, over 630,000 new jobs were required to meet employment demands each year, rising to 869,000 by the year 2000. TFR below 5 children per family, could have lowered this number to 420,000 by the same year. These figures imply considerable financial investment in job creation. In Kenya, about 1,700 Kenya pounds must be invested for each new job created. If high levels of fertility are maintained, a staggering Kenya pounds 1,480 million would require to be invested to meet job demand by the year 2000, as compared to Kenya pound 715 million that would be spent under a slower rate of annual population increase.

An important problem affecting the labour force in Kenya is the issue of dependency. About 25 per cent of Kenya's population is aged between 15 and 24 years. This represents about 6.7 million youths, a figure that is expected to be over 8.3 million by the year 2000. In Kenya today, there are estimated to be 184 dependants for every 100 economically active members of the population. This statistic is, of course, much higher, since not all economically active workers are gainfully employed. With population increasing at its current pace this dependent population would rise with a resultant high decline in standard of living within the family.

In view of the stated policy of curtailing guaranteed employment for those graduating at various levels from educational institutions, the school leavers problem becomes even more significant and worse. As might be expected, the number of school leavers who cannot get employment is progressively larger under high fertility, than under lower fertility levels. Under a high fertility projection, about 858,500 school leavers would be expected in Kenya by the year 2000, against a modern sector job availability of only 121,900 jobs. Over 1.3 million school leavers would be competing for jobs between 2000 and 2010, while about 550,000 fewer competitors would be present under a lower fertility projection.

4.4.3 POPULATION POLICY

The population policy in Kenya comes under the general rubric of Strategies and Priorities in Sessional Paper no.4 of 1984 (Kenya/NCPD, 1984). The basic strategies and priorities entail the documentation and evaluation of population activities, research in demography, fertility determinants and contraception, the provision of population education, and the improvement of the family planning and health service delivery system. These areas are generally viewed as the weakest and most in need of support in implementing Kenya's population policy goals, as set out in the population policy guidelines:

(a) to reduce population growth rate from estimated annual rate growth 4 per cent per annum to 3 per cent by 2012;

(b) to encourage all Kenyans to have small families;

(c) to reduce fertility levels that sustain the high rate of population growth and at the same time assist couples, as well as individuals, who desire but are unable to have children;

(d) to reduce mortality further, particularly infant and child mortality, because such reductions would ultimately lead to lowering of fertility levels;

(e) to reduce rural-urban and rural to rural migration which creates unplanned settlements in marginal lands, and so assist in easing the pressure on basic needs services in both rural and urban areas;

(f) to encourage and motivate Kenyan males to adopt and practice family planning;

(g) to improve the status of women through equal opportunities and access to higher education, training and remunerative employment;

(h) to improve general education attainment levels for both males and females, and enhance the educational institutions' capacity to provide relevant skills for Kenyan young people;

(i) to provide Kenyan young people with information on sex, unprotected sex and sex education concerning population matters;

(j) to ensure availability of contraceptive services for those women, men and young people who are ready for and need them;

(k) to ensure adequate counselling, examination and follow-up for contraceptive users;

(1) to train, re-train and supervise health and other contraceptive workers in the provision of contraceptive services;

(m) to train all health workers to be vigilant about the type and quality of contraceptives being provided in the service delivery points.

4.4.4 POPULATION IMPLEMENTATION STRATEGY

In its activities on population policy programmes, the NCPD works closely with six leading Kenyan NGOs, namely the Family Planning Association of Kenya (FPAK), the National Council of Churches of Kenya (NCCK), the Kenya Catholic Secretariat (KCS), the Maendeleo ya Wanawake Organisation (MYWO), the Protestant Churches Medical Association (PCMA) and the Salvation Army (SA). Among the NGOs, the NCCK has been particularly active in developing a Family Life Education (FLE) programme directed towards Kenyan youth, both within and outside school, and extending the same type of education as adults through programmes such as marriage counselling. The NCCK, whose programmes are apparently well planned and managed, has so far succeeded in attracting experienced personnel of long service to the communities where it is actively working, as well as maintaining close rapport with teachers, parents and young people. Within the government and nationwide, its initiatives have been particularly appreciated, and the introduction of (FLE) into the formal school curriculum by the Ministry of Education, owes much to the example set by the NCCK. This new educational programme requires certain support in the publications field, and seems to represent an area, where donors' assistance could be considered.

The implementation of population policy measures falls under the aegis of the National Council for Population and Development (NCPD). The implementation of these measures involves the participation of all central government ministries and some six leading NGOs. These include the Family Planning Association of Kenya (FPAK), the National Council of Churches of Kenya (NCCK), the Kenya Catholic Secretariat (KCS), the Maendeleo ya Wanawake Organisation (MYWO), the Protestant Churches' Medical Association (PCMA), and Kenya Salvation Army (SA).

In the implementation of NCPD activities, the Council has extended its financial and technical assistance to all the NGOs mentioned above. The NGOs have in turn made considerable progress in assisting the Council to achieve its objective, within their respective policy and ethical constraints. The contributions and expertise of each of these NGOs has been immense and highly appreciated by all Kenyans.

4.4.5 NGOS CONTRIBUTIONS TO IMPLEMENTATION PROGRAMMES

4.4.5.1 NCCK

The NCCK has been supported in its efforts by NCPD to develop and implement a Family Life Education (FLE) programme, directed at both the in and out of school youth. The Council extends the same type of education to adults through offering programmes such as marriage counselling. The range of activities the Council engages in, with the aim of implementing the population policies of NCPD, include teacher in-service training in family life education, educational material development, programme monitoring and evaluation and logistic support to field workers, especially transportation and office equipment.

The overall aim of the Council is to provide a form of education that can help young people acquire values and an ethical system, which will enhance their sense of responsibility in the family context. The Council is concerned to extend the FLE to out of school youth, in order to assist both the in and out of school youth to understand factors that influence their physical and sexual development, and to appreciate the means within their reach which may help them adapt to such change.

The NCCK supports the use of contraception in the population context, but through the institution of marriage, that is assumed to apply only to adults.

The NCCK project activities have so far managed to attract experienced VSO and other overseas voluntary personnel and others of long service to the communities in which they are working, as well as considerable rapport with teachers, parents and youth. Its programmes are well planned, managed, monitored and evaluated. The NCCK approach constitutes a major boost to the introduction of Family Life Education into the formal school curriculum, which is likely to provide the foundation on which the entire FLE curriculum will stand.

4.4.5.2 Family Planning Association of Kenya (FRAK)

Outside the Ministry of Health (MOH), the FPAK is the main implementing agency for family planning in Kenya. The assistance it has received from both the government and various international organisations, is geared towards the production and adaptation of family planning educational materials, the development of media approaches to the adoption of a small family size, the training of its workforce in effective communication, and programme monitoring aimed at the improvement of project operations.

The FPAK programmes are characterised by strong coordination at national level and an efficient support team in the field. It has been able to produce various types of educational materials, run family planning clinics and field motivation for family planning and FLE for youth. One of the important achievements of the FPAK is the translation of popular booklets, e.g. 'Ukipanga Uzazi' into Kikamba, Kalenjin, Kisii and Kimeru, with a production of 2,000 copies in each of the above languages, and over 40,000 copies in Kiswahili (Gatara and Murungaru, 1984). But, overall the EPAK's operations and programmes still leaves much to be desired.

4.4.5.3 Protestant Churches' Medical Association (PCMA)

The main effort of the PCMA in the implementation of population policy is directed at both the in and out of school youth. The evolving strategy of PCMA aims at assisting young people in FLE, reducing the incidence of teenage pregnancy and parenthood, instruction in reproductive physiology for young people, and the preparation of youth for responsible parenthood. PCMA also aims at establishing a competent information, sex education and communications team to manage its various centres in the country, and at the same time encourage the development of teams of voluntary educators, from among teachers, youth, church and peer group leaders. In addition, the PCMA has a strong programme monitoring system based on activity planning, scheduling, projections and evaluation.

4.4.5.4 Mandeleo ya Wanawake Organisation (MYWO)

The MYWO is one of the main organisations operating a family planning programme in Kenya, and also the major body dealing with all activities relating to the improvement of the status of women in the country. The central thrust of the MYWO activities in regard to population policy implementation, entails informing Mandeleo leaders about the population objectives of the organisation, and promoting the increased acceptance of MCH/FP among women in the rural areas.

The organisation is currently running MCH/FP activities, a motivation programme for family planning use, and the development of Community-Based Distribution of (CED) of contraceptives in western Kenya, reportedly with some success. The MYWO constitutes a crucial, but completely un-utilised channel for both attitude and behaviour change with regard to contraceptive use in Kenya.

4.4.5.5 Kenya Catholic Secretariat (KCS)

The importance of this body for the implementation of population policy measures in Kenya is for a number of reasons of particular significance. Firstly, it runs the only 'effective' Natural Family Planning (NFP) programme in the country, recording an acceptance rate up to 15 per cent. Secondly, the acceptance of NFP in Kenya may pose problems for other forms of contraception, given the influence of the Catholic Church and its doctrine and stand on family planning in the country.

The entire response of the KCS rests on the motivation of couples to adopt and use NFP, an approach which in Kenya dates back to 1965. In two districts, Embu and Meru, over 1,000 couples have been reported as accepting and using NFP (Ga tara and Murunga, 1984). The organisation also aims at training nurses and placing them at strategic health service delivery points to provide NFP.

4.4.5.6 *Salvation Army (SA)*

The response of the Salvation Army to population policy implementation, is perhaps the least developed of the agencies under discussion. The main aim of the Salvation Army is to increase the knowledge of, and support for, family planning among young people. The Salvation Army provides a limited supply of those contraceptives that require no medical attention, e.g. condoms. The SA prepares population and FLE training materials, and uses materials developed by other organisations, such as IPPE, IFPA, and FPIA. The SA works mainly through its own network of youth councils, which organise seminars on FLE. Through this approach, over 5,000 young people have been reached to date by SA initiatives.

4.4.6 ASSESSMENT OF NGOS ON IMPLEMENTATION PROGRAMMES

In principle, the implementation of the entire population policy programmes in Kenya, hinges on two broad assumptions:

(a) that unmet family planning demand exists, and that if met, required population management goals will eventually be achieved,

(b) that people are educated in population subjects, and appreciate how these relate to both their daily lives and to the use of resources in society.

The various NGOs have gone a long way in promoting the latter. With regard to meeting demand for FP services, the NGOs will trail behind the efforts of the MON for some time to come. This is due to the continued presence of major financial, management, research and personnel bottlenecks in all the NGOs. A critical weakness of NGOs is the almost total lack of inter-agency cooperation and coordination, even though they are carrying out similar tasks, frequently involving the same clientele. Further, the problems of these NGOs reflect those of NCPD. Because the NCPD has structural and personnel deficiencies, it cannot give sufficient back-up support to implementing NGOs, as a complement to the financial assistance which it provides.

4.4.7 MORBIDITY–MORTALITY – IMPLICATIONS FOR FERTILITY

Mortality is one of the population dynamics through which population changes occur. Mortality is affected by morbidity, social, cultural and economic conditions. It is also influenced by fertility dynamics, which are in turn affected by mortality.

The trends in mortality in Kenya (see Table 4.4.1) show that the Crude Death Rate (CDR – number of deaths per 1,000 population) has been in decline since 1948, the CDR stood at 25 deaths per 1,000 population, after which a rapid diminution occurred to 20 in 1962, 17 in 1969 and 14 in 1979. Infant mortality rate (IMR) levels decreased from an estimated 184 infant deaths per 1,000 in 1948, to 119 in 1969, and about 87 in 1979. This decline in mortality has resulted in increases in life expectancy at birth, which has risen from about 35 years in 1948, to 44 years in 1969, and 53 in 1979.

Table 4.4.1   Mortality and Life Expectancy Trends in Kenya 1948–1979

Year	CDR	IMR	Life Expectancy
1948	25	184	35
1962	20	NA	44
1969	17	119	49
1979	14	87	53

Source: Central Bureau of Statistics, 1962/1969 and 1979 Census Report.

The decline in both adult and infant mortality levels is mainly attributable to improvements in public hygiene and medicine, eradication of major infant diseases, and changes in living conditions. Kenya's IMR is still more than three times the average for developed countries, and ranked among the few African countries with an IMR below 110 per 1,000 live births. In Kenya, infant mortality also seems to be a curvilinear function of birth order and a direct function of mother's age. The IMR stands at 103 for mothers of first birth order, 96 for those of 2nd to 3rd order, 83 for those of 4th – 6th order, and 106 for those of birth order 7 and beyond. For mothers aged less than 20 years, the rate is 104 infant deaths per 1,000 live births, 70 for those aged 20–29 and 75 for those aged between 30–39 years (World Bank, 1986c). Available data on infant mortality show general decline between 1962 and 1979, for all age groups of childbearing mothers (see Table 4.4.2). The mortality levels of male children are persistently higher than those for female of all ages (see Table 4.4.3). But that opulent picture is now distorted due to the horrors of AIDS, acute poverty and IMF SAP.

Table 4.4.2   Estimates of the Mortality Rate (Death in the First Year of Life per 1,000 Live Births) for Kenya by Feeney's Method 1962/1979

Age Group of mothers	census 1962 Infant Mort Rate	Yr	1969 census Infant Mort Rate	Yr	1977 NDS Infant Mort Rate	Yr	1977–78 KFS Infant Mort Rate	Yr	1979 census Infant Mort Rate	Year
20–24	131	1959	113	1966	86	1974	103	1975	98	1976
25–29	141	1957	119	1964	86	1972	100	1973	97	1974
30–34	150	1955	126	1962	100	1970	99	1971	105	1972
35–39	161	1952	137	1959	105	1967	103	1968	109	1970
40–44	171	1949	145	1956	115	1964	103	1965	120	1967
45–49	168	1946	150	1953	123	1961	117	1962	126	1963

Source: Central Bureau of Statistics.

Table 4.4.3   Proportions of Children Dead by Age Group of
              Mother and Sex of Child in Kenya

Age Group	Proportion of children Dead	
	Male	Female
15–19	0.1227	0.1094
20–24	0.1294	0.1200
25–29	0.1476	0.1344
30–34	0.1725	0.1589
35–39	0.1923	0.1765
40–44	0.2247	0.2099
45–49	0.2626	0.2433

Source:Central Bureau of Statistics

The geographical distribution of IMR shows a low IMR in
Central Kenya, with Central Province generally recording rates
below 1,000 population, and Nyeri District having a rate of 47
deaths per 1,000 population. A high IMR zone is also detectable
in Coast Province, where rates exceed 200 deaths per 1,000 live
births, and Nyanza Province, where countrywide it is the highest
with 266 deaths recorded (this is understandable due to a
deliberate freeze on development programmes in the Province
following the death of Tom Mboya, Dr Robert Ouko etc., and the
Province's opposition to President Kenyatta/Moi's authori-
tarianism). Rates between 100 and 200 are recorded for the
districts of Eastern Province, with Kitui District recording the
much higher, live births. It should be noted, however, that some
figures might be much higher, had the data available to compute
these rates been more reliable (Kenya/Central Bureau of Statistics,
1990).

The general influence of infant mortality on fertility levels in
Kenya, is that as long as such high rates of infant mortality persist,
Kenyan women will not see the need to have fewer children, and
would not be inclined to have small families. High fertility levels
persist in the area with high IMR, while transition to lower
fertility levels is predicted in Nyeri District, where IMR has fallen
to below 50. It is, however, true that a decrease in IMR will not

necessarily lead to an immediate diminution in fertility levels, but reduced IMR will be an important determinant of eventual fertility decline.

Morbidity statistics in Kenya are of poor quality and often unavailable and not reliable. However, it is possible to formulate a general prevalence scenario on the basis of (see Table 4.4.4) which shows the predominance of AIDS, respiratory, malaria and skin diseases, with diarrhoea and intestinal ailments in following order. Generally, the disease pattern shows AIDS, malaria, respiratory diseases, diarrhoea and measles prevalent in high IMR districts where, despite the relatively low rates of infant mortality, severe protein energy malnutrition is prevalent and affects about half of rural children (Kenya/Central Bureau of Statistics, 1980a)

Table 4.4.4   Outpatient in District Hospitals, Health Centres, and Dispensaries in Kenya, 1978

Disease Type	Number of cases '000	Per cent of total cases
Acute Respiratory Infections	5,881	31.2
Malaria	4,417	23.4
Skin Disease	3,262	17.3
Diarrhoea	1,664	8.8
Intestinal Worms	1,126	6.0
Accidents	1,120	5.9
Gonorrhoea	507	2.7
Measles	292	1.5
Pneumonia	288	1.5
Other	350	1.7

Source: Ministry of Health, Health Information Bulletin, Vol. 3, 1979.

4.4.8 A SIMPLE EXPLANATION OF FERTILITY TRENDS

A bald description of fertility in Kenya is that it is high, was high in the past, and will continue to be high in the future, unless different strategies can be adopted. The FTR in 1948 is estimated to have been 7.0 children per woman. This changed to 7.6

children per woman in 1976, and 8.1 by 1977/1984. A number of reasons may be advanced to explain this trend.

At an individual level, two major factors seem to be central. The first is that belief systems, norms and values favouring large families continue to exist alongside efforts to persuade Kenyans to adopt a small family size.

The second is that, despite ample demonstration that the adoption and practice of contraception use is a critical determinant in fertility transition, its adoption and use in Kenya remains generally unsatisfactory and ineffective. This is explained by reference to the status of women, strong male influence against birth control, women's educational attainment, the prevalence of high infant mortality and tribal politics in the country. The contention that modern occupational roles prevent women from pursuing fertility goals, is at least valid in urban Kenya. In rural areas, however, it is possible for women to achieve familial goals alongside work roles. The educational hypothesis, that the standard of women's education influences fertility level positively, is partial explanation of fertility in Kenya, in the sense that only educational attainment beyond four years, seems to make any difference in fertility levels.

With respect to infant mortality, the general hypothesis, that high IMRs encourage high fertility, may apply on a long-term basis. In the short run, however, there is an incongruence between high infant mortality and fertility levels. As shown in (Table 4.4.5), the FTR for the Coast Province, where infant mortality is high, are lower than those of Central Province districts, where infant mortality levels are low. In the light of these figures, fertility may be predicted to be high for some time in districts where IMRs are high, even after a decline occurs to these IMRs.

The cost of children are also one of the key determinants of high fertility in Kenya. The country does not have a comprehensive old age security system, and hence many parents find it necessary to rear large families, in the hope that some of their children may support them in old age. This comes in addition to a number of other reasons, such as continuation of lineage, and honour and pride derived from parenthood.

Table 4.4.5   Infant Mortality and Fertility Levels in Selected Districts

	Districts	IMF	FTR
	Kiambu	84	6.9
Central	Kirinyaga	115	7.3
Province	Muranga	89	7.8
	Nyeri	85	7.0
	Kilifi	246	5.8
	Kwale	226	5.4
Coast	Lamu	215	5.8
Province	Mombasa	142	4.8
	Taita/Taveta	144	6.4
	Tana River	202	6.3

Source: Central Bureau of Statistics, Census Report 1979, Volume II; Kibet & UNICEF, IMR Map, 1983.

At the national level, it seems that independence ushered in an era of economic prosperity that translated into large family formation. This prosperity was accompanied by major public undertakings to improve basic needs services, especially health, and thus reduce the traditional morbidity patterns in Kenya. (Part of these changes should also have included deliberate action to educate Kenyan males about fertility management.) If this general theory is true, then it means that high fertility levels may be expected to persist in those districts where such prosperity is only starting to take root. In the leading districts, a fertility transition to a lower fertility level may be expected.

4.4.9 MIGRATION PATTERNS AND FERTILITY

In dealing with the issue of migration, attention is devoted exclusively to rural-urban and rural to rural migration, without reference to international migration whose role in population changes in Kenya is expected to be minimal.

As shown in Table 4.4.6, Nairobi, Coast and Rift Valley Provinces are net receivers of migrants, while all the other provinces are net senders of migrants. This situation is mainly attributable to the location of the major urban centres of Nairobi, Mombasa and Nakuru in the Rift Valley Provinces, in addition, it provides ample farming opportunities. Migration is generally a phenomenon affecting the working population, is male-dominated, i.e. over 94.5, and affects the more educated job opportunity seekers in the country.

It might have been expected that in the receiving districts, fertility levels would increase in the future, due mainly to the availability of better resources for the maintenance of large families in these districts, and to the fact the migrant population consists of young and potentially fecund people. In urban areas, however, migrants are unlikely to foster large families due to the rising costs of living, and the heavy financial responsibility of providing a family with basic needs, such as health and education. Already, only people with small families tend to migrate to urban areas with their families, or if they have large families, they leave them in the rural areas.

Table 4.4.6   Lifetime Migrants by Province

Province	Enumerated in Prov. Born Outside	Born in Prov Enumerated Outside	Net Migration
Nairobi	615,942	91,570	+524,373
Central	191,102	665,253	–274,151
Coast	222,229	47,983	+174,246
Eastern	89,966	263,957	–173,991
North Eastern	14,998	30,347	–15,349
Nyanza	109,130	375,596	–266,466
Rift Valley	625,594	146,385	+479,209
Western	103,181	390,808	–287,627

Source: Central Bureau of Statistics.

4.4.10 NUPTIALITY PATTERNS AND FERTILITY LEVELS

Changes in marriage patterns in Kenya are important indicators of what could happen to fertility levels, especially in the light of the assumption that it is within marriage that family formation occurs. In this context, age and marriage is of particular importance for fertility determination.

Data on marriage patterns in Kenya show that about 25.8 per cent of young women aged 15–19 years have had marriage experience (see Table 4.4.7). By age 20 to 24, 76.5 per cent of women have had marital experience, and by the age of 30, close to 90 per cent have already experienced marriage. The proportion married does not exceed 90 per cent, and hence about 10 per cent of women in Kenya never marry. The implication of these figures for fertility is that the institution of marriage to a great extent determines fertility, and the age at first marriage remains well below 20 years for the majority of Kenyan women, thus ensuring their lengthy reproductive span to contribute to fertility before they reach menopause.

From these figures, it is apparent that in 1984–1985 the average age of first marriage was lower among the currently younger than currently older women, which implies that women of earlier generations married later than women of the current younger generation. The figures also show that more than 50 per cent of women of all ages are married by the age of 19. If early marriage is an indicator of fertility performance, then high fertility levels may be expected in the future. The raising of the legal age of first marriage is one policy area, which the government has at its disposal to influence fertility patterns in Kenya.

Table 4.4.7   Percentage of Women Married by Current Age

	Current Age						
Current Age	15–19	20–24	25–29	30–34	35–39	40–44	45–49
Never married	73.8	23.5	6.2	3.6	2.1	0.5	1.4
Past married	2.3	6.2	7.3	10.0	12.1	10.6	16.0
Married now	23.5	70.3	86.6	86.4	85.8	88.8	82.7

Source: Central Bureau of Statistic, Contraceptive Prevalence Survey, 1984.

Available evidence on the incidence of polygamy indicates that polygamous unions are generally on the decrease see Table 4.4.8.

Polygamous marriages are more common for older than younger women. As for the effects of these unions on fertility, it has been shown that polygamy is not a key determinant of high fertility levels in Kenya, or anywhere else in the world. Indeed, polygamy has actually been shown to have a depressing effect on fertility. It is quite common to find that polygamous marriages in the country that have produced lower average family sizes than monogamous households.

With respect to the prevalence of polygamy in urban centres, no conclusive evidence exists to show it is growing in these areas. Available evidence indicates that polygamy is still a predominantly rural phenomenon (see Table 4.4.8). It is prevalent especially among younger women aged less than 40 years and levels are highest among those without formal schooling, notably among the Luo and the Luhya.

Table 4.4.8 Percentage of currently Married Women in a Polygamous Unions by Current Age and Place of Residence, 1984

Current Age	Per cent 1977/78 KFS Mombasa	Per cent 1984 CPS			
		Total	Nairobi	Other Urban	Rural
15–19	24	21.9	27.0	16.4	22.0
20–24	22	17.3	12.2	18.3	17.7
25–29	28	22.4	10.3	24.2	23.8
30–34	28	23.8	15.2	7.6	25.4
35–39	33	30.1	26.6	34.1	30.2
40–44	38	30.1	29.6	53.5	29.2
45–49	42	34.3	34.7	67.7	33.5
Total	30	24.5	16.7	22.5	25.2

Source: Central Bureau of Statistics, Contraceptive Prevalence Survey 1984.

4.4.11 CONTRACEPTION – ATTITUDES AND PREVALENCE

Evidence exists to show that some 81 per cent of Kenyan women are aware of at least one method of contraception, with the pill being the best known contraceptive, and quoted by 72.8 per cent of women. With regard to attitudes towards family planning, the most significant features of these in Kenya is that women wishing to practice family planning, consider they have not received enough support from their husbands (see Table 4.4.9). Only about 49 per cent of those women, who are currently not using any form of contraception, are married to men who approve of family planning. This figure is slightly higher at 51 per cent in urban areas than in rural areas.

Family planning attitudes in Kenya, whether favourable or not raise important issues with regard to fertility behaviour. The existence of favourable attitudes is not necessarily a guarantee that fertility change will follow. At the present time, the issue of what comes first between attitude change and behaviour modification, is one that current fertility data in Kenya do not answer adequately.

Table 4.4.9   Percentage of currently Married Non-Users with Knowledge of Family Planning by Husband's Attitude to Family Planning, 1984

Husbands' attitude to family Planning	Total	Nairobi Mombasa	other Urban	Rural
Approves	48.9	51.9	51.0	48.1
Disapprove	18.9	18.1	19.2	19.0
Says it depends	3.6	4.6	4.6	3.4
No opinion	3.5	4.9	1.9	3.5
Do not know	25.1	20.5	23.2	25.5

Source: Central Bureau of Statistics, Contraceptive Prevalence Survey 1984.

Concerning contraceptive use, existing data show about 15 per cent of Kenyan women aged between 15 and 49 years are in fact using contraceptives. About 8.1 per cent use modern methods, and the rest traditional practices. Figures on prevalence by method (Table 4.4.10) show that the pill, the rhythm method and abstinence are the most widely practised contraceptive methods in

Kenya. Contraceptive methods, such as vasectomy and female sterilisation, have the lowest incidence of use.

Table 4.4.10 Contraceptive Prevalence by Method, Per cent

Method	Per cent
Pill	2.9
Condom	0.2
Female Scientific	0.1
Injection	0.4
Male sterilisation	0.0
Female sterilisation	1.9
IUD	2.5
Rhythm	3.8
Douche	0.0
Abstinence	2.6
Other	0.1

Source: Central Bureau of Statistics, Prevalence survey 1984.

Contraception is used most by women aged between 35 and 39 years (see Table 4.4.11). This group of users comprises 21 per cent of women of reproductive age. Young people, aged between 15 and 19 years, use contraception least, i.e. only 6 per cent.

Table 4.4.11 Contraception Use by age, Per cent

Age Group	Per cent Users
15–19	6.0
20–24	13.5
25–29	18.2
30–34	21.1
35–39	21.7
40–44	19.8
45–49	18.3

Source: Central Bureau of Statistics, Contraceptive Prevalence Survey 1984.

Regionally, the figure is depressing (see Table 4.4.12). Central Province has a lead over all the other provinces in contraceptive prevalence. Where 34 per cent of women are current users, followed by 28.3 per cent in Nairobi and 26.3 per cent in Eastern Province. It is in the leading districts in contraceptive use that onset of fertility decline is now expected, e.g. in Nyeri District of Central Province.

Table 4.4.12 Current Contraceptive Users by Type of Method and Region, 1984

| Province | Per cent Current Users | | |
	Any Method	Modern Method	Traditional Method
Central	34.1	20.7	13.5
Nairobi	28.3	22.9	5.4
Eastern	26.3	14.2	12.1
Rift Valley	15.1	5.4	9.6
Coast	10.5	6.8	3.7
Nyanza	8.6	5.5	3.0
Western	4.8	3.5	1.1

Source: Central Bureau of Statistics, Contraceptive Prevalence Survey 1984

Contraceptive use by ethnicity is of particular interest to demographers because of its significance as a proxy for persistence of belief systems, values and norms that continue to favour large family sizes in Kenya (see Table 4.4.13). The leading ethnic group in contraceptive use is the Kikuyu with 31.9 per cent prevalence, followed by Meru and Embu with 30.0 per cent, and the Kamba with 22.6 per cent. Contraception is least evident among the Mijikenda with only 3.5 per cent prevalence. The leading area tends to be more modernised than others, and also portray modernised fertility behaviour.

The overall, present low level and very modest use of contraceptives, gives Kenya an increasing annual rate of population growth. The reasons for this state of affairs are wide and varied, and call for more closely focused analysis than was envisaged in either the KFS and CPS, of 1978/1979 and 1984/1985 respectively. The interrelation between attitude change and fertility behaviour modification needs deeper analysis.

Table 4.4.13: Per cent of Currently Married Women Using a Contraceptive Method by Ethnic Group, 1984.

Ethnic Group	Use Any	Use Modern	Use Traditional
Kikuyu	31.3	16.8	14.5
Luo	8.7	5.2	3.5
Luhya	6.9	5.4	1.5
Kisii	23.3	8.2	15.1
Kamba	12.3	10.0	2.3
Meru-Embu	30.3	22.7	7.6
Mijikenda	5.5	2.7	2.8
Kalenjin	9.9	4.2	5.6
Taita-Tavets	22.8	16.2	6.6

Source: Central Bureau of Statistics, Contraceptive Prevalence Survey 1984.

4.5   Conclusion

In his Principle of Political Economy (1873) Mill emphasised the need to protect nature from unfettered growth if we are to preserve human welfare before diminishing returns begin to reverse the growth swing of the pendulum. Malthus, before Mill, had warned of the stresses imposed by the increasing numbers of humans on the carrying capacity of the planet, though his primary concern was with the potential collapse in food supplies, rather than a collapse of the global environment. In other words, what environmentalists perceive as inherent problems were being dismissed, for a considerable period of time, as 'eternalities', factors separable and separate from 'real' economics.

Economic growth is, indeed, the only engine which can pull countless millions from their present hopeless plight in the poverty trap. But it is also true that it is precisely the unthinking, limitless over-consumption by another part of the world's population which perpetuate this entrapment and makes it even worse - structural adjustment programmes notwithstanding. Both rich and poor need development (humanisation). For the rich, it is a question of recapturing what has been cast aside so foolishly, or carelessly lost in the intoxicated rush towards production's sake and growth as if there were no tomorrow. This headlong path ultimately must lead to disaster, even for those who may have benefited originally or in the short-term. For the poor, it is often a question of trying to preserve, defend and reinforce what they still have: their cultural and ethical values, their capacity to think and act autonomously, their artisan skills and oral prowess (oracy), and above all, their ancient wisdom and civilisations.

Population issues and family planning in Kenya can only be properly grasped if Kenyan traditional modes of reproduction, social structures, attitudes, values and ideological imperative are properly understood. According to Kenyan views, fertility, i.e. the capacity to produce offspring is more important than all other human endowments, and is valued primarily as the indispensable condition for the achievement of parenthood. The personal misery, often accompanied by social stigmatisation, of childlessness is a recurrent theme in studies of African family systems. Parenthood is not merely a matter of personal fulfilment; it is also a fulfilment of fundamental kinship, religious and political obligations and represents a commitment by parents to transmit the cultural heritage for the community.

It is parenthood, much more than marriage, which carries significance in Kenyan society: a woman does not gain full status until she is a mother, not just a wife. Her future depends not on an old age pension, but on having sons who will win for her the respect of her husband and mother-in-law. Indeed we might add that in Kenyan society, it wins her the respect of her whole lineage and her society. For women in Kenyan traditional society, marriage and motherhood are not matters of choice or chance, it is a life-cycle stage, as inevitable as puberty or death.

These strong pro-natalist attitudes inform the Kenyan world-view and are enshrined in the social values and norms as well as the unspoken assumptions and norms of the kinship system, the property laws and social structure and national ideology of African Socialism. In the economic sense, the Kenyan in traditional society wants to recoup himself for what he has invested in his children – hence the importance of 'bride-price'.

All kin groups believe that more children enhance their importance, and economically, it clearly benefits parents to increase the number of children and there increase manpower, production and consumption.

Given the fact that fertility is valued above all other human endowments, that motherhood carries great honour and prestige and that large families are preferred, it follows that the best way of achieving this social desideratum is to give girls away in marriage at an early age so that they may begin reproducing in their late teens. The median age of marriage in Africa generally is 16 and this means that a woman begins to bear children in the late teens until the late 30s. This gives a woman a fertile span of 20 years. In Kenyan society generally, the range of children per woman is from 7–10 produced at two yearly intervals. This figure decrease in polygynous households for reasons already given above.

One other factor must be taken into consideration when discussing population growth and fertility in Kenyan society. This is the fact of universal marriage for men and women. This factor alone casts doubt on the validity of extrapolations from western societies where celibacy, bachelorhood, spinsterhood or homosexuality are acceptable social states. In Kenyan society, an unmarried man has to contend with social disapproval and ridicule. He is often asked the question of where and how he entertains since he has no wife or home. For a woman the pressures are also unbearable and suicidal, and might even carry implications of moral turpitude, genital malformation, social scorn and even worse.

Understandably, population education is an extremely emotional issue in Kenya because it touches on sex and sexual practices. All one has to do to grasp the full import of this fact is to read the reports of speeches made in parliament or hold discussions with Kenyan parents on the issue. It is emotional because it touches on deeply held views about sex, fertility and the social values which surround these subjects as well as values relating to large families. It is also particularly sensitive because it offends the sensibilities of the most powerful section of the population: men; who regard it as an impious intrusion from outside into the Kenyan social scene in order to disturb the traditionally honoured status relationships between men and women. It is seen as an attempt to foster the egalitarian theories which outsiders promote in order to disrupt peaceful social and family relations. The parents also see family planning and birth control as a subtle means of encouraging promiscuity and prostitution among women and girls.

In terms of our study, we identified two groups as best targets for concerted efforts at education. There was the adult urban group which has adjusted to the urban environment and among whom the factors of education and industrialisation have become important factors in the decision making processes. In terms of population problems, they showed a high sensitivity to economic factors. They had a high degree of ideological change as supported by their rejection of traditional ideology. They are the ones who know about and use contraceptive devices and socially, they are the reference group in terms of being pace setters. The second group which is important in this education process was the teenage group of over fifteen years olds. This group may still be at school or they may be school drop-outs. The popular and comfortable belief is that school going teenagers are safe and that they do not need to be taught family planning and birth control techniques yet. This assumption is wrong. Kenyan sexual norms allow for sex relations between youth outside of marriage, with, of course, traditional safeguards against pregnancies. At the present, however, the old time controls, which were meant to prevent pregnancies outside of marriage, have broken down. The old system of examining girls for virginity has disappeared, mainly because it strikes the modern sensibilities as both obscene and degrading to womanhood.

There ought to be programmes developed for the young teenagers who are still at school and others developed for the adult women and the over-fifteen school drop-outs. The best form of presentation is the audio-visual approach. Great care should be taken however not to allow any materials which are of doubtful social taste to be shown. The whole subject should not be trivialised and turned into an occasion for lewd or even mildly sexy jokes. In the social climate of rural Kenya this could set the whole educational effort back.

In this rather difficult task of teaching, obviously men are not the best persons to choose to teach. The best teachers for this would be female nurses or properly trained females. It is also important for this purpose to use public media: that is, the newspapers, radio and television.

In considering educational strategies, we cannot overlook the possible uses of informal channels of education. In our research on this aspect of the problem, we found that in a predominantly Kenyan pro-natalist society where large families are the rule, all non-formal avenues stressed high procreativity. The songs and games played stress many children. The language idioms also give great stress to this aspect, e.g. 'to bear children is the extension of one's reach or the extension of one's personality'. Clearly, family planning information could be an integral part of two government ministries – health and community development programmes.

Finally, the issue of population is very closely linked to the issue of the status of women in Kenyan society. As we pointed out earlier in discussing the traditional background, a woman is a perpetual minor, under the control first of her father and other male relatives and later under the control of her husband. This has always meant that life choices were limited. Women in Kenyan society, as in many other African traditional societies had only one option, that of being a wife and mother as soon as she was socially deemed to be ready.

With the introduction of western-type education, Christianity and the growth of industrialisation and urbanisation, new opportunities have been opened to women so that a girl of between 14 and 18 years now does not have to be a wife and mother immediately. The opportunity to go to high school, teacher training colleges and to university have had the immediate effect of postponing marriage and delaying fertility. The inculcation of higher social ideals has meant a much more selective and responsible womanhood. It has not, of course, meant that the women do not ultimately get married, nor has it given respectability to spinsterhood. It has, however, given them much more leverage in social and family negotiations. It has greatly enlarged the range of professional choices which become available as a result of enlargement of society. They can now be nurses, school teachers, doctors, secretaries and lawyers, for example. As a consequence, women have had their status enhanced. Now there are women who are in positions of authority over men and whose self-image has been so enhanced that they assert their independence. Clearly education and the new status influence women's attitudes towards fertility. It is with the educated women who have reached high levels in their professions who are in a better position to control fertility and who can resist husband pressures mainly because of their financial independence.

Chapter V

EDUCATION AND ENVIRONMENT

5.1 Education

5.1.1 EDUCATION AIMS

> The future has always been the province of those who planned for it.
>
> Tex Thornton

In any analysis of the experience with modern education on the African continent, the year of independence for a given country is historically a critical watershed between two periods: between an era of a pre-independence slow-moving, sometimes reluctant process of formal schooling guided and controlled by the colonial administration and, on the other hand, a highly fuelled, highly charged post-independence process of education controlled, guided and often influenced if not actually driven by the national political machines.

The formal education systems in Kenya today have been in existence for some three decades, a period long enough to warrant celebration of its maturity or its 'coming of age', as has already happened in some countries; but more important, the period is long enough to allow for a dispassionate introspection and self-criticism in an attempt to assess the achievements registered so far, the problems created in the process, and the possibilities open for the future.

Because of the loud and visible difference there was supposed to be shown between the pre-existing colonial situation and the new situation of independence and nationhood, the system of education devised and fashioned in Kenya in the 1960s and 1970s was consciously designed to be a vehicle for:

(i) creating and stamping an international image for the newly independent state through both construction of highly prestigious institutional structures and expanded pupil and student enrolment in existing educational institutions;

(ii) reducing and eventually eradicating mass illiteracy;

(iii) producing well-educated and functional middle and high-level manpower to man the various sectors of the national economy;

(iv) creating within the community a literate, innovative, productive and self-reliant cadre who would have gained and mastered skills of producing and boosting the national wealth in the years and decades after completing their school education.

Have these four major goals in the post-independence educational undertaking been achieved? To what extent? To some varying extent there have been achievements in connection with these original nationalist ambitions. They deserve a mention here before any entry into a more engaging, perhaps more provoking discussion of problems that have arisen.

Accordingly, this section attempts three tasks, namely to give an overview of the acclaimed achievements or successes in the education sector of the post-independence period in Kenya, to highlight the major and critical problems faced today, and to propose some possible alternative or 'reforms' for the future.

5.1.2 THE EDUCATIONAL STRUCTURES AND SYSTEM

The common assumption in Kenya, perhaps the most conspicuous response to the new stage of national independence was the sensitised need and action to send children to school in much greater numbers than hitherto were permitted or engineered. While professionalism at that stage was at the base of the response and confidence in the undertaking, the actual drive towards the new need was more politically motivated than otherwise, orchestrated as it was by the desire to push the new Kenya to the newly defined echelons of national importance and pride beyond the hitherto stigmatised with mass illiteracy and ignorance.

The assumptions in undertaking and operating a massive full primary education in Kenya was that by the end of the primary school cycle, the youths would have gained education in the sense of (a) a definite mastery of the 3Rs (Reading, Writing and Arithmetic), (b) a demonstrable development in an enquiring mind, leading to creativity and innovativeness, (c) acquired attitudes of cooperative and industrious life in the community, (d) a definite mastery of practical skills that in conjunction with an acquired scope of knowledge would enable young people to apply them in their everyday lives. This would assist them to produce goods and services, to solve common environmental problems and/or engage in gainful employment in productive ventures or some other way. The young people would thereby have been transformed into useful self-reliant citizens of today and of the twenty-first century.

For most part, these assumptions and hopes have not come true. The education system Kenya inherited from its colonial masters, was like a train which travels on a single track bound for one destination but which ejects most of its passengers without stopping at several points along the route. In other words, the system favours a small minority who are believed to be the most able academically, at the expense of the vast majority of others. By doing so, it promotes a spirit of selfish competition rather than cooperation. It breeds individualism, elitism and class consciousness, since material wealth and the comfortable life seem to be the goal at the end of the academic ordeal.

As a consequence, a continuously growing army of primary school leavers began to reach an unprecedented scale in the early 1970s. The actual drama began in earnest after the mid-1970s. Since then, in practically every year the proportion of those who could not be absorbed either into secondary schools or some other form of post-primary regular institution became larger and larger. In Kenya, concern about the magnitude and dim prospects of the primary school output was registered in early 1983:

(1) Every year, at this time of the year (January), a great number of Kenyan children undergo a traumatic experience that affects their individual lives for ever. It

is at this time of the year that our country witnesses with bleeding heart, a great mass of the leaders of tomorrow and the twenty-first century, youths, suddenly becoming the paupers of tomorrow and the twenty-first century: they are the so-called drop-outs.

(2) The tragedy of this whole saga is that, in the year 1983 alone, over 200,000 Kenyan children who are still at the tender age of 11, 12 and 13, are suddenly thrown out in the cold, cruel, merciless, and vicious world to fend for themselves.

(3) The school system as it is at the present turns out every year youth who can only read and write basic English/Kiswahili, but are totally unproductive. Thousands of these children find themselves in the street every year with absolutely no hope of ever getting a good livelihood, their social problems also increase. What the present system is producing are gangs of half-educated savages, thieves, rapists and robbers, not because these children want it that way, but, because the society into which they came, which is supposed to protect them has failed them, and because they have no other means to survive in this cruel and dangerous world at that tender age. (*Weekly Review*, February 1983)

On 27 February 1984, the Minister for Education, Science and Technology launched the 8–4–4 System of Education, in conformity with the recommendation of the Working Party on the Establishment of a Second University in Kenya. This system, whose designation refers to eight years of primary education, four years of secondary education and a minimum of four years of university education, became operational in January 1985. Apart from its change of structure, the essential elements of the new system were an improvement in curriculum content, with a greater orientation towards technical education, and a movement away from a traditional examination-centred form of education.

The old structure adopted from the colonial period was seven years primary, four years lower secondary, two years higher secondary and a minimum of three years of university education. Little technical education was offered at primary, secondary and higher levels, and the measure of success at each of these levels was on the basis of examinations which took little consideration of a child/student's progressive development at school. The quality of this system, which relied mainly on rote learning and memorising, was said to have declined to a certain extent in the late 1970s and early 1980s.

The new system, apart from doing away with the bottleneck of the two years of higher secondary education, had a heavier emphasis on technical education in the last two years of primary, and a technical channel in the post-primary phase for most pupils, parallel with a purely academic channel for 20 per cent of pupils. Assessment at every stage, from the early classes in primary school onwards, was to form part of a yardstick for judging success or failure. In order to place the formal post-independence education structure in proper perspective as regards the changes introduced in January 1985, it is necessary and relevant to look back briefly to the evolution of educational policy during the pre-independence period.

Here, it should be recalled that the British Colonial Office issued its first statement on educational policy in 1925 (Education Policy in British Tropical Africa), to the effect that an education system should render the individual more efficient, and promote the advancement of agriculture, the development of 'native' industries, the improvement of health, the training of people in the management of their own affairs, and the inculcation of true ideals of citizenship and service.

The policy sowed seeds of suspicion among Kenyans, as to the real motives underlying the practical skills content in the curriculum at that time. Dissatisfaction with the types of education offered grew as Kenyans came to resent the emphasis on technical and vocational education, feeling it was intended to restrict them to an inferior position, and culminated in the formation in Kenya of the Independent School Movement (ISM). When the state of Emergency was declared in 1952, the ISM became an important instrument for mobilising the Mau Mau movement towards Kenya's freedom, and after independence in

1963 the ISM became known as the 'harambee' schools. The Kenyanisation of the economy became the overriding policy objective, requiring manpower equipped with the requisite vocational technical skills, and the consequent expansion of the educational system at all levels.

In the First National Development Plan (1964–1970), it was pointed out that 'we must provide education and training to prepare Kenyans to take advantage of new opportunities and to prepare a new generation of responsible, active Kenyan citizens. Our plan places particular emphasis on the expansion of secondary education.' This policy, which continued during the Second Development Plan period (1970–1974), had the overriding objectives of '...producing sufficient numbers of people with the technical skills, knowledge and expertise to support an independent modern Kenyan economy at a high rate of growth.'

The third National Development Plan (1974–1978) noted that the educational system had been charged increasingly with the tasks of expanding educational opportunities and the production of high level manpower. In doing so, the system had come to provide the most accessible route for an individual's social and economic advancement in the modern sector of the economy. Subsequently, during the Fourth National Development Plan period (1979–1983), it became increasingly apparent that there were serious problems growing within the system: (a) the dilemma of inflated primary school enrolment and the associated issue of internal inefficiency, (b) the primary school leaver problem, or output wastage in the system, (c) the problem with the medium of instruction and the language policy as a factor in cognitive achievement and task performance levels and (d) the problems of unemployment and poverty had been compounded by the mismatch between education and job requirements – there was a skills shortage). There was by then a pronounced degree of imbalance between an educational system, basically aiming at qualifying graduates for the next step in the system, and the availability of jobs in the modern sector of the economy.

The Fifth National Development Plan (1984–1988) contained many references to modifications in the focus of education, in order to provide the recipients with income-earning professions. The need for modification had in fact been evident for quite sometime. The National Committee on Education Policies and Objectives, set up in 1976, observed that the policy adopted at independence, and carried forward through all subsequent development plan periods, had created unanticipated problems: thus, '…a strong attitude had been established that formal education automatically led to high wage employment in the modern urbanised sector of the economy.' (Kenya Government, 1976). This committee concluded that 'Education and training will in future, need to be modified and diversified, so as to cater for the majority of students who terminate their education at any one level…Vocation and technical skill training was needed to be oriented increasingly towards self-employment in rural areas.' The recommendations of this first committee were, however, not implemented, until the 'Working Party on the Establishment of a Second University' came forward with similar recommendations in 1982.

5.1.3 SCHOOL ENROLMENT

Since independence in 1963, the education system in Kenya has undergone a remarkable expansion. The number of primary schools has increased from about 5,000 to about 13,000 in 1985, while the enrolment figures over this period rose from 1 million to some 4.7 million. The ratio between boys and girls over the same period dropped from 1.80 to 1.04.

There have been two major upward movements in enrolment figures. The first took place in 1974, with the abolition of fees for standard 1 to 4, when enrolment increased by 900,000. The second rise of 700,000 occurred in 1979, when free school milk was introduced and the remaining fees were waived. The increase in 1974 was somewhat higher for the boys than for girls, while the opposite was the case in 1979. This indicated that, by 1979, many districts in Kenya were close to universal primary education for boys and girls.

Compared with the estimated population in the 5–12 years group, the enrolment of 4.7 million in 1985, gives the impression that Kenya had virtually reached universal primary education. This would, however, be an overstatement, since the enrolment figures included drop-outs, over-aged and repeating pupils. The importance of these factors can be illustrated by the fact that, of the cohort that started standard 1 in the middle of the 1970s, 20 per cent dropped out during the first year, and less than half reached standard 7. The repetition rate for those who reached standard 7 was some 10 to 15 per cent. Even with these reservations, Kenya in 1986 had the highest primary school rate among eastern, central and southern African countries.

There are, however, considerable regional inequalities in school attendance. In 1977 an estimated 72 per cent of school-aged children attended schools in Nairobi, but only 4 per cent in North-Eastern Province. Considerable improvement has taken place in recent years in the semi-arid and sparsely populated regions, but school attendance still remains much lower in these regions than in the rest of the country, especially in the case of girls. As regards western Kenya and the Lake region, school attendance is close to being universal for both girls and boys alike.

Since independence, secondary school enrolment has expanded even faster than primary. In 1964 enrolment in the 244 secondary schools covered 21,000 boys and 10,000 girls, while in 1985, approximately 300,000 boys and 200,000 girls were enrolled in some 2,400 secondary schools then functioning. This implied that a ratio of over 20 per cent of the relevant age groups attended secondary schools. The regional inequalities were, however, even greater for secondary schools attendance than for primary.

As regards Western Kenya and Lake region secondary schools the attendance ratio for both genders is slightly above the national average, although somewhat below for girls alone. In addition to the more traditional secondary schools, 19 technical secondary schools were established during the 1970s and the beginning of the 1980s with some 10,000 pupils.

Enrolment in higher education still represents a small fraction of the relevant age group. In 1985, there were 5,900 students in the two polytechnic colleges, and 9,000 students in Nairobi University and Kenyatta University College

5.1.4 THE ROLE OF HARAMBEE (COMMUNITY) SCHOOLS

The rapid expansion of the school system after independence, was only possible because of the popular support for the policy of the government, by which local communities created and maintained the necessary infrastructure, school buildings, dormitories, workshops and staff houses. The government then provided the requisite teachers, as and when the schools had been constructed. Practically all primary schools and youth polytechnics, and 75 per cent of secondary schools built and equipped after independence, were initially the result of harambee (community) efforts. The construction of some harambee secondary schools and youth polytechnics, were however, supported by donors and NGOs.

The introduction of standard 8 classes required construction of some 13,370 additional classrooms, and the provision at each school of a workshop and a home economics room. This building programme was also scheduled for financing through harambee efforts.

Over the years, capital resources equivalent to some 4 to 10 per cent of government's annual development expenditure, were mobilised through 'harambee'. In some areas, the 'harambee' contributions at times equalled 30 per cent of government development expenditure in the district, mostly for schools and clinics. This impressive mobilisation of local resources for social infrastructure projects, where government was committed to supplying the necessary staff, however, created problems for a balanced form of development and it had some undesirable social effects. In this context, it should be recalled that in 1985/86, 34 per cent of the recurrent budget went to cover the Ministry of Education's commitments, while another 4 per cent was used to fund teaching staff coming under other ministries.

The response from the Kenyan public to the development of educational facilities, had also outstripped the government's ability to recruit trained teachers. Before the introduction of the new school system, approximately a quarter of the teachers in primary schools, and nearly half of those in secondary schools, were untrained. In 1984, the government recruited 11,500 untrained teachers for the requirements of standard B classes.

This brought the total staff of teachers up to approximately 195,000, of whom more than one third were untrained teachers. It was hoped that within five years' time, a more reasonable balance would be struck between the provision of trained teachers and effective requirements for these, by adding in-service trained staff to complement graduates from teachers' colleges. This, however, had budgetary consequences, which for example, conflicted with government policy of bringing the recurrent budget of the Ministry of Education down to 30 per cent of total government recurrent expenditure.

Some of the socially undesirable effects were linked to the fact that the capacity to finance social infrastructure through mobilisation of local resources, varied from district to district and amongst people within any one district. Consequently, the development of basic social infrastructure differed significantly district-wide, with the poorer districts getting less support from government in the way of teachers, than the better endowed. The pressure on parents to participate in 'harambee' projects' contributions for the construction of primary schools, in addition to the costs of school uniforms and textbooks, seriously affected the social profile of 'free primary education'. Now that 'harambee' had de facto become a special tax, initiated by the majority of a community or sometimes by a local official, it retained little of a 'voluntary' character for the poorest sections of the community. When less resourceful communities had succeeded in building a secondary school or a youth polytechnic, the standard of construction and equipment had usually been at a very low level, and frequently below the minimum standard needed to keep these facilities functioning properly. In particular, many of the girls' harambee secondary schools seemed to be very poorly equipped with laboratories and staff houses, compared with government schools, where most of the pupils were boys. This placed the girls, who made their way through secondary schools, at a disadvantage in qualifying for higher education in fields where there still was a demand for skills, and obliged them to choose liberal arts subjects, where there was a surplus of job seekers.

5.1.5 PROBLEMS OF IMPLEMENTING THE 8–4–4 SYSTEM

Given the short time span between the initial introduction of the 8–4–4 system and its full implementation, the government was faced with various difficulties and constraints in putting this major policy change into effect. Here it would appear that to an impressive degree the local communities managed to construct the additional classrooms needed, but not the workshops and home science classrooms. Bungoma (western Kenya) was a typical example. Of the 447 standard 8 classrooms required, 426 were completed in time, and the remaining 21 were under construction. However, of the 360 workshops needed, only 32 were finished, while 88 were being constructed. Similarly, of the 360 home science rooms required, only 18 were completed, while 80 were under construction. It therefore, took some time before a more practical orientation of teaching took effect, even in circumstances where trained teachers became available.

As a direct consequence of the abruptness with which the new school system was introduced, another serious internal inefficiency arose from the inadequate educational material provided in terms of essential textbooks, supplementary readers, teaching-learning aids and facilities ranging in some cases from chalk, exercise books, charts and illustration maps to major items such as classroom desks; to enable pupils to sit properly and comfortably, to write aesthetically to ensure the effective implementation of the new curriculum. The change in the curriculum necessarily created a demand for new books, and led to a business boom for private publishers. They cashed in on the new developments to market new and hastily prepared titles of poor quality textbooks. Meanwhile the Ministry of Education was responsible for an inadequate teacher supply situation created by the radical educational changes to meet a progressively expanding yearly enrolment. This resulted in the optimal pupil–teacher ratio being set too high. Such a pupil–teacher ratio clearly outraged all professional expectations of teachers in relation to their pupils as it physically as well as psychologically prevented the teacher giving close attention and individualised attention to the pupil, from supervision of child conduct to the monitoring of pupil progress. It also clearly fatigued the teachers.

An inadequately prepared teaching force for implementing the Kenya Government's new educational policy on 8-4-4, was further complicated by the haste with which the Ministry of Education had to look for and train individual teachers for the many children enrolled. For example, the massive implementation programme launched in 1985 demanded, in addition to the normal preparations, contingency measures such as redeployment of retired teachers, withdrawal of regular teacher trainees in their second or third year in order to teach children, redeployment of untrained teachers whose contracts had been terminated and employment of auxiliary teachers, including Primary Grade VII teachers.

The Government's policy assumed that, in the preparation and publication of the main course books, the curriculum specialists at the Kenya Institute of Education (KIE) would write the new textbooks, while the government-owned Jomo Kenyatta Foundation (JKF) would publish them. Since the two organisations are non-commercial, and the authors at KIE are civil servants, no royalty was paid, and their books were therefore cheaper than their equivalent from commercial publishers. Up to the end of 1984, the two institutions had published some 232 titles, and in 1984 sold 1.5 million copies of KIE-prepared books. Some of the profits made by KJF through these sales were used for scholarships.

KIE and KJF were not able to cope with the considerable task of publishing all the new textbooks required to meet the demands made by changes in the curriculum. In order to assist providing the necessary capacity, another government publisher, the Kenya Literature Bureau, which so far has been publishing books by local authors, collaborated with KIE, in producing textbooks. In order to speed up the publication of these books, there was a need for manpower skilled in writing, illustrating and printing of additional textbooks. The same was true in the preparation of textbooks for secondary schools. In this case the Ministry of Education agreed that schools should continue using the old textbook. The Government Printer also needed to be technically upgraded to meet the new challenge. Commodity technical aid, such as printing paper was of valuable assistance in getting the new school system off the ground.

5.1.6 VILLAGE YOUTH POLYTECHNICS

One important proviso should be made regarding the neglect of the majority of primary school leavers within the Kenyan educational system, who generally go short of opportunities for further education, training or gainful employment. Even as early as 1966, the National Christian Council of Kenya (NCCK) had set up two pilot 'village (youth) polytechnics', where primary school leavers were to learn skills for self-employment or jobs within the informal sector in their communities. The venture was considered so important that by 1973 the government decided to give a measure of support to these so-called village youth polytechnics, by supplying them with instructors. By 1985, there were approximately 300 of these polytechnics, with some 17,000 school leavers, which received government support by way of instructors, while many more were operating on a 'harambee' basis with fees paid by pupils' parents. Under the 1984 educational reforms, it became government policy that these polytechnics should play an important role in complementing the changes in the primary school curriculum which had a more technical orientation, and in preparing school-leavers for self-employment or jobs in the informal sector. The redesignation of the village polytechnics, as youth polytechnics, reflected the increased importance which government attached to these institutions under the new educational system; with the growing significance of the informal sector in combating the problems of youth unemployment, disaffection and social exclusion. The adequacy and the relevance of the training given at the youth polytechnic, became vital for the success of this policy.

However, one of the problems, which had to be addressed in this connection, was related to the fact that in many of these polytechnics, the workshops and dormitories were well below standard. Most of the youth polytechnics were grossly inefficient and under-supplied with training tools, equipment, materials and capital. In most cases, the original concept of these schools was based on innovation and self-reliance, i.e. they would be able to recover part of their operating costs, through sales of their products and services to the local community, this was quite unrealistic. As a result, the polytechnics were unable to provide their students with proper training, due to lack of capital and materials. Many of the technical instructors provided by the government were not qualified and therefore were not included in the Ministry of Education's establishment. Instead the instructors' salaries were covered by the Ministry of Culture and Social Services. The employment conditions were much inferior to those of teachers in ordinary schools, and their jobs were thus not considered very attractive. The instructors were usually recruited from the local community by friends of some big men in the KANU party, or among people who had found difficulties in making a living by imparting the skills of their trade, and consequently the standard of tuition given by these instructors was very poor.

This is not to say that Kenya does not have technical colleges that offer relevant training for potential instructors at youth polytechnics, but the capacity for the majority of these colleges seems to have been inadequate, and employment conditions at youth polytechnics were unattractive. The subjects taught were usually in traditional trades, such as carpentry, metal work and masonry, regardless of whether or not there was a demand in the market for such skills in the local community concerned. Girls were usually taught home economics or tailoring, neither of which holds much prospect of self-employment or job openings. Hardly any of the youth polytechnics taught the youngsters how to be innovative, creative or inventive of new ideas. There were no programmes for introducing information technology training courses and computer skills or how to manage small business enterprises. In addition, some means were needed during an 'infant period' to support these young polytechnic graduates, either as a group or individually to help them establish themselves in a small business, after having passed their trade tests.

The problems that would need to be addressed systematically, if the youth polytechnics are to play their assigned role of making school leavers better equipped to find a living in the informal sector, should, I suggest, include the following:

(a) the selection of subjects for instruction, which should be more directly relevant to the local demand for skills;

(b) the upgrading of tools and equipment and the provision of adequate materials in order to mount effective technical courses;

(c) the provision of relevant instruction to students in setting up and managing small businesses and training of skills in information technology and computer technicians.

(d) the creation of effective arrangements for supporting and backstopping those trainees, who either as a group or individually, try to establish a small business, after having passed their trade tests.

5.1.7 ADULT LITERACY RATES

Adult literacy rates in 1985 were estimated to be significantly above 60 per cent for males, and 40 per cent for females, which put Kenya well above the average among neighbouring countries and other developing countries.

There has been a remarkable advance since independence in reducing illiteracy. A measure of progress is the fact that, according to the 1979 census, 51 per cent of men and 83 per cent of women in the age group 45–49, has had no schooling, while 18 per cent of men and 38 per cent of women in the age group 20–24, belonged to this category. Since the census in 1979, a comprehensive campaign has been carried out to raise the level of literacy. In 1982, no less than 12,845 adult education centres were recorded, with 347,800 learners. By 1985, these figures had declined to 10,161, with 184,000 learners, of whom remarkably 77 per cent were women.

NGOs both national and international working together have played a very important role in this literacy campaign, and have been responsible for teaching programmes at approximately a fifth of the centres. However, the distribution by district of the government-sponsored centres, was not well matched to the levels of illiteracy, and the NGOs did little to rectify this imbalance. As a result, some districts seemed to have benefited much less than others. The reduction in the number of centres and

learners since 1982, was probably a reflection of budget constraints, but it was also said to be due to lack of teachers. The
turnover of the 13,000 or so teachers employed in 1982, were very
high, and it was difficult to replace those taking up other assignments.

5.1.8 HIGHER EDUCATION

Although in terms of mass involvement not as much as the
primary – secondary education sector, higher education has
benefited from both internal and external resource inputs spread
over the last three decades. It has witnessed the establishment of
university institutions, leading to a multi-university development.
This development is contingent upon a very early independence-
charged drive for the new Kenya to construct an elegant
university institution as a national status symbol of a 'victorious'
post-colonial situation.

While for most of the 1970s internal resource inputs
concentrated on primary and adult education, much of the
external bilateral as well as multilateral was geared towards higher
education largely in terms of technical assistance – teachers,
advisers, study fellowships and training awards, accounting for 13
per cent between 1970 and 1975 (World Bank, 1980). It is partly
because of this that the need for technical assistance in the
developing countries after 1975 declined for the increase in the
number of students and trainees must have at least partially offset
the number of advisers and teachers for tertiary (including
university) education institutions.

Notwithstanding the detected shortcomings in effective manpower allocation, deployment, utilisation, and productivity by
many of those individuals who had reached higher education
levels, there were some indications of success deriving from
higher education in Kenya. The underlying assumption was that
from those who had been allocated appropriate jobs
commensurate with their professional training, who had therefore
not been frustrated into quitting their places of work; from others
who despite possible job-labour mismatches had stayed in Kenya
to work in various capacities, there had been a positive influence
in terms of work performance, habits and professional ethics, on

the coming generation. On the strength of this assumption, the area of higher education can be described as an achievement of the last three decades of Kenya's independence.

5.1.9 RECOMMENDATIONS AND CONCLUSION

There are several other problems one could discuss in relation to educational enterprise in modern Kenya, such issues as increasing numbers of illiterates (World Bank, 1980) and decreasing levels of productivity and production of goods and services in the public sector, as an expert on Kenya's primary education has amply summed up the unhappy situation now obtaining in Kenya:

(1) …When one considers the hordes of half-illiterates being produced by unmotivated, un-dedicated and untrained teachers who are themselves without basic salaries … I accept… that Kenyans are the first to admit that, very serious short-comings remain. Young 10, 11, 12 year-olds who cannot write their own names or read their mother tongue, let alone multiply or do some basic shopping accounts, abound in our schools today… The inspectorates are almost totally ineffective in supervising teachers at the work-place. It is true, refresher courses are available. But these only perpetuate the traditional model of more paper qualification for teachers rather than some truly refreshing learning experience which one can take back to the classroom.

(2) …the most important lesson is that, ultimately universal education, no matter how defined, is a political issue in all societies, and, because politics rule, politicians should be made aware of the 'quality' issue at stake so that appropriate resources can be set aside for educational purposes. Otherwise, universal education becomes what Goodman (1973) called compulsory miseducation. (Kenyan School Inspector Report, 1997)

What has been discussed, does at least show positive sides of educational achievement in Kenya. But, the deeper problems cannot be ignored at the moment as their solutions seem to depend on other basic policy reforms.

Three problematic issues are discussed below, require

immediate government intervention now by way of reforms towards the direction of preventing greater crises and chasms in the future:

1. With regard to expanded formal primary schooling and the trends to universalisation of primary education (UPE), Kenya should now focus more on qualitative improvements and backups (such details as production and procurement, efficient distribution and proper use of teaching-learning materials and school equipment, redressing the current grossly in-optimal pupil–teacher ratio, etc.) than about mere quantitative expansion that leads to another undesirable vice of publicised access to inadequate and visibly frustrating educational facilities. Without a proper balance, the publicised quantitative achievement could soon turn out to be sheer political propaganda that is self-deceiving and intellectually self-defeating.

    This submission is based on the truth that:

    A UPE without (classroom) desks to sit on, books to read, and chalk for blackboard work; a UPE without articulately trained teachers; a UPE without the necessary professional and pedagogical support may – indeed – fall short of basic functional education it was meant to be...

2. With regard to the problem of primary school leavers, there are pertinent possibilities as seem to be suggested from relevant research:

    (i) More attention now should be paid to the establishment and institutionalisation of technical schools and vocational training centres in order to equip primary school leaving youth with more relevant practical skills in important areas of active adult life. Necessary tools for the trades they prepare for should be made available upon graduation and at reasonably affordable prices.

    (ii) Alongside these innovations, the public secondary school sector could be expanded only to the extent the government could meet the expense for more places than are currently available. For most part, however, the government ought to willingly transfer the burden of the secondary and higher education industry to the shoulders of the private sector, namely the parent associations, the local communities and voluntary organisations who would have or would mobilise sufficient resources and run the schools more efficiently. These different groups in the private sector could (and indeed should) be challenged and encouraged to think of various productive and employment-generating ventures that could in the end serve to absorb young school leavers.

It is a pity that, so far, the Kenya Government has been the biggest single employer and yet, unfortunately, the slowest employment generator. Considering the many civil tasks governments should do, the trend of thinking now is that there should be deliberate efforts to activate and encourage cooperative organisations and the private sector, in the areas of production of goods and services and in the generation of gainful employment for the young people coming out of the school system.

3. As for the language policy for education in Kenya, the question 'What medium of instruction?' remains a sensitive and controversial one, as there are different contending political and professional groups and views. But where the question has not yet come even nearer to settlement, a compromise on the older (ex-colonial) language could be struck. This is guided by realistic, hence scientific, observation that at the post- formative (in this case at the post-primary) level, the learning and performance capacity of an individual will be greatly enhanced by the language type, which is not only familiar in vocabulary but also has had tested years of experience in grammatical and structural development and stability. The process is made faster and more effective by the prevalence in the same language medium of the necessary textbooks and follow-up reading materials in the various content subjects.

Realism of this can be verified by India's experience. In 1938, Shri E W Aryanayakam, President of the Hindustani Talimi Sangh

(Cultural Society) in Savagram, and a contemporary of Mohandas Gandhi and Vinoba Bhave, had scathing criticism for the colonial English language:

(a) ...Up to the age of twelve all the knowledge I gained was through Gujarati, my mother-tongue. I knew then something of arithmetic, history and geography. Then I entered a high school. For the first three years the mother-tongue was still the medium. But the schoolmaster's business was to drive English into the pupil's head. Therefore more than half of our time was given to learning English and mastering its arbitrary spelling and pronunciation. It was a painful discovery to have to learn a language that was not pronounced as it was written..., to have to learn the spelling by heart...

(b) ...The Pillory began with the fourth year. Everything had to be learnt through English – geometry, algebra, chemistry, astronomy, history, geography... I now know that what I took four years to learn of arithmetic, geometry... I would have learnt easily in one year, if I had had to learn them not through English but Gujarati...

(c) ...I must not be understood to decry English or its noble literature... but the nobility of its literature cannot avail the Indian nation any more than the temperate climate or the scenery of England can avail her... (Aryanayakam, 1938:2–4)

His powerful criticism and argument are likely to have had the political influence and support of nationalists and must have been championed by his contemporaries. But one is compelled to wonder why, for about fifty years since then, has India's official language and the medium of higher education not reverted to one of the Indian languages? Why has English persisted? A compelling answer lies in India's ethnic diversity, the convenience and efficacy of a pre-existing language of formal education and its ability to place the subcontinent into the web of international relations – that, among other reasons, also lies behind the choices Kenya and the African continent have to face today. Yet India is now far ahead of many developing countries in scientific inventions, in technology, business and in self-reliance in a number of ways.

This section has attempted a survey of the development and

issues in formal education in Kenya over the last three decades or so. It has touched upon a few achievements such as increased access to educational opportunities and increased higher-level training opportunities for expanded economies. It has, however, highlighted some of the most critical areas and bottlenecks that, if unattended to, may frustrate balanced national development as we advance into the twenty-first century. Such problematics include uncontrolled and quality-unconscious universal primary education, an unemployed and intellectually stunted mass of primary school leavers, and an under-estimated and politically ambiguous role for the medium of instruction.

Finally, knowledge has increasingly become an international commodity, and the belief that knowledge can be and must be produced by (politically) neutral, objective and detached observation, and owned, transmitted, distributed and certified by official, neutral bodies, is part and parcel of the myth which shores up the artificial separation of a certain class of intellectuals from the uninformed masses; the world of mental from that of physical labour thus reinforcing the power wielded by the owners of knowledge. Scientific research is premised on separation: the object of research may be an atom or a chemical compound, but it may also be people in society or a living organism. The whole is presumed to be the sum of the parts. Hence, the understanding in depth of each segment becomes all important: the 'chop it up and study the parts' method of research triumphs. The active agency of the scientist as knower becomes separated from the object and superior to it in its separation. In the last resort, the much vaunted objectivity and neutrality of science can be little more than a sophisticated form of partisanship, geared to the maintenance of power bestowed by claimants to a monopoly over knowledge. The scientist him/herself is culturally, socially and politically grounded and part of a historical context: neutrality – simply washing one's hands of the conflict between the powerful and the powerless – means to side with the powerful, not to be neutral.

Genuine knowledge (wisdom) is holistic: it is not just 'produced', but continuously created. In a sense, we are all intellectuals, educators, professionals and researchers-creators, not just producers of knowledge. That is the deeper meaning of

Gramsci's concept of the organic intellectual. People already have practical knowledge of their reality, they have a 'feel' for it. The world is not simply divided into owners and receivers of knowledge. All humans have the innate capacity to create new knowledge which allows the understanding of reality in order to transform it. For Unesco, education is more than the provision of instruction and skills. It is the awakening of human creative potential, the building of endogenous capacities. It is also about the acquisition of the ability to master one's own destiny. Or as Unesco puts it:

> ...the value of such (conventional, professional) knowledge stands and falls with the paradigm which premises structural subordination as the basis of development. If the people are the principal actors, the relevant reality must be people's own, constructed by them only (Unesco, 1994).

5.2   Environment and Policy

5.2.1   ENVIRONMENT

The United Nations has been concerned about population, resources, environment and economic development for many years. This led to the creation of a trust fund in 1982 to encourage joint research among different organisations of the United Nations system. In the same year a project put forward by the Food and Agriculture Organisation of the United Nations (FAO) and the United Nation Education, Science and Cultural Organisation (Unesco) was approved.

FAO had already carried out some work through its Agro-ecological Zone project that could be applied at various levels of agricultural input. This was achieved by assessing the productivity potential and quantity of inputs required to meet self-sufficiency in food. Kenya was one of the countries where this study was carried out and, from the study of Kenyan agriculture, a database was developed. Unesco, for its part, had evolved a means of quantifying all aspects of the economy; in effect how national carrying capacity could be enhanced over time.

Kenya has come to experience many serious forms of environmental degradation as the population grows dramatically and more and more people seek incomes and subsistence from a declining resource base. It is true, as many UN resolutions often declare, that a fundamental cause of much environmental degradation in a predominantly rural country like Kenya lies in poverty. Landlessness, for example, leads to cultivation of unsuitable land, which in turn generates soil erosion and desertification. Landlessness raises political questions relating to land tenure and reform, and to the equality of income distribution. But clearly, if many Kenyan environmental problems are the result of poverty, they do in turn cause further impoverishment through the destruction of the productive base itself. Economic development in Kenya should, therefore, be seen as essential to the alleviation of many basic environmental problems.

Economic development and growth in Kenya are absolutely essential. In the process of development, natural resources, ecological balance and human well-being are all often compromised or damaged by unplanned action and exploitation. The concept of sustainable development, where a balance is struck between nature's resilience and the exigencies of human needs over time, has been recognised by UNEP, among others, as the best approach to environmental protection. Such tools as Environmental Impact Assessment (EIA) and Cost Benefit Analysis (CBA), have been generally accepted in the appraisal of projects and environmental protection measures. While EIA is eminently suitable in all instances, this is not the case in respect to CBA. The Kenyan economy has major distortions that render the monetary value of environmental protection largely meaningless. In the case of soil and water resources, specific value judgements of a qualitative nature must be made to justify protection measures, so precious are these resources for the future. Many development projects in Kenya are donor-funded. An examination of certain of these, focusing on road construction and its effects on soil erosion, show that design and implementation processes do not adequately incorporate environmental requirements. This situation now appears to be changing, as the United Nations Environment Programme (UNEP) persuaded donors to apply environmental guidelines, and the Kenya Government enforces existing legal instruments. The National Environment and Human Settlement Secretariat (NEHSS) and the Permanent Presidential Commission for Soil Conservation and Afforestation (PPCSCA) have now become more effective in certain areas of soil conservation affected by road construction, e.g. the Thuci–Meru road. However, no adequate legal instruments exist. The lack of these constituted a major flaw, but it was reportedly soon to be rectified by the introduction of new legislation.

Donors and consultants need to be convinced that environmental protection should be undertaken at the design stage, and not dismissed as an incidental contingency to be tackled following project completion. The so-called contingency fund that MOTC claims is used for soil conservation work, has many other calls on its resources. The ratio of this fund to total project cost stands at 7.5 per cent of the total cost of any project, but will soon be raised to 10 per cent. The 2.5 per cent increase is to be reserved exclusively for environmental protection work. Nor is it adequate to assign environmental protection to post-commissioning maintenance work, whose reliability is now increasingly uncertain, due, *inter alia*, to budget constraints affecting ministries. Rural access roads and special purpose roads, both public and private are major culprits in land degradation. In Central Province, Machakos and Meru districts and elsewhere, these roads have caused much siltation of valley farmlands, gullying of sloping lands, and damage to water systems.

According to the Declaration of Environmental Policies and Procedures Relating to Economic Development (UNEP, 1979)

> ...the major environmental problems of the developing countries are not necessarily of the same nature as those of the developed countries in that (they are) problems which often reflect the impacts of poverty and the lack of economic development which not only affect the quality of life but life itself economic development is essential to the alleviation of major environmental problems (...) in the long run environmental protection and economic development may not only be compatible but interdependent and mutually reinforcing.

The review of Environment and Development looks at various environmental problems that result from economic development activities in Kenya, and at the possibilities in this context of applying current theoretical and methodological tools for project evaluation, in order to minimise environmental damage. Attention is directed towards examining the role and effect of engineering projects, especially road construction in producing soil erosion and siltation. The use of environmental appraisal tools will be discussed in this regard. The role of certain donors and of the Kenya Government in project implementation and environmental protection (especially soil conservation) will also be examined. In addition, a brief look at the environmental implications of agricultural intensification will be included.

5.2.2 ENVIRONMENT AND SUSTAINABLE DEVELOPMENT

Since the 1972 Stockholm Environment Conference and the founding of UNEP, it is now widely accepted that economic development and growth:

(a) exact a severe toll on the biosphere, thus endangering the current and future welfare of mankind, but

(b) it is possible to avoid excessive ecological damage or even enhance the environmental impact of development projects by including strict environmental elements at the design, planning and execution stages.

This is a recent state of awareness. In the past, when a false sense of an 'infinite earth' or 'growth at all costs', were the principal premises, projects were designed and implemented with little consideration for ecological risks and damage. The literature abounds with examples of such attitudes and their consequences. In East Africa many projects with serious ecological side effects can be found.

Well before the Stockholm conference, a few governments and agencies had already issued ecological guidelines for the exploitation of natural resources and enhancement of the human environment. For instance, the path-breaking US National Environment Policy Act (NEAP – US Congress, 1970) forced US government departments to formulate environmental impact statements, prior to initiating any large scale action in natural resources use.

It is now accepted, at least in theory, that the biosphere is finite, which with proper management can be largely self-generating. It is accepted, too, that the interdependence of natural components of the earth, or of an ecosystem, is such that any manipulation of one component, as happens during the development process, will necessarily result in effects on all the other components. Usually these effects are detrimental, but often their harmful qualities can be deliberately reduced, or even rendered beneficial. Ecosystems are at once resilient and fragile.

Thus human intervention in nature for the purpose of economic development has an ecological cost, which slowly, if not dramatically in some cases, reduces immediate welfare, and may even bring about permanent and irreversible damage in some forms of resources (e.g. extinction of species and desertification), thus endangering future economic choices. How can Kenyans reconcile their current and future search for welfare with the inherent fragility of ecosystems? Is the solution to minimise or stop economic activity? Are there possibilities of reducing adverse ecological effects?

The notion of sustainable development has now come to receive high priority on the list of development issues and it occupies an important place on environment and development. Here sustainable development is defined as 'development that meets the needs of the present Kenyans, without compromising the ability of future generations to meet their own needs'. It is recognised that since Kenya's rapid population growth adds pressure on resources and slows improvements in living standards, 'sustainable development can only be pursued if population size and growth are in harmony with the changing production potential of the ecosystem'. The imbalance between population growth and resource development will worsen unless deliberate measures are taken.

The strategy to achieve this goal recognises that some quite radical changes will be required if the concept of sustainable development, including the linkages between population, resources and the environment, is to be taken seriously into account in national planning. Not only will production have to be linked with conservation measures and social and economic goals defined in terms of sustainability; fundamental institutional changes will also need to be made within the Kenya Government's structures. They should aim to overcome long habits of decision-making based on compartmental concerns and which for the most part exclude agencies concerned with population or natural resource issues from top-level participation in economic planning. While, however, significant attention is given to institutional change, the problem of necessary innovation in development planning methodology remains. The question therefore still remains: on what basis can the Kenya Government identify the trade-offs between, say, population growth and standard of living or between intensification of agriculture and soil conservation? How can the Kenya Government determine development strategies through which actions taken in different components of the economy are mutually reinforcing, guiding the economy towards sustainable development? To Kenyans, such development is required not only to meet the basic needs of all but to increase opportunities for fulfilling people's aspirations for a better life.

5.2.3 ENVIRONMENTAL IMPACT ASSESSMENT (EIA)

Environmental Impact Assessment (EIA) is now universally accepted as the methodology by which the effects of any proposed intervention affecting the natural environment can be foreseen, investigated and rectified, before a project is actually implemented. Briefly EIA, in attempting to examine how a proposed activity will affect a given environment, sets up the following categories of criteria and questions:

(i) What is the expected degree and effect of ecological and social disturbance both on-site and off-site?

(ii) Are there any irreversible effects?

(iii) What identifiable cumulative effects does it entail?

(iv) Are there chain reactions or secondary effects?

(v) Are the effects and reactions mentioned above localised or generalised?

(vi) Is the particular resource unique or rare? EIA should therefore include:

   (a) a detailed description of the proposed action and of the environment it will affect, including the social environment;

   (b) probable impact of the proposed action on the total environment (including both positive and negative effects, primary and secondary as well as direct and indirect consequences);

   (c) alternative to the proposed action (including no action);

   (d) any proposed environmental effects which cannot be avoided;

   (e) any irreversible and irretrievable commitment of resources that would be involved.

Much of the above has been modified from the early efforts in the USA to formulate EIA methodologies to set out new laws and guidelines for resource use and protection, issued by the US Congress's Council on Environmental Quality. UNEP and many governments have since refined, and continue to adapt, the procedures in different ecosystems (UNEP, 1984).

In addition, many books and case studies now address the issue, including the very important question of how to quantify invisible or slow microscopic cumulative effects over the long-term and evaluate the benefits of non-market qualities of non-quantifiable amenities. (Ray, 1984, Swartz *et al*., 1982). Of particular relevance to Kenya is the analysis provided in Ahmed and Sammy (1985), which specifically addresses appraisal problems in developing countries.

In theory, the EIA has been widely accepted as an excellent instrument. In practice, EIA seems to have proved much more difficult to implement than had been anticipated, and mere lip service is often paid to the investigation of environmental effects.

5.2.4 AID DONORS AND GOVERNMENT ATTITUDES TO EIA

Although UNEP persuaded donor countries and their aid agencies to make EIA a precondition for all their projects, many of these agencies did not generally have specific guidelines for environmental damage assessment or avoidance in their development programmes. In their own home countries by contrast, it was obligatory for all projects to have EIA statements. In the case of the USA, even public enquiries were held on crucial issues. UNEP put great efforts into making donors maintain similar standards 'abroad' and organised numerous intergovernmental Expert Meetings on all aspects of impact analysis and ecological damage-avoidance, including cost-benefit-analysis (UNEP, 1979; UNEP/CIDIE, 1986). The World Bank similarly did set out environmental guidelines and methodologies, and were perhaps among the leading donors involved in policy discussion, if not always in the practical application of policy (Lee, 1985).

In a study to examine the position on EIA of seven major government donor agencies (Germany, Canada, Netherlands, Sweden, UK and USA), the International Institute for Environment and Development (IIED) found that many of them did not include any environmental protection/enhancement measures at any stage in their aid activities, despite ready acceptance in theory of the EIA procedures by the agencies and their own governments. In only three of the agencies studied, were there clearly defined focal points for environmental responsibility.

> ...In only one country do procedures exist to ensure that projects are systematically screened for environmental impact and where necessary subject them to environmental examination. Environmental considerations are not included in the initial conception and design of projects, thus often unnecessary environmental damage or lack of protection and enhancement are built into project design. (UNEP/WG.31/2, 1979)

Attempts to obtain specific guidelines for particular projects in Kenya for the agencies concerned, were met with some resistance, or at least with the provision of general and perhaps unsuitable guidelines, formulated for projects in their own countries. At other times, reference was made by agency officials to the lack of environmental specificity in the Kenya Government's proposals, and the virtually complete absence of guidelines for specific projects. A case in point was road construction before 1982, where the Kenya Ministry concerned simply did not provide any significant environmental guidelines, beyond purely minimal road protection provisions of an engineering nature.

In this connection, it is certainly true that Kenya did not have a coherent environmental protection/enhancement policy. This default provided donors with the opportunity, if not excuse, to undertake dubious projects in terms of ecological damage. Clearly the agencies had overwhelming responsibility (and in funding, some powerful leverage) to ensure that their aid resources went towards environmentally sound projects. Indeed, they had committed themselves under international agreements to fulfilling such objectives (UNEP/CIDIE, 1986).

But commitments, while high-sounding and readily acceptable, were often impractical for several reasons:

(a) Project implementation has severe budgetary and time constraints often making it necessary for project managers to literally 'cut corners' in order to meet pressing deadlines and to avoid excessive extra costs.

(b) Implementers often have to show visible accomplishments to their own respective governments, which in turn are under understandable political pressure to provide visible evidence of money spent. Environmental protection measures are frustrating in being undramatic, often invisible and difficult to justify in the short run terms of most project cycles.

(c) Environmental issues are trans-disciplinary in nature and while 'idealistic' EIA may have been undertaken by precisely such trans-disciplinary teams prior to implementation. During the actual project the situation often reverts to uni-disciplinary approaches by single managers. Engineering projects are notorious for this.

(d) Most environmental benefits, while important, are intangible and diffuse in time, often in space and within society and are thus easily ignored.

5.2.5 COST BENEFIT ANALYSIS (CBA) AND ENVIRONMENTAL APPRAISAL

The whole question of Cost-Benefit Analysis (CBA), as an appraisal technique for evaluating choices in resource use or in environmental protection, remains largely unresolved. In a large, relatively free and well defined market, CBA may have great advantages. In small rather distorted economies, such as Kenya's, which have vast income differentials and large non-market sectors associated with rural poverty, CBA is a highly questionable tool. What for example is the meaning in Kenya of 'willingness to pay' – a crucial parameter in CBA calculations? There are also likely to be such gross imperfections in the monetary estimates of costs and benefits in the Kenyan economy that the resulting analysis is only at best a rough indicator of environmental damage, especially in the long-term. Related to this, is the inherent unreliability of the statistical database for such a sophisticated analysis.

Under the present conditions in Kenya, one is forced to the conclusion that, in a country so constrained by limited arable land resources and high population growth rates and densities, the basis for environmental protection and conservation must necessarily be considered more subjective and qualitative than CBA allows. This is not, as in Europe and North America, because of problems such as, 'How do you quantify amenities or aesthetics?', but because in Kenya's case, soil and water are such critically vital and severely threatened resources. From this perspective, it may be preferable to defer or even forego some new development activity, if the slightest doubts about soil protection arise. Alternatively, the strictest steps should be taken to build into such projects as are judged essential, the highest standards of soil and water conservation, almost irrespective of initial cost.

The gravity of the situation was recognised by some sections of government, and, as stated elsewhere, between 1980 and 1985 important measures were forced upon some donors, ministries and contractors, who previously had not been amenable to this type of constraint. In addition, the National Environment and Human Settlement Secretariat (NEHSS) became an enforcing, as well as a 'watchdog' body under parliamentary legislation at drafting stages. The Ministry of Transport and Communications (MOTO) was similarly required to incorporate total soil and water conservation measures (including road rerouting) into all road developments at the design, budgeting and implementation stages. Already, even without such legislation, the Permanent Presidential Commission for Soil Conservation and Afforestation (PPCSCA) used its presidential authority to require, on an entirely ad hoc basis, that ministries carry out conservation measures, beyond those originally proposed in the initial budget estimates.

Strict adherence to CBA allowed little consideration for unique situations and resources in Kenya, and paid grossly inadequate attention to ('under prices') slow, momentarily invisible, yet irreversible process, such as land degradation and desertification. However, in other areas, e.g. basic processing, industrial pollution control alternative, CBA was eminently suited to dealing with short run problems.

The impression gained from donors interviewed, was that projects are evaluated on a cost-effectiveness basis, with figures derived from the current national data base or simply from donor estimates. If one did not question the accuracy of such figures, the calculations for most projects would look impressive. Few environmental conservation/control measures are separately identifiable as such, and until 1984 none at all in the case of road construction. In any case, most donors followed the practice of funding a project package, as requested or proposed by the recipient government, without evaluating its component parts. Future mandatory EIA preconditions may change this practice, and require stricter specifications under CBA for protection measures, where these are applicable. The World Bank has already moved towards such a policy in its checklist approach, first issued in 1973, and since revised (Lee, 1984).

In addition to environmental standards being identified and specified in all development projects at all stages, Kenya's environmental database clearly also require considerable improvement in order that CBA can move beyond the guesswork stage. The International Statistical Institute at its 42nd session in Manila, 1979, prepared both conceptual framework and a unified approach to the presentation of environmental statistics. In Environment and Development (Kenya Government, UNEP & UNDP, 1981), alternative views are set out as to the possibility of applying CBA in the context of environmental evaluation work in Kenya (Ray, 1984).

5.2.6 GOVERNMENT AND ENVIRONMENTAL ASSESSMENT

While agencies and donors assumed the type of the specific responsibilities outlined above, it seemed even more necessary that the Kenya Government should exercise authority and contractually oblige, rather than merely expect, both international aid donors and project implementing agencies to adhere to environmental guidelines at the design, and all subsequent project stages. This unfortunately was not the case in 1998, although on paper, Kenya is party to all the major UNEP agreements and guidelines on environmental protection.

Nevertheless, compared to other African or Third World countries, Kenya has probably done more to rationalise its institutional arrangements and to institute a system of impact assessment and environmental protection. The 1984–1988 Development Plan incorporated many recommendations of the 1981 study on Environment and Development, referred to earlier.

The NEHSS, charged with the coordination of all national environmental matters, has now been operating for 20 years. Despite its existence, many ministries still continue going about their business in their customary way, with only minimal coordination with either the NEHSS or other departments. It is not unusual to be referred to the NEHSS by, for example, the Ministry of Water and Development on an issue concerning guidelines for water quality protection, only to be referred back to the same Ministry by the NEHSS. Overall, one is left with the impression of many good intentions and exhortations of a general character, but of little concerted action or sense of direction on the ground. A beginning has been made, however, and these initial foundations should now be consolidated.

The Kenya Government recognised relatively early the case in principal for integrated environmental protection. The 1979–1983 Development Plan took a clear stand on this question, and broached the future need for EIA for all projects. In 1981, the government organised with UNEP and UNDP a major multidisciplinary seminar and study project on Environment and Development, where flaws in past project design, planning and implementation were examined, and recommendations were submitted regarding the introduction of improved methods and procedures (Kenya Government, UNEP & UNDP, 1981).

The 1984–1988 Plan accepted this approach, as a basis for administrative action (Kenya/Government, 1983a). In practice, however, it is not always clear as to what extent these recommendations have been translated into specific development guidelines, particularly since no legislation has been passed to enforce the recommended practices. The examination of some recent projects, however, serve to highlight the problems that can arise, both in environmentally conscious project planning, and in the implementation of recommended EIA guidelines.

5.2.7 CONSULTANTS' ROLE IN DEVELOPMENT

Any discussion of environmental protection in aided development projects, would be incomplete without a brief mention of the role of the consultants. The Kenya Government and many donors have depended on large international specialist firms for an extensive range of pre-investment, feasibility and supervisory consulting services. Among these companies, several engineering firms involved in road building in Kenya were interviewed. While one may be impressed with the competence of their engineering skills, there is general evidence of a great deficiency in environmental awareness on their part. Some even think environmental concerns are a 'feminine fad' or a 'passing chic' to quote one extreme, if not a frivolous case.

In other instances, foreign consultants and 'experts' with little knowledge of Kenya, are often hampered by an inability to penetrate a mass of words and official obfuscation to understand the real concerns and functions of the Kenyan administration and its components. Consequently, the services they provide could simply be described at times as a 'waste of time and money for both, the donor and the Kenya Government'.

Thus, consultants may mistake policy for real intentions, and declared intentions for realities on the ground. In certain cases, local consultants can help to penetrate these difficulties, as they have a readier understanding of many of the intricacies of Kenyan governance and political processes.

In the course of one interview, a consultant expressed amazement as to how much was left to the discretion of consultants under the detailed terms of reference for particular projects. A case in point was environmental protection, where no guidelines existed, and where decisions were left to the conscience and good faith of the consultant on the spot.

There is a dearth of crucial data on most aspects of Kenyan life, and those figures that exist, are often surrounded with uncertainty, thus jeopardising the validity of both analysis and conclusions. A case in point was hydrological data for the Kapenguria and Kerio escarpments. Veidekke-Furruholmen and Norconsult engineers designed a road traversing these escarpments with minimal historical data. Following the construction of this road, parts of it were soon washed away by normal flash floods. Unfortunately, some donors specify that only their own citizens can carry out consultancy assignments relating to their aid projects. The US AID provides a typical, if extreme, example of this position. The International Institute for Environment and Development (IIED) have done an interesting study of consultants' roles in international development aid work (Horberry and Johnsen, 1981).

In the last three decades, the Kenya Government has, however, carried out some EIA both through consultants and the NEHSS. In most of the larger projects, where EIA have been made, donors were instrumental in supporting the necessary studies. For example, EIA for hydro-power projects at Gitaru and Kamburu, were financed by the World Bank and SIDA (Odingo 1975). An EIA was done locally (TARDA/ADAEC, 1983) for the proposed Kiambere hydro-power scheme, while the proposed massive Tana project in the lower Tana river, became the subject of an ecological assessment (EcoSystems Ltd, 1985).

But in general, donor agencies and government merely undertake economic as distinct from environmental studies. In many cases, no studies of a social impact character are carried out. The Kapenguria–Lodwar–Sudan road project, which will have such a profound effect on the Turkana people's future and on their traditional environment, was not assessed before and only partially after completion. In this regard, it may be observed that the Ministry of Transport and Communication (MOTC) considered the post completion evaluation of roads project to turn on the preparation of traffic flow studies, and on investigation into road surface stability (e.g. Parsely, 1986).

5.3 Kenya and Soil Erosion

5.3.1 SOIL EROSION AND ITS IMPACTS

It is evident that the soil erosion effects of roads and road construction were not fully appreciated in the environment and Development study (Kenya/Government, UNEP, & UNDP, 1981). In an extensive section discussing various national river catchment systems and their respective sediment loads cum siltation the following paragraph appears on page 111:

> Because it is a separate problem, some attention needs to be given to the management and construction of rural roads in order to develop technology for minimising soil loss from roads and construction sites. The application of this technology to roads and settlements in the Upper Tana catchment, as well as elsewhere in the country, would prolong the life of roads, human settlements and reservoirs, and enhance the importance of water reserves not only of the Tana River but also of the whole country.

While this paragraph refers to the Upper Tana catchment, and in particular to the high rate of sedimentation/siltation of the hydro-power lake system in the lower reaches of this huge catchment, significantly the general view of the study team was that roads (including tracks) contributed proportionately far less to erosion and siltation, than do increasingly destructive changes in land use and agricultural/livestock practices. The following changes in land use practices were identified in this connection:

(a) increase in the area of land used especially for subsistence agricultural purposes by clearing of sloping forest land in high rainfall areas and bush-land in marginal rainfall areas;

(b) increase in the proportion of steep and valley bottom land under crops;

(c) increase in the area of crop-land under continuous cultivation due to decline in shifting cultivation, shortening of fallow periods and decreased use of pastures in rotation with crops;

(d) change in cropping patterns due to emphasis on cash crops;

(e) changes in crop production methods, due to increased use of inputs such as improved crop varieties, fertilisers, insecticides, irrigation and mechanisation;

(f) change in land tenure from communal to individual owner-ship in medium and high potential areas, or communal to group ownership in rangelands, coupled with demarcation of boundaries and registration of title. Reduction of holding size due to subdivision of former large farms and fragmentation through inheritance of a restricted area of land by an increasing population.

The net effect of these changes has been increasing de-vegetation, higher run-off due to reduced infiltration, and consequently more and more soil washed away and sedimented elsewhere, resulting in the following types of deterioration:

(1) depletion of plant nutrients e.g. due to removal in crop erosion or by leaching without replacement through fertilisers, manure, or organic matter;

(2) reduced availability of nutrients;

(3) reduced soil depths as a result of erosion leading to decrease in the nutrient reservoir or the root zone and moisture stor-age;

(4) deterioration in soil structure due to continuous cultivation, exposure of soil to rain-drop impact and loss of organic matter;

(5) loss of cultivable area due to gully erosion;

(6) reduced accretion and drainage.

5.3.2 DEFINITION OF SOIL EROSION

Soil erosion has been a concern of many scientists especially since the early twentieth century. Erosion (Latin, erodere, to gnaw away), in its general use, is a comprehensive term applied to the various ways in which the mobile agencies (water, wind, glaciers) obtain and remove rock debris. There are four aspects of erosion. They are, following Thornburry (1964), designated as: (1) the acquisition of loose materials by erosional agency, (2) the wearing away of solid rock by impact upon it of materials in transit, (3) the mutual wear of rock particles in transit through contact with each other, and (4) transportation.

'Soil', according to Bushnell (1944) cited by Thornburry (1964), which we adopt for our purpose, 'is a natural part of the earth's surface, being characterised by layers of soil material parallel to the surface, resulting from modification of parent materials by physical, and biological processes operating under varying conditions during varying periods of time.' Thus soils are the result of biochemical and physical processes operating upon earth materials under various topographic and climatic conditions.

At the outset, in the analysis of soil erosion two distinct processes have been recognised:

(a) normal geological erosion;

(b) accelerated soil erosion.

Geological erosion takes place as a result of the actions of water, wind, gravity and glaciers. Water causes erosion through run-off, stream flow, wave action and groundwater flow. Wind picks up and transports soil particles, thus causing a general mixing of soil at the surface. Gravity causes mass movement, such as soil creep, rock creep, mud flow, rock slide and subsidence of the soil surface. This erosion process include both soil-forming as well as soil-eroding processes and thus, to some extent, maintains the soil in a favourable balance.

The problem of accelerated soil erosion is mainly induced by human actions usually associated with changes in natural vegetation cover. Though such changes are mainly caused by human activities there are also the intrinsic properties of climate, land form and the soil erosivity and erodibility, which influence the rate of accelerated soil erosion and thus make it a very complicated issue involving natural physical phenomena and human activities.

The severity of soil erosion varies from place to place, mainly depending on the nature of the topography, vegetation cover, climatic conditions, and management practices. The conventional view was that soil erosion is generally attributed to physical factors denoted by the functions of erosivity and erodibility. Since erosivity was assumed to be related to the intensity of the eroding forces (e.g. the actions of wind, running water, rain, waves, glaciers) the effects could be evaluated by calculations based on kinetic energy. Similarly as erodibility was taken as a quantitative measure of resistance to erosion, the effects could be calculated from measurable soil properties such as cohesive forces, soil structure, and the like. The resistance to erosion was taken as being influenced by the natural relief (slope, shape, and length) the quality of the protecting natural vegetation, and land and crop management.

In his study of erosivity, Cook (1936) realised that the energy associated with raindrop impact is an important factor in the soil erosion process. In his classic study of raindrop splash, Ellison (1947) indicated that the raindrop was an initiator of the erosion process. Barnett (1958) determined the relationships between individual intense storms, run-off, and developed methods that express the erosivity of intense storms. Wischmeir (1962) suggested that the quantity of soil eroded from a field depends to a large degree upon kinds of rainstorms and the extent to which the soil is protected at the time erosive storms occur.

Thus what is known as 'the Universal Soil Loss Equation', developed by Wischmeir and Smith (1965) expresses the relationship between the contributing factors, quantitatively, in the following form:

*A = RKLSCP

where   R is the resistance to erosion,
            K is the kinetic energy,
            L is the length of the slope factor,
            S is the slope gradient factor,
            C is the cropping management factor, and
            P is the factor related to erosion control practices.

Based on this theoretical ground, it is often proclaimed that: 'to control erosion on arable land, of the factors influencing erosion, we can do nothing about erosivity or land form and nothing significant about erodibility, and so control must be achieved through management'. Since the main causes of soil erosion are attributed to water and wind, these physical forces are considered as constraints. In order to overcome the constraints and solve the problems of soil erosion judicious management efforts are sought.

But the question of judicious management, even in countries of the most developed technology in the twentieth century, has resulted in paradoxically unprecedented problems, since it is well known that the case of 'windbowl' in USA and Canada in the early 1920s and 1930s caused serious soil devastation. The case of the 'windbowl' in North America was an example of where a shift to large, heavy equipment and enlargement of fields, which eliminated many natural boundary constraints on erosion of soil by both wind and water brought about indisputable problems. It is now recognised that 'intensification, development and mechanisation bring new erosion hazards, for which the solutions are not always available'.

To control soil loss caused by erosion it is important to understand the forces that cause material to move or to resist movement because there must be an understanding and awareness of the problem to provide a thorough solution. But, in Kenya, the effective control of erosion problems, which demands judicious management effort, is influenced by many factors, of which social–political relations, social–cultural structure and government policy play the dominant role. Thus the management issue becomes complicated as problems of government policy, socio-economic set-up, and political complications are intermingled with the technical complexity of the problems of soil erosion.

In Kenya the most common types of soil erosion result from the effects of running water. Wind-related erosion does play a certain role, especially in drier areas and localised situations, but it seems appropriate here to focus basically on water-related erosion.

In this context, there is a direct relationship between soil erosion and vegetation cover. Other things being equal, vegetative soil cover (from roots through the humus/litter layer to the above-ground growth) is perhaps the single most important insurance for surface soil stability and protection against erosion. Where vegetation has been removed with no equivalent substitute, the impact of rainfall, which is normally cushioned by plants and their debris on the ground, effectively loosens soil particles, which are then washed away. Without vegetation cover, run-off is itself greatly increased to the detriment of infiltration. Up to 60 per cent of annual rainfall can be lost from eroded soil surface in many areas of Kenya.

As in many part of the tropics, Kenya's rainfall, especially in the drier lowlands, comes in powerful downpours which can cause massive loosening and erosion even overnight. Almost the whole of Kenya is subject to the dangers of acute soil erosion through climatic hazards of this kind.

By causing losses of productive topsoil, organic matter and nutrients, water soil erosion is a most destructive process. In Kenya, soil erosion is already recognised as the greatest ecological hazard. It is the beginning of a process that, if unchecked, leads ultimately to desertification, which is largely an irreversible condition, involving the most substantial social costs. Combating soil erosion now ranks among the highest of government's declared priorities, and in 1981 the PPCSCA was created to coordinate all soil-related activities. It was a measure of the immensity of the conservation problem that, after five years the rate of erosion was and is evidently still increasing, despite the adoption of closely concerted measures.

5.3.3 SOIL CONSERVATION MANAGEMENT

When referring to the soil erosion problems in Kenya, most

researchers emphasise that the failure of proper management and cultural practices are the causes of the predicament. But very few seem to care to analyse the impediments posed by production relations, and by government policy and external intervention.

True, in order to understand the historical processes of such effects, it is not sufficient to limit one's study to the physical phenomena. One must also study the social ties and relations to which people enter to produce material things, because it is in the process of production of material things that the process of accelerated soil erosion is induced. That means it is also necessary to take into account the effects of socio-politico-economic relations, i.e., the overall policy of the government, within which resources management decisions are made.

In addition to its destructive on-site consequences, soil erosion also brings about undesirable off-site effects, the most important of which are sedimentation of reservoirs and other water bodies, siltation and swamping of farmland, and reduction in quality and volume of ground water, and its distribution over time. Good soil conservation invariably involves water conservation, as the two are inseparable in hydrological terms.

The concept of soil conservation normally includes:

(1) protection of the soil against physical loss by erosion against chemical deterioration, i.e. excessive loss of fertility either by natural or artificial means;

(2) a combination of all management and land use methods which safeguard the soil against depletion or deterioration by natural or by man-induced factors.

Soil conservation means, therefore, the preservation of the remaining good qualities inherent in the land, and the restoration (or reclamation) of those qualities which may have been destroyed:

(a) 'Soil' is a basic resource, for the present and future generation of Kenyans. As such, the value of its conservation goes far beyond what can be expressed in monetary terms;

(b) the damage caused by severe soil erosion is frequently irreversible. It is consequently desirable to take conservation measures to prevent onset of erosion, rather than acting after it has begun.

5.3.4 KENYAN ROADS AND SOIL EROSION

Like many major engineering projects, road construction involves considerable alteration in topographic features, e.g. filling valleys, cutting through hills and slopes, thus rerouting surface run-off from natural drainage channels to new artificial ones. This change in drainage and in the natural catchments disturbs established equilibria between storm-water run-off and the natural channels. It creates new situations of highly concentrated run-off directed to single-channels, thus boosting water velocity and force, and creating an urgent need for a new equilibrium. This process immediately results in massive gullying, as the accelerated flow of water seeks to escape downhill. In effect, such gullies constitute a new equilibrium in the making. In a short time, these new 'channels' widen, deepen and get scoured by increasing sediment load. This material is then deposited in the valley bottoms or carried to river systems, where it again scours river beds, cuts the river banks (interfluvial erosion), and may end up as silt in reservoirs. Gullies may also cut back and destroy the very roads whose construction originally led to their formation.

According to Megahan (1977), some causes of accelerated erosion following road construction are:

(i) removal of protective soil cover;
(ii) increased slope gradients created by reconstruction of cut and fill slopes;
(iii) decreased infiltration rates on compacted or paved parts of the road itself;
(iv) interception of subsurface flow by the cut slope;
(v) decrease or increase of sheer strength on cut and fill slopes;
(vi) concentration of generated and interrupted water.

In Kenya it has been variously estimated by Ministry of

Agriculture officials that roads directly or indirectly cause between 20 and 40 per cent of all land gullying and river sedimentation. In fact, the figure is perhaps higher in some specific localities, of which Machakos, Muranga and Meru districts are good examples.

In a major study for the Machakos Integrated Development Project (MIDP), Ecosystems Ltd found that roads of all classes especially the higher order roads cause gullying at very rapid rates, and contribute disproportionately to sediment load (Ecosystem Ltd, 1981).

There are relatively few known studies of specific roads or districts but at the University of Nairobi, Department of Soil Science, several masters' theses have investigated some road-related erosion issues. In his thesis investigation into causes, of Gullying and Gully Control in Kandara Division of Muranga, Damba (1981) found that roads studied had directly caused substantial degradation of farmland, (and therefore siltation, flooding etc., of valley bottom farm sites), because of poor design or storm water disposal systems by the road authorities and contractors.

In a similar thesis, Anyona (1981) investigated certain roads in Muranga and Baringo, and found road drainage designs and construction woefully wanting, as they were often related neither to specific site requirements nor to the need for soil protection on the steeply sloping farmland, particularly in Muranga. As a result, extensive gullying and destruction of very high potential land have occurred. Other studies have examined the performance of specific types of engineering innovations or designs in safely controlling or channelling concentrated storm run-off (Gacheru, 1985). At the national seminars on soil conservation, roads were singled out as major culprits in gully-damaged farmland in Central Province.

5.3.5 MOTC – RESPONSIBILITIES AND ATTITUDES

MOTC uses Road Design Manual Part 1: Geometric Design of Rural Roads, attachments, published by the Ministry of Works in 1979 (Kenya/Ministry of Works 1979). In this manual, the entire range of environmental factors is dismissed cursorily in a single page. The prevention of soil erosion and sedimentation is mentioned fleetingly, together with preservation of roadside beauty on page 3.3. This is reinforced, feebly, by some guidelines included on pages 4.9 and 4.10 regarding standards for specific types of side-ditch and cut-off ditch. But these particular ditches, while relevant in soil erosion control, are mainly intended for road protection within the road reserve (i.e. within the immediate vicinity of the road). Soil erosion beyond the road reserve is not in any sense, fully addressed in the manual. Many consultants use this document as their basic guidelines for the development of new road projects.

The MOTC, under whose jurisdiction the road system falls, maintains that the department's terms of reference are to build good roads inexpensively, in order to carry specified levels of traffic. There is a strong implication, in this legalistic approach, that what happens to storm water run-off beyond the road reserve limits, is not really their business in the MOTC, and that therefore they can take no responsibility for its effects outside their immediate domain. Any drainage works they may carry out in connection with road construction and maintenance, is primarily intended for the protection of the road itself, and not, unless fortuitously, for general soil protection or land improvement. This attitude, which encapsulates the traditional practice of the MOTC, accounts for much of the current road related soil damage in Kenya.

Where gross soil damage occurs after construction, MOTC leaves the work, of structural rectification to their Road Maintenance Division. By 'failing to attend to the regular repair or replacement of' culverts (sometimes wilfully blocked by farmers in desperation), this division, under-funded and absolutely incompetent, is the major cause of a great deal of soil erosion in Kenya, particularly in the mountain districts.

Road maintenance in Kenya has deteriorated since 1979 to such an extent, that many storm drains no longer function because of blockages. Soil protection should be built into initial road design, and operate at the project post-completion stage, and not left to the unreliable, incompetent maintenance staff.

Little sympathy is found within MOTC for the non-engineering issues of off-site damage occurring as a result of run-off, gullying and sedimentation. If anything, conservation measures are often discounted in order to reduce total road building costs, because of understandable financial constraints. There is evidently no Act of Parliament or legal instrument that obliges MOTC to assume a more responsible attitude towards soil conservation. It is no surprise that 'the El Nino Phenomenon 1998', caused havoc with Kenya's roads. The flood damage was worse than anything ever imagined by Kenyans, destroying all the road infrastructure completely and thereby sending the prices of goods and services sky-rocketing. However the MOTC's role, if not attitude, must soon change if Kenya's 'basic resource' (soil), is to be protected from total destruction.

In 1979/1980, before the PPCSCA was created, the National Steering Committee on Soil and Water Conservation was already in existence. Its recommendations regarding the adaptation of road design to conservation needs were accepted by the MOTC in inter-ministerial consultations and thereafter the construction work on various roads positively reflected those concerns, e.g. the Ruiru–Githunguri and Kiambu–Kianaiko roads in Kiambu district and the Thuci–Meru road, which even the Ministry of Agriculture and Livestock Development (MALD) officials regarded as an exemplary pointer to the future. In the case of the latter road, 'gabion mattresses' and the waterways (paved in some area), were constructed all the way to the valley bottoms, together with mechanisms for reducing water flow velocities. In addition, extensive revegetation was undertaken on the earth walls and slopes of cut banks. However, in many cases due to the nature of the mountainous terrain, these provisions are still far from adequate. In this regard, the consulting engineers blame new access roads as the main cause of erosion.

There has not, however, been any formal change in the functional responsibilities attributed to the MOTC. In fact, MALD claimed that for lack of alternative recourse, it still often had to make a specific request to the MOTC to include conservation specifications in road design. However, in late 1989, the MOTC reverted to its traditional reluctance to cooperate with other departments. Construction work on the Bahati–Ndondori road smacked of this new attitude, as did that on the Tambach–

Kabarnet road. The demise of the original Steering Committee, and its replacement by PPCSCA helped to explain this lapse, although the latter applied its full presidential status to enforcing many conservation measures, especially on the Thuci-Meru road.

5.3.6 RECOMMENDATIONS

There is a need for legal instruments which, to be effective must, *inter alia*, take account of the following considerations.

(a) Oblige the MOTC and others concerned to view roads and road building as part of the total natural/human environment, and not as an isolated exercise in applied physics.

(b) Require all concerned ministries to undertake inter-disciplinary EIA studies and to build project design specifications all necessary measures for environmental (especially soil) conservation, so that the road design and total road cost reflect these measures integrally, not as ad hoc contingencies.

(c) Re-train and strengthen MOTC's maintenance division staff to ensure regularity of work, conducive to the permanence of protective structures and their efficacy.

(d) Require the MOTC to oblige contractors to effectively revegetate and landscape road environments after construction. Quarries and other scars should be remoulded into natural forms to facilitate natural revegetation in the same way strip mines etc. are reclaimed elsewhere in the world (Law, 1984). (In addition to being eyesores, abandoned quarries can become hotbeds for disease vectors, especially mosquitoes. The Road Design Manual recommends this type of landscaping and reclamation, it is rarely enforced, even as an incidental contingency. The result is many gaping scars and needless ugliness along Kenyan roads.)

(e) The Kenya Government should take note of a consultancy report on Soil Water Conservation Programme Masinga Dam Catchment Area (TARDA/Atkins, 1984) where the following recommendations were made to MOTC:

devise road design criteria in relation to alignment,

geometry and drainage;

provide more numerous small culverts with due regard to outfall conditions;

improve drainage channel linings;

reduce the velocity of road run-off;

establish grass on all embankments and cuttings;

eliminate roads on 'cut-lines', which take no account of topography.

(f) Note in addition that special design specifications are required for such special case as the transverse roads across natural drainage, as in Muranga where they act as run-off collection drains, and cause most road-related erosion.

(g) Require the introduction of a moratorium on rural access road construction, which have the most destructive effects, until new guidelines are issued. The construction should never be left to untrained technicians, as is sometimes the case. MOTC should also have regulatory or statutory power to oversee design standards for non-classified and temporary roads on private land, which can cause much land degradation.

(h) Urgently to carry out or commission holistic post-completion studies of major donor engineering projects, in order to gain insights into any current flaws in design technique, implementation and management practices.

5.4   Social Amenities and Utilities

5.4.1 ACCESS TO WATER

Kenya having a mean annual precipitation of about 500 mm, would seem to indicate that the country is well endowed with rainfall. However, the pattern of precipitation shows greater regional variations ranging from below 200 mm in the arid areas to well above 200 mm in the highlands. Reliability of rainfall is also highly erratic from one year to another, and within any single year.

The Ministry of Water Development (MOWD) is responsible for water development, catchment protection and water pollution control, as well as for the maintenance of most water supply schemes. At present, more than 300 gazetted schemes are operated and maintained by MOWD. While the government aims at providing clean water to all Kenyan citizens by the year 2000, above 75 per cent of the 1981 rural population has been catered for under existing arrangements.

Natural streams and lakes are the principal sources of water for rural people. A study carried-out by NORAD in 1982 on the socio-economic aspects of Minor Urban Water Supply Programme (MUSP) found that over 50 per cent of those questioned, stated streams and lakes to be their main alternative source of piped water. The IRS-2 (1976) indicated that 88 per cent of rural households had a water source within a distance of 2 NBS km (Kenya/Central Bureau of Statistics, 1981a). Drawing water is considered the task of women and children.

The larger cities operate water treatment facilities, and supply the greater part of their inhabitants with clean water. IRS-4 (1987) showed about 95 per cent of urban households has access to piped water. By comparison the corresponding figure was about 12 per cent for rural households (Kenya/Central Bureau of Statistics, 1982a).

To satisfy the water requirements of the population in Kenya's minor urban centres and rural areas, it was estimated that a total annual water supply of 227 million m^3 is necessary. In 1982, the Ministry of Water Development's (MOWD's) total production was 60 million m^3, equivalent to some 26 per cent of the required volume (Business and Economic Research, 1982). Looking ahead towards the year 2000, it was estimated that Kenya's population, outside the major cities, would then be of the order of 35 million. To meet its objective of supplying all Kenyans with clean water by that time, MOWD would have needed to increase its capacity ninefold over the last fourteen years. An even more discouraging picture emerges from a study undertaken in 1982, which suggested that only 6 per cent of the Kenyan population living in rural areas and minor urban centres, were actually served by MOWD schemes. This implies that a distinction should be made between availability and accessibility for different user groups.

For metered water consumption per month, the gazetted tariffs for urban and rural water supply schemes, were respectively K.shs. 21.50 and 18.50 up to 9m^3, and K.shs. 2.65 and 2.00 per m^3 above that level. For unmetered water, a flat rate charge was imposed of K.shs 36.00 and 15.00 per month, again respectively for urban rural areas. Total monthly water consumption levels for metered and unmetered connections are shown to have averaged 20 and 32 m^3, in respect of each type of source. This implies that a metered rural connection is charged on average more than four times as much per m^3, as the unmetered flat rate and rural consumer. It also suggests a certain water wastage by the unmetered consumers.

The most glaring inequities are apparent in the tariff differential between unmetered and metered connections. In addition, the tariff structure for metered connections clearly favours consumption above 9m^3, i.e. the large users over the smaller, and presumably poorer consumers.

Thus, the present water tariff structure in Kenya favours the large consumers, encourages wasteful consumption and places a burden on the operations and maintenance budget of MOWD, as only a small proportion of actual production costs are recovered from user fees.

Given the present organisational weaknesses in the system and tariff structure, the provision of piped water supplies to all Kenyan consumers countrywide, is not considered feasible under the present administration in the foreseeable future; without the institution of communal water kiosks, combined with waterbore-holes and shallow wells exploiting groundwater resources, the situation looks bleak. While an approach of this kind will not have achieved the stated objective by the government of providing all Kenyans with clean water by the year 2000, and loopholes in the organisational structure remain, nonetheless it represents a methodology and focus of working towards this goal.

5.4.2 ACCESS TO ELECTRICITY

The Ministry of Energy and Regional Development is charged with policy formulation and coordination of energy development, while the operation and maintenance of the national electricity grid is entrusted to the Kenya Power and Lighting Company (KPLC).

The Kenya electrical power grid was first developed in the larger towns and cities, which contained the highest proportion of consumers with an ability to pay for the use of electricity, either as individuals or on a corporate basis. The combination of low distribution costs, relatively easy maintenance, manageable transmission losses, few natural hazards and readily available and a viable group of consumers, also made the densely populated urban centres a catalytic agent for subsequent electrification programmes in Kenya. At the same time, it should be borne in mind that Kenya currently obtains only 4 per cent of its energy consumption from electricity, compared with more than 60 per cent from fuel-wood and charcoal (Kenya Energy consumption, 1996).

While domestically generated electricity has grown from 263 GWh in 1963 to 2,155 GWh in 1985, representing an average annual increase of 10 per cent over this period, electricity will continue to be greatly restricted in its use, because of the high cost of power lines required for distribution in the rural areas. A power sector master plan was adopted and geared to a low cost programme for the 1985–2005 period. Like an earlier Rural Electrification study Programme, the master plan recommended that electrification should be limited to areas of sufficient high population density, or possessing energy intensive industries. The presence of such factors might be expected to limit installation costs to between K.shs. 5,000–15,000 per KWh, and at the same time enable the KPLC to obtain a satisfactory rate of return through the application of competitive tariffs. At present (1998), about 8 per cent of Kenya's total population have access to electricity. As regards rural households, only 1 per cent of these had access to electricity in 1976, and those were in the main, relatively high income groups, living on the urban periphery (Kenya/Central Bureau of Statistics, 1981a).

Over the period 1980–1985, the average tariff level for electricity decreased in real terms by 12 per cent. According to the World Bank report (World Bank, 1986a), this decline resulted in the tariff level falling in 1984 to 22 per cent below the long-run electricity consumption. It should be noted, however, that the subsequent tariff increased in 1985 and 1986 to 17 per cent and 11 per cent respectively, restored the sector's overall financial viability (World Bank, 1986a).

While the present tariff structure has certain built-in bias, favouring domestic low quantity consumers, this particular charge is still well above the rates offered to large industrial users, a situation not peculiar to Kenya.

Larger regional hospitals, offering a complement of diagnostic and curative medical services, depend on the use of modern and technically advanced laboratory equipment which cannot function properly with the unstable power supply provided by diesel-generated systems. For hospitals of this kind, grid electricity is of crucial significance.

Despite the relatively low per capita level of installed capacity for electricity generation, amounting to some 110 KWh per annum, the rural electrification of Kenya will remain a relatively far distant prospect as long as political power remains with the corrupt and degenerate administration under the KANU government. Future increase in demand for electricity will probably come from established or growing urban centres, large energy-intensive industries, and major centres in the health sector.

Chapter VI
ECONOMIC DEVELOPMENT AND SELF RELIANCE

6.1 Economic Aims

Before encouraging swimmer to dive, one must first fill pool with water.

(Attributed to Confucius)

The economic aims of the new government were carefully set out in the 1963 KANU election manifesto, and subsequently in sessional paper no. 10 of 1965, 'African Socialism and its Application to Planning in Kenya'. These objectives were seen by international observers to be orthodox enough, 'to achieve high and growing per capita incomes equitably distributed so that all are free from want, disease and exploitation' (Burrows, 1975). The particular approaches envisaged in attaining these aims were considered to be more specifically Kenyan, in that the government proposed to call upon the best of African tradition, including the mutual social responsibility of the extended family system, in pursuing a new path to African Socialism. While initially seeking to distance Kenyan policies from foreign influence, the architects of Kenya's early development programme were fully prepared to use foreign technology, personnel, and capital, where these could be used to the national economic advantage.

In this context, the main thrust of government strategy was to promote rapid economic growth through public sector programmes, the encouragement of both smallholder and large-scale farming, and the pursuit of accelerated industrialisation by policy incentives to encourage private (including foreign) investment in modern industry. The Kenyan development model might therefore be described as a 'mixed economy', in the sense that it embraced a wide range of organisational structures and incentives, and associated private, cooperative and non-governmental institutions with a substantial element of government involvement and direction.

In this situation, there was a remarkable continuity in the functioning of the economy and system of government between the previous colonial period and the post-independence years. For many foreign countries, arriving for the first time in Kenya, the existence of a relatively strong and stable administration in Nairobi, committed to carefully articulated development programmes was a positive factor in negotiating initial cooperation arrangements.

The first decade of the 1963–1976 period underlined the comparative strength of the Kenyan economy, the 1973–1976 years served to pinpoint certain fragilities in the country's economic situation and structure. As a result of the 1973 Organisation of Oil Exporting Countries (OPEC) decision on oil prices, and the general inflationary trends of that period, Kenya encountered a serious deficit in its balance of payments, which had to be funded by a combination of short-term borrowing from the IMF, programme support from multilateral and other sources, commercial borrowing and a drawing down of foreign exchange reserves. Since the inflationary impact on import prices appeared largely irreversible, for the first time since Kenya's independence, the government and donors became seriously concerned about the country's long-term payments position.

Consequently, this period also heralded the beginning of intensive economic policy discussions between Kenyan authorities, the IMF and the World Bank, which were to be a central feature of the 1976–1986 decade, and which were initiated in the publication by government of sessional paper no.4 of 1975 'on Economic Prospects and policies' (Kenya Ministry of Finance and Planning, 1975).

Among its major recommendations were lines of action, which were to affect donor policies throughout the 1976–1986 period, notably in the emphasis accorded to agricultural programmes, water supplies and rural access roads, and to curtailment of those outlays that would not make immediate contributions to economic productivity.

In the wake of the 1973 oil crisis, growth slackened to some 4 per cent per annum, with virtually no increase in per capita incomes. These developments were attributable to the consequences of the 1973 oil crisis, including an important deterioration in Kenya's terms of trade, and also to various structural problems, which were to intensify during the 1976–1986 period. Thus agricultural problems began to increase, due to the declining significance of those factors which had helped to sustain rural development in the 1960s. Notable among these was the access which many smallholders had to the acquisition of farmland, and to the use of supporting economic services. For a period in the 1970s, official policies turned the internal terms of trade against agriculture, while inadequate marketing arrangements had adversely affected domestic trade in agricultural products.

Growth in the industrial sector also declined, and was pushed forward at rising cost in terms of capital-intensive production and low employment creation. There was, too, a certain burden on the balance of payments from this sector, which imported significant quantities of intermediate goods for limited forms of assembly or processing, but in itself exported very little. These developments resulted from official policies favouring substantial measures of domestic protection, and inadequately planned public involvement in industrial projects. In the export field, volume increase was frequently less than 1 per cent annually, and exports became more sharply focused on coffee, tea and petroleum items. Finally population growth increased to one of the highest publicly recorded rates in the world, as a result of a fall in mortality and improved health conditions permitting fertility to approach its natural limits.

Three major aspects of the Kenyan economic system assumed a special significance during the 1976–1986 period. First of all, the open nature of the Kenyan economy, with a total volume of its export–import trade accounting for some two-thirds of GDP, rendered it particularly susceptible to the impact of abrupt changes in international market conditions. Secondly, while the

Kenyan administration appeared increasingly committed to a free market system and competition, outside the normal economic and social infrastructure and services, it was apparent that further significant elements of Kenya's industrial and commercial activities were being brought into the public sector. And thirdly, the willingness and ability of the authorities in Nairobi to maintain continuing and serious economic policy discussions with international institutions, such as the IMF and the World Bank, became an important element in the evolution of economic policy, during the 1976–1986 decade.

As in other parts of Africa, much of the initiative for such consultation came from the IMF and the World Bank, with whose activities and conditions the American and British development aid agencies increasingly came to link their own decisions on their respective bilateral programmes. Between the work of the IMF and the World Bank, there was generally a high degree of complementarity, with the former devoting its attention to monetary, fiscal and budgetary issues, and to questions of demand management and stabilisation, while the World Bank focused mainly on longer term structural adjustment and sectoral policy issues.

In Kenya, IMF conditionality has been primarily directed towards curtailing the budget deficit, restraining public borrowing from the banking system, and re-establishing the external balance. To this end, the IMF has sought to secure a range of fiscal and monetary reforms, including higher interest rates, trade liberalisation, wage restraint, realistic exchange rates, increased taxation and certain reduction in both development and recurrent expenditure. While the IMF has been primarily concerned with broad policy measures, the World Bank has linked the implementation of its structural adjustment programmes in Kenya to more detailed forms of conditionality; including, for example, incentives for infant industries, export promotion schemes, agricultural pricing and marketing arrangements, land and population policies, supervision of agricultural schemes, forward budgeting in the public sector, and the curtailment of investments in parastatals and public companies. There has also been a certain complementarity in the supervision of procedures monitoring numerical results of the IMF and the World Bank, and the World Bank assessing policy actions.

6.1.2 RECENT ECONOMIC TRENDS AND OUTLOOK

The introduction of major economic reforms in early 1993 resulted in considerable liberalisation and deregulation across a number of key areas, notably agriculture, trade and finances. Economic activity responded to the more favourable commercial environment and a three year period of economic advancement took place. However, economic activity slowed sharply in 1996 in the wake of a number of adverse developments. A severe drought in late 1996 and early 1997 affected crop production, while there was business uncertainty ahead of the end-year general election. An escalation of political violence in mid-1997 had an adverse effect on investment and decision-making and in particular had a negative impact on tourism. The mid-year disagreement with the IMF over the latter's concerns about good governance, state accountability, transparency and corruption triggered a freeze on other official financial flows and further dampened investment sentiment; while the continuing difficulties with a weak infrastructure, notably power supplies and poor conditions of roads hampered economic activity.

These difficulties made it difficult to achieve economic stability over the past few years. The economic slowdown was a contributory factor in a larger-than-estimated budget deficit for the 1996–1997 year as revenues were lower than expected. Inflationary pressure also persisted and resulted in a sharp rise in interest rates towards the latter part of 1998. The currency, however, remained fairly stable until August 1997 when it fell sharply but subsequently regained some value and stability. The political situation and how President Moi would win the 1997 election tended to dominate government thinking and as a consequence there was little progress in market reform, notably on privatisation; while donors concerns over the standard of good governance, accountability and transparency remained. Externally, improved commodity terms-of-trade enabled Kenya to narrow its trade deficit in 1997 following two years of sharp imbalances and lower tourism receipts, allowing the current account to return to surplus.

Despite continuing grave concern over the 1997–1998 performance of the agricultural sector, owing to fears of adverse weather, economic growth favouring the few urban rich Kenyans and foreigners was forecast to improve slightly in 1998 while, in the Kenyan rural heartland, there was a terminal decline even as a gradual peaceful political environment and business confidence began to return. Inflationary pressures are likely to persist and, despite a tight monetary policy, continuing high interest rates and a less volatile exchange rate, inflation is expected to ease slightly. Heavy rains towards the end of 1997 caused considerable damage to crops and infrastructure, an unbudgeted teacher's pay settlement and a continuing donor freeze were likely to widen the 1997–1998 fiscal deficit despite enhanced revenue collection methods by the Kenya Revenue Authority. With elections over, the administration's effort were directed to seeking an early resumption of IMF support. The government, as a consequence, will be under pressure to expedite parastatal and civil service reform, the former through speedier privatisation (particularly key service utilities) and the latter through labour retrenchment, as well as by efforts to clamp down on endemic corruption. However, it is very likely that the IMF and other official donors will wait to see progress before releasing further support, suggesting that the restoration of IMF funding is conditional and would not be forthcoming until the latter part of 1998 or early 1999.

Despite further growth in exports, the balance of payments recurrent account is expected to return to deficit this year as the trade gap widens. With a continuing donor freeze, a slow rise in external debt is expected over the outlook period. A resumption of donor support would have eased any debt-servicing difficulties that would have been encountered this year and 1999.

6.1.3 NAIROBI BOMBING – A BLOW TO THE ECONOMY

As relatives continued to bury well over 247 victims of 7 August 1998 Nairobi bomb blast, Kenya was beginning to measure the impact of the country's worst terrorist attack on an economy already hit by crisis. Coming after an 18–month slump, the timing of the explosion could not have been more damaging. 'Things were limping along badly anyway', said an economic analyst. 'This is the final shot in the head.'

Even before the blast, stagnating foreign investment, an aid freeze by donors exasperated by top-level graft, El Nino's ravages on agriculture and the near collapse of the tourism industry had prompted many economists to predict that growth in 1998 would be under 1 per cent after an already disappointing 2.3 per cent in 1997. Now even that scenario looks optimistic. 'I'd be surprised if growth isn't in the negative,' said Robert Shaw, director of the Institute of Economic Affairs. 'Overall this will increase momentum towards greater slowdown' (*Daily Nation*, 13 April 1998).

The immediate damage to Nairobi's infrastructure has still to be assessed although, while touring the bomb site, Kenya's President Daniel Arap Moi said the total cost could reach $800M. The bomb – coinciding with a similar blast in Dar-es Salaam – seriously damaged at least 30 buildings in the business centre and it is expected many small businesses will be bankrupted, as insurance policies in a city with no history of guerrilla attack rarely catered for terrorism. The Association of Kenya Insurers, under public pressure to be lenient, met to consider how to react.

Tourism is likely to suffer the biggest blow. The industry, accounting for up to 20 per cent of foreign exchange revenue, was just beginning to pick up after what Henry Kosgey, tourism minister, called its worst year since independence. The Kenya Tourist Board has appealed to the US government to review the travel warning issued after the bomb blast, which advised nationals to avoid Kenya and Tanzania because they would find no local back-up in countries where both US embassies are out of action.

The warning, which contrasted with advice from the British Foreign Office recommending travellers to leave their plans unchanged as 'repeat incidents' seemed unlikely, triggered fury in Kenya that already sees itself as the victim of a dispute between Islamic Fundamentalists and the US. An editorial in the Daily Nation newspaper blasted what it described as an 'impolitic and callous' move, saying Kenya took 'great offence' at the advisory.

'We trust that Americans are intelligent enough to treat this piece of ill advice with the disdain it deserves,' it said (*Daily Nation*, 11 August 1998).

American visitors rank only sixth in importance for Kenya, with the greatest share coming from Europe. But tour operators worry that even without the negative advisory, TV coverage of the blast's aftermath will compound the negative image of Kenya arising from 1997's ethnic clashes, university students' killings by police and a spate of gangster attacks in which westerners have died. Kenya was estimated to have lost up to $700M in tourist revenue in the 12 months to July, 1998. Hotels on the coast were closed and 50,000 people in the industry lost their jobs.

The latest bad news come just as European customers turned their attention to winter bookings. 'The tourist board has been busy promoting Kenya abroad and there were hopes we would see bookings up for the November to March high season,' said an industry operator. 'This knocks it all for six.' The government is poorly placed to ride out any further slowdown in economic activity. It is struggling to control a budget deficit likely to reach 4 per cent of gross domestic product against a target of 2.4 per cent. It is also desperate to reduce the huge domestic debt fuelling cripplingly high interest rates (interest rates on treasury bonds are about 25 per cent).

Kenya's government will hope that, given the exceptional circumstance, the US and other governments will soften the hard line taken since development aid was frozen in 1997 by the IMF and bilateral donors. Madeleine Albright, the former US Secretary of State, promised following the bomb blast, that Washington would discuss with Tanzania and Kenya ways the US could assist. But given the widespread perception Mr Moi is reluctant to crack down on corruption, and weak and despotic leadership, a sea change in international attitudes to Kenya looks unlikely.

6.1.4 KENYA'S ECONOMIC POLICY

6.1.4.1 *Fiscal Strategy*
Kenya's budget deficits have been financed largely by internal borrowing and external aid. The key objective of fiscal policy in

recent years has been to bring down the budget deficit as a proportion of GDP and to eliminate the deficit in the near future. Reducing the central government borrowing requirements is seen as promoting economic stability and allowing the private sector greater access to domestic credit.

6.1.4.2 Budget Estimates

Largely because of an economic slowdown in 1996 and lower than anticipated revenues, official estimates revealed a larger-than-expected deficit in 1996–1997. Although the 1997–1998 tax-cutting budget, geared towards promoting investment and employment, sought to lower the fiscal deficit to below 2% of GDP, this appears optimistic in the light of a recent pay award to teachers, government assistance for flood-related damage and the continued withholding of official donor assistance. There may be a need to cut-back further on public expenditure and/or raise taxes to meet budgetary targets. Although in August 1997, a series of indirect tax measures were announced to bridge revenue losses associated with the suspension of IMF funds, and efforts to boost revenue collection procedures by the Kenya Revenue Authority (KRA), a larger deficit was anticipated for 1997–1998. The government is under considerable pressure by the World Bank to expedite public sector reform, notably a privatisation programme which includes the restructuring of key service utilities, particularly the energy sector and telecommunications. In addition, the government is seeking to redress past financial mismanagement and endemic official corruption by pursuing improved state accountability and transparency. There is a continuing urgent need for public investment to rehabilitate a seriously deteriorating public infrastructure.

6.1.4.3 Monetary Policy

Monetary policy has two principal and connected aims; the maintenance of a stable exchange rate and achieving low inflation. Both objectives are linked policies and strategies for tackling one goal which helps indirectly to meet the other. In Kenya, following a series of measures in 1993, there was a noticeable fall in inflation by 1995, but inflation started to creep up slightly, largely because of cost-push factors. The 1996–1997 drought-related impact on food supplies caused inflation to rise sharply in early 1997 and

301

although inflation eased in the middle of the year, helped by increased food supplies, the currency depreciation in August and supplementary tax increases have maintained inflationary pressures and the authorities raised interest rates. The lagged effects of these recent cost influences may hinder the achievement of the single figure inflation target in 1998. Instead, a slower decline is anticipated although a tight monetary strategy suggests little room for an early reduction in interest rates.

6.1.4.4 Kenya's Currency Outlook

Although the Kenya shilling was relatively stable in the first half of 1997, it suffered a sharp fall on the international market in August in the wake of the IMF loan suspension. However, the currency soon regained much of its earlier losses, helped by strong inflows of export receipts and higher interest rates, and thereafter has remained stable. Forecasts for 1998 suggested that with correct monetary stance and lower inflation the shilling should depreciate slightly and would draw support from a resumption of official aid flows.

6.1.5 NEED FOR LONG-TERM ECONOMIC DEVELOPMENT PLANNING

There has been an instinctive tendency to rely on economics and economic modelling to solve the Kenyan problems of bringing population and environmental issues into development planning, but so far traditional techniques appear to have failed to meet this challenge. Conventional economic models are constructed to reflect the workings of the market economy where growth is determined by market expectations and the values attributed to goods and services. They are concerned with the internal logic of the economy rather than with external physical influences which may ultimately affect the direction of growth over the long term. As long as resource and environmental constraints do not have to be considered, it is perfectly reasonable to proceed, say, by setting a target for economic growth and then deciding on the fiscal and other economic policies needed to achieve that target. The trouble, however, begins when attempts are made to forecast over the long term, for it involves estimating the values underlying prices over a long period ahead and with increasing uncertainty.

A United Nations task force on long term objectives (1981) touched on these problems when it referred to the uncertainties involved in estimating the long-term price and supply of oil which would justify investments in alternatives. What the task force really implied was that the physical as well as the economic determinants of oil availability needed to be understood before prices could be estimated with any degree of accuracy. Economic planning techniques can serve their function admirably over the short-term, but they cannot guarantee the objectives they pursue are compatible with physically realisable development over a long period. There may be environmental implications which are concealed because environmental factors are 'externalised'. There may be physical restrictions affecting the supply of resources as these become harder to access. If economic forecasts are taken too far ahead, they may be leading the national system towards a state which is ultimately unsustainable.

This does not imply that governments are doing nothing to take account of the demographic and resource trends underlying the development of their economies. In a number of developing countries national planning has managed to adjust to a certain extent. Some efforts are being made to improve individual aspects of resource management, particularly in the case of water, and attention is being given in certain quarters to the question of incorporating the environmental and social costs of production. Long term population forecasts are beginning to be used to calculate school enrolment, housing or health needs, although generally on a sectoral basis only. A start has been made to quantify factors outside the formal and informal economy, such as fuel-wood gathering as it contributes to energy consumption.

When a long-term planning horizon is adopted it turns our attention to anticipated problems which may not be justified or which appear superfluous in the context of short-term planning, but which cannot be postponed to a time when action is too late or prohibitively expensive. Increases in population, deterioration of soils or land lost through desertification are examples of such changes which are barely perceptible over five or even ten years, but over longer periods become increasingly evident. By this time they may well be compromising a nation's prospects of attaining sustainable development.

Certain long-term targets may be found in national plans, when common sense dictates that action is necessary. This includes the setting of population growth targets which, generally speaking, are determined on the basis of the likely response to family planning measures. In other areas, including the following, targets for action are most likely to be lacking:

(i) the allocation of heavy initial investments which may be required, for example, to build up the infrastructure necessary for ensuring the transition to a new energy regime (perhaps based on renewable energy systems), or to maintain environmental quality – an activity which is easily discounted by economic accounting methods;

(ii) the husbanding of natural resources to ensure the sustainable productive capacity of renewable resources and to plan for the rate of exploitation of non-renewable in a manner which will allow for the availability of substitutes and give time for social adjustment;

(iii) the formulation of material goals which accord with long-term prospects of physical development;

(iv) the planning of research and development to meet problems identified in advance and taking account of relevant lead times;

(v) the creation of a basic understanding of the overall national situation, as it affects both present and future generations, so that people may realise the importance of, and give support to population and other policies designed to secure a satisfactory life both for themselves and for their children and descendants.

Now that the notion of sustainable development is gaining ground in Kenya and many developing countries, the understandable reaction of both the international community and of individual governments has been to seek as much improvement as possible on all fronts: economic growth through the intensification of agriculture and industry, the stepping up of family planning programmes, and greater attention to the control of environmental degradation and to the conservation of natural species. An instructive example is taken from a sessional paper No.1, issued by the Government of Kenya (1986), which proposed a development strategy destined to form a basis of the 1989–1993 development plan. The paper recognised that anticipated rapid population growth constituted a serious problem, stating that at the end of the century Kenya would have a population of some 35 million people, 75 per cent more than in 1984. The threat of increasing strain on the environment – land, water and forests – was similarly recognised. In response to this situation, an economic growth target of 5.6 per cent annual increase was set to generate the means of satisfying basic needs and to create employment opportunities. This was to be accompanied by stricter attention to resource management and conservation.

The question which immediately arose, quite apart from that of the feasibility of maintaining a 5.6 per cent growth rate, was whether these different goals were mutually consistent. Could agriculture be intensified to the point of maintaining a population one-and-three-quarters as large as that of 1986 (and without danger to the productivity of the soil)? If so how will the necessary inputs be obtained, through local industry or through imports? If it were to be through imports, would these be through cash crops? And if through cash crops will this mean that land would have to be taken from food production, limiting yet further arable land or that which might be used for fuel-wood plantations or other purposes? Such questions could only be answered if the dynamics were understood of the entire national system, and of the feedback obtained from different components of the system. The sessional paper had the merit, though, of pointing out that a trade-off existed between rates of population increase and standard of living expressed in GNP per capita.

Table 6.1 indicates that if the (4%) 1986's total fertility rate (TFR) were to remain constant at 7.9 per cent (projection A), average incomes between 1984 and 2000 would only increase by 2.7 per cent, assuming that there was an average annual growth rate in GNP of 4.5 per cent. Incomes would increase by as much as 21.4 per cent if a GNP growth rate of 5.6 per cent could be maintained. If instead a fertility rate of 5.6 per cent could be achieved (projection B), then incomes would grow by 13.6 and 34.1 per cent respectively. The sessional paper concluded, naturally, that the next fifteen years economic growth was the only way to make a significant impact on average income and on employment, given anticipated population increase. Family planning undertaken would have had a marked effect. It was not within the scope of that report to ascertain whether those methods would prove to be sufficient or not. An annual economic growth rate of 5.6 per cent, however, appeared to be an extremely ambitious target.

Table 6.1   Kenya Population and Income per Capita in 2000

	1984	2000 Projection	
		A	B
1. Population (million)	19.5	38.5	34.8
2. Fertility rate	7.9	7.9	5.6
3. Implied average growth rate (%/year)	–	4.4	3.7
4. Dependency ratio	1.22	1.24	1.04
5. GDP per capita in 1984 prices with GDP growth			
(1) 4.5%/year	220	226	250
(2) 5.6%/year	220	267	295
6. 16–year increase (%) in income /capita			
(1)		2.7	13.6
(2)		21.4	34.1

Source: Government of Kenya Sessional Paper No.1 of 1986, citing Development Plan 1984–1988.

Attempts have been made to assess the somewhat longer-term impacts of population growth on different components of a nation's economy. In a report on Jordan's development prospects, made by the Futures Group on behalf of USAID, the effect of alternative population growth variants were calculated in relation to a number of other variables (see Table 6.1.2).

A series of discontinuous snapshots were obtained in this way of what the future scenario might be. Again, there was no feedback of output to input data. The question was not addressed as to whether the economy, considered as a total system, could have generated rates of growth without damage to the fragile environment and provided for the needs of the population indefinitely; that is, on a sustainable basis.

Table 6.1.2 The effect of population growth on selected Variables
Current fertility 2 child families

1. Population 2025	9.8×10^6	3.5×10^6
2. Social Service expenditure to 2025 to maintain current standard	14×10^6★	$50x\ 10^6$★
3. Water deficit by 2010	$370 \times 10^6\ m^3$	$220x\ 10^6\ m^3$
4. Arable land per capita 2025	0.037 ha	0.11 ha
5. Food imported to feed population to current standard	increase	reduction
6. Males in labour force	1,250,000	900,000
7. GNP/capita (1976 units)	500	1000

Source: Jordan report to USAID by Futures Group, Washington DC Population Growth.
★ Values in Jordan dinars, 1JD (1984) – $US 2.72.

6.1.6 FISCAL AND MONETARY THEORY

When John Maynard Keynes wrote his book, *The General Theory of Interest and Employment*, he became famous because the world saw his theory of financial manipulation by the government as the solution to the problem of unemployment. This is not to imply that Keynes was the only, or the first to advocate such ideas, but to a large extent his name has become associated with them in academic and government circles. Ever since then, virtually all of the economists trained in the Western universities, have been taught the Keynes' Theory. It has become the Bible of the economic establishment. It is true that there have been dissenters, classical and neo-classical economists, including the Marxists, but these dissenters have received little attention within the halls of government 'decision makers' in the capitalist economies.

At the risk of over-simplification Keynes' 'monetary' and 'fiscal' policies which are the basis of what is often called a 'managed economy' all add up to trying to stimulate the economy if it is sluggish or slow it down if it is over-stimulated. The economy is stimulated or cooled off merely by increasing or decreasing taxes (fiscal policies), or by printing money to create inflation or reducing the supply of money if inflation is getting out of hand (monetary policies) Keynes said, 'a little inflation is a good thing'. By this he meant that, with inflation, people are encouraged to spend more, and spending stimulates the economy. He did not, of course, explain that inflation can lead to disasters, perhaps worse disasters than unemployment. In the same way, reducing taxes is supposed to give the consumer more spendable money and therefore stimulate the economy, or vice versa.

Keynes' ideas seemed to work for a time, because of the need to do something about massive unemployment during the Great Depression, the enormous stimulus to demand that occurred during the Second World War, and the changes in technology, especially communications and transport, that made it possible to exploit the entire world's resources at an ever-increasing rate.

Today the situation has changed and it has become increasingly clear that high technology is beginning to reach a plateau of development and the limits of the world's resources have begun to loom on the horizon. Thus have 'stagflation', with increasing unemployment and increasing inflation occurring simultaneously; a condition which has confounded most Keynesians, although Keynes himself may have foreseen it with his famous statement 'for a time we must pretend that fair is foul and foul is fair'. Whether he meant this way or not, we have been depleting the world's resources and polluting the environment as the means to maintain the value of the dollar or sterling. His devotees have forgotten the first part of the statement and are puzzled over what to do now since he left no further instructions.

There is, of course, still some slack in the system for the

economists and politicians to use in postponing galloping inflation for a while. There is still a large portion of the world's population which is not well fed, well clothed, or well housed, and direct government subsidies – if politically possible – to those groups may continue for a time to prop up the system and stave off runaway inflation. This is only relatively true, of course; government subsidies for real needs are not necessarily as inflationary as guns and bombs, but bureaucratic red tape can add enormous inflationary costs. But these subsidies cannot forever be advanced without a reduction in the subsidies to the big corporations in the form of defence spending. We cannot much longer have 'guns and butter' too.

To the discredited Keynesian economic theory can now be added the equally implausible underlying proposition of supply side economics – the Monetarists, namely, that radical tax reduction will so stimulate economic growth as actually to boost government revenue, thereby eliminating budget deficits, while simultaneously generating enough jobs to keep everybody employed at decent wages. Under President Reagan in the U.S., and Mrs Thatcher's Britain, the trickle down policy became a cruel hoax for soaking the poor to benefit the rich.

The Monetarist Controversy – on the other hand, had its origin in the pioneering work of Milton Friedman, at the University of Chicago, on the demand for money and the role of monetary policy. Friedman and his followers stressed the importance of the money supply in determining the behaviour of prices and the level of economic activity and hence argued the case for the revival of monetary policy, which at the time had fallen into disrepute. Consequently, they became known as monetarists. The participants on the other side of the controversy formed two distinct, but not unrelated, groups. Those who challenged the theoretical, empirical and methodological basis of the monetarists' arguments, and those who set themselves up as the defenders of the fiscal policy, which they thought was under attack by the monetarists. This latter group became known as the Keynesians.

With hindsight it is clear that participants on both sides of the controversy were responsible for creating confusion. To avoid adding to this confusion we will describe the monetarist position, and the main issues involved in the controversy, by means of a set of straightforward propositions.

1. The demand for money function is a stable function of a relatively small number of economic variables.

2. The relationship between the demand for real money balances and the nominal supply of money is one of the key macroeconomic relationships.

3. There is a predictable relationship between changes in the supply of money and the level of nominal income, the money multiplier relationship.

4. The money multiplier relationship is at least as good a predictor of the response of the level of economic activity to changes in the supply of money, as the fiscal multiplier is for changes in the level of autonomous expenditure.

5. Changes in the supply of money exert their influence on nominal income with a long, and sometimes variable, lag.

6. In the long run, the influence of changes in the supply of money is mainly on the price level and not real output. Money is neutral in the long run.

7. The interest rate relevant to economic decision making is the real and not the money rate of interest. Because the real rate of interest depends upon price expectations, it is unobservable. Consequently, variations in the money rate of interest do not provide a good indication of variations in the real rate of interest, nor of the strength of monetary policy.

8. The target variable of monetary policy should be the supply of money (a monetary aggregate) and not the rate of interest (credit market conditions).

9. Because of lags in the transmission of monetary impulses, steady growth of the money supply is likely to be more stabilising than discretionary actions.

10. Fiscal policy is important, but in using fiscal policy allowance must be made for the monetary consequences of different fiscal policy actions.

11. Monetary expansion is essential for the continuation of an inflationary process. Control of the money supply is an essential ingredient of any policy to stop inflation.

This rich menu of monetarist propositions clearly demonstrates why it is inappropriate to appraise the monetarist controversy solely in terms of monetary versus fiscal policy. It also dispels the myth that monetarism is synonymous with crude quantity theory predictions. Monetarism is concerned with the role of money in the economy, and the appropriate monetary policy for minimising monetary and real disturbances in the economy. It does not imply that money alone is important, or that monetary policy is more important than fiscal policy. It recognises that both are important, but stresses that to use them effectively they must be used to attain the ends to which they are best suited. It further emphasises that because changes in the supply of money, for whatever reason, exert specific and pronounced effects on the level of nominal income, the monetary consequences of fiscal policy actions must be allowed for. That is, monetarists recognise that in some cases the terms monetary and fiscal policy refer to the same policy actions, in that policy actions involve changes in the supply of money.

6.2 Self-Reliance and Economics Embedded in Culture

6.2.1 SELF-RELIANCE AS A DEVELOPMENT STRATEGY

Self-reliance as a development strategy has five key elements which are organically linked and answers the key questions development of what? Development by whom? Development for whom? Development how? It also contains the following key elements:

1. Need-oriented, i.e., geared to human needs, both material and non-material, starting with the needs of the majority of Kenyan inhabitants, the dominated and the exploited. Ensuring the humanisation of all human beings in Kenya by

311

the satisfaction of their basic needs for expression, creativity and conviviality and to understand and master their own destiny.

2. Endogenous, i.e., stemming from the heart of Kenyan society, which defines in sovereignty its values, objectives and its vision of the future.

3. Self-reliant, i.e., implying that Kenya's society relies primarily on its own strength, weaknesses and resources in terms of its members' energies and its natural and cultural environment.

4. Ecologically sound, i.e., utilising rationally the resources of the biosphere in full awareness of the potential of local ecosystems as well as the global and local outer limits imposed on the present and future generations.

5. Based in structural transformation/modernisation, people are required, more often than not, in social relations, in economic activities and in their spatial distribution, as well as in the power structure, to realise the conditions of self-management and participation in democratic decision making by those affected by it.

One answer to the despair and frustration generated by failure of 'mainstream' economic ideas lies in the opportunity of revitalising communities by rebuilding their economies, literally, from the bottom up. It is a melancholy fact of life that in order to bring about significant change, conditions have to get bad enough for a sizeable proportion of people to accept, if not work for it them-selves, a meaningful environment as the centre of their concern.

The position of pre-eminence achieved by contemporary economics in development is such that other disciplines are considered important only from the moment their economic impact and benefits can be demonstrated. This is one of the principal reasons why, until very recently, so little attention was paid to ecological, cultural or ethical dimensions of development. The case of education is somewhat different. Schultz *et al* in the mid 1960s, were able to demonstrate the economic benefit of 'human capital', 'human resources' and 'investment' in education, and its capacity to process successive age-cohorts into skilled 'manpower'. The moment education transformed itself into the Economics of Education it started gaining respect and status as a genuine development discipline. Community development, media and management studies achieved prominence because of their function as pioneers of the age of development and accelerators of the passing of traditional society. Patterns of speech and vocabulary have undergone such a profound transformation that not only education, but also other services such as health, transport or tourism now uniformly use the language of competition and of the market. Even culture, though apparently less susceptible to economic dictates, is now confronted by market forces which do not stop at auctioning a Van Gogh but engage in cost-benefit analysis of leisure activities or the environment. Nothing is sacred. The relentless logic of market economics demands that human relations and values once prized for their own worth be turned into commodities which can be bought and sold. Happiness is predicated on consumption and the only virtuous activity becomes material enrichment.

Research into the linkages between culture and development economics is virtually non-existent and yet,

> ...what would be interesting and therefore highly unorthodox, would be to turn the received epistemological relationship between economics and culture on its head, i.e. to think of the former in function of the latter... This inversion would be all the more necessary as the autonomous economic hegemony continues to spout models which look consistent on paper, but which are utterly destructive for those societies which blindly put them into practice, particularly in the Third World. (Zaoual, 1989)

Since the dawn of humanity, culture has paved the way for and supported economics: 'there is an undeniable dialectical relationship between the two' (David, 1993). Even the IMF has conceded that a purely rational, 'logical' application of development comes up, time and again, against the brick wall of local resistance. This resistance owes nothing to economic rationality or logic. It is more significant than what anthropologists call, 'cultural lag', but has everything to do with the cultural determinants that economists prefer to call 'externalities', processes imputed to be outside the field of economics 'proper'. Macro-economic (i.e. the study of the total economic activity in a nation) models are part of an idealist construct only partially rooted in actual reality: the importance and the intractability of the so called 'informal sector' in Kenya, as well as the irrelevance and untranslatable nature of the development concept itself are symptomatic of this.

The micro-dynamic economics (i.e. study of smaller decision-making units of the national economy e.g. firms and consumers) of the informal sector operate and proliferate with little reference, if not altogether in opposition, to the imperatives or 'organised' development as it is currently orchestrated by the United Nations institutions and the World Bank. The world of the informal sector is characterised by a mixture of local cultures and technologies with certain infusion of outside imports which, after assimilation, take on an entirely localised character. This renders them virtually immune to universalist development. Everything points in the direction of the co-existence of two entirely different economic practices that stem from disparate cultural understandings of economics and, by implication, society itself.

Amidst so many paralysing economic-isms inherited from the nineteenth century, only culture allows each generation and nation the possibility of autonomously ascribing meaning and direction to its future. As the unitary New World order model is being imposed with increasing vigour, increasingly it will be resisted. Popular resistance and popular ingenuity – as exemplified again by the recent Chiapas uprising in Southern Mexico – have been a constant obstacle to the march of modernity, which made its inroads largely at the expense of the peasantry. And no impositions can ever prevent economic and social life from continuing to re-invent itself. Not for nothing has the informal sector of the economy been called the 'invisible economy', it remains invisible to the production indicators that yield the statistics of the formal economy.

A new practice rooted in the principle of Human Scale Development (HSD) has come to be known as 'ecological economics', holistic or 'barefoot economics'. HSD is based on the imperative of the satisfaction of fundamental basic human needs, the generation of a growing level of (economic) self-reliance and the construction of organic articulations of people with nature and technology, global processes with local activity, of the personal with social, of planning with autonomy and of civil society with the government. People are, as they always have been and ought to be, the real champions of their own development and future. In other words, HSD is sympathetic to autonomous human agency: development cannot be built on imposition, on transfers, plans or interventions. The essence of development is creation, innovation and invention, not just pre-planned and pre-targeted economic growth. Economics, which etymologically shares its root 'oikos' ('home' in Greek) with ecology (the art of managing the home), is by definition 'ecological'. There is nothing intrinsically wrong with oiko-economists, or by implication, with development economics as such. The multiple crises of development find their origin not in economics, but in the heads of the economists who, for reasons best known to themselves, did not take up the challenges thrown in their path, or who have concentrated increasingly on issues which, in the end, do not make sense, even on the basis of purely economic criteria. Economics, it must not be forgotten, is the daughter of moral philosophy, which in turn, is concerned with the Aristotelian 'summum bonum', or the pursuit of human happiness. The idea of a 'human scales is at the very core of economics, and has always been' (Max Neef *et al.*, 1989).

Ecological economics is the economics of the future, if only because the economics of the future has to be ecological for there to be a future at all. It will allow the refocusing on the economics of well-being, displaced for so long by the economics of well-having. The all-consuming question of classical economics: 'how to have more of the same?' will turn into subordinate questions such as: 'How much is enough?' In other words: 'Are people happier?' 'Do they feel more realised?' 'Do they feel more in ownership and control of their lives?' In the name of reform and modernisation and the irresistible march of market forces, innumerable economies, otherwise perfectly capable of looking after themselves and of providing precisely, the quality of life hinted at in the questions of above, have been obliterated or have become extinct. The destruction of the peasantry and its mode of production is at the root of most social upheavals in this century: dispossessed and marginalised people become totally vulnerable and dependent. Rural areas in Kenya, once self-sufficient, were invaded and re-settled by immigrant commercial farmers intent on cash-crop production, squeezing the food-producing interests and potential of women and their children. When the same market forces caused a collapse in the price of those crops, people lost everything they had. A displaced peasantry on the fringes of large towns and cities was bound to be the outcome: in real terms, a 'humanisation of the landscape' happening in reverse.

When the term 'informal sector' was coined – as usual by economists, who are quite adept at such negativism (see Table 6.2.1) – as usual, the focus was on Africa. From an HSD perspective, the informal economy is synonymous with the resistance of traditional society to the incursions of an alien transplanted development model. There is no compelling reason for not referring to it, positively, as 'popular, vernacular, convivial, relational or barefoot' economics. It was the discovery of this positive dimension of the informal sector which made Max Neef decide to break with the conventional economics and, as he recalls – 'step in the mud'. He had come to conclusion that:

> ...continuing to be engaged (as a conventional economist) in efforts to diagnose poverty, to measure 'it' and to devise indicators in order to set up a statistical and conceptual threshold... then to participate in even costlier conferences in order to communicate the findings, to interpret the meaning of the findings, and (my God!) criticise the methodology behind the findings... all this made me feel at a certain point that I was happily engaged in a rather obscene ritual (Max-Neef 1992).

Barefoot economics may, in material terms be the economics of the poor. In the eyes of the barefoot economist, they are rich in relationship, creativity, innovation, and inventiveness.

How come the informal sector has been discovered particularly in the Third World, when it exists everywhere and always has? It is as though someone wanted to accuse developing countries of delinquency relative to economic rationality.

Table 6.2.1   Informal Sector: an Economic of the Delinquent

Latouche, 1992: 'Should what is known as':	The 'informal' sector The non-structured sector The non-organised sector The outlaw economy The parallel economy The bazaar economy The a-legal/illegal sector The not-to-be-taken-seriously sector
'be called':	The substantive sector Subsistence economy Vernacular economy Convivial economy Folk economy The economics of solidarity Barefoot economics The Relational economy/society Popular economics The economy of affection (Hyden) The Tontine economy (Sizoo) The grocery economy (Zaoual) The economy of the 'symbolic sites' (Zaoual)

For the barefoot economist ready to 'step in the mud', people are not problems, they are the solution: this fundamental wisdom has been expressed by various cultures in their proverbs. For the Wolof of West Africa, people are a remedy for people. And: 'the lack of means is already a means' (Pradervand, 1989). Max Neef, taking Chile as an example of self-reliance, demonstrates that:

...in every community, one finds resources from within: Mama Emilia has an absolutely extraordinary garden here: she produces a variety of at least fifty or sixty things which allow her family, as far as food is concerned, to be totally self-reliant, and on this tiny plot, she produces virtually everything she needs. What we are trying to do is to motivate her to teach other women to organise a little farm like this, in order to contribute to the improvement of everyone's quality of life. (Max Neef, 1992)

The invisible world of barefoot economics – on paper, Mama Emilia's family has the income of a street-beggar in Calcutta, but in reality there is little that they have to do without: 'they weld, they weed, they construct, they plant'. All this does not appear in the national accounts. It does not contribute, in the rubrics of conventional economics, to economic growth nor to 'development'. In other words, the wealth of such a family cannot be measured by the yardsticks of conventional economics: the conventional economics cannot even 'see' them, nor translate the quality of life which is the family's daily experience into statistical data, even if it tried. This is consistent with the fact that none of the things which fundamentally matter to the quality of people's lives, can be 'provided for' or bought. Economics assumes a direct correlation between the subjective-particular and economic goods. This correlation is assumed to manifest itself in market demand which can be quantified and provided for by the production of goods. As needs are conceived of as particular to each individual person, there is no reason to believe these needs (wants) should not change over time, differ according to culture and environment, and indeed be virtually unlimited, bearing out Gandhi's famous dictum that: 'there is enough for everyone's need, but never enough for everyone's greed'. The main factor missing from this logic of the market is the differentiation between needs and satisfiers.

Satisfiers: HSD analysis drastically breaks with this mechanistic correlation between needs (wants) and goods by introducing the concept of satisfier. The need for subsistence (Table 6.2.2) is a fundamental need which tops the list. But it is just one of a total of nine fundamental needs. Food and shelter, often described as needs, and on which development economics under the trickle-down principle almost exclusively concentrates, are not needs as such, but satisfiers of the fundamental need for subsistence. In much the same way, education is a satisfier of the need for understanding. The concept of 'satisfier', is thus at odds with mainstream Basic Needs Approach (BNA) orthodoxy which has been with us since it was introduced by the ILO in the mid-1970s. BNA, 'the provision of a minimum level of basic needs for all the people', was identified as a new development objective. According to the original ILO documents, Basic Needs involves:

> ...the setting of basic level of needs for all the people. This will involve the setting of: (a) minimum standard of household consumption, i.e. food and nutrition, housing, clothing etc., (b) minimum targets for the provision of essential services, particularly clean water, sanitation, public transport, education and health services and (c) the opportunity for productive and satisfying employment as a means of generating the production and incomes needed to meet the above 'goals' and as an end in itself. (ILO, L976a)

It is symptomatic of development economics as we know it to concentrate on 'basic' needs such as clothing, food, shelter, and health – the economics of survival – and call this development. At best they may be said to form a basis for development. In a 'developed' world, therefore, people do not have needs, but wants and desires which have to be pandered to. Those desires and wants are in essence infinite (as well as insatiable) because they are based on purely transient, fashionable preferences (Kamenetzky, Mario 1992). The real basic need, however:

> is not any of these, it is to do things for themselves, i.e. to create, for being human is creative, innovative and inventive and this is what distinguishes the human from the animal in oneself. The animal, indeed, needs to be fed and clothed and sheltered and medically cared for and taught how to find all these, but the human needs to be fulfilled by creative, innovative and inventive acts. (Rahman, 1992)

A multi-dimensional taxonomy of needs Table 6.2.2 establishes a clear-cut distinction between needs, goods and satisfiers:

1. Needs not only encompass human deprivations (for example, poverty as deprivation of consumption goods) but also individual and collective creative, innovative and inventive human potential.

2. Satisfiers are individual forms of being, having, doing and interacting which 'actualise' those needs in the present space and time. Satisfiers may include forms of organisation, political structures, social practices, subjective conditions, values and norms, spaces, context and modes and various types of behaviour and attitudes. A satisfier is, ultimately, the way in which a need is expressed.

3. Economic goods, finally, are objects or artefacts which affect the efficiency of the satisfiers. Satisfiers are to be historical, and cultural manifestations of needs just as economic goods are their material manifestation.

Table 6.2.2   Matrix of Needs and Satisfiers*

Needs According to existential /axiological categories	Being	Having	Doing	Interacting
Subsistence	1/Physical health, mental health, equilibrium, sense of humour, adaptability	2./Food, shelter, work	3/Feed, procreate, rest, work	4/Living environment, social setting
Protection	5/Care, adaptability, autonomy, equilibrium, solidarity	6 Insurance systems, savings, social security, health systems, rights, family, work	7/Cooperate, prevent, plan, take care of, cure, help	8/Living space, social environment, dwelling

Affection	9/ Self-esteem, solidarity, respect, tolerance, generosity, receptiveness, passion, determinatio n, sensuality, sense of humour	10/Friendshi ps, family partnerships relationships with nature	11/Make love, caress, express emotions, share, take care of, cultivate, appreciate	12/Privacy, intimacy, home, spaces of togetherness
Understandi ng	13/Critical conscience, receptiveness, curiosity, astonishment , discipline, intuition, rationality	14/Literature, teachers method, educational policies, communicati on policies	15/Investigate , study, experiment, educate, analyse, meditate	16/Settings of formative interaction, schools, universities, academies, groups, communities, family
Participation	17/Adaptabili ty receptiveness, solidarity, willingness, determinatio n, dedication, respect, passion, sense of humour	18/Rights, responsibiliti es, duties, privileges, work	19/Become affiliated, cooperate, propose, share dissent obey, interact, agree on, express opinions	20/Settings of participative interaction, parties, associations, churches, communities, neighbourho ods, family
Idleness	21/Curiosity, receptiveness, imagination, recklessness, sense of humour, tranquillity, sensuality	22/Games, spectacles, clubs, parties, peace of mind	23/Day-dream, brood, recall old times, give way to fantasies, remember, relax, have fun, play	24/ Privacy, intimacy, spaces of closeness, free time, surroundings , landscape

Creation	25/Passion, determination, intuition, imagination, boldness, rationality, autonomy, inventiveness curiosity	26/Abilities, skills, method, work	27/Work, invent, build, design, compose, interpret	28/Productive and feedback settings, workshops, cultural groups, audiences, spaces for expression, temporal freedom
Identity	29/Sense of belonging, consistency, differentiation, self-esteem, assertiveness	30/Symbols, language, religion, habits, customs, reference groups, sexuality, values, norms, historical memory, work	31/Commit oneself, integrate oneself, confront, decide on, get to know oneself, actualise oneself, grow	32/Social rhythms, everyday settings, settings which one belong to, maturation stages
Freedom	33/Autonomy, self-esteem, determination, passion, assertiveness, boldness, rebelliousness, tolerance	34/Equal rights	35/Dissent, choose, be different from, run risks, develop awareness, commit oneself, disobey	36/Temporal/spatial plasticity

★The column of BEING registers attributes. Personal or collective, that are expressed as nouns. The column of HAVING registers institutions, norms, mechanisms, tools (not in a material sense) laws etc., that can be expressed in one or more words. The column of DOING, registers actions, personal or collective, that can be expressed as verbs. The column of INTERACTING, registers location and milieus (as times and space) Source: Max Neef: 1989.

The interrelationship between those three – needs, satisfiers and economic goods – is dynamic: needs are not, simply, either fulfilled or unfulfilled, satisfied or unsatisfied. Because they exist in dialogical tension with the satisfiers and goods, needs should be conceived of as forever in the process of being 'realised', 'experienced' or 'actualised'. In Table 6.2.2 needs have been subdivided along existential categories (horizontal axis; being, having, doing and interaction) and axiological categories (vertical axis) the needs for (1) subsistence, (2) protection, (3) affection, (4) understanding, (5) participation, (6) idleness and (7) creation, innovation, or invention. These needs have existed since the dawn of time, probably since *homo habilis*, and certainly since *homo sapiens* first roamed the earth. The need for (8) identity may have appeared much later and the need for (9) freedom possibly later still. The existence of another fundamental need (10) transcendence, is not yet recognised as universal, but may become so at some time in the future.

Economism, and its close relative, developmentalism, assume that human needs (wants) are infinite, that they change all the time, and that they differ according to a host of local and historical determinants: the moment one need is satisfied, ten others jostle to take its place. Fundamental needs, by contrast, are finite and few. This way of reinterpreting needs is fundamental if the economics of the future is to be sound in ecological and ethical terms. The answer to the question 'How much is enough?' is contained in embryo in the fact that needs are not infinite. If a distinction is made between needs and satisfiers, then, for example, food and shelter are more than mere basic needs: they are, at the same time, satisfiers of the fundamental need for subsistence. Allopathic and preventive medicine satisfy the fundamental need for protection. Education, literacy, orality, orature, communication and learning satisfy the need for understanding. The liberating aspect of thinking in terms of fundamental needs are finite and few. Over-consumption and over-development are symptomatic of the frantic search for satisfaction of basic needs *ad absurdum*. Genuine development 'knows its limits', in material terms; when it comes to what is both desirable and possible from the 'perspective of becoming' the sky is the limit. If it is the limit accepted that human agency is at the core of what it is to develop, then it is of secondary importance whether this agency operates in a resource-rich or a resource-poor environment. Even if, hypothetically, society were able, by dint of the most sophisticated breakthrough technologies, to keep pace with the whirling vortex of the consumption needs and wants of a multi-billion world population, this would not necessarily mean that the resulting society would be any wiser or any more humane: development is not just about 'coping' (a term increasingly used by population experts) or 'surviving' (used for example in the title of the Brandt Report: a blueprint for survival) or 'muddling through'. It is about life, and about the space and freedom we create.

6.2.2 ECONOMICS OF SELF-RELIANCE

The basic principles of self-reliance are: first, some mechanism in addition to the free market must be found for the satisfaction of basic human needs, while at the same time not limiting economic activity a priori to the basics. The satisfaction of people's basic needs is obviously the only way to self-reliance. The present opposite tendency is still to equate a demand backed-up with money as a basic human need, because at least one human being 'needs' it, or at least demands it.

Second, we have to ask ourselves: how we can produce what is needed, relying on ourselves, on our own production capacity, meaning nature, (land, raw materials, energy); labour – skilled and unskilled; capital – liquid and fixed; research – basic and applied; management and administration? All these factors of production, as well as the output, the goods and services, come in crude and refined versions. In conventional theory, protected by a misapplication of Ricardo's ideal comparative advantage, a division of labour takes place with the centre applying refined factors for the refined production of refined products, and the periphery applying crude factors for the crude production of crude products, exchanging these with each other. Thus, the centre treats the periphery as an external sector of its own economy; as a place to fetch or use nature and dump pollutants; as a place to use cheap labour and dump excess labour from back home (a major function of colonialism); as a place to export excess, tied capital for specific investment purposes and from which to import profits, in a broad sense, as untied capital; as a place to carry out research projects that could not be done at home, while at the same time importing researchers trained at the expense of the periphery country, and as a place to administer, but not be administered by issuing SOPs (Standard operating procedures) from the centre. Self-reliance implies a total rejection of this 'division of labour', a rejection of the use of others as an external sector for dumping the negative externalities and of denying them the positive externalities in a production process. It means treating others like an internal sector.

Hence the basic rule of self-reliance is: 'Produce what we need in Kenya using our own resources, internalising the challenges this involves, growing with challenges, neither giving the most challenging tasks (positive externalities) to somebody else on whom we become dependent, nor exporting negative externalities to somebody else to whom we do damage and who may become psychologically dependent on us.'

By producing what we consume and consuming what we produce, rather than doing either through exchange, by definition we keep the externalities, positive and negative, for ourselves. The justification for so doing is clear: we will enjoy the positive externalities, rather than giving them away, and at the same time we will be responsible ourselves for the negative externalities (e.g. pollution, depletion, dirty, degrading, boring work, highly inegalitarian income distribution, top-heavy social formations). We can fight the negative consequences ourselves, the distance between cause and effect being a short one.

For instance, an obvious way of preventing pollution of rivers from riverside factories will be to force the management of the factory to drink downstream water; the rule would have an immediate impact. Moreover, there is another hidden moral behind this little example: it is not enough that the effects are localised in the sense of being this side of the horizon. They also have to hit high up where decisions are made or at least can be more easily made. Those who have made the beds have an obligation to lie on them.

Thus self-reliance cuts both ways: it preserves the positive externalities by trading much less upwards, and protects against the negative externalities by trading much less downwards. It is a measure of economic defence as well as a pact of non-aggressiveness. In self-reliance there is both an element of enlightened egoism (do not give away the positive externalities) and enlightened altruism (do not damage others by exporting negative externalities).

Yet the third consideration is that there may well be a discrepancy between the list of what is needed and the list of what can be produced on a local basis even with the best possible use of human imagination. If only one factor of production is missing or is in inadequate supply, the production will not take place. The solution to this problem is, of course, exchange and trade. And this is where self-reliance spills over the local borders and becomes international and global interdependence. Nothing in self-reliance is against trade, provided it takes place according to the following two rules:

1. The exchange should be carried out so that the net balance of costs and benefits, including externalities, for the parties to the exchange is as equal as possible. In practice this will point to the direction of intra-sectorial rather than inter-sectorial trade; in other words exchange of primary products (raw materials, commodities, agricultural products); or exchange of secondary products (manufactures, industrial goods including high technology); or tertiary products (services). The moment one exchanges primary products for secondary products or tertiary products there is a problem: the externalities may be extremely different and very difficult to compare or equalise. Provided that the parties to the interaction stick to the exchange within a single sector of production, they need not necessarily be at the same level of technical economic development. But if they are at the same level, the proportion of primary/secondary tertiary outputs is more equal, and equitable exchange would come more easily. A useful rule of thumb is that the total degree of processing involved in the items for exchange should be at about the

same level in both directions.

2   One field of production – production for basic needs –
     should be carried out in such a way that the country is at least
     potentially self-sufficient, if not self-reliant. This includes the
     production particularly of food, clothing, shelter, energy and
     whatever is needed for health, education, and home defence.
     If production exceeds consumption, then there is no problem
     – provided one does not make others dependent on oneself
     through trade in this field of basic needs. If production is
     short of consumption, there has to be exchange according to
     the preceding rule, which again would be in order, provided
     steps are taken and concrete plans are made so that in times of
     crisis society can nevertheless be self-sufficient. The crisis
     planning of Switzerland is a good example of such plans.

Fourth, typical of the theory of self-reliance is its scope for
transcending the nakedness of economic relations. There is a
strong normative injunction, based on a feeling of compassion
and a will to resist threats and the actual exercise of violence,
direct or structural, from the outside. At the same time, it puts
some limitations on the kinds of contractual relations that should
legitimately be entered into. Self-reliance is psycho-politics as
much as economics, it presupposes, and builds self-respect. It
does not mean more or less splendid isolation, but spins a web of
interaction that is mainly horizontal rather than vertical.

Self-reliance will not be a theory only for the Kenyan
government, but equally for village communities, locations,
divisions and districts. This is where the theory of global interdependence starts, as part of, and not separate from, the theory of
self-reliance, which thus aims to avoid being or becoming
dependent by fostering both independence and inter-dependence.

6.2.3 ENCOURAGING HOME-GROWN VILLAGE ECONOMY

It is now more than two hundred years since the famous French
Revolution occurred. An important task for political and
economic philosophy at the ending of the twentieth into the
twenty-first century is to reinterpret the role of democracy,
liberty, equality, freedom, social justice and solidarity – in an

economic order pervaded by processes of enabling and self-development.

One aspect of economic development in Kenya's twenty-first century must be a systematic approach to village community development on 'home-grown economy' lines. This will involve campaigns and constructive action by local people at the levels of district, division, location and village levels, and also in the cities, towns especially in the squatter/slum settlements and mixed rural/urban towns to build a self-reliant economy. It will mean people in the district themselves working out:

(a) ways in which a greater proportion of local needs can be met by local work programmes using local resources;

(b) ways by which a greater proportion of local income can be encouraged to circulate locally (instead of leaking out of the local economy, in order to generate local work and local economic activity;

(c) ways in which a greater proportion of local savings of all kinds can be channelled into local investments or loans, in order to contribute to local economic development.

In non-financial terms more self-reliant local economic development will involve households, villages and squatter/slum settlements becoming places where goods and services are produced by the residents for themselves and one another; and in most villages, locations, divisions, districts, towns, cities and regions, it will involve a degree of local import substitution, i.e. some replacements of goods produced coming from outside Kenya by locally produced goods and services. This will affect the production and distribution of food and energy, patterns of industry and employment, the role of education in the local community, health planning and housing, and many other aspects of economic and social life.

A good example, which could be replicated in Kenya, is the 'Home-grown Economy' project in the city of St Paul, Minnesota, USA. Under this project, described to me by the Mayor's office, 'job creation remains an important goal, but the project broadens the focus by emphasising the most efficient management of all local resources. Its goal is to extract the maximum value from the village community's human, natural and technological resources. Its aggregate result is significant increases in local wealth, added employment, a more diverse and resilient economic base, increased citizen efficacy, and a self-reliant orientation among St Paul's institutions'. In supporting new enterprises, emphasis is given to local ownership, diversifying the local economy, direct benefit to the local community in terms of the products and services offered, and other criteria related to local economic self-reliance. A local fund to provide local venture capital at rates of return lower than the prevailing market rates is supported by the investment portfolios of a group of local insurance companies, which recognise that they have a direct economic stake in their own local village economy and have a revolving fund to provide loans to businesses that meet the 'Home-grown Economy' criteria.

There are three key principles for this new economic order geared to creating self-reliance and well-being for the Kenyan people. Firstly, self-reliance must be enabling i.e. decolonising peoples' minds, by the economic and social development where there is a space for the flowering of human creativity and the 'right to invent their own future', secondly, self-reliance must be conserving i.e. enabling Kenyans themselves to manage Kenya's environment, biodiversity and all diverse cultural forms and thirdly, self-reliance must be organised and understood as a multi-level traditional Kenyan system. An important task for all Kenyan leaders in the twenty-first century, will be to clarify and put in practice these principles and their practical applications and implications. These are dynamic principles in the sense that they indicate a direction for development and progress. Their application will still be valid in two to three hundred years time, but the practical ways of applying them will be different from the year 2003.

Enabling people to understand and master their own destiny, and conserving their environment and management of resources, are not precisely symmetrical. Enabling Kenyan people to develop their creative and innovative capacities and potential is more positive, conserving is linked to class struggle, gender and the environment – women's bodies and nature were both colonised by patriarchy and capitalism operating in tandem (Mies, 1986). Enriching Kenya's natural environment, biodiversity and resource base would be the counterpart to 'enabling'. Our mission and aim is to leave Kenya's natural environment better when we depart from it than it was when we came in. This is certainly a worthy mission and aim for human life on this planet. Environmental conservation shades into environmental enrichment, just as to take an example of enabling – preventative health care shades into health promotion. Environmental conservation and environmental enrichment both represent environmental investment, just as preventative health care and health promotion both represent social investment. They are all concerned with safeguarding and creating the environmental or social wealth of our country.

(a) Enabling – Kenya's economy in the twenty-first century must be systematically enabling. Instead of systematically creating and extending dependency, it must systematically foster self-reliance and the capacity for self-development. Self-reliance does not mean self-sufficiency or selfish isolation. Self-reliance requires the capacity to cooperate freely with others. Self-development includes the development of the capacity for cooperative self-reliance.

Enabling and self-development, as a two-sided process like teaching and learning, should pervade twenty-first century Kenyan economic and social life. Our policy of greater self-reliance, not greater dependency should be a continuing aim of economic units – persons, cities, towns and villages – at every level of the nation's economic system. Enabling smaller units - villages and towns to become economically more self-reliant and to acquire the capacity to develop themselves, should be one of the main functions of the larger units which contain them – such as districts and the whole country. Many of the tasks in Kenya for the twenty-first century will involve working out ways of applying the two-sided process of enabling and self-development through-out the nation's economy, in all its component sub-units including the lives of individual Kenyans which must be improved and enriched in the shortest time possible.

Enabling and self-development represents a fundamental change from the conventional pattern of economic development. That has created and reinforced dependency and domination. 'Development starts in the mind, and the greatest tool of domination has always been the colonisation of people's minds' (Ngugi wa Thiongo, 1986). What is happening in Kenya today is a repetition of what happened three centuries ago in the early stages of industrialised countries' development. First people were excluded from a self-reliant subsistence way of life and forced to be dependent on paid labour. Then, as development proceeded, dependency widened and deepened. People became conditioned to depend on employers for work. As consumers they became dependent on businesses, professional organisations and government agencies, which then persuaded them to regard an ever expanding range of goods and services as necessities of life.

By developing a more self-reliant economic and social attitude, and thereby taking more control of our economic destiny, Kenyan people and localities will be able to secure a materially adequate and sustainable standard of living, a socially acceptable and psychologically rewarding quality of life – for our families, for one another, and for all Kenyans in the succeeding generations.

This will bring more justice and equality in our economic life than we have today; not the kind of justice and equality that is administered to subordinate people by those from on high. In the new economic order – self-reliance, justice and equality will be brought about by liberating our people from dependency, helping them to provide for themselves and for one another as Kenyans irrespective of tribes, ethnic origin, colour or race and enabling them to take more control of their own economic destinies, rather than making the less fortunate depend on transfers of welfare and aid from those who are richer and more powerful than themselves. The decolonisation of the mind, therefore has to be the first precondition of development which starts 'from where people are, who they are, what they can do and know how to do' (Bernard Ouedraogo, 1984).

(b) Conserving – all Kenyans must be systematically conserving, and self-reliant instead of systematically wasteful and polluting. Conventional economic thinking treats material economic activities as if each one were a separate linear process, starting with the extraction of resources (from an infinite pool of resources in the natural world, which is seen as being outside the economic system altogether), continuing with the use of the resources in the production of the goods, and ending with the disposal of wastes (into an infinite sink in the natural world, which is again seen as outside the economic system). The result is that today's economic system operates as if it were a machine designed to take resources out of the Earth, convert them into wastes, and return them to the Earth as wastes. By its very nature, it is systematically wasteful and polluting.

The new self-reliant economic order by contrast, must see the whole of economic activity as a single continuing cyclical process, consisting of countless inter-related cyclical sub-processes, with the wastes from each providing resources for others. It must design the economic system as an organic part of the natural world not as a machine external to it, a reintegration which will also mean giving up the converse assumption that the natural world is a limitless pool and sink external to the economic system. The economic system must thus be systematically conserving. 'The point to emphasise here is that a more conserving approach and a more enabling and self-reliant approach to economic life will be mutually reinforcing'.

Using resources efficiently and conservingly contributes to self-reliance. The more a city, a town or a village or other local economy can recycle its own flows of food, water, energy, wastes and money within its own closed-loop system i.e. the more conserving, as opposed to wasteful and ecologically damaging and polluting, a local economy can become, the more self-reliant it will be. The more it can supply itself with food, energy and materials by using its wasteland for food growing, by capturing energy from internal sources, and recycling its wastes, the less dependent it will be on imports of food, energy and materials; and the more its people's income will circulate within the local economy and generate activity there. As urban/rural planners are becoming aware, it makes sense – from the point of view of socio-economic as well as physical planning – to think of a city's economy as an ecosystem (Tan Douglas, 1983).

The connection between local economic autonomy and ecological sustainability runs the other way too. Local people who control their own local economy are less likely to waste their resources and pollute their environment than distant decision-makers with no local roots. As the Brundtland Commission found, the integration of economic and ecological goals is

> ...best secured by decentralising the management of resources upon which local communities depend and giving these communities an effective say over the use of these resources. (Brundtland Commission, 1990)

Meanwhile, the World Health Organisation's work on Health For All by the Year 2000 has been reaching similar conclusions. WHO's 1986 Charter for Health Promotion stresses the empowerment of communities, their ownership and control of their own endeavour and destinies as the heart of the process of strengthening community action on which health promotion ultimately depends; and the concept of the self-reliant, ecological city is providing a focus for WHO's international Healthy Cities programme.

Cities and other localities are not the only economic units to which the ecosystem concept applies. We have to treat households and nations and the global economy itself as ecosystem economies, and work out new approaches to more self-reliant and sustainable development for them. Investing in self-reliance and sustainability will be increasingly relevant to them all.

Conventional economic thinking has classified social and environmental measures as wealth consumption, not wealth creation. This has been reflected by the fact that such measures have always been largely remedial. So health policies and health services have been more concerned with remedying sickness after the event than with positively improving the public health and enabling people to be healthier. As the Brundtland Commission put it, 'environmental management practices have focused largely upon after-the-fact repair of damage: reforestation, reclaiming desert and arid lands, rebuilding urban environment, restoring natural habitats, and rehabilitating wild lands' (Brundtland

Commission, 1990).

The twenty-first century economic order rejects these conventional perceptions and conventional policy orientations. The idea that economic policies are wealth-creating and social policies are wealth consuming, and that economic policies should therefore be given priority over social policies, is simply not realistic. In that context, the need for an improved social environment, work opportunities, affordable housing, health care system, education, leisure facilities, and improved income, and above all, an improvement in the capacity and confidence of local people to do more for themselves, clearly has to be approached as a single constellation of need, not a collection of distinct and separate needs to be met in distinct and separate ways – some economic, some social. In the context of sustainable development for example, in countries such as Kenya, the Brundtland Commission asked these governments to consider abandoning 'the false division between "productive" or "economic" expenditures and "social" expenditures. Policy makers must realise that spending on population activities and on other efforts to raise human potential is crucial to a nation's economic and productive activities'.

Investment to create social and environmental wealth will have a vital role in the new twenty-first-century economic order, and an important economic strand will be to develop the practice and theory of social and environmental investment. New criteria and procedures for evaluating, accounting and auditing such investments will have to be worked out. New institutions will be needed to enable people, as well as public sector agencies, to channel their savings into this investment.

6.2.4 SELF-RELIANCE AND INTERDEPENDENCE

Self-reliance starts with the idea of producing things for yourself rather than getting them through exchange. In some ways exchange is the lazy way out: 'I have something in excess, send it down to the storehouse, ship it out, get in return something somebody else has in excess provided we both agree on the prices,' and that is it. This is simplistic to the point of irresponsibility – it does not ask what additional impacts the agreement reached might have on both parties, on nature and on the rest of the world. We should be able to do better than that.

A more positive argument, however, would be that it may be easier for the peripheries to develop their autonomous technical and economic capacity if they are only left free to do so, benefiting from all the challenges and positive externalities and being themselves responsible for the negative externalities they create. Is it not our experience as teachers and parents, that children develop best, not by being perennially dependent, all the time receiving 'advice', ready-made products (food, shelter, pocket-money) and services (care) and never having to fend for themselves 'to swim or sink', but through self-reliance they develop ultimate self-sufficiency? Why should the above theory of communities, countries and regions be different? Could it be that the centre countries want periphery communities to remain dependent on the capital cities, or they want periphery countries to remain dependent on centre countries and periphery regions on centre regions? Are the centre countries afraid that otherwise they in the centre might themselves decline?

That is not to say that self-reliance and global interdependence is the formula for the centre's premature demise. Except for those at the very top, it is thought that, this is a formula for the centre's regeneration. Thus, there is no reason at all why the rest of the world should be dependent on Japanese/American electronics of all kinds, cameras, watches, cars and motorcycles. Why should others deny themselves the growth they could obtain through their own production of these challenging goods? And even those at the very top may contemplate whether it is not also in their interest to seek arrangements with some built-in stability, being neither dependent on them in a situation from which, sooner or later, they may want to withdraw, possibly in a very violent manner. Ultimately, dependency is very unpleasant for everyone involved. Yet it is the consequence of conventional economic theory and practice. A new economic practice based on self-reliance has to be based on a whole new economic theory. Here we are only at the beginning.

The shift from dependency to self-reliance, involving individuals, communities, countries and regions endeavouring to meet as much of their consumption from their own production as possible, will reverberate throughout every aspect of economic and social life, i.e. working patterns, food production, the use of energy and other resources, education and training, new technology, modern communication systems, entertainment and politics. All these areas can be very rewarding and useful to a community doing things for themselves and between individuals, even in an informal economy and working without being paid. Furthermore, the fact of a person's very existence as an individual human being, are given value by a community that is seeking maximum internal self-reliance at every stage before looking to the next level for the provision or exchange of resources beyond the capacity of the stage in question.

An emphasis on self-reliance has special implications for public expenditure, especially that part of it which is communal expenditure at an outer level (e.g. the national level) designed to meet needs at an inner level (e.g. the inner city), which that level is unable to provide for itself through its own self-reliance. With self-reliance as its objective, this expenditure would be subject to very different evaluative criteria than at present. It would seek to serve three main purposes.

First, it would be exclusively geared towards the satisfaction of basic needs, as agreed in the context of the society in question. Second order wants and, even more, luxuries, which a level could not provide directly for itself, would have to be obtained through the exchange of surpluses i.e. through trade. Self-initiated local exchange systems of these kinds can be seen either as a way of facilitating multilateral barter among local groups for whom money is in short supply, or as a way of providing an alternative form of money. In practice these come to the same thing. It would be unrealistic to exaggerate the impact which these experiments with new local currencies and related forms of self-financing for small-scale economic activities can make or to forget that, because they still have to swim against the prevailing tide, they will meet with many practical difficulties. But they do suggest that, along with other local financial innovations like local investment funds, local government bonds, and so on, local currencies and quasi-currencies can have a significant role as an aspect of local self-reliance.

Second, it would be expenditure that was either especially appropriate to the outer level, i.e. providing goods and services which, by virtue of their nature, an inner level could not provide itself; or was redistributive, i.e. resulting in a transfer of resources from a richer inner level to a poorer one. Gone would be the wholesale levying of taxes on an inner level by an outer level, for the outer level either to give the money back with strings attached or to provide a central control service for the purposes of the outer level, which the inner level could perfectly well have provided for itself.

The third main purpose of public expenditure would be 'enabling'. The emphasis would shift away from public expenditure on the delivery of benefits and services to dependent clients, towards measures that enabled people to meet their own needs more self-reliantly. Thus, welfare benefits would be of such a form as to reduce the recipients' need of them. They would, as far as possible, increase the ability of recipients to make future provisions for themselves. The basic income guarantee is one such benefit, positively encouraging those unable to find full-time jobs to engage in any part-time or voluntary work of their choice, and to enhance their income or their skills. This is in sharp contrast to unemployment benefit, which, in the UK at least, actively discourages people from doing anything but looking for possibly full-time employment which does not exist.

'Our monetary and banking system is the product of harmful restrictions imposed by governments to increase their powers. They are certainly not institutions of which it can be said they have been tried and found good, since the people were not allowed to try any alternative.' In support of a free money movement comparable to the free trade movement of the nineteenth century, Professor F A Hayek has argued that the government monopoly of money has been the cause of four major defects – inflation, financial instability, undisciplined public expenditure and economic nationalism. He has proposed the denationalisation of money. The government monopoly should be replaced by competition in currency supplied by private users who, to preserve public confidence, will limit the quantity of the money they issue in order to maintain its value.

Hayek has also suggested that 'it will be through the credit card rather than through any kind of circulating token money that government monopoly of the issue of money will ultimately be broken'. The significance of electronic and plastic money has now begun to make itself fully felt, with credit cards and cash cards becoming accepted as a feature of economic life. The practical feasibility of proposals like Hayek's for denationalising money now needs to be established in the light of our new understanding of money. That is of money, not primarily as paper or metal items which physically circulate, but as a scoring arrangement made up of a system of accounts, in which the provision of metal and paper tokens that can be physically transferred from payer to payee is becoming a secondary feature – to facilitate particular types of transaction, especially those that are occasional and small. Monopoly control of the money system is the most basic impediment to greater economic self-reliance.

6.2.5 CONCLUSION

We started with the conventional economics, about Kenya's economy, then, the taken-for-granted 'informal sector', the so-called non-structural sector, that illegitimate alien in constant rebellion which insists on standing out as a sore thumb against the healthy, organised, classified and quantified backdrop of the world of mainstream economics. The choice obtained by market driven development is stark: either invisibility and oblivion or outlaw status for the nondescript, the non-structured, the non-organised, the illegal, not to be taken too seriously. The hope is that, like a bad headache, this misfit will 'pass away' or now regulated, integrated and up-rooted from its cultural moorings will become a culturally neutral and therefore a legitimate partner in the development business. In other words, the end result of the radical uprooting of the cultural from the economic will be extinction or co-option. Reality, however, is never neutral. Nor is the newly restructured, formalised parallel economy ever neutral, it has simply become part of a dominant world order which, for all its dominance and hegemony, is none the less culturally, politically determined. A culturally embedded economy becomes disembedded to the point of extinction or it is embedded into another, dominant, master-culture. Latouche typifies the process at work as 'the Westernisation of the entire world', under the guise, perhaps, of cultural and political neutrality, but in reality under the ethnocentric assumption that 'West is best'.

Riches and wealth come from diversity: uniformity means regression and ultimately extinction and death. This is a truth contained in the commonplace process of the life of sexual reproduction which allowed species to evolve, diversify and thrive for billions of years. But now in the twentieth century version of alchemy, economics, the attributes of diversity and non-conformity are negatively loaded: why else should what is different invariably be described in negative language? Considering the energy, brain-power and financial resources that go into research into economic development, the development enterprise is remarkably slow and inefficient.

It is not only inefficient, but also destructive – of values, of a sense of balance, of proportion and propriety, of a sense of justice, of the imperatives of the environment, of cultural identities, of everything which gives meaning and direction to human life. Development has shaken humanity, literally, to its very core: it has triggered the 'crisis of the foundations' (Max Neef, 1992).

The situation would be hopeless if indeed the culture of power were hegemonic but hope springs eternal in the realisation that there always will be the countervailing power of culture. This culture has the power to resist. It also has the power of building and rebuilding the artificially transformed economy autonomously. Culture means people, their ways of life, the 'matrix' in which their very cultural identities are shaped. Interest in cultural aspects of development does not stop at revealing some religious or sociological traits relating to custom or folklore. It demands the recognition of the existence of, and the entering into dialogue with, countless manifestations of culture – or a coming together of 'symbolic sites'. In that sense, development is the very opposite of all notions of trans-culturalism, globalism, and universalism which pretend to be valid for all people and all time: universal human rights, 'democracy', 'basic human needs' and so on. It is a time- and culture-sensitive notion such as satisfier which can bridge the gap between 'animal', 'dead' basic need and fundamental human needs, highlighting the notion that the essence of development is not provision but creation. And creation, 'the making of something out of nothing' (Oona King, 1998) lies at the heart of the meaning of culture.

Development in a country like Japan is more and more understood, not simplistically in terms of imitation of Western practice and patterns, but as an inner process directly linked to specific cultural values. The West, which has been delivering a cultural monologue for decades, not to say centuries, has to face up to the new Third World generations with a decolonised mind and the realisation that, in order to be acceptable and accepted, it is necessary first to become literate in the culture (and language) of 'the other'. The ethnocentric, mono-cultural interpretation of universality of science, technology, economics and development is well past its sell-by date. A new 'universal universality' has to be generated in mutually respectful dialogue. In the Golden Rule, the bedrock of universal ethics – we are called upon to treat others as we would want to be treated, this includes respect for human dignity.

Chapter VII
AGRICULTURE AND SELF-RELIANCE

7.1 Agricultural Development

7.1.1 AGRICULTURE AND RURAL DEVELOPMENT

> ...Genius is ninety per cent industriousness. The remaining ten per cent account for everything else.
>
> (Helmut V. Moltke)

History does not repeat itself, and as Kenya pursues its development efforts today, the circumstances are very different from those which confronted the now-developed countries when they began their industrialisation. Perhaps, the main difference is the rapid population growth in Kenya, which is without parallel in history. In the coming years, the most dramatic manifestation of this population explosion will be unprecedented increase in food deficits, as well as a rapid surge in the labour force, at a rate which the country will never be able to absorb. These two factors only reinforce the argument for giving greater priority to the agricultural sector. More than a passing fad or an obedient, self-serving response to the whims of aid donors, this new orientation must signify a profound change in Kenya's development strategies. Only when this priority is translated into action will it become a concrete reality rather than a mere good intention.

The major constraint affecting agricultural development in Kenya is the shortage of good quality arable land, exacerbated by already high population densities and continued rapid population growth. Only 33 per cent of Kenya's 570,000 km^2 can be considered high or medium quality land; another 9 per cent can produce crops, but is subject to periodic drought, and the remaining land area is suitable mainly for cattle production. Kenya's good quality arable land is situated in a relatively compact highland area, running south-east to north-west through Nairobi. The semi-arid country is located principally in the north and north-east and in parts of southern Kenya.

Agriculture is the dominant sector in Kenya, employing nearly 80 per cent of the population and contributing close to one-third of GDP. More than one half of output is produced on subsistence farms. Sustained growth in this sector is vital in generating food and employment for Kenya's rapidly growing population, in increasing agricultural exports (which currently account for one-third of total exports), and in providing raw materials for Kenya's largely agro-based industrial sector. Compared with other states in the region and developing countries elsewhere, the growth in Kenya's agricultural GDP over the last ten years (of about 3.5 per cent per annum) has been respectable. However it has been below the targets set in recent plans. Export crops have performed much better than food crops, and unless there is a substantial increase in the production of domestically consumed crops, the country faces the prospect of spending an increasing proportion of its foreign exchange earnings on importing its food supplies. With the limited availability of good land, future growth will, therefore, depend crucially on programmes and policies that promote the intensification of production through the greater use of inputs, particularly by small farms, as well as on research and extension services that are orientated towards food crops and the needs of small farmers.

In the years since independence, the increased production of cash crops and the growing commercialisation of smallholder agriculture have resulted in a certain movement of production structures from large-scale to small-scale farming. Three major groups of producers can be identified in the agricultural field, namely the subsistence sector consisting of smallholder and pastoral producers; a commercially orientated smallholder sector, producing both food and cash crops, and a large and medium farm sector. The growing significance of smallholder agriculture has provided a continuing stimulus to growth, and future agricultural development will depend largely on facilitating expansion of this sector. The altogether arbitrary cut-off point between small and medium/large farms, used in statistical analysis in Kenya, is a 20 NBS ha area. Defined in this sense, small-holdings including subdivided large and medium farms, account for three quarters of total agricultural output, some 55 per cent of marketed output, two-thirds of land devoted to arable agriculture, over 85 per cent of total agricultural employment, and about 70 per cent of total employment in Kenya. Smallholders have quickly adopted innovations, such as hybrid maize and grade cattle. By 1980, smallholders were producing about 60 per cent of marketed coffee and beef, 50 per cent of marketed milk, 45 per cent of marketed maize and sugar cane, and 35 per cent of marketed tea, and almost all the marketed production of cotton, pyrethrum, rice and tobacco. The average size of a smallholding is about two hectares, but over half of all smallholdings are under one hectare, and three quarters under two hectares.

There has been a significant decline in the size of the large and medium farm sector since independence. Large farms over 50 NBS ha now account for some 2.5 million NBS ha, with another 1 million NBS ha in the medium size range (20 to 50 NBS ha). Large and medium mixed farms produce mainly grains and livestock, with plantations growing sugarcane and sisal, and part of Kenya's coffee and tea.

The agricultural marketing system, which like the land tenure arrangements, is an inheritance from the colonial period, has been the subject of critical appraisal in the post-independence years. Prior to 1982, official prices for major domestic commodities (maize, wheat, milk, meat, sugarcane and cotton) lagged behind world prices and the agricultural sector's terms of trade deteriorated relative to the rest of the economy. Prices for the major export crops, coffee, tea, are not controlled. In 1982, government took deliberate steps to raise official prices for major crops. However, these prices remain somewhat inflexible, applying uniformly throughout the country, and allowing little seasonal or quality variation. Many farmers do not receive the full benefit of the official price, due to lengthy delays in payment by monopolistic parastatals and cooperatives, excessive handling charges often unrelated to commercial activities, and inefficient marketing systems. In providing consumer subsidies, government has also frequently set retail price ceilings for major foodstuffs (maize, meat, wheat flour, vegetable oil, milk, coffee, tea, and sugar), with a resultant squeezing of parastatal distribution margins, and consequential operating losses.

The government has generally restricted participation in the marketing and processing of maize, wheat, cotton and milk to parastatal marketing enterprises, whose operations are frequently inefficient. Of particular importance is the National Cereals and Produce Board (NCPB), which plays a central role in the food security field. Its relatively poor performance is characterised by large and increasing losses, and weak financial management. The 1980s formed Kenya Grain Growers' Cooperative Union (KGGCU) would appear to be concerned mainly with primary grain marketing, but its exact role in this area remains poorly defined, and it has also been experiencing financial difficulties. Even without legal barriers to entry, the private sector and cooperative have encountered difficulties in developing their marketing channels, due to long-term credit limitations, the administrative regulation of investment, export and imports, and the lack of support from government for small-scale enterprises in this area.

7.1.2 LAND USE AND CLASS STRUCTURE

The existence of social class is quite marked in Kenya. The single most important distinguishing class factor is land ownership, which has been at the core of political conflict in Kenya since the arrival of foreign settlers in the country. This struggle took a particularly acute form in the 1950s during the so-called Mau Mau uprising. The transitional period from colonial rule to independence saw some redistribution of land through settlement schemes (Abrams, 1979), but the general pattern of land ownership was largely carried over into the post-independence era, albeit with indigenous Kenyans replacing the departing white settlers, as the landed class. The pre-independence class structure has been indigenised. The privatisation of land ownership introduced by the Swynnerton plan in the mid-1950s, meant that land had become a commercial commodity to be bought and sold, and to be put up as collateral when seeking credit. The commitment to private ownership of land, was reiterated in the 1983 KANU Manifesto (KANU, 1983). Since the post-independence period, the concentration of land ownership has accelerated, resulting, *inter alia*, in small plots being bought up by large landowners. This happens with growing frequency, when defaulting small peasants, who have put up their title deeds as loan collateral, are compelled to sell their land through forced auctions to meet their debt obligations. This holds true in spite of some sub-division of large farms by land-buying companies, which has occurred in recent years. Despite the dearth of reliable and updated data on this sensitive and explosive issue of land ownership, studies and surveys are virtually unanimous in their view that land distribution in Kenya is extremely uneven and is in need of urgent and radical reform (Kenya/Central Bureau of Statistics, 1982; Godfrey, 1986).

As in the colonial period, land as a means of production is a leading source of capital accumulation. Generated capital may either be reinvested in agriculture or invested outside that sector, e.g. transport, services and manufacturing. The extremely skewed distribution of land ownership obtaining at independence and later, has thus tended to reinforce class division, as capital investment has expanded beyond the confines of agriculture. Studies of non-agricultural activities have, however, been associated with a higher degree of collaboration with international capital than has agricultural production. An unresolved controversy has, as a result, arisen as to the nature of the Kenyan bourgeoisie (Kitching, 1985). The first school maintains that it is a genuinely 'national' and 'developmental' bourgeoisie, capable of taking Kenya along the road to autonomous and self-reliant capitalist development (Swainson, 1980; Leys, 1978). The second, contending school asserts that the present Kenyan bourgeoisie is merely a 'comprador' class whose interests are the same as those of the centre countries and which thereby profits from the relationship established with the latter countries. This bourgeois leadership imposes a development model that serves its own interests and those of the centre, to the detriment of the Kenyan

Population. It is a 'dependent' class, without dynamism required to bring about self-reliant national development (Leys, 1975; Kaplinsky, 1980). The implications stem from consequences of Kenya's psychological dependency, much reliance on development aid and foreign multinationals rather than on national self-reliance and self-sufficiency.

As to a particular class, the concept, is only meaningful when seen in relationship to other classes. In Kenya, the classes contending with the bourgeoisie (landed, commercial and industrial) are the peasantry and the proletariat. Class division are often blurred and fluid, but such terms may justifiably be used in the Kenyan context. Numerically, the peasantry is undoubtedly the largest in Kenya. According to the Integrated Rural Survey from 1976, 1978 and 1979, the mean land holding size dropped from 1.6 NBS ha in 1976 to 1.3 NBS ha in 1978, and further to 1.2 NBS ha in 1979 (Kenya/Central Bureau of Statistics, 1981a). The average shamba is shrinking. These figures disguise the skewness of land holding. In 1978, 21.6 per cent or rural households had no land under cultivation, as compared with 13.7 per cent in 1976. In 1978, 66.9 per cent of rural households had holdings less than one hectare, compared to 59 per cent in 1976 (Kenya/Central Bureau of Statistics, 1981a). This serves to show that the overwhelming majority of the peasantry are small-scale agricultural producers. It might be reliably assumed that, since 1978, the mean holding size has dropped even further, due to the high population growth rate and the on-going subdivision of land from one generation to another. Inheritance rules do not prevent subdivision of parents' plots between sons. The fact that men inherit and own land does not mean that they work on the land. An overwhelming proportion of the labour inputs into agriculture come from women. Due to its high degree of social differentiation and dispersed settlement pattern, the peasantry has hitherto not been a potent political force in bringing about change in post-independence Kenya.

The pastoralists, comprising some 2 to 3 million, depend on livestock in the semi arid and arid areas of the country, which constitute about two thirds of the total land area. Their small number and acephalous social structure make them politically vulnerable. Historically they have lost vast tracts of land to agriculturalists (Sandford, 1976). This encroachment on pastoral land is continuing today, as is evident, for example, in the case of Turkana and Maasailand.

The proletariat is relatively small in number. Total wage employment in Kenya was about 1.1 million in 1984, out of which only some 200,000 can be considered an industrial proletariat proper in the manufacturing and construction sectors. Due to extensive labour migration the households of most of these workers also derive an income from agriculture. They are thus only semi-proletarianised, i.e. not entirely divorced from the land. The general pattern is that the husband in the household will seek wage labour, while the wife attends to the shamba (Tostensen, 1986). The fact that the proletariat is actually a 'peasantariat', makes it a vacillating political force. The class consciousness of industrial workers tends more to be that of a peasant, than that of proletarian. In providing the membership basis for the Kenyan trade union movement, however, the industrial workforce has constituted the support base for many political initiatives and careers.

The remainder of those in wage employment, some 900,000, are found in the non-manufacturing public and private sectors - agriculture, finance, trade and services. Despite their limited number, some of these groups can be articulate, and play a significant role in the political life of the country.

Kenya's economic and social problems derive in part from mismanagement and inappropriate policies. In an agriculturally dependent economy, the government's primary concern should be to safeguard and expand agricultural production. Yet just the opposite effect is created by certain policies. Price controls on foodstuff, low producer prices for agricultural exports, overvalued currencies and high protective tariffs on manufacturers turn the rural–urban terms of trade decisively against agricultural producers. Tax revenues, drawn disproportionately from the primary sector, are allocated disproportionately to the urban areas in the form of subsidised public credit to commerce, industry and public investment. The results are negative: the production of foodstuffs and cash crops is discouraged and a massive rural exodus to the cities is stimulated. Together, agricultural stagnation or decline and urban growth escalate black-market food prices and restrict foreign exchange and government revenues.

Deeper probing reveals that Kenya's failure lies as much at the level of policy implementation as formulation. Kenya Government ministers are unaware of the need for policies to stimulate agricultural production. Many politicians in Kenya know that farmers will produce only if they are promptly and adequately compensated and if they believe their goods can and will be marketed. Year after year the Kenya Government offered solemn promises – agriculture was declared to have a top priority. But, the same problems persisted: (a) low producer prices, (b) delays in payment, and (c) deteriorating market organisations and infrastructure. In practice, reform laws have been completely ignored. Hence, the credibility of the government has sank even further. The present government is currently more part of the economic and social problems than a solution.

The Colonial administration and white settlers left Kenya with a relatively efficient agricultural producer system, but in the late 1960s and early 1970s, the pattern was emerging, which one frustrated critic wrote in 1983, 'policies have been outlined, often published and even elaborately launched, but have failed to be properly implemented'. The National Food Policy (launched in Sessional Paper No. 4, 1980), for instance, fully accords with current thinking that agricultural productivity must be motivated through material incentives. In practice, however, maize and wheat farmers had been forced into long waits before they were compensated by inefficient and corrupt marketing boards. Consequently, the inevitable happened; production of these commodities fell in the 1980s while imports rose. Clearly the central issue revolved around how to reverse the government management slide, because no amount of policy statements or promises of improved efficiency will ever make any real difference until this is done.

In Kenya, agriculture is one important case. But fundamentally, the public sector is incapable of maintaining most of the conditions which foster economic growth; they are overwhelmed by their own incoherence, indiscipline and shrinking fiscal base. Potential investors (many are still willing to invest in Kenya) both foreign and indigenous – are not willing to gamble on a climate of political instability, political violence and unequal applications of the law. A rational and predictable administration encourages capitalist accumulation, but public mismanagement which grows out of systemic corruption, incompetence and demoralisation are all negative. Essential services deteriorate. Public corporations operate at a loss. Inequities and inconsistencies in tax administration encourage fraud and vitiate sound fiscal policy. Public officials seem unwilling or unable to create the delicate balance between attracting and squeezing foreign investors. The stage is set for the aborting of capitalist development in Kenya.

7.1.3 LAND TENURE

Rousseau advanced the argument that original sin rose with the first man who saw fit to appropriate land from the rest of the community by delineating his own boundaries with stakes effectively pronouncing 'This is mine'! Such proprietary attitudes have placed land in a special category when it comes to the framing and execution of land-use policy on physical environment, and planning policies, for undeniably, as a scarce resource, land possesses certain distinctive characteristics, some in common with other exchangeable commodities, some unique to land. Orthodox economic analysis asserts that land is relatively fixed in supply, although the quantity may be increased by limited and partial reclamation or marginally decreased by flooding and erosion. The quality can be improved by efficient land use planning and management and the adroit application of capital.

In absolute terms, land is considered irreplaceable for no one piece of land is like any other. This notion has material repercussions, when we base the equity of compensation for compulsory acquisition on simple open market values, when exact replacement is impossible. It is maintained that there is no cost involved in the creation of land, nor in the long run is it used up; there are thus 'original and indestructible powers of the soil'. Besides being immobile, land is also said to be subject to the law of eventual diminishing returns to scale, whereby past a particular point additional inputs of other factors produce successively lower outputs of the final product.

Although the supply of land to particular uses is not so inelastic, it is nevertheless apparent that given conditions of long-term economic growth throughout an economy, the relative fixity of supply in conjunction with an escalating demand produces exceptionally inflated prices in comparison with other more adjustable sectors. The lack of homogeneity, paucity of knowledge, and dearth of many buyers and sellers competing at the same time has led to the land market being repeatedly labelled as imperfect. It is not without justification that it has also been described as chaotic, irrational, monopolistic and therefore not amenable to empirical generalisation.

One last recognisable characteristic of land, and one of some relevance to strategic planning in particular, is the difficulty encountered in quantification. This relates not only to measurement in terms of area, productive capacity and value, but also refers to the almost insuperable problems involved in calculating the economic consequences of various land policies.

The system of land tenure in Kenya embodies those legal, contractual or tribal/customary arrangements whereby individuals or organisations gain access to economic or social opportunities through land. The precise form of tenure is constituted by the rules and procedures which govern the rights and responsibilities of both individuals and groups in the use and control over the basic resource land.

The effect of redistribution of land on output is controversial. The subdivision of large farms of good quality might normally be expected to increase yield per hectare. Of those who have studied the potential effects of redistribution in Kenya, Diana Hunt, (1984) goes further and suggests that a 'radical redistribution of land both in the large and small farm sectors, with a 3 ha ceiling on existing farms in the high potential areas (larger in the low potential areas) might... generate some 3.1 million new farms and some 1.55 million man/woman years of employment'. Hunt regards land reform as 'the single most urgently needed measure in the Kenyan rural economy,' which would also contribute to an expansion of the domestic market for manufactured goods.

The World Bank voiced similar concerns as early as 1981. The bank insisted on a 'systematic consideration of outstanding land policy issues' as one of the formal conditions for the second structural adjustment loan in 1982. However, the furthest the government moved in this direction, was to formalise the spontaneous subdivision of large farms owned by groups. It is difficult not to come to the same conclusions as Hunt's that 'the prospect of radical reform under Moi's administration looks bleak', when one considers what was stated in Sessional Paper No.1 (Kenya/Government, 1986) under the heading 'Land Tenure and Use':

(a) In this situation, private owners have a social obligation to put their land to its best use. The sanctity of private land ownership will be respected in Kenya. But, it can also operate if private land is used in socially responsible and productive ways. Mis-users of land must be prevented, if the strategy of agricultural and economic growth presented in Paper No.1 is to be realised now and in the future. First, despite growing population pressure on the land, there must be limits to the subdivision of small farms. Subdivision should be prevented beyond the point where total returns to land begin to diminish, Second, Kenya cannot feed itself and produce sufficient exports if land is allowed to lie idle or under-utilised in large land-holdings. Steps must be taken to induce land owners to put under-utilised land to more productive use. The Government recognises the sensitivity of land issues. But the economic future will be bleak unless these twin problems are faced and solved.

It was, however stated in the Sessional Paper that:

(b) There has not been a major review of Kenya's land policy since independence. The existing situation combines colonial land tenure laws with recent practices in a complex pattern that makes it difficult to operate a land policy. To correct this situation, Government will appoint a high-level commission to review the land tenure laws and practices of the country and recommend legislation that will bring the law into conformity with Kenya's development needs. The Commission's terms of reference will include consideration of the following elements of a land policy:

(1) taxation and other measures that provide an incentive to use land more productively;

(2) regulations limiting the extent of subdivision to ensure that farmland can produce adequate income for a family unit, including potential criteria governing subdivision, which must vary by agro-ecological zone;

(3) laws that could encourage and protect holders of large tracts who lease their land to those able to farm it more intensively.

7.1.4 LAND USE PLANNING AND AGRICULTURAL STRATEGY

Land use planning is a reconciliation of social and economic aims, of public and private objectives. It is the allocation of resources particularly land, in such a manner as to obtain maximum efficiency, while paying heed to the nature of the built and natural environment, and the welfare of the community. In this way planning is therefore the art of anticipating change, and arbitrating between the economic, social, political, cultural and physical environment that determine the location, form and effect of urban development. In democracy it should be the practical and technical implementation of the people's wishes operating within a legal framework, permitting the manipulation of the various urban components, such as transport, power, health, housing, education, employment, facilities for amenities etc, in such a way as to ensure the greatest benefit to all.

Creating a Land-use Planning Policy in Kenya, therefore presents great opportunities but also great responsibilities and challenges. The verdict of Kenya's future generation will depend not only on the handling of large and small developments but also their size, positioning and aesthetic qualities, the conservation measures, use of open space, and reclamation of arid and semi-arid areas in all parts of the country.

The current planning system and land-use policy is based on the old colonial urban oriented system and is welcomed by land speculators in Kenya. It aims to identify the areas of prospective development, and so reduces the level of risk speculation. The present planning system by itself is helpless to prevent inner-city decay, slums, squatter settlements, and urban sprawl, as it is all too obvious. Land-use regulations in its present form provide untold spoils for the rich owners.

None of this is to argue against land use planning *per se*. Planning laws are easily incorporated into the land value taxation model. Where regulations alter market prices, tax obligations are automatically adjusted up or down. For example, a preservation order on an historic building would restrict the economic use to which the land could be put. The economic rent of that land would be assessed downwards by the market, and the tax collector would have to follow suit. The re-zoning of land to an apparently more valuable use would not automatically raise the tax obligation, however, if the planner was ahead of the market; that is, if people did not express a need for the alternative use through the price mechanism taxes would not rise.

Advocates of public sector planning and spending should in fact be among the first to recognise the benefits of land value taxation. Justice surely requires the community as a whole should be the net winner of increased values arising from investments in infrastructural and social amenities and the enhancement of the ecological environment, schools, highways, pollution-control, open space conservation, etc. Indeed, this fiscal instrument would provide scope to undertake more of those projects, because the projects, through the increase in land value that they generate, would be self-financing.

Within the agricultural sector, the Sessional Paper No.1 of 1986 looked further ahead to the year 2000, and built its agricultural strategy around seven commodities, tea, coffee, maize, wheat, milk, meat and horticultural products. It set particularly ambitious targets for coffee and tea, with coffee exports expected to grow at an annual average rate of 7.3 per cent to 354,000 NBS tons by the year 2000, and tea at 5.2 per cent to 262,000 NBS tons. Real agricultural export earnings were projected to expand at an annual average rate of 5.9 per cent. The long-term target for the increase in production of food crops was set at 5 per cent per annum, well above the increase in population. The basic anxiety behind these ambitious targets for the agricultural sector and for the Kenyan economy in general, lies in the exceptionally high rate of population growth.

It would be wrong to suggest that Kenya has reached its ultimate land frontier, but the pressure on land in certain parts of the country is undoubtedly severe. Available statistics on the distribution of high, medium and low potential land, and of population by province, bring out the contrast between Kenya's apparently favourable population/land ratio of 0.3 NBS persons per hectare, and the corresponding ratio, when only land in areas of reasonable rainfall is included. Pressure on land is particularly acute in Western, Central and Nyanza provinces, and can be expected to grow, since these are the areas where the highest natural population increase is expected. The situation could also become critical in Eastern Province, partly as a result of internal migration.

A recent policy document emphasises the possibility of expanding the supply of agricultural land through irrigation, drainage or the conversion of forests and pastures. However, scepticism seems to be growing as to the cost effectiveness of large scale irrigation, as an escape route from land constraints. The result of such projects have so far been somewhat uncertain. Apart from Kenya's showpiece, the Mwea scheme, which technically is working well, the rate of return on most projects of this kind has been low. Drainage, which could also add an estimated 600,000 NBS ha to the land area, is cheaper, but Kenya has little experience in this field. In short, while there is certainly some cultivable land at present lying unutilised, particularly in Coast province, converting it to productive use would not be a straightforward agricultural process. Consequently, neither irrigation nor drainage appears to offer promising possibilities for any immediate extension of the cultivable land area.

Kenya's two major export crops, coffee and tea, are grown on less than 5 per cent of the agricultural land. Consequently, a 70 per cent extension in the area used for cultivating these two crops, would reduce land available for food production by just over 3 per cent. It is believed that such an expansion, together with measures to increase yields of coffee and tea on already planted land, should make it possible to realise the growth target for export crops, without creating an insoluble conflict with plans for food production.

The long-term growth in output of maize, wheat, milk and other food stuffs largely depended upon increased yields from land, already committed to producing these commodities. To achieve an annual increase in their output of 5 per cent, and a much more rapid growth in marketed output for urban consumption, government intended to pursue three broad policy initiatives simultaneously. Firstly, agricultural inputs, and especially fertilisers were to be made more widely available in convenient packages, and at appropriate locations. This initiative required attention to the agricultural input supply system, including its improvement and further development. Secondly, farmers, and especially small farmers, were to be made aware of improved farming practices by a more effective extension service, and to be encouraged to practise better husbandry, through price and other incentives. According to Session Paper No.1 of 1986, these two policy initiatives were only capable of sustaining adequate increases in food production for less than a decade. After that, it would become necessary to introduce new, higher yielding varieties of maize and other grains in order to sustain growth and provide for continuing food security. Thus the third key initiative was urgently to focus Kenya's research capacity and attention on the development of new cereal varieties, particularly of maize, for introduction within the next decade.

As mentioned above, seven commodities were regarded as crucially significant, in achieving the development goals which government had established for agriculture. In this context, the expansion of coffee and tea production was seen as the foundation for growth in both agricultural incomes and exports, while the production of maize, wheat, milk and meat was geared primarily to food security objectives. Horticultural crops were to serve both goals. According to the 1986 Sessional Paper, the envisaged concentration on these seven commodities was justified, because success in these programmes should ensure that agricultural income can grow at 5 per cent a year to the end of the twentieth century. Other commodities – especially sorghum, millet, rice, tuber crops, sugar and oil crops – will remain important for farmers, and also in terms of government support measures. Furthermore, it was considered in government that if these seven intensification and expansion programmes were not to succeed, there would be no alternative investment package of comparable magnitude that could raise Kenya's agricultural prosperity so effectively in so short a period.

Two implications follow from this strategy. Firstly, rapid growth of rural incomes and production would be served by increased output of coffee, tea and vegetables, through both an expansion in acreage and the use of more intensive methods of production. Secondly, in maintaining self-reliance and self-sufficiency in maize, milk, meat and most other basic foods, it would be necessary to intensify production on existing lands, without encroaching on other areas devoted to higher income-earning crops.

Other development considerations point in the same direction. Even after allowing for labour-saving innovations, coffee, tea, vegetables and pyrethrum employ between 1.4 and 2.0 person-years per hectare, compared to only 0.3 to 0.6 for milk, maize and beans, root crops, sorghum and millet. Thus employment objectives also broadly dictate an expansion in high-value crops. Similarly, the need to raise agriculture's export earnings also required an increase in tea, coffee and horticultural production, and in that other cash crops. Coffee, tea and vegetables earn five to ten times the foreign exchange per hectare that can be saved through import substitution resulting from increased cereal production.

7.1.5 LAND REFORM AND SUSTAINABLE AGRICULTURE

Land is a fundamental factor of production of comparable importance to labour or capital. Access to land is at the heart of self-reliance not only for home food production, but also for agribusiness and food exports. Virtually all social and productive activities e.g. water, agro-forestry, energy, health, production, homes, conservation, offices, business, transport, education and urbanisation etc., require land. The methods and efficiency of agriculture are of crucial importance to Kenya, both at local and national levels in the quest for self-sufficiency in food. Self-reliance will inevitably involve people having access to land and communities having more control over their land. This will entail a significant measure of land reform in Kenya and care in how land is owned, farmed and used, thus needing a wide measure of land use planning.

The approach to Kenya's land reform and land use will involve three main elements:

(1) Structural changes in agricultural policy and support to change the direction of agricultural development with a marked improvement in the efficiency with which agricultural inputs and outputs are researched, planned, managed and marketed; that give far more people the chance of being involved in land use.

(2) A clear policy direction which explains possible means of enabling and encouraging the development of technical pack-ages, pest and disease control, development in animal husbandry, joint-holding and working of land – the cooperative land bank – which combine private ownership of improvements to land with community ownership of the land itself.

(3) The quest for a balance between private and social ownership of land, seeking its efficient use according to ecologically sound, socially agreed criteria will be taken further in discussions of land value taxation. Underlying each of these three elements is a perception that land is not just another financial asset. It is the basis of food, work and life for the majority of Kenyans. As such, the whole concept of ownership of land is replaced by that of stewardship, seeking the management of land not just for the benefit of the person who owns or works it, but also for the community as a whole, while safeguarding it for the future generation of Kenyan children.

Under District Focus Policy (DFP), each district will be required to produce a development strategy – a plan for the environment and programme for the District's food requirements to be produced to:

(a) promote tree planting especially among small-scale farmers in order to make village communities self-sufficient in fuelwood, building and fencing materials;

(b) promote informal environment education in such activities as preventing soil erosion and flooding. Environment education sessions to consider desertification, cultivation along river banks and sloping areas, indiscriminate cutting-down of trees, burning and clearing of bushes for crop-land;

(c) create employment for the physically handicapped, young school leavers, the aged and those grossly handicapped by poverty. These should be engaged to plant and care for tree nurseries, horticulture and promote the movements in the field;

(d) make seedling production an income-generating activity, especially for women and school children;

(e) promote agricultural practices that enhance food production;

(f) introduce practices of good livestock management;

(g) promote need of the other village land uses, in particular agro-forestry, landscaping and aesthetics;

(h) meet needs for conservation, eco-tourism, planning, recreation facilities and amenities, promotion and marketing of such facilities;

(i) meet need for stability and prosperity in rural areas and equity of income distribution – within the district;

(j) meet the nutritional needs of the population in the district;

(k) monitor and ensure the long term productivity of the soil;

(l) promote environmental protection and the use of non-renewable resources;

It is assumed that the following DFP policies will be achieved without imposing an undue burden upon the taxpayer or consumer within the area, and having regard to agricultural and nutritional needs of people living in other areas.

Sustainable agriculture lies at the heart of the solutions to Kenya's agricultural problems, food production and adopting radically different kinds of agricultural development objectives for a self-reliant economy. It does not necessitate a return to a backward tribal way of farming, using uneconomic, old-fashioned methods, but looks forward to a modern type of ecological agriculture, which utilises scientific knowledge for the development of appropriate technology and advances traditional farming practices that are applicable for an agriculture not based exclusively on short-term economics, but which also takes ecological considerations into account.

(1) Kenya will organise the production of crops, livestock, and the management of farm resources in such a way that they harmonise rather than conflict with natural systems. This does not mean that one must always decline to use man-made or synthetic resources.

(2) There will be pursuit of optimum (not necessarily maximum) production through planned diversity.

(3) There will be pursuit of optimum production, through the achievement and maintenance of high soil fertility, relying primarily on renewable resources.

(4) There will be the development of new, small-scale technologies, based upon a better understanding of biological systems.

(5) There will be pursuit of the optimum nutritional value of staple foods.

(6) There will be the development of locally based systems of processing, distribution and marketing.

(7) There will be concern for the social well-being of the people who live and work on the land and of their communities.

(8) Kenya's land-use policy will create a system which is aesthetically pleasing both for those working within and for those viewing land from the outside. Thus, it should enhance rather than scar the landscape of which it forms a part.

Some of these objectives would also be met by organic farming, defined as follows (USDA, 1980)

> ...Organic farming is a production system which avoids or largely excludes the use of synthetically compounded fertilisers, pesticides, growth regulators and livestock feed additives. To the maximum extent feasible, organic farming systems rely upon crop rotations, crop residues, animal manures, legumes, green manures, off-farm organic wastes, mechanical cultivation, mineral-bearing rocks and aspects of biological pest control to maintain soil productivity and tilth, to supply plant nutrients and control insects, weeds and other pests.

Bateman and Lampkin conclude that:

> ...there is evidence that an extension of organic farming would, compared with conventional farming, offer quite clear advantages in relation to some of the objectives: output would be lower, the environment would benefit, soil erosion would be reduced and some nutritional fears (particularly those associated with the use of pesticides) would be allayed.

They go on to argue that a modest expansion of organic farming is in fact likely in any case, but its poorer overall financial performance compared to subsidised conventional farming makes it unlikely that this expansion will be significant without positive policy changes to redress the balance. First and foremost such policy changes should include research and advice. As they point out:

> In the past, there has in effect been positive discrimination against organic farming – no doubt by default rather than by design. Research has been directed towards varieties that are dependent on chemical inputs and the use of artificial fertilisers. Advice has been similarly oriented. The high rate of 'technical changes which is the obvious feature of modern agriculture since the war is the direct result of these activities,' and it is they, much more than those other elements of policy which generally receive most attention, that have been influential in shaping agricultural development. It is from changing attitudes in this area that the biggest change in the competitiveness of organic agriculture is

likely to spring. A reorientation of research is the aspect of policy change that should be pressed hardest by those who wish to see an extension of organic farming. The provision of advice directly relevant to organic systems must also be considered as an Urgent priority. (Lampkin and Bates, 1985)

7.1.6 USE OF FERTILISERS

Increased application of fertiliser is essential for achieving higher yields from food and cash crops. While the use of fertilisers grew very rapidly during the 1960s and early 1970s, the rate of growth in the 1980s was much lower as the availability fell well below estimated requirements. Furthermore, it would seem that most of the growth during the earlier period, was associated with the estate and large farm sectors, with relatively little fertilisers being used by smallholders. It has, been estimated that in 1983 smallholder maize producers accounted for 6 per cent of total fertiliser use. If maize producers applied the recommended rates of fertiliser, it is estimated that a further 100,000 tons would have been required. This compares with the 1909 annual imports of around 200,000 tons.

There is wide variation in fertiliser use per hectare from one part of Kenya to another, and the large shortfalls from recommended applications testify to the need for improved fertiliser availability. A case in point is that maize growers in Ryanza use as little as 5 per cent of recommended levels, but in Trans Nzoia the rate is as high as 60 per cent.

Fertilisers provided under aid programmes made an important contribution to total fertiliser supplies. However, coordination of aid supplies and commercial imports have in the past left much to be desired. The government took various steps in the past to tackle the problems and, according to the major donor interviewed for this study, substantial improvements have taken place. Further measures should include: greater reliance on commercial importers and distributors; coordination of fertiliser provided under aid programmes with commercial supplies; timely allocations; packing in small bags; offering sufficient retail margins, as incentives to distributors, and establishing a credit scheme for smallholders.

7.2 Cooperative Land Banks and Housing the Poor

7.2.1 COOPERATIVE LAND BANK CONCEPT

It is expected that the agricultural policies just outlined would result in a significant increase in the number of those involved in farming. Many of the new units would be in family, but it is also likely that there would be a demand for joint land holding. Moreover, it is not just a question of increasing access to agricultural land. Measures are also needed to enable those with low incomes and little capital to build their own houses/homes and to plan and build their village communities. For example, in Britain, two such current schemes are already in existence or being formed: the Lightmoor Project at Telford New Town, and the Greentown Project at Milton Keynes. One possible mechanism for facilitating these developments which could be replicated in Kenya is the establishment of a cooperative land bank, described below, which seeks to strike a balance between individual ownership of property on the land and community ownership of the land itself.

The cooperative land bank concept is designed to combine the efficiency of private property rights with the equity of public ownership. It is however, more than just a land tenure system. It is also a grassroots structure of village community self-management in the tradition of Sir Ebnenezer Howard's concept of self-governing garden cities (Howard, 1902). As such, the cooperative land bank is a basic building block of a new type of political system which will be called here 'social capitalism'. The ability of the cooperative land bank to become self-financing provides the basis for it to become financially independent of higher levels of government. It thus provides a means for creating a grassroots self-reliant local government structure on a decentralised democratic basis. It is important, therefore, that the constitution of the cooperative land bank should prescribe that only individuals may have the right to vote so as to exclude corporations. All individuals who meet residency requirements and are of voting age would obtain only one vote, no matter how many shares they own in the cooperative land bank.

The self-financing feature of a cooperative land bank is especially important for low-income developing countries like Kenya. In low-income areas a cooperative land bank would provide land without cost to its initial or pioneer members who would build or buy their home with security of tenure provided by a cooperative land bank's perpetual lease. Squatter settlements and slum areas in cities and towns often have strong internal self-reliant organisations and the cooperative land bank concept provides a means to institutionalise and reinforce such informal social organisation and cohesion into a permanent settlement.

Indeed, the concept of cooperative land banks and their operational financial efficiency and effectiveness is very much dependent upon a strong grassroots self-reliant social organisation and sense of community. Local self-government traditionally exists in many Kenyan tribal institutions. The cooperative land bank provides an innovative and skilful means of building a new economic structure on old tribal traditions, while breaking down tribal cohesion and tribalism from within. Typically, development along the capitalist path will result in a less expensive organisation, the cooperative land bank concept also provides a non-exploitative private alternative to commune or state cooperative, collectives, and kibbutz for building a decentralised society in Kenya.

This system proposes an alternative method of urban/rural land ownership and housing policy in Kenya which, will reduce the inequities and inefficiencies of the present system and facilitate both self-financing development and greater access to land and housing to the majority of poor Kenyans in the squatter slum settlements in cities, towns and in rural village communities.

The inequities of private land ownership are generally widely understood. Existing private land owners obtain benefits both in terms of monetary wealth and exploitative power from improvements and increases in value created by others. The alternative – public ownership – introduces gross inefficiencies, as neither the tenants nor their bureaucratic landlords have sufficient incentive to diligently maintain and improve housing stock. The same inefficiency arises with concentrated private ownership, which requires a private bureaucracy to manage the tenants and the housing stock. The results of such inefficiency are dramatically illustrated in the United States of America, where extensive urban areas have become devastated due to the alienation between tenants–occupiers and owners of property.

Recent research both in the UK/EU countries and the former Soviet Union countries show that owner-occupation of dwellings provides the most efficient method of maintaining and improving the housing stock. Without private ownership there is no incentive for individuals to contribute either their funds or their labour to improve the value of the housing stock where they live. Only owner-occupiers are in the best position and have the greatest incentive to enhance both their standard of living and their equity through their own labour.

Such 'sweat equity' is often the only means available to the poor to either build or maintain their shelter. Indeed, on a global basis, this is how the majority of the world's housing stock has been created and maintained.

Any system for owning land and housing must mobilise 'sweat equity' if it is to have any significant practical effect on a global scale. Sweat equity is not only the most universal and efficient means of creating or enhancing the housing stock, but it also creates the most satisfying shelter for the consumer. Ideally, then, all occupants of housing should also own their houses. The tenure system proposed here allows this to occur. But human settlements still require provision of public expenditure to improve community facilities and services. This introduces two problems: how to fund such improvements and how to overcome the new inequities created by the public expenditure generating windfall gains for owners.

The common theoretical answer to these problems is to fund public expenditure by imposing rates and taxes on those owners who benefit from the public expenditure. By this means, the inequities created by the expenditure should be offset by the charges imposed to finance them. This may be true in theory but it is difficult to implement in practice. The most serious problem is cash flow. The public expenditures create diffuse capital gains rather than offset flows. The unrealised capital gains may or may not be convertible into cash. If they cannot be fully converted into cash required, then the charges imposed on property owners to recover the cost of community improvement may introduce unreasonable financial burdens. This is especially so in poorer communities. Indeed, it is a fundamental problem in financing public services in any low-income area. It is commonly overcome by resorting to a higher level of government, which is then asked to pay for the improvement as a subsidy. This in turn can create political tensions within the government.

Even when it is practical to impose community charges to recover community expenditures, the charges imposed may not relate to the benefits. As a result the basic inequity of the public authorities creating windfall gains for some is further complicated by the added administration costs of assessing the charges and making collections. The windfall benefits accruing to private property owners or, for that matter, to long-term lessees, are not just created by public expenditure but also by all private expenditure in the neighbourhood/village. Shopping, commercial and secondary industries are the most obvious examples. Less obvious but more pervading is the extent of home maintenance and improvements undertaken by other property owners. Another benefit is the sense of community created in the village neighbourhood by residents.

External factors, especially government regulations and public utilities may reduce rather than enhance property values. Such reductions are referred to as wipe-outs and create further inequities. Various proposals have been put forward to capture windfall gains and to use them to offset wipe-outs so as to mitigate the inequities of both. The capture, pooling and sharing of all windfall gains and wipeouts within a community is an important feature of the tenure system of a cooperative land bank (Hagman and Misczynski, 1978).

7.2.2 BUILDING OF COOPERATIVE LAND BANK

It can be expected that the agricultural policies outlined will result in a significant increase in the number of those involved in farming. Many of the new units would be in poor family farms, but it is likely that there would also be a demand for joint land holding. The tenure system of a cooperative land bank would be created wherever a sufficient area of land can be aggregated and vested in a suitable legal entity such as a cooperative, company, or a common law trust. In order to assist in land aggregation the entity could be formed to create not just two types of equity interests but others which may be required during the formative period of the cooperative land bank.

Rather than borrow money to pay cash for land aggregation, the cooperative land bank may wish to issue redeemable participating non-voting preference shares in exchange for land and/or its improvements. Such shares could also have special conversion rights if required. In this way the vendor of the land can participate in the development profits but not in the management of the cooperative land bank. The cooperative land bank, on the other hand, can minimise its immediate requirements for cash. If the vendor is a low-income home-owner or a squatter whose home has to be relocated then her/his preference shares should be redeemed not into cash but into a new home in the cooperative. This would be represented by a perpetual lease over her/his new living area and a pro-rata issue of shares in the cooperative.

In both examples the need for cash is avoided by battering property rights. The second example has many similarities to the land pooling/readjustment techniques described by Doebele (1976) and Archer (1976). These techniques can be used for aggregating either bare land or land with improvements. There thus exists a number of possibilities for converting any area of land and its improvements into a duplex tenure system to form a cooperative land bank without further consideration. Like the land pooling readjustment procedures in South Korea and Australia, this may require the authority of the central government.

Indeed, such arrangements would appear to have considerable political attractions compared with either proposals for making land available for housing low-income families. In particular, proposed land ceiling legislation in South and Southeast Asia aimed at limiting the size of unused land holdings in and around cities, would appear to be far more contentious both politically and technically. The transformation and aggregation of such land into a cooperative land bank tenure system would immediately make land available at no cost to the government or to the poor, who could be allowed to build their own homes on the land. This, in turn, would create development value for the existing landowners to share. Existing landowners would not have to find the funds to develop their land and would be assured that their land would not be bypassed for development.

Another possible mechanism for building cooperative land banks is dynamic tenure. Dynamic tenure can increase the efficiency, equity, effectiveness, and self-governance of a cooperative land bank. Dynamic tenure is created when property rights are defined to flow from one party to another with the passage of time at a prescribed rate. There need not be any cash compensation paid or received by the parties involved.

The rationale for adopting the concepts in a cooperative land bank is that it is the occupier of property, and not the owner that maintains and creates property values. Thus, if the owner is not an occupier, the rights of ownership should flow from the landlord to the tenant. In practice it is suggested here a twenty-five or fifty year transfer period for rental housing. This would involve a 4 per cent to 2 per cent transfer of equity each year by the landlord to the tenant. The landlord would consequently increase her/his rental charges from 4 per cent to 2 per cent. However, the tenant would be acquiring without cost a pro-rata share in the land occupied by her/his home. In a cooperative land bank, this would already be owned by the community.

The pragmatic effect of these arrangements is to ensure that all residents of a cooperative land bank will automatically, with the passage of time, become owners of leasehold improvements in the cooperative. It should thus increase development values by mobilising sweat equity. By this means it should protect itself from the destruction caused by the alienation between landlords and tenants as demonstrated in the dilapidated areas of North American cities.

A cooperative land bank is in many ways similar to a condominium or company title system for owning apartment buildings. In both condominium and company tenure systems two related interests in property are created. One defines the ownership of improvements to the land which may be used exclusively by the owner, and this would represent his/her particular apartment. This interest could be considered to be in the nature of a perpetual lease. The other related interest represents an ownership share in all the common areas such as hallways, stairs, laundries, garden, swimming pool and other amenities which the owner of a leasehold title has the right to use on a non-exclusive basis. This joint interest could be represented by stock units or shares in the corporate entity which owns all the rights to the land. A cooperative land bank has a number of features which distinguishes it from most condominium and company title systems. At this stage it will only be necessary to introduce here those relevant concepts.

(1) A cooperative land bank would operate in Kenya on a larger scale than a typical condominium, representing a village, squatter/slum settlement, neighbourhood or community containing roads, gardens, schools, hospitals and commercial activities with a residential capacity of 300 to 50,000 people.

(2) The owner of each perpetual lease representing her/his house or apartment would obtain a share in the cooperative land bank and so in all common areas, proportional to the area occupied by her/his leasehold improvements.

(3) Unlike condominium and company title systems, there would be no restriction to whom a member of the cooperative land bank could sell her/his shares and lease. The price of the property she/he owns (the leasehold improvements) will be directly negotiated with the buyer. The price of her/his shares and the leasehold improvements will be determined by the market price paid elsewhere for similar types of residence.

(4) Only real persons (not corporations, institutions, or governmental bodies) would be allowed to hold either titles or shares. Corporations, institutions, governments and their agencies would only be able to obtain lease from title holders or the cooperative land bank for a time period of less than fifty years. This would allow any residual value in improvements made by such organisations to revert to

individuals on the termination of the lease. In general, such organisations do not need the capital gains on property in order to operate efficiently. Traditional private property ownership systems usually provide them with economic rewards in excess of the necessary incentive.

Since a house and its plot in a cooperative land bank can not be sold without its shares, the price received by a member for her/his house would depend upon the price at which the buyer had to purchase the associated shares in the cooperative land bank. While these shares represent the pro-rata share of the land value; their cost could be considered to be of the nature of 'key money' representing the cost of entry to the community. This would be a fair representation as the cost of land is really the market value of its location and this, in turn, depends upon the nature of the physical and social environment of the village neighbourhood. The services, amenities and facilities creating the physical and social environment of the community would be created and managed by the cooperative land bank. The price received by the vendor for her/his house would be determined by how much the purchaser had to pay in key money to enter the community. The total proceeds received by the existing members would be the price she/he obtained for her/his house, plus the price she/he obtained from the cooperative land bank for her/his shares. The price paid by the cooperative land bank for the existing member's shares could be considerably less than the price at which the bank sold the shares. It is by this means that the bank will obtain cash from the development gains it captures.

As a cooperative land bank would own all the land in a sizeable community/village it would have a substantial asset base and income-earning potential. It would thus be in an excellent position to compete in the capital market for long-term debt funds. This would overcome the cash-flow problems inherent in financing community improvements. By financing community improvements with debt finance their cost can be repaid in the future from the cash flows generated by the improvements.

The self-financing capability of a cooperative land bank would be considerably greater than the traditional type of local government organisation found in the UK and other western societies. This arises from a number of income-generating activities in such an organisation, in addition to the income from the sale of shares, mentioned above. These include: income from all commercial enterprises, which would be only able to lease their premises:

(1) Savings on community improvements, because of the incentives in the structure of a cooperative land bank for residents to contribute their own labour enterprise;
(2) The ability to levy a rate, as commonly already pertains to local government bodies.

These means of income generation can be adjusted as necessary to ensure an adequate cash flow for community improvements.

7.2.3 CAPTURING DEVELOPMENT PROFITS

The ability of the cooperative land bank to capture and obtain cash from land development profits is one of its most valuable features in terms of both efficiency and equity. The price at which the shares in the cooperative may be purchased by new members is determined in the same way as the price for shares in a real estate investment trust, that is, by dividing the number of shares, units or stocks on issue into the total value of land owned by the cooperative land bank. The valuation of the land would be tempered by pragmatic pressures in much the same way as countries now manage their exchange rates. If the price becomes too far out of line, market pressure would force an adjustment to more realistic levels.

The price at which the cooperative land bank would buy shares back from members would be discounted according to a formula. This formula would need to be embedded in the constitution of the cooperative land bank so that it would require no less than 75 per cent of the members to agree on a change. The formula would need to maintain equity between short- and long-term members of the cooperative and to inhibit speculation.

The appreciation in the land value of the cooperative land bank and its shares would be created by the consumer demand for its sites, services and facilities. The greatest contribution to consumer demand for both public and private goods and services in the cooperative land bank would be the long-term residents. The members who suffer the greatest discount (or exit tax) should thus be short-term members. There could well be a zero discount for long-term residents. A suitable formula would therefore be a sliding scale discount reducing with years of residency. A twenty-year period, for example, could reduce the discount applied by 5 per cent for each year of residency.

In Australia and the United States of America, the average period of owning a particular home is only around six years even though purchase finance is obtained for twenty-five to thirty-five years. Such a rapid turnover of members would make a cooperative land bank self-financing simply from this mechanism alone. One of the most important features of the cooperative land bank is its ability to capture for the community any increase in land values due to development. This is also one of the principles underlying the next mechanism of land reform discussed below – land value taxation will enable the village community to benefit from the value of its land, and to profit from any increase in such a value, by taxing land on the basis of its economic rent; that is, the surplus wealth earned by the land over and above the income earned by labour (wages) and capital (interest from assets on the land). It is, in fact, the oldest fiscal mechanism employed by human societies and would reinstate ancient principles in the modern context. It would fulfil the roles formerly played by custom and moral suasion, in preventing people from possessing more land than they needed for production and recreation; and it would ensure a fair and equal distribution of the value of nature, through the public sector (Gorge, 1979)

The proposal is for a tax on the site-value of all land in Kenya, the site value being the value of any plot or area of land in its unimproved state, i.e. excluding the value of any building on it or other man-made improvements that have been made to it. The tax will be paid annually by owners of the land. It will be calculated as a percentage of the capital value of the site or its annual rental value. This will, in effect be a tax on every piece of land at the point just before it contributes to any economic activity. It will therefore, enter into the cost of every activity involving that piece of land, including the cost of leaving it idle. Not only will it capture for the community a proportion of any communally created increase in land value. It will tend to encourage efficient land use, to reduce the value of land in relation to other forms of capital, to redistribute wealth as well as income from those who own valuable city-centre and agricultural land to those who do not, and make it easier for more people to own a piece of land.

Apart from the equitable arguments favouring recoupment of that portion of community-created land value, it is the existence of an economic rent or surplus, unique or otherwise, that renders land an attractive proposition for taxation. Because taxes on marginal transactions disturb optimum conditions of production an ideal neutral tax should be either non-marginal or lump-sum. The most commonly advocated non-marginal taxes are those imposed on economic surplus, of which land is a prime example. A tax is neutral and most efficient if it places the least burden on the person to be taxed and does not interfere with the functioning of the market. In this context it can be argued that among the range of practicable taxes there is none which is so economically 'efficient' as a tax upon land.

The incidence of land taxation can be traced back to 2697 BC and the Huang-Ti dynasty in China. Thomas Spence in 1775 described the problems of the 'unearned increment' and published recommendations for the appropriation of the rent from land. Malthus, following Ricardo and encouraged by both Mills', when appointed the first professor at Imperial college (London), induced young colonial administrators to establish a 'land revenue' in India whereby a detailed cadastral survey, linked to records of agricultural yields over preceding years, was employed to institute a tax imposed at a reasonable non-confiscatory level on surplus. Nevertheless, Indian experience served to illustrate that a land tax is not always unshiftable and that, with the soil of India for the most part being less productive, the 'original and indestructible powers' may not in fact endure.

Furthermore, in imposing a liability related to hypothetical developed value, landowners are encouraged to release or develop vacant sites. From experience gained in Australia and South Africa, land value taxation is said to encourage not only development but good development; although it appears that quality is often equated with quantity. Perhaps the most attractive characteristic with which a system of land value taxation is endowed is that relating to social justice, for it can be said that the fundamental purpose of land value taxation is the apprehension of capital gains.

On the other hand, land value taxation is not similar to the UK rates on 'improved' property values which is a familiar form of local taxation. Having been in existence since the sixteenth century, rates account for 34 per cent of local government income. It can be varied according to circumstances and locality, is readily identified with local government areas and is easily administered. At a cost of 2 per cent of yield it is cheap to collect and difficult to evade. In addition, it is a relatively simple task to alter the rate poundage in order to gain an increase in revenue. On the other side of the coin, it has been criticised for not being related to an individual's ability to pay and, while mitigated by social security and rate rebate schemes, the UK rating system displays a certain regressive element. Furthermore, besides penalising improvement, discouraging development, and possessing a degree of inconsistency and inequity by fluctuation through time, the very basis of original valuation is questionable.

The implementation of an effective land value taxation policy is, however, fraught with difficulties as the introduction in Jamaica aptly demonstrates. The taxation base requires detailed land-use zoning and continuitive cadastral survey. There is the inherent problem of measuring base site value, although the use of a standard rate has been suggested as a means of ameliorating this enigma, the designation of optimum use probably presents the most Herculean task of all if the system is to be truly used as a proper planning tool, a development incentive and an economic stimulus, rather than just a pragmatic method of revenue collection. Inevitably the fixed, certain and rigid nature of the cartographic base for taxation purposes is destined to be contrary to the spirit and purpose of strategic planning. The horrendous valuation and revaluation procedures; the eventual lack of cleared-site comparables in developed areas leading to the use of arbitrary ratios; the economic and political delicacy regarding exemptions; and the ever-present dilemma that emerges with any rating system where rich areas grow richer; where values are low and rates inordinately high; all militate against a smooth and expeditious introduction.

But, despite these forebodings regarding the introduction of some kind of site value tax or rate, there can be little doubt that the valuation of all land at the free market rate is the first step, and is an important factor in planning policy, an exercise that will be swiftly performed by the District Valuers once Parliament has sanctioned the reform of the rating (property tax) system. The Land Register would be opened to the public and the process of compulsory registration of titles to land would be accelerated to cover all land in Kenya, including tribal holdings. The next decision is to fix the rate of taxation as a percentage of the annual economic rent. Some, for example the United Nations (1968), have advocated a tax rate well below 100 per cent. In Kenya that the rate ought to be 100 per cent. Anything less leaves a margin that encourages speculation and waste. A full capture of rent would enable the government to reduce taxes on labour and capital, which penalise people who work or invest.

This fiscal policy reform will force speculative hoarders to relinquish vacant land in favour of those who wish to use it. Both unemployment and the speculatively high level of rents will be reduced, thereby increasing the real living standards of many Kenyan people who are today trapped in poverty, despair, alienation and lack of means to break out the institutionalised cycle of deprivation and acute poverty.

Indeed, it will encourage individuals to use land that they possess to produce the best returns consistent with the expressed wishes of the consumers and society at large. In the agricultural sector, land value taxation will lead to a break-up of inefficiently managed large foreign owned agricultural estates in favour of smaller, family size holdings. In the cities and towns, high-value vacant land will be brought back into use. Buildings will be constantly renewed, which is the best way to recycle urban land and so prevent squatter/slum settlements and the premature spread on to greenfield sites. Compact living environment would reduce the capital costs of infrastructure (thereby reducing the need for government revenues on the present scale), reduce the private costs of transportation (thereby increasing the real standard of living without having to push for higher money wages), establish integrated communities (thereby reducing psycho-social stress), and conserve the rural environment and landscaping to enhance its aesthetic value. It is a bright prospectus for just one change in the system of taxation.

7.2.4 CONCLUSION

Most of the small rural towns in Kenya have failed to fulfil a positive function in modern society. At present their narrow economy is still based on the provision of a few services to the hinterland, petty trade and subsistence agricultural labour. Lack of sufficient employment opportunities has prompted the young and the more enterprising element to emigrate to the larger towns, leaving the small rural community without adequate leadership, and limiting even those functions which they have traditionally performed for the farming community. Far from slowing down the rate of migration to large towns, they at best serve as a stepping stone for the flow of migrants.

The task of modernising and rejuvenating rural towns in Kenya is by no means a simple one. Confronted by formidable problems, particularly shortage of capital and skilled labour, the planner is justified in questioning the relative advantage of diverting a part of the national development effort to small towns rather than concentrating it entirely in large urban city centres and allowing for trickle-down effects.

Studies of costs of urbanisation for cities of varying sizes in the developed and developing countries have generally shown that development of small and medium sized towns can be less costly than metropolitan urbanisation. For one, the required investment in infrastructure is lower. Cheaper land and the possibility of using low rise buildings will also lessen the cost of housing.

The shortage of skilled labour in the rural hinterland is a problem that can be solved by the provision of vocational training facilities which would be programmed into the regional development strategy, so as to ensure that as the factories are built and the various services established, that trained people are available to man the new positions.

Regional development calls for an integrated rural and urban development cycle into a comprehensive and balanced strategy so that the improvement of the one has a positive effect on the other and vice versa. Development cannot take place in a vacuum unrelated to specific social and economic objectives. Many of these are already embodied in the proposed agrarian reform setting out land ownership policies, minimum desirable income levels etc. The process involves adjustment between planned agricultural output and urban development until a state of dynamic equilibrium is achieved, and subsequent stages of rural and urban development are implemented and the level of the regional development spirals upwards, retaining more and more of its people in the region and giving them a higher and higher standard of living. It would be unrealistic to presume that development of small towns would put a complete stop to the migration to large cities in Kenya or anywhere.

The cooperative land bank on the other hand, is a concept designed to combine the efficiency of private property rights with equity of public ownership. It is however, more than just a land tenure system. It is also a grassroots structure of village/community self-management in the tradition of Sir Ebenezer Howard's concept of self-governing garden cities (Howard, 1902). As such, the cooperative land bank is a basic building block of a new type of political system, which will be known as 'social capitalism'. The ability of the cooperative land bank to become self-financing provides the basis for it to become financially independent of a higher level of government. It thus provides a means for creating a grassroots (village) self-reliant and sustainable local government structure on a decentralised democratic basis. It is important, therefore, that the constitution of the cooperative land bank should prescribe that only individuals may have the right to vote so as to exclude any corporations, institutions or government. All individuals who meet residency requirements and are of voting age would obtain only one vote, no matter how many shares they own in the cooperative land bank.

The self-financing feature of a cooperative land bank is especially important in low-income rural poor, urban shanties, slums and squatter settlements in Kenya. In the rural poor and shanties, slums and squatter settlements a cooperative land bank would provide land without cost to its initial or pioneer members to build or buy their home with the security of tenure provided by the cooperative land bank's perpetual lease. Squatter/slum settlements and rural villages often have a strong internal self-reliant organisation and the cooperative land bank concept provides a means to institutionalise and reinforce such informal social organisation and cohesion.

Finally, the operating financial efficiency and effectiveness of the concept is very much dependent upon a strong grassroots self-reliant social organisation and sense of community. Local self-government is traditional to all Kenyan tribes. The cooperative land bank would provide an innovative and skilful means of building a new economic structure on old tribal traditions, while at the same time breaking down tribal cohesion and tribalism from within. Typically, development along either the capitalist or socialist path has resulted in an expensive organisation. Village self-governance, on the other hand, is a most economical way to organise society, as it substantially reduces government costs. The cooperative land bank concept provides a non-exploitative grassroots village development alternative to Chinese commune, state-cooperative, kibbutz or Soviet collectivism for building a decentralised society.

Chapter VIII
MANUFACTURING AND TRADE

8.1 Industrial Development Sector

8.1.1 INTRODUCTION

> Reading makes a full man, conference a ready man, writing an
> exact man.
>
> Francis Bacon

The international division of labour was modified in the
1950/1960s as a belated though limited process of industrialisation
got underway in tropical Africa. Only a few colonies such as
Senegal, Kenya, the Belgian Congo and Southern Rhodesia
(Zimbabwe) gained much manufacturing investment before the
late fifties. These pioneers offered their foreign investors
relatively large expatriate markets and advanced economic
infrastructure. It was not until independence that most ex-
colonies were able to progress much beyond the manufacture of
beverages, food and cigarettes. Even thereafter, manufacturing
investment typically extended only to some local processing of
raw materials and local assembly or fabrication of formerly
imported consumer goods. Contemporary Africa continues to
supply mainly primary products to the world markets. Its flow of
imports has somewhat altered; industrial economies now provide
fewer manufactured consumer imports, concentrating instead on
machinery, high technology, intermediate goods and locally
available raw materials. Of prime importance is the import of
technology.

This pattern of exchange has presented considerable problems for capital accumulation in Africa. Most obviously, African latecomers cannot exploit factors that facilitated the industrial revolution in Europe, Japan and the United States – captive markets for industrial exports and raw material imports cheapened by slave labour or low wages. In contrast, Africa must compete in world markets already dominated by technologically sophisticated transnational corporations. Is this challenge insurmountable? Yes, but, judging by the recent successes of the Newly Industrialising Countries (NICs) in East Asia and Latin America, the task is extremely complex and one calling for a great deal of acumen, vision and ingenuity.

In Kenya the industrial sector accounts for some 13 per cent of GDP, and has been among the fastest growing areas of the economy, and one which has attracted significant private capital and public donors aid from external sources. Informed discussion of Kenya's industrial policies occurred between the administration, the World Bank and to some extent the ILO. In particular, government policy towards industry has lain at the heart of much of the structural adjustment consultations between the World Bank and the administration. In 1984/1986 the World Bank was involved in a detailed study of the Kenyan industrial sector, which formed the basis for an industrial sector programme in Kenya. It is understood that the resulting report formed, the basis for an industrial sector programme which was to be funded by the World Bank and the IFC in association with other donors and investors. The development of the manufacturing sector in Kenya has been a major element in structural adjustment consultations between the government and the World Bank over several years. Industrial development in Kenya has also long been associated with regional markets and various regional perspectives in Kenya's development policies.

This study provides a brief description of the problems facing the industrial sector in Kenya, and also considers the position adopted by the government and the World Bank to the future policy in the twenty-first century. The growth, structure and problems of this sector are discussed in the section below, which also looks more closely at questions relating to Kenyanisation, the export of manufactures, and the informal sector, role of small-scale industrialisation and artisan industries and the work of Kenya Industrial Estates (KIE), which have received significant support from international development aid. Particular reference is made to Kenyanisation and self-reliance objectives, and the World Bank detailed study (1984/1986),

8.1.2 INDUSTRIAL SECTOR: DEVELOPMENT

In many areas, the Kenyan industrial sector is still grappling with problems inherited from the pre-independence period, when the entire sector was dominated by European, Asian and transnational interests, limiting Kenyans involvement to semi-skilled and labouring work, and largely excluding Kenyans from ownership, management and skilled employment. Since 1963, the government has made determined efforts to rectify this situation involving Kenyans in all departments, levels and functions of industry, while maintaining a continuing relationship with other local and international groups, either still traditionally involved in this sector or which could contribute to its future development.

In these complex and challenging circumstances, it is a tribute to Kenyan good sense that the administration has succeeded in maintaining a viable and expanding manufacturing sector, and that it has in recent years been prepared to consider and take action on economic policy advice from international institutions (the World Bank, the OECD and the ILO) as to the restructuring and future development of this crucial area of the Kenyan economy.

Amidst the many technical aspects of the structural adjustment discussions in the 1982/1986 period which inspired so much of Kenya's forward planning, certain policy initiatives continued to form the hard core of government endeavour. These basically relate to Kenyan advancement, both in the informal sector and in major industrial undertakings, in the boardroom and the artisan's workshop, in the industrial areas of Nairobi and Mombasa and in the remotest districts of the country. For the moment, any policy reflection on Kenyan advancement in the twenty-first century should appear to focus on closely interrelated fields, namely (a) industrial ownership, (b) entrepreneurial and industrial skills and employment, (c) reforms, modernisation of the sector and (d) market access arrangements.

(a) As to ownership, in the years since independence Kenyan business people, cooperatives, transnational companies and parastatals have acquired and developed substantial segments of the industrial sector, to such an extent that, by 1980, it was estimated by the World Bank that less than 10 per cent of total employment in large-scale manufacturing firms (fifty plus employees) was provided by a majority of foreign owned companies. But significant problems remained. Major parastatal acquisitions of the late and early 1970/1980s, were not adequately funded or properly managed within the industrial and commercial sectors. As a result, there was continuing international advice to the government, endorsed in the WPGE report of 1982: (1) to curtail further parastatal expansion; (2) to improve public sector management; (3) to rationalise production; and (4) to divert particular industrial acquisitions to the private sector. The administration responded, in some degree, to these representations, but significant problems arose in disposing of parastatal companies acceptable to private sector purchasers. This difficulty was clearly evident in the case of a major transport group (KENATCO), where no acceptable sale could be arranged by government. It appeared that an extensive parastatal sub-sector was likely to remain active within the Kenyan industrial economy, and one which will require to be provided with an effective complement of entrepreneurial and technical skills and with adequate industrial funding.

In the private industrial sector, there are increasing pressures from small Kenyan firms to take over certain specified industrial processes, currently handled by larger companies. The World Bank offered certain technical advice in this connection, and the matter was placed under consideration by the government in the context of its small industry programme. However, the present administration lacks clear policy guidelines in the industrial field, and there is little constructive initiative on the part of the leading industrial parastatals, such as the Industrial and Commercial

Development Corporation (ICDC) and the Industrial Development Bank (IDB), which tend to pursue largely risk-free policies of buying into well established and successful enterprises. The uncertainties surrounding government policy towards the private sector have in turn given rise to anxieties among investors, including the Asian business community, who are concerned to defuse the sensitive issues inherent in this problem. One frequently canvassed solution to the ownership question is for such enterprises to follow examples set by certain major transnational groups, namely to incorporate themselves as public companies within Kenya, and then to make over the majority of equity shares to Kenyan investors. It is felt that a pragmatic solution of this kind could meet both the Kenyanisation interest, and the original investors' concern to retain some involvement in their respective companies.

(b) Possibly for more intense public concern than industrial ownership, is the acquisition by Kenyans of entrepreneurial skills, which, at all industrial levels from major firms to the work of the 'jua kali', is a subject of constant political discussion. Here it is increasingly contended that successive national development plans have been primarily concerned with creating the appropriate economic climate and infra-structural services for the emergence of local entrepreneurs. Since this somewhat passive approach is thought to have yielded rather limited results, it is now argued that a more positive and professional initiative is necessary, aimed at the purposeful development of Kenya entrepreneurial skills (Nzomo, 1986).

The constructive criticism of official policy has received general support from the government itself, the international bodies, such as the ILO and the World Bank, Kenyan academics, and business. The World Bank strongly advocates the development of programmes for training African entre-preneurs and managers, in business education management, administration, engineering, biotechnology, microelectronics etc, and research at all levels, including on-the-job training, and through actively encouraging project development in the informal and small scale manufacturing sector, high performance and high investment by strengthening support services, including vocational training in middle management, information technology, credit, accounting technicians, banking and finance, insurance and consultancy advice etc, (World Bank, 1986)

It is now apparent that traditional policies associated with Kenya Industrial Estates (KIE), have come under growing serious criticism, and that increasing attention is now required to be given to alternative approaches to the professional training of entrepreneurs in Kenya. Since small scale industry and artisans have been traditionally regarded as the main nursery for producing Kenyan entrepreneurs for the entire industrial sector, the KIE itself has come to assume even greater prominence in Kenya's economic life. In launching further initiatives in entrepreneurial development, the KIE does of course provide a relatively strong institutional base, with a solid background experience throughout different parts of the country. But, the time and political circumstance has come for the KIE to change the direction and relevance of its programmes, in the context of new priorities, to a more systematic approach to the training of Kenyan entrepreneurs.

Perhaps the most serious constraint on further industrial development in Kenya is the slow growth in both domestic and foreign markets. Small-scale industries have been facing stiff competition from large scale companies, as well as from imports (Carlsen, 1980). This suggests that the marketing dimension must be a central feature of any assessment relating to support given to the small scale industry sector.

Again, in the industrial marketing field, there are two further areas of immediate policy concern in Kenya. The first relates to rural–urban balance, where public purchasing, tendering arrangements and other policies will need to be adjusted, to encourage the development of village craftsmen and small-scale industries outside the wider main urban centres discussed below under self-reliance strategies. The second areas of policy concern relate to the wider perspectives of markets in Eastern, Central and Southern Africa, where the government will be particularly anxious to strengthen trade links with the Preferential Trade Area for Eastern and Southern Africa (PTA).

8.1.3 INDUSTRIAL SECTOR: GROWTH, STRUCTURE AND PROBLEMS

The development of the industrial sector represents a major aspect of Kenya's forward planning, where the Sessional Paper no.1 of 1986 foresaw a target growth rate of some 7.5 per cent per annum over the next fifteen years. Although Kenya is the most industrially developed country in Eastern Africa, manufacturing represents only 13 per cent of GDP. Since independence, industrial growth and diversification have been relatively rapid, and by order of contributing to GDP, and in addition to the processing of oil products, the most important branches now are: beverage and tobacco, textiles, miscellaneous food products, motor vehicle assembly and automobile products; electrical and electronic appliances and machinery; basic and secondary metal products, printing and publishing; pulp and paper products; sugar and confectionery, canned fruits and vegetables, chemical products; rubber; clothing, cement; meat and dairy products; wood and cork products; and leather goods.

Conditions favouring the expansion of the Kenyan manufacturing sector in the 1960s and 1970s, included the country's climate, and general political stability linked with a strong commitment towards industrial development embracing private capital and parastatals, foreign investors and the local business community. This was assisted by a relatively generous system of government incentive and protective measures.

During this period, manufacturing was among Kenya's fastest expanding sectors, with production in real terms increasing by more than 9 per cent per annum, and total output growing almost fourfold between independence and 1979. Subsequently in the 1980–1984 period, manufacturing growth fell to less than 4 per cent per annum. While there was a significant reduction in the volume of manufactured exports during this period, there was a certain expansion in production for the internal market, where the substitution effects of exchange rate depreciation and of a more intensive application of quantitative restrictions on consumer imports, more than offset slackening domestic demand. Much of the impetus for this growth in industrial output came from textiles and clothing and transport equipment, which benefited from tariff increases, and in the case of motor vehicles from virtually complete prohibition of importation of assembled products.

As regards capital formation in the industrial sector, the 1980s saw a significant decline, with manufacturing investment in 1984 down by more than a third on 1980 in real terms. The trend was particularly evident in the private sector, where there also appeared to be no significant proposals for new investments, and production increases resulted largely from more effective capacity utilisation. By the 1990s, net private long-term capital inflow drastically declined to some 37 per cent of capital formation by enterprises. Meanwhile the gross outflow of investment income, which always tended to exceed net private capital inflow, had risen to almost double the level of this inflow.

Recorded wage employment in the manufacturing sector increased at more than 6 per cent per annum from some 60,000 in 1966 to 130,000 in 1978. In the 1980s, growth slackened to some 2 per cent per annum, and by 1984 employment in this sector amounted to some 153,000 or approximately 13 per cent of employment in the modern wage sector.

In a situation where import substitution represented the driving force behind industrialisation, it was expected that imports of manufactured goods, as a percentage of domestic supplies, would fall over time. This was the case in Kenya in the 1960s and 1970s, where the ratio of manufactured imports to domestic production declined to more than 40 per cent in 1964 to some 30 per cent in 1974, and less than 20 per cent by 1984. It is questionable whether all import substitution investment during this period made a net contribution to Kenya's balance of payments. In several industries, particularly those with sharply increasing returns over a scale of output larger than the Kenya market (motor vehicles assembly, pharmaceutical and synthetic fibres), domestic production has involved a higher foreign exchange cost than would have resulted from importing the products concerned.

Because effective protection has been for final goods rather than intermediate goods, a significant proportion of production has been in the assembly type of industries. There has been a continuing trend in Kenya toward production of 'final touch' goods, as substantial as the certain decline in the ratio of value added to gross output within the large-scale manufacturing sector.

During the 1960s and 1970s, capital goods were frequently imported at over-valued exchange rates, and financed at low interest rates. As a result, the Kenyan industrial sector became dominated by large and medium firms that produced relatively capital intensive products, with a decreasing employment-to-output ratio, and did not utilise a substantial proportion of their capacity. Large firms in Kenya contribute about 90 per cent to manufacturing value added, and also employ about 90 per cent of workers in the industrial sector. These shares are much higher than in low and middle income developing countries generally, where large firms on average contribute some 68 per cent to manufacturing value added and employ some 56 per cent of the workforce. In the composition of production, the share of capital-intensive commodities also appears relatively high, given Kenya's stage of development.

Large enterprises and production of capital intensive products often imply low-capacity utilisation and low employment–output ratios. While no systematic data for capacity utilisation across the Kenyan industrial sector is available, the steel industry shows a capacity utilisation varying between 13 to 48 per cent for different branches of production.

8.1.4 EVOLUTION IN THE INDUSTRIAL SECTOR

The growth and direction of manufacturing industry in the 1960s and 1970s were shaped to a marked extent by government policies and parastatal programmes. Public policy in relation to industry included the curtailment of imports by quantitative restrictions and protective import duties, a range of fiscal and other incentives to stimulate investment, and the development of an extensive parastatal sector involving both loan finances and equity participation from public sources.

During the 1970s the Kenyanisation of the manufacturing sector was pursued through increased public investment, and the 1982 Working Party on Government Expenditure (WPGE) (Kenya Government, 1982a) found that government had either an exclusive, controlling or minority interest in some 176 enterprises, including the majority of firms with more than 200 employees. Notwithstanding the favoured access, these firms or parastatals enjoyed with a wide range of incentives and assistance, few projects with public sector involvement were financially successful. Moreover, as this favoured treatment was available essentially to large- and medium-scale enterprises, private sector African entrepreneurship involved mainly with smaller firms, came to feel that government's industrial policy conflicted with their interests, and it was noted that the proliferation of commercial activities by the government had been an impediment to true Kenyanisation.

In accepting the recommendations of the WPGE, the government subsequently initiated a programme to rationalise and improve the efficiency of the parastatals through a dual strategy involving, on the one hand, the divestiture of certain investments to the private sector and, on the other, strengthening the capacity of those parastatals remaining in the public sector. Progress in the ensuing implementation of this strategy was somewhat hesitant, but further parastatal expansion was held in check through the exercise of budgetary controls. In addition, under the Fifth Development Plan 1984–1988, government policy moved decisively away from public investment in commercial activities towards strengthening the private sector environment for Kenyan enterprise.

Specific problems, nonetheless, remained in the implementation of these policies. For example, fundamental difficulties arose in reconciling divestiture policies with Kenyanisation objectives. This was apparent in the case of Kenatco, a publicly owned transport service firm, which government sought to divest by selling off the company assets to the Kenyan private sector. In the event no satisfactory financial offer was forthcoming from Kenyan private investors, and government was obliged to abandon this particular privatisation exercise. Given the limitations on local financial resources, it is probable that government retained a significant parastatal component within the industrial and commercial sectors, and consequently more attention was needed to effect industrial rationalisation processes through such organisations as the ICDC and the IDB. But, there are no clear indications of the latter taking a decisive lead in this area. On the contrary, it appeared that the ICDC and IDB were pursuing largely risk-free policies into well established and successful enterprises.

The probable continuance of a large parastatal element in the industrial and commercial sectors, which was implicitly recognised in the state corporation legislation, clearly underlines the need for a more professional approach to management issues. The World Bank emphasised this, reinforcing the entire range of programmes concerned with the development of entrepreneurial skills. And as the crisis in local financial institutions has demonstrated, such programmes have a relevance to many areas in the private sector as well as to parastatal activities.

8.1.5 KENYANISATION AND INDIGENOUS CAPITALIST CLASS

By 1980, less than 10 per cent of total development employment in large scale manufacturing firms (fifty plus employees), was provided by majority foreign-owned companies. Since then, direct foreign investment and private long-term loan capital have both declined in real terms, and practically all new foreign investment has been made from retained earnings, rather than external sources.

In the case of the private sector, the government's approach to new external investment has not always been precisely defined. On the one hand, the government anxiously encouraged the inflow of private capital, and relevant technical skills not immediately available within Kenya. In this regard, efforts have been made within the administration to ease certain constraints inhibiting the inflow of private capital, which are broadly understood to include provision for repatriation of dividends and capital, domestic borrowing limits, income tax rates and permission to use expatriate skills. A more general problem, raised publicly by certain diplomatic missions, related to delays to decision-making within the administration, which is said to discourage certain foreign interests from further expansion or even continuing their activities, and by the same token inhibit potential investors. In this general regard, Session Paper no.1 of 1986 and World Bank Report (World Bank, 1986) made certain proposals for resolving administrative and other constraints affecting foreign investment.

On the other hand, problems of this kind to some degree reflected in the government's concern for the general advancement of Kenya's participation in both ownership and management, a social and economic priority which became the subject of public attention. In this situation, and with no clearly articulated lead from the government or the parastatal institutions, there was a matching concern within the private sector, including the Asian business community, defusing the sensitive issues inherent in this problem. One solution to the ownership question frequently canvassed was for foreign enterprises to follow an example set by certain major groups, namely to incorporate as public companies within Kenya, and then to make over the majority of equity shares to Kenyan investors. It is felt that a pragmatic solution of this kind could meet both the Kenyanisation interest, and the foreign investors' concern to retain some involvement in their respective companies.

A more open debate focused on the Kenyanisation of entrepreneurship and management, where it is contended that successive national development plans have been primarily concerned with creating the appropriate economic climate and infrastructural services for the emergence of local entrepreneurs. Since this somewhat passive approach is felt to have yielded rather limited results, it is argued that a more positive and professional initiative is necessary, aimed at the purposeful development of Kenyan entrepreneurial skills (Nzomo, 1986).

This constructive critique received general support from government and international bodies such as the World Bank, the International Labour Organisation (ILO) and the Organisation for Economic Cooperation and Development (OECD) which actively advocated the development of African entrepreneurs and managers through reinforcing business and engineering education at all levels, including on-the-job training, and positively encouraging project development in the informal and small-scale manufacturing sectors by strengthening support services including vocational training, information technology, credit and consultancy advice etc. As the numbers of successful African entrepreneurs increase, it is felt that there could be a diminution in concern over foreign and expatriate involvement in the industrial sector (World Bank, 1986).

In this context, Kenya Industrial Estates (KIE), took a particular interest in the development of training programmes, especially for women entrepreneurs. Similar training was taken with the Norwegian Agency for International Development (NORAID) support, through the Kenya Women's Finance Trust; although it was not only limited to developing entrepreneurial and management skills in manufacturing, but included trading and services. There would also seem to be possibilities for developing KIE, perhaps in collaboration with the Kenya Women's Finance Trust, as a resource centre in this field, with experience drawn from European/North American/Japanese and Taiwanese development of small scale industries by women.

Leys (1975) observed: 'when circumstances permit an indigenous capitalist class to establish itself effectively, as in the Ivory Coast and perhaps Kenya, the conditions for capitalist development at the hands of both foreign and domestic capital are enormously enhanced.'

First, here then, is the clear image of the new Kenya Government in the 1960s and early 1970s as 'importantly conditioned by a domestic class with substantial capital of its own at stake'. At independence the indigenous Kenyan bourgeoisie acceded to power and rapidly accumulated capital aided by a favourable combination of circumstances. For one, the indigenous, largely Kikuyu, accumulators from the colonial period survived. This group had exploited opportunities in the interstices of the settler-controlled economy, and formed the kernel of Kenya's dominant class. A second beneficial factor was the settlers' success at undermining pre-capitalist forms of production and subsistence agriculture, by forming a large labour market, building an advanced economic infrastructure and accumulating capital in farms and factories. On this groundwork, an indigenous bourgeoisie was built, helped by the post-colonial state it controlled. Its members assumed positions formerly held by Europeans and established control over Kenya's petty bourgeois, peasantry and labour. Bourgeois class consciousness was apparent, not only in the use of the state, but also in the parallel development of bourgeois culture.

Thirdly, there is the question of hegemony. To establish itself effectively in power, a bourgeoisie must control a state that governs through the consent of the lower classes. This in turn means that the values of the rising class must suffuse society to the point that they are held universally. Hegemony in this sense contrasts with supremacy based on domination, that is, the state's reliance upon forced obedience. But, this is not so in Kenya, no social class has become hegemonic. Wealthy business men/women are the envy of many peasants, workers and unemployed, who dream of joining their ranks. This does not mean, however, that they have absorbed the instrumental and individualistic ethics of capitalism. Individual competition, personal accumulation, thrift, rational calculation of means and ends, efficiency, innovation – these Calvinist values have not penetrated deeply into a Kenyan peasant society rooted in an 'economy of affection'. Its values are traditional ones such as solidarity with kin, the minimisation of risks and household autonomy.

The Kenyan radical group of critics has observed: 'the Kenyan bourgeoisie have no bourgeois values suffused in them' and the critics then dismiss them as a tribal 'ruling oligarch' in stinging and contemptuous terms:

Indifferent to the bourgeois values that made European society so dynamic in the nineteenth century – to a respect for thrift, hard work and punctuality – Kenyan leaders operate with a pre-capitalist mentality. They embrace the type of conspicuous consumption which is the hallmark of the feudal ruling caste, where the patron has to impress his dependent clients with hollow pomp and lavish signs of wealth and influence. They respect the big belly squeezed under the steering wheel of the

Mercedes far more than they respect talent, quality and productivity. Perpetual parasites, they are simply not good enough to be truly bourgeois.

Two factors make the Kenyan bourgeoisie's class power seem comparatively formidable to an outsider: First, is the cohesiveness and cultural distinctiveness of this group. But, this owes much to the Kikuyu domination of African big business. Kikuyu preponderance can be attributed to several factors: their head-start in education and jobs during colonial rule, their numbers (twenty per cent of the population); and, the ethnic favouritism under Jomo Kenyatta's system of personal rule, their domination of the ruling Kenya African National Union (KANU) which they used in 'Mafia style control' as an instrument for self enrichment at the expense of other ethnic groups.

Second, the Kikuyu elite benefited from the considerable assets built up in colonial Kenya by white settlers, Asian capitalists and transnationals. This political elite used state power to displace or ally itself with European or Asian capital. Its members accumulated a substantial economic stake during the 1960s and 1970s under the protection of Jomo Kenyatta's presidency.

But the Kikuyu bourgeoisie is not a dominant or ruling class in the Western European mould. The Kikuyu elites' political power, derived from the struggle to generate an anti-colonial movement, allowed it to build its economic power, not vice versa. This economic power was limited by the fact that the Kikuyu bourgeoisie was not a national class, but a tribal clique. Under the Presidency of Daniel Arap Moi, a Kalenjin, it became disadvantageous to be a Kikuyu. By 1983, the Kikuyu were a minor force within Moi's system of personal rule. President Moi has surrounded himself with his own clan and the leaders of smaller tribes, who in turn, have used the state apparatus to displace the Kikuyu bourgeoisie. Based as it was on patronage and force, Kikuyu dominance proved vulnerable to the turns of political fortune.

Specifically, the exigencies of contemporary capitalism requires the state to create and maintain a number of conditions. First and most fundamental, the general socio-political and legal framework must be conducive to market relationships. An environment of security of property and predictability is basic to encourage investment; in turn, this requires political stability and a minimum degree of social harmony. Otherwise, entrepreneurs cannot calculate that an investment today will bear fruit tomorrow. A legal code that protects the prerogatives of the owners and is officially respected (hence calculable) is another element. Such a code must, of course, create and protect a unified national market by limiting or eliminating the taxation power of local authorities. And it should foster a stable and rational taxation system that encourages investment. Also vital is the protection of the institution of private property through such steps as: limiting the claims of employees, abolishing traditional land tenure, safeguarding the sanctity of contracts and guaranteeing full compensation in the event of nationalisation.

Secondly, a range of economic conditions must be fostered by the state. Services that directly facilitate production – roads, railways, ports, airports, electricity, water and telephone communications – are some of the essential basic public services that indirectly assist production. They promote a skilled, healthy, motivated labour force. Services also include schools, technical education, public housing, sanitation and facilities for sports and health. The public sector may also intervene directly through subsidy or investment in industries which are essential to expansion of complementary industries but are too risky to attract private investors. Publicly owned steel, transport or cement factories may sometimes play a significant economic role even if they are not profitable in themselves.

Finally, the government should attract and regulate inward investments in order to maximise the local benefits. This is a most delicate task, for example, the government should strive to attract foreign investment to particular regions in the area, and should negotiate favourable trading arrangements with investors. If the conditions sketched above were met, the multinationals would probably be drawn to invest – provided some local economic potential existed. On the other hand, the government should defend the national interest in the local accumulation of capital, foreign exchange, employment and expertise. This would require, at the minimum, some regulation of the multinationals' economic activities; for otherwise the latter's global profit considerations would jeopardise the achievement of local economic priorities. To attract and regulate foreign investment – this is the challenge confronting public officials or a political leader, who wish to push capitalist development in the context of the existing world economy.

8.1.6 INDUSTRIAL SECTOR AND STRUCTURAL ADJUSTMENT

The heavily protective nature of Kenya's industrial promotion system, its economic weaknesses, its administrative shortcomings, skill shortage and the consequent need for adaptation, structural reforms and modernisation, emerged as a matter of major concern to the government and the World Bank in the structural adjustment consultations of the early 1980s. The major thrust of the World Bank's approach, which was broadly accepted by the government, was to shift from a highly protective import substitution strategy to industrial policies which would encourage self-reliance, increased use of local resources, greater emphasis on employment creation and the encouragement of exports through enhanced institutional support and more effective incentives.

While the necessary policy measures were introduced some-what hesitantly by the administration, and could not be expected to yield immediate results, there were, nonetheless, notable changes in leading economic parameters. Thus, in the monetary field, there was a significant and continuing depreciation of the real effective exchange rate throughout the early 1980s. Real interest rates turned positive in 1984, while real wages continued to fall. In the area of international trade, imports of intermediate and capital goods were liberalised, although extensive restrictions on consumer imports remained in place.

However, as was clearly explained in the World Bank report on Prospects and Policies for Restoring Sustained Growth, the future outlook for Kenyan industry depended on certain further adjustments being made. This challenge was immediately taken up by the government in its planning document, Sessional Paper no.1 of 1986, where two dominant policy themes emerged, directed towards export and small industries.

There was, first of all a determination to increase export earnings and to diversify Kenya's export base, with a particular focus on the further processing of local commodities, in conditions of increasing productivity. Secondly, there were interrelated commitments to increasing employment and to encouraging the advancement of African entrepreneurs within small industry and the informal sector. The latter is seen to be the optimum area, both for the creation of off-farm jobs and for nurturing African entrepreneurial and managerial qualities. Both major policy themes touch on fields where the government is particularly anxious to secure new continuing support from donors development aid. This would help to advance its developmental and commercial goals within the parastatal, private and informal sectors, in the Kenyan context, as well as in regional and international contexts.

Both major policy themes are also being pursued within the structural adjustment framework, which continues to indicate a move away from direct government involvement in manufacturing and other fields, where it is argued the private sector could operate more efficiently. Under the proposal of Sessional Paper no.1 of 1986, the framework itself was to be further strengthened, notably in relation to tariffs, where, since 1981, fiscal policy had focused on duty reductions on imported inputs to help domestic industry lower its costs. In the next phase of the tariff reform programme, action was intended to gradually reduce a range of exceptionally high duties on consumer goods, thus slowly exposing the domestic sub-sectors concerned to competition from imports, as an incentive to become more efficient.

8.1.7 WORLD BANK APPROACH TO INDUSTRIAL SECTOR

The fuller implications of this particular programme were spelled out in the 1986 World Bank report on Prospects and Policies for Restoring Sustainable Growth, which suggested that the arrangements for the phased reduction in tariff protection should be coordinated with a programme for restructuring specified industrial sub-sectors. It envisaged that this process would include financial and management operations directed towards improved capitalisation, liquidity and staff development priorities, linked as necessary with new physical investments. It foresaw that when most of the specified sub-sectors had been treated in this way, protection for domestic production would be rendered relatively uniform at a generally acceptable level. It is not altogether clear what institutional procedures would be used in effecting these rationalisation programmes, but the crucial significance of such initiatives to the future evolution of Kenyan industry and society, suggests that the process should not be left entirely to outside financial institutions or to private business interest, but should quite definitely involve suitably strengthened public bodies, with clearly defined objectives, goals and responsibilities in this area, such as the ICDC and the IDB, and where appropriate the KIE.

In the World Bank view, Kenya has practically completed replacement of those imported consumer goods which can be manufactured economically on a modest scale by local manufacturers, as well as establishing the normal backward linkage industries, which can be set up without major capital investments and with limited labour skills. The Kenyan industrial sector is now largely dominated by enterprises producing 'machine-orientated' products, which require little skilled labour input apart from machinery maintenance. Remaining backward linkage steps, from these operations, led to industries with a very large minimum economic size (e.g. steel and non-ferrous metals), and most of these, in a fully integrated form, are still out of market reach for Kenya.

Given these very real constraints, a possible approach to leading areas of the industrial sector was set out by the World Bank in its 1983 report (World Bank, 1983a), which reviewed Kenyan industry under four main heads, namely intermediate processing, engineering, light consumer goods and major consumer goods and durables, and also considered the development of new industries with strong backward linkages. This analysis is concerned, in the first instance, with the domestic market, but is complemented by a parallel review of export implications.

Under processing industries are grouped standard intermediate goods, such as steel, paper, chemicals, petroleum-refining, glass, cement etc. Here Kenya is advised that unless relevant new plants can be constructed on an efficient scale, and complete with imports with the help of lower transport costs, they should generally be avoided. Within these constraints, specific recommendations are made regarding possible development in the plastics industry. Since intermediate products are by definition used as inputs for other manufactures and sectors, their cost structure can have extensive price implications for the economy and for industrial competitiveness. Where new investments are made in intermediates processing, the products should be sold, in the World Bank's view, at import equivalent prices, and in exceptional circumstances, could be subsidised by government.

In the engineering field a more positive view is taken, since in this area small countries like Kenya can often compete effectively on the international market, as sub-contractors and parts producers in certain specialised lines, while within the Kenyan market, there are still feasible import substitution possibilities. Given the availability of imported primary metals at competitive prices, the Kenyan engineering industry could, in the World Bank's view, be fostered through encouraging broad processes or classes of production including foundries, forging operations and machine shops. It is emphasised, in this regard, that efficiency in engineering depends to a large extent on work organisation, operational planning, and the effective use of skilled workers, technical managers and engineers – factors which are the subject of detailed World Bank recommendations.

In the case of light consumer goods and processed food products, the basic strategy should be to improve their efficiency to move from import substitution to exports, which may frequently be feasible, given the requisite resources and relatively inexpensive labour. As in engineering, work scheduling is again regarded as crucial to productivity, but since the product mix is usually simpler, the processes in this area are generally more straightforward.

As regards remaining import substitution possibilities, there are indications that small electrical appliances could become increasingly viable for local production with certain export possibilities. It would also appear that, in certain instances import substitution did not prove possible because of technical, organisational or policy problems relating to the supply of requisite domestic inputs, particularly from the agricultural sector. Within this category fall items such as animal and vegetable oils, whose production could be substantially increased by improved organisation.

In the case of major consumer durable and motor vehicles, it is suggested that an appropriate strategy might be to encourage import substitution, only where relevant developments could be effected at moderate cost to the consumer, and if there were realistic presumption that they could become competitive over the longer term. Activities in this field could be used to build up the engineering industry through appropriate backward linkages.

Turning to potential new industries, it is suggested by the World Bank and the ILO that certain of these, and more specifically prefabricated low cost housing of non-traditional design, could have strong backward linkages. If a carefully planned programme were implemented, the demand for domestic inputs for this branch of the building and construction industry and for home furnishing could increase, while it is felt that various other industries could become viable, and existing operations expanded in this general area.

8.1.8 EXPORT OF MANUFACTURES

Among the leading objectives of Sessional Paper no.1 of 1986 was a determination to increase exports over forthcoming planning periods at a real growth rate of some 6 per cent. In working towards this target, particular attention was to be given to diversifying the range of exports, to processing local commodities, and to improving productivity. Structural adjustment discussions identified three broad categories in Kenya's manufactured exports. Firstly, there is a group of standard products, including paper and cement, which are made in relatively large modern plants, and exported competitively over an extensive regional market. Secondly, there is a series of manufactured exports based on distinctive natural resources such as soda ash, leather, and processed agricultural products including fruits and vegetables.

Finally, there are products identical to those produced for the domestic market, which may be exported in limited quantities to neighbouring states by virtue of market linkage and transport cost advantages. It is estimated that this last group accounts for some two thirds of Kenya's manufactured exports.

Industrial products with a relatively high manufacturing content (SITC 5–8 less 68) represented some 15 per cent of Kenya's total traded exports. Export performance in manufactured items has been generally disappointing, with decline of some 37 per cent in volume between 1980 and 1984, resulting in a fall in the proportion of exports to total manufacturing, from 7 per cent to less than 5 per cent. Among the main reasons for this decline, was a shortage within Kenya of foreign exchange to secure imported inputs and spares during the 1982–1983 period, and declining incomes and inadequate convertible currency resources within many PTA countries.

Under the East African Community (EAC), Tanzania and Uganda were the leading markets for Kenya's manufactured exports, and in 1983 they still accounted for about a quarter of such exports strictly defined. The Tanzanian market for Kenyan exports peaked in the 1970s, and these were already declining prior to the 1977 border closure, which ushered in six years of very limited bilateral trade. The reopening of the common border in late 1983 led to a certain resurgence of Kenyan exports to Tanzania in 1984–1985, which indicated a potential for further growth.

Unlike the situation in Tanzania, the volume of Kenyan exports to Uganda was not radically affected by the EAC's dissolution, and these, in fact, tended to continue growing in the wake of political difficulties. To some degree, Kenya benefited from the de-industrialisation of Uganda under Idi Amin, which provided new export opportunities off-setting the adverse effect on market growth in Uganda, resulting from the disruption of cash crops and marketing arrangements. By 1985, the level of total Kenyan exports to Uganda had reached some US$50 million, and in the case of Tanzania some US$20 million.

8.1.9 STRUCTURAL ADJUSTMENT ON EXPORT DIMENSIONS

The promotion of Kenya's manufactured exports has represented a leading element in the various structural adjustment discussions between government and the World Bank, which could on occasion take a less sanguine view of Kenya's prospects. Apart from the economic policy adjustments that the World Bank considered necessary, it is also preoccupied with factors such as the availability of appropriate skills, labour costs and transport constraints, which affects Kenya's competitiveness in richer world markets outside Eastern Africa. Nevertheless, the World Bank considers that by developing country standard, Kenya has a strong infrastructure particularly in transportation, power and communications, favourable location for industry, a well developed financial system, and a positive attitude to foreign investment. In a regional context, the World Bank considers Kenya should fully exploit its transport cost and accessibility advantages in exporting manufactures within the PTA area, although it also felt that the volume of these exports have been most adversely affected by foreign exchange problems in the region (World Bank, 1986a).

Looking at Kenya's performance in manufactured exports in a more fundamental sense, the World Bank attributes many of Kenya's difficulties to more deep seated domestic problems, including a certain discrimination against exports in the country's industrial incentive system. Thus the well protected industries supplying local needs, are frequently not sufficiently competitive to hold their own on international markets while, at the same time, their domestic profitability results in their diverting resources from areas that appear to have an economic potential for exporting.

More generally, the World Bank emphasised that the success of official measures to promote manufactured exports depends on government's political commitment to this objective. If the national leadership is ready to throw its full weight behind efforts to expand exports, then the administrative cadres would take the necessary action and bureaucratic and other obstacles might be overcome.

The Kenya Government's response to the challenge from the World Bank came in a succession of policy initiatives, and most directly in the cabinet's strong endorsement of Sessional Paper no.1 of 1986, which set out the various steps that the administration proposed to take in regard to export promotion. In the sessional paper it is acknowledged that the best incentive for export industries is the flexible management of the exchange rate, which might be expected to yield a profitable margin from export earnings over production costs. However, the government also accepts that additional incentives would be necessary to encourage potential exporters to move into foreign markets, and the sessional paper set out a range of government commitment in this area.

First of all, under the Kenyan export compensation scheme, a 1985 decision was reconfirmed, whereby companies engaged in exporting, received reimbursement from government of an amount equivalent to 20 per cent of the export value of the item concerned, (as compared with a previous 10 per cent). The purpose of the reimbursement was to compensate the exporting firm for increase production costs, resulting from tariff payments on imported inputs, and from high cost elements in domestic supplies. In this general context, the sessional paper indicated that there would be further improvements in a special programme permitting industrialists engaged exclusively in a particular export line to manufacture under bond, that is under conditions where the duties are entirely waived on specified imported inputs. In addition, it was indicated that a green channel system to simplify administrative procedures was being introduced for exporters, who might also benefit from a system of special concessions.

In the field of export financing, it was indicated that government was prepared to facilitate the creation of an export credit insurance scheme by the commercial banks, although for financial reasons government would not be able to participate, either as a source of capital or a guarantor, but hoped to attract foreign assistance to get the scheme started.

In this context, it may be recalled that in 1983 the World Bank advised the government that an important component in Kenya's industrial export drive should be to provide potential exporters with services such as export credits, grantees, insurance, and relevant trade and marketing information. It was also suggested by the World Bank that in view of the relatively small volume of many individual exports, it might be desirable to pool resources for marketing, by creating a central marketing organisation in Kenya, possibly in collaboration with the Kenya external Trade Authority (KETA), with a related external marketing structure.

8.2   District Focal Policy and the Informal Sector

8.2.1 INTRODUCTION

Under Kenya's District Focus Policy (DFP), development programmes will require investment into each district. Is this to come from outside or from within the district? An integrated approach, involving a combination of the two, is desirable. But each presents a series of problems, which leaves a dilemma to be resolved.

Reliance on the outside for commercial investment to stimulate local development has inevitable consequences. The outside investment has to earn a return, in the form of money paid out in future years from the locality to the outside world. This means that regular flows of new money have to be brought into the locality to match the money being paid out, and this requires an increase in exports out of the locality in order to generate the new outside earnings. So new external investment inevitably makes a locality more dependent than it was before on earnings from products and services exported to the outside world – as well as usually increasing its dependence on employment created and controlled from outside. But this is not precisely what self-reliant development is about. To avoid this problem, outside investment in local economic development must be made in a form which requires no new export earnings to service it or pay it back – in other words, external investment must be made either as a gift or grant to the local economy; or as 'immigrant' investment which is not itself, or the earnings from it, subsequently taken out of the local economy but is spent and reinvested within it.

The nature of the problem can be seen more clearly if we look at present external investment in Kenya's development programme. In this case, external loans from the IMF or World Bank and private loan investments have to be serviced and repaid in foreign exchange. By their very nature, therefore, they cannot be used to reduce the Kenya's dependence on foreign exchange earnings. They have at least to generate the extra foreign exchange needed to service and repay the debt. The imposition of a necessity of this kind is the reverse of self-reliant development. Self-reliant development involves producing home-grown substitutes for imports, which reduce the need to earn foreign exchange.

In the case of a district focussed development, foreign exchange would not be involved. But the principle is exactly the same. Under Kenya's District Focus Industrial policy, the following practical and 'holistic' approach would be directed to all rural districts, divisions, locations and villages:

(a) to provide enabling, rather than dependency-reinforcing, forms of village support and incentives for family care, village community initiatives and industrial programmes;

(b) to encourage village architecture and landscape plan for housing, health, education, and leisure initiatives, and information centres for each as possible starting points for a wider range of grass roots village initiative and creativity on which local communities can be built;

(c) to encourage village community initiatives in recycling, conservation, agricultural farms, horticulture and energy saving, as steps towards developing more resourceful and conserving village communities;

(d) to enable policy-makers and professionals to help village community groups with local projects that cut across sectoral boundaries (employment, health, housing, tourism, leisure etc);

(e) to develop techniques of social accounting and social audit in order to measure the benefits produced and the costs saved by village community businesses and other conserving village communities;

(f) to evolve an effective financial and administrative framework for supporting village community initiatives;

(g) to shift the emphasis in public sector social spending from programmes that deliver dependency-reinforcing services to programmes which enable local village communities to meet their own needs;

(h) to adapt the structures and procedures of central government and local district administration to their increasingly important functions as enablers of village enterprises and initiatives;

(i) to expand the role of the voluntary sector to include churches and charities, schools etc., in local regeneration initiatives;

(j) to enable traders, administrators, councillors, police and unions to play a positive role in village community initiatives;

(k) to develop management education for village community enterprises and initiatives, recognising the crucial role of social entrepreneurs whose enterprise is committed not to making money for themselves but to creating social wealth.

Each of these needs is a need for social investment or, to put it another way, for investment in the village socio-economy. However, there is also a problem about a strictly self-reliant approach to District Focus Policy programmes. That would mean relying wholly on district generated capital for investment in the district and its capacity to make import substitution possible. But, the very places where this approach is most necessary are likely to be those districts where local capital is least available, and where local investment facilities are least developed. The mobilisation of local savings on the required scale may be difficult without outside help.

So there seems to be a dilemma – either investment in dependency-generating development based on export-dependent growth, or no investment in local development at all. How can this be resolved? This situation can only be resolved by a form of socially directed investment.

Socially directed investment in a self-reliant programme is

investment in the capacities of local people, to enable them to do more for themselves and one another. In other words, it is investment to create local social wealth. Conventional economic investment aims to create direct financial returns for the investor. In socially, directed investment, the investor is concerned primarily with non-financial objectives rather than with maximum financial returns. There is need for new opportunities for people to direct their savings into socially benign enterprises, such as production for use, to meet directly the needs of the producer or the producer's family, friends and neighbours, without any payment taking place. Investment in self-reliant local development is one example of socially valuable investment into which people and organisations might wish to direct their funds, if given the opportunity.

Some of the potential sources of socially directed investment in local economic self-reliance are outside the local economy. Others are within it. Potential external sources include agencies of national government. An example might be a national health department promotion that will genuinely enable a village, a location, a division or a district, to become less dependent on nationally supported health services in future years. Potential internal sources include local residents and local organisations, including local government agencies. There are many ways in which they might be prepared to invest some of their money to develop and improve their own area if the facilities existed for doing so, rather than investing it in ways that mainly benefit other places. And experience shows that poor people, especially in developing countries, are prepared to save – through credit unions, cooperative land bank and other types of saving institutions – for investment in their own economic future, if they are given the opportunities.

An important task for the twenty-first-century is to develop a concept of socially directed investment in local self-reliance, including:

(1) new priorities for national government spending on local programmes; and
(2) new financial facilities for channelling local savings into local

investment.

In a sense the world is at a trading cross-roads today: there is a certain retreat from free trade, which might be intensified, or could be reversed. This is true for developed and developing countries. Developing countries are under considerable pressure from the international community (the IMF and the World Bank and the major donor countries) to move towards freer trade, but their financial crises reinforce protectionist tendencies, while giving the international community considerable leverage to secure liberalisation. This is a time, therefore, when a great number of countries are facing choices in their trading strategy, based on three broad options.

(1) Free trade – one option is to aim to reverse the move towards protectionism, and promote free trade. This option may be interpreted as involving free trade for all, both the developing and developed countries; or it might consist in free trade for just some category, such as developed countries, and not developing countries; or it might be selectively operated by particular countries. The argument then becomes somewhat complex because what is best for any one country or group of countries depends in part on what policies other countries are adopting. From developing countries' perspective, genuinely free trade access to developed country markets would offer an enormous extension of markets: all middle-income countries, which have already established an industrial capacity, would be likely to benefit, as their lower-wage costs would enable them to undercut developed countries in many lines. The sheer size of developed countries' markets, which account for nearly two-thirds of world markets, means that developed-country markets offer significantly more potential in some respects than other possibilities; more, for example, than trade between Third World countries. Genuinely free trade extended to primary commodities, such as sugar and grain, would benefit a number of the poorest developing countries as well. However, there are a number of qualifications that need to be made before concluding that this option offers

most countries the best prospects.

The first concerns political realism. The industrialised countries have resisted free trade in agricultural products and textiles, even in the apparently free trade era of the 1950/1960s. While the new moves towards protectionism might be halted, it is extremely unlikely that totally free access would be permitted for 'Developing Countries' exports. It is more likely that rich countries will seek to impose free trade on developing countries, while at the same time protecting the most vulnerable of their own industries.

A second qualifying factor is economic vulnerability. Even with totally free access to industrialised countries markets, developing countries would become even more vulnerable to fluctuations in the world economy, since an increasing proportion of their markets would be external. Experience during recent world fluctuations has shown: (a) that countries most dependent on exports of primary products, for example, many African economies, are very vulnerable to world fluctuations, (b) that countries which have been successful exporters of manufactured goods are better able to defend themselves against world fluctuations than less export-oriented economies, because their potential to adjust into new markets and into import substitution, appears to be high. South Korea, until the recent economic crisis, and Taiwan have provided good examples. However, large countries, such as India and China, which do not trade or borrow a great deal internationally, are probably the least vulnerable, but this is not a realistic possibility for small countries. From the point of view of reducing vulnerability, then, it appears that reduced dependence on primary products is desirable, but an increase in manufactured exports need not increase underlying vulnerability.

A third qualification concerns the need to protect infant industry. In order to compete in the world economy, countries have to build up a strong competitive base in manufacturing. To do this requires time, both for industry as a whole and for particular industries. Hence, some protection is essential; in the early stages of industrialisation, the whole industrial sector needs protecting from competition from abroad; in the later stages, selective protection is necessary while a country builds up a capacity in particular industries. Consequently, developing countries must retain the ability to impose some protection. If the price of free access to developed countries' markets is completely free trade, then it will only benefit those countries which have already established themselves as industrial economies such as those (NICs) – but, will perpetuate under-development in the less developed economies.

A fourth major qualification concerns dependence. It is often argued that increased trade with developed countries also involves increased dependence. This may be variously defined as: (a) dependence on markets; (b) dependence on multi-national companies (MNCs); (c) dependence on international banks; and (d) dependence on advanced countries' technology.

Whether or not a free trade strategy involves more dependency on MNCs and on international banks depends on the strategy adopted, and also on the alternatives considered. For example, many import-substituting countries, with high levels of protection, have used the multi-national company as the vehicle of development and are highly dependent on it. It is also the case that many of these same countries became heavily indebted to the international banks as in the 1970s. Consequently, an import substitution (IS) strategy does not necessarily mean reduced dependency. Moreover, the countries exporting manufactured goods – Taiwan, South Korea – have not in the past been as closely involved with MNCs as some of the IS countries. Taiwan has not borrowed heavily, although South Korea did and is doing so now. So we may conclude that dependence on MNCs and international banks is neither a necessary nor a sufficient condition of export-oriented strategy, nor of an IS strategy, since countries like India and China did not make use of MNCs nor borrow heavily.

(2) The main reasons for adopting autarchy – a complete retreat from free trade – are: (a) to protect employment; (b) to

reduce vulnerability to international fluctuations; (c) to permit the development and adoption of appropriate technologies.

These justifications apply to both developed and developing countries. The disadvantage of this strategy is that it is likely to lead to lower levels of income for the countries concerned, and levels which become increasingly reduced relative to the rest of the world. Essentially, the option would involve giving up the advantages, in productivity gains, of international specialisation and economies of scale. These losses would be particularly great for small economies, and for economies lacking a large technological capacity. In a way this strategy has been followed by China, but that country is now turning away from it because of the costs involved. India, too, which had until recently taken a very selective approach to free trade and technology, tried to develop its own self-reliant capacity for production of goods and technology and is now opening the economy more to foreign technology and, to a lesser extent, specialisation in trade.

(3) Trading Blocks and Selectivity – there are obviously a huge number of variants within this option. Basically, the reasons for selecting this approach may be twofold:

   (1) because a free-trade policy is not possible, given the restrictions in trade and finance in the world trading system;
   (2) to permit countries to enjoy some of the advantages of trade without some of the disadvantages.

In practice, at this moment, both reasons apply. The many restrictions in being, especially in payments, mean that many countries in payments difficulties cannot afford to import because they have no ready access to foreign exchange. If two or more of such countries get together and offer swap arrangements, they will be able to expand their markets and their imports, resulting in increased incomes and employment for them all. The growth in counter-trade is a way in which this coincidence of interests among countries in difficulties may be realised in selective trading arrangements. For example, Brazil and Nigeria have made arrangements whereby Brazil exchanges machinery for Nigerian oil. Indonesia buys the refined oil products it needs, like kerosene and diesel, from Singapore, in exchange for other oil products where it has marketing difficulties, such as low sulphur waxy residue. Malaysia has bought two naval patrol boats from South Korea in exchange for crude oil, refined palm oil, textiles, timber and electrical products.

Trading blocks may also assist smaller countries to stimulate the conditions of the larger economies, and may be organised in a number of ways. Regional arrangements between economies of similar levels of development is one possibility. Problems often emerge in these arrangements due to differences in stages of development so that one member of the group may come to dominate the whole. The problems are compounded by political problems between neighbours. Among developed countries, however, these arrangements have been very successful (e.g. the European Community, EU); and in some cases among developing countries also (e.g. the Preferential Trade Area, PTA or the Latin American Free Trade Area).

Another possibility is North–South blocks; the EU arrangements with Lomé countries is an example, as are the US arrangements with the Caribbean countries and the old UK arrangements with Commonwealth countries. These arrangements may benefit the richer countries, providing protected trade outlets; the poorer countries may secure a greater share of finance. Normally, the arrangements have not permitted less developed countries better market access to any significant degree. If they did, then these arrangements would offer the particular group of countries some of the advantages of market access to developed countries. Their advantage over more general free trade arrangements would be (a) protecting the lesser developed countries over the more developed one e.g. Africa in the EU as compared with Asia (NICs products); and (b) they might be easier to negotiate than more general arrangements, but history does not give this hypothesis much support.

There are very strong grounds for favouring a selective approach to trade, especially one that promotes trade among countries at a similar stage of development and with similar objectives. This selective approach should permit countries to realise their objectives better, compared with both the autarchic approach and a free-trade approach. A selective approach is in fact emerging, to some extent, from the present crisis. It is not the most rational of selective approaches, in many cases; it needs investigation and rationalisation, but it may offer countries some potential for realising their development objectives.

8.2.2 PREFERENTIAL TRADE AREA (PTA)

In the Sessional Paper no.1 of 1986 the Kenya Government underlined the significance that it attached to membership of the Preferential Trade Area (PTA), which is believed could eventually have a profound impact on Kenya's export trade. In this context, the sessional paper did usefully examine the wider policy implications, and notably the fact that Kenya's best interests were better and most effectively served by extensive economic development, throughout the Eastern and Southern Africa region, stimulating not only competitive forces, but also some measure of cooperation in the industrial field.

As the Governor of the Central Bank of Kenya pointed out, what is required in African regional cooperation is properly managed equitable distribution of diverted trade, which should include deliberate measures for dealing with polarisation effects (Ndegwa, 1985). Despite the improved performance of the PTA clearing house arrangements, it is clear that a significant constraint to the growth of trade within the PTA, remains an acute shortage of convertible currency resources among most members. Unless relevant financial arrangements can be found to tackle this problem effectively, possibly with donor aid support, then notwithstanding the PTA provisions, Kenya could well be obliged to negotiate bilateral counter-trade arrangements with its neighbours, if it is to develop, maintain and expand its export markets within the region.

8.2.3 THE INFORMAL SECTOR AND SMALL-SCALE INDUSTRY

The sessional paper guidelines devoted special attention to the needs of small industries, and in particular to the requirements of informal sector entrepreneurs in manufacturing, transport and housing, and also of those entrepreneurs with a capacity to make the transition to large-scale production. Beyond the normal structure of incentives, special initiatives were proposed to expand access to credit for informal sector enterprises, to disseminate relevant information on marketing and production, to expand youth polytechnic training and focus such programmes on appropriate skills and management techniques, and to relax certain restrictions on informal sector activities.

Within small industry in Kenya, a distinction is customarily drawn between two broad and interrelated categories, namely unregistered traditional artisan production and registered non-traditional small-scale industry. While this distinction may be more apparent than real, certain broad characteristics are frequently attributed to these two branches of small industry.

8.2.4 INFORMAL SECTOR AND ARTISAN PRODUCTION

Traditional artisan production is normally defined as including small undertakings employing less than ten workers, not registered with the Registrar of Companies, and using forms of production which require limited specialisation and management capacity. These traditional operations are based for the most part on skills, technical knowledge and raw materials, which are all quite readily available. There are seldom on taking up traditional enterprise, production risks, but competition is frequently intense. A large proportion of traditional artisan production is directed to satisfying basic needs, namely the provision of low income consumer goods and services, for which available substitutes normally, although not invariably, sell at significantly higher prices. Foremost amongst these items are clothing, furniture, foodstuffs and motor vehicle repairs.

While data for this sector is not entirely adequate, it is estimated that there are approximately 16,000 enterprises, certain of which may be semi-dormant, and provide total employment for some 61,000 persons. However, within the urban informal sector, artisan production accounts for little more than 18 per cent in retail trades. In addition to some 4,500,000 persons working in the urban informal sector, there are estimated to be 2,300,000 people involved in rural non-farm production, which generally consists of part-time work performed by family farm workers. In urban areas, employment in the traditional artisan field is thought to be increasing more rapidly than in the modern manufacturing sector, with wider distribution outside Nairobi and Mombasa.

While employees incomes in the traditional artisan sector are generally below the official minimum wage, artisans, for the most part, normally have net earnings above this level. Although small traditional enterprises as unregistered bodies, rarely have access to many of the incentives and other advantages available to larger undertakings, they benefit to some degree from the subsidy conditions inherent in the non-enforcement of many official regulations and fiscal charges in the case of their particular activities. While traditional artisans have in the past often complained of harassment by local officials and police, their economic role in society now receives generous recognition from the Presidency, which has given particular encouragement to the work of the 'jua kali'.

8.2.5 SMALL-SCALE MANUFACTURING

In the related area of small-scale industry, which comes within the formal economy, the sectoral definition is generally based on employment levels of up to 50 persons, associated with significant specialisation and supervision requirements within a registered enterprise. In this modern small-scale manufacturing sector, where the relevant knowledge, skills and material inputs are often not initially available in the requisite form, greater priority is given to qualities of enterprise and innovation, in conditions of economic uncertainty. Since entry to this sector tends to be restricted by access to capital and knowledge, there are generally fewer participants and less competition than in the traditional field. Enterprises in the modern small-scale category manufacture a much wider variety of articles than traditional artisans, including wood and metal products, glass and pottery, clothing and leather items, furniture and fixtures: products generally designed to meet the needs of low-income households.

According to recent estimates, the modern small-scale manufacturing sector, which is centred mainly in the Nairobi and Mombasa areas, consists of some 4,000 registered enterprises (certain of which may be semi-dormant), employing approximately 14,000 persons representing some 4 per cent of total wage employment and 3 per cent of value added in modern manufacturing. It is in this sector, and in the employment range up to 100 persons, that the great majority of Kenya's one-person family enterprises are to be found, as also are the 150–200 African firms located in industrial estates. This sector has hitherto been seen as the main focus for the development of African entrepreneurs, although the enterprise capacities of the 'jua kali' are also increasingly stressed, as is a professionally programmed approach to the cultivation of entrepreneurial skills.

8.2.6 KENYA'S INDUSTRIAL ESTATES (KIE)

Responsibility for assistance to small industry is vested for the main part in Kenya's Industrial Estates (KIE), whose original aim and in large measure continuing purpose, lies in the advancement of African entrepreneurship through the development of nursery-style industrial estates. KIE has three main operations, namely the Rural Industrial Development Centre (RIDCs), the urban industrial estates, and a capital loans programme, and has received significant support from Scandinavian Countries and other donors. An interesting feature of the KIE was the appointment of a woman as its managing director.

There are about some sixteen RIDCs geared to the needs of entrepreneurs manufacturing traditional small industry products. The RIDCs have emerged from a scheme to foster enterprise skills through extension work, which was expanded to include the provision of workshop and supporting facilities, and the selection of potential entrepreneurs in specific branches of industry. Most undertakings assisted under this programme have been relatively successful, particularly in the production of traditional artisan items.

The industrial estates programme consists of some five major schemes, each with a Technical Service Centre (TSC), and together providing approximately 150 units let out on subsidised terms to small entrepreneurs. Most of these enterprises have been established on the basis of project identification and developmental work undertaken by KIE staff. The latter subsequently assist selected entrepreneurs, who are required to put up to 10 per cent of capital costs, with all aspects of project development. Within the industrial estates, the TSC's capabilities have not always been fully utilised, and they have become increasingly and usefully involved in outside technical work with small businesses.

The loans programme for small firms, dating back to the 1950s, was taken over in 1978 by KIE, which lends up to 90 per cent of the total fixed and working capital required, with collateral being provided through loan-funded equipment.

8.2.7 WORLD BANK ASSESSMENT OF KIE

Among published assessments of KIE activities was a World Bank report (World Bank, 1983a), which suggested that the KIE programme had attained differing degrees of success. On the positive side, KIE is seen to represent an exceptionally comprehensive approach to small industrial development, with willingness both to experiment with new methods and to provide the most thorough support for projects in their charge.

On the other hand, it appears that the KIE has devoted a relatively large measure of assistance, with varying results, to the development of a limited number of new projects. In this regard, the World Bank correctly recommended that the KIE should aim to widen its activities by devoting an increasing part of its attention to the needs of traditional artisans. While emphasising the case for introducing economic charges in certain areas, the bank assessment gave limited consideration to the funding of training programmes sponsored by the youth polytechnic or related extension schemes. Nor was reference made to the place of women in the KIE programmes, who received increasing support through Scandinavian and NORAD development aid assistance.

8.2.8 TECHNOLOGY AND SUB-CONTRACTING

Further issues discussed by the World Bank in its report (World Bank, 1983) concerned the upgrading of technology and the sub-contracting by small industry, a subject which assumed a new relevance in the context of government initiatives on entrepreneurial development and rural-urban balance. In the World

Bank's view, a critical element in strengthening the enterprise capacity of Kenyan business persons is to raise the level of technical and organisational knowledge they apply to the management of their firms. Formal training institutions, such as the Kenyan Industrial Training Institute, the Management Training Advisory Centre, and the youth polytechnic clearly has a significant role to play in this context, especially when technical knowledge relates to an industry that is comparatively new to Kenya.

In this regard, the bank suggested that the proper starting point for a programme of promoting technological advance, would be an extensive analysis of the relevant market conditions, including the constraints these impose on product upgrading and on changes in production methods. The results of such an investigation would then provide the necessary parameters around which a technological programme can be designed. More specifically, industry by industry 'state of the art' field surveys of this kind should constitute an effective basis for curricula reform, for new initiatives in the use of appropriate technology, and for technical assistance work.

In this context, both the World Bank and the ILO underlined the significance of sub-contracting in relation to technology development. Where it operates effectively, sub-contracting can offer three important advantages to the small producer, namely (a) an assured market, (b) technical backing not otherwise obtainable to develop manufacturing processes, and (c) strict quality control. In the sub-contracting field, which would appear to represent an increasingly significant element in the development of Kenyan industrial policy, the World Bank recommended a realistic and careful approach. Firstly, the emergence of an efficient sub-contracting system is seen to require a relatively extensive supply of middle-level organisational and technical skills. Secondly, except where capital is short, there would often appear to be little enthusiasm on the part of large-scale companies in forging sub-contracting links with small emergent producers with limited technical capacities. And thirdly, it is argued that sub-contracting is rarely consistent with geographical dispersion, since it is generally only where small enterprises are nurtured near parent companies that they can operate at a capacity level and mobilise the necessary range of technical skills.

However, with such limitations in mind, the World Bank believe a start can be made in a modest but practical sub-contracting programme. Here, in addition to the very specific 'state of the art' studies mentioned above, a key ingredient would be an inventory of potential sub-contractors and of their respective technical capacities, which would form the basis for negotiations between designated government agencies, such as the KIE, and representatives of large-scale firms regarding the establishment of a sub-contracting programme. It assumed that this useful proposal would have been the subject of further discussions between the government and the World Bank, following the completion of the latter's industrial sector review.

Finally, it is understood that in its final report the World Bank industrial mission referred to reorganising part of the KIE operations in a single output delivery system, the provision of credit facilities on the basis of character rather than collateral, and certain modification of interest charges for informal sector operations.

Chapter IX
CONCLUSION AND A THIRD WAY

9.1 Introduction

Is capitalism the best basis on which Kenya can build its economic future? The widespread view that experiments in socialism have largely failed lends credence to this position. Of course, one might counter that many capitalist experiments have also gone awry. But the force of this argument is vitiated by the common attribution of capitalist failure to governments' fondness for public economic intervention – that is, to the supposedly socialist elements of a mixed-economy approach. Whatever the merits of their case, world recession and general economic decline clearly exert a firm pressure on African governments to free market forces and rely on private investment. All of them desperately need to obtain loans, development aid and investment from international organisations, especially the IMF and the World Bank, bilateral agencies, private banks, and corporations that favour such policies. Therefore, even socialist-oriented regimes are inexorably pushed in a capitalist direction as they seek a workable economic path in the midst of economic, and often, social and political chaos. Capitalism's potential in Africa thus remains a crucial question.

This is not only a question about which particular bundle of economic policies is likely to prove most effective in Kenya. Consideration of the appropriate degree of export orientation, the pros and cons of concentration on small-scale peasant agriculture, or the proper extent of reliance on direct foreign investment is of course necessary and valuable. But there is also a more fundamental question: how conducive is the African environment to capitalist development, irrespective of any particular policy approach? It is clear that capitalism in sub-Saharan Africa, in comparative Third World terms, has not been particularly resilient and successful since the 1960s. Is this principally a matter of inadvisable policy formulation, implementation and management, or do more fundamental constraints operate?

I argue that the latter is the case and that socio-political factors, in particular, place severe limitations on economic development. Elsewhere (Germany, Japan and NICs) the state has played a central role in capitalist development, indirectly through the provision of a conducive framework of political order, rational law and administration; directly through the provision of adequate infrastructure, subsidies to promising firms, sectors, even productive public investment in strategic industries. But African states are not, in any real sense, capitalist states. The peculiar conditions of post-colonial Africa impels an adaptation of unworkable colonial inspired political, administrative structures and processes in a patrimonial, or rather neo-patrimonial direction. The omnipresent danger in this adaptation is the degeneration of neo-patrimonialism into an economically irrational form of 'personal rule'. This decay is manifest in political instability, systemic corruption, maladministration, mismanagement, and introduces irrationalities into economic life. Nonetheless, it is shaped by a particular political logic.

Personal rule, a form of patrimonialism, is the system of governance best adapted to these conditions. Unable to depend on the willing compliance of bureaucrats and citizens, African leaders turn to mercenary incentives and force. The typical scenario goes something like this: a strongman (President Kabila/Mobutu type) emerges; his rule is based on managing a complex system of patron-client linkages and factional alliances. He personally maintains loyal and corrupt armed forces, police and foreign mercenaries to support him at every turn.

Personal rule can be dangerous though. Inherent in this system is the likelihood that no one harbours the will or capacity to keep in check its destructive features. The cynical tactics of political support-building and self-enrichment undermine the state's already fragile authority, and demoralise even the most honest and loyal public officials. One of many African writers who have lamented this condition is a Nigerian, Chinua Achebe.

The narrator of *A Man of the People* expresses this disenchantment:

> ...They (the villagers) were not only ignorant but cynical. Tell them that this man (the Minister) had used his position to enrich himself and they would ask you – as my father did – if you thought that a sensible man would spit out the juicy morsel that good fortune placed in his mouth. (p.2)

Chinua Achebe, *A Man of the People*.
Reprinted by permission of Heinemann Educational Publishers, a
division of Reed Educational and Professional Publishing Ltd.

The omnipresent danger of political decay – decline in the political and administrative institutions of the state – is shown through the prevalence of political violence, constant instability, bureaucratic incompetence and corruption. Like a disease, political decay attacks the well-being of the people. The economy will not attract investors who are naturally frightened of violence, instability and arbitrary administration. A political logic of survival dictates the allocation of public jobs and resources, but this is totally irrational from the viewpoint of capital accumulation. In summary, the state cannot maintain the essential conditions for a thriving capitalism.

A self-reinforcing downward spiral of political decay and economic deterioration is the principal danger. Once underway, this pattern gathers momentum and is difficult to reverse. Political violence and bureaucratic ineptitude lay waste to the modern economy. *Pari passu*, a parallel economy or black market flourishes outside the state's control. This, in turn feeds on bureaucratic corruption, the avoidance of regulations and taxes. The state is undermined further by the erosion of public revenues and the ineffectiveness of the civil service.

At the nadir of this spiral lies chaos. A fictitious state of armed political thugs detaches itself from society and preys upon a dying economy and its people. This conclusion is a grim one; but it can be reversed.

9.2 A Third Way

Both in spirit and letters, autonomy ought to be understood as a

political counterforce and definitely not a withdrawal or en-
trenchment behind the walls of naive self-sufficiency or
impossible autarchy. Autonomous agency consists of the action of
citizens who:

> ...perceive that the essence of history is the endless effort for
> emancipation by which we grasp towards mastery of our own
> destiny, an effort which is, in the final analysis, coterminous with
> humanisation of man/woman (in the generic sense).

The idea of an autonomy which is both desirable and possible
emerges from the realisation that a 'third way' is eminently
feasible. It is also based on the irresistible logic that in a situation
of overall maldevelopment, only a common effort of mutual
adjustment will do, and not a one-sided reliance on transfers,
interventions and structural adjustment measures imposed by the
economically and militarily powerful on those who can least
afford it. Autonomy means that the:

> ...Third World does not become self-reliant by imitating the First
> World and Second Worlds, nor by exploiting a kind of Fourth
> World... Self-Reliance implies the autonomy to set one's own
> goals and realise them as far as possible through one's own
> efforts, using one's own forces, including economic factors.
> (Galtung, 1980)

It is this interpretation of development which gave rise to the
Manila and Arusha declarations of 1990, the gist and thrust of
which can perhaps best be summarised as: yield space to the
people. According to the Manila Declaration, there is a need for a
'fundamentally different' development model based on the
following three principles:

1. Sovereignty of the people, the 'real actors' of positive change.
   The legitimate role of government is to enable people to
   pursue their own agenda.
2. People's control of their own resources, their access to
   relevant information, and the creation of machinery by which
   people can hold government officials accountable and trans-

parent. It is a government's elementary duty to protect those rights.

3. Those who would assist the people with their development must recognise that it is they who are participating in the support of the people and not vice versa: i.e. the interventionist principle and interventionist arrogance turned on its head.

This analysis and these principles were echoed by the Arusha Declaration in the same year as the Economic Commission for Africa (EcA, 1990). The Arusha conference defined popular participation as:

> in essence, the empowerment of people to effectively involve themselves in creating the structures, in designing the policies and programmes that serve the interests of all, as well as to effectively contribute to the development process and share equitably in its benefits. (EcA, 1990)

This requires 'action on the part of all, first and foremost the people themselves'. But equally important are the actions of the government concerned which must act as a catalyst 'to create the necessary conditions' and the international community must support where necessary. To achieve economic and social justice, 'a redirection of resources is necessary'. As for the 'orthodox Structural Adjustment Programme', it is said to 'undermine the human condition and disregards the potential and role of popular participation in self-sustaining development'. The African Alternative Framework to Structural Adjustment Programmes for Socio-Economic Recovery and Transformation (AAF-SAP) aimed to adopt these principles as a firm basis for Africa's development in the 1990s and into the twenty-first century. Popular participation means, no more and no less, the positioning of people's power alongside government power; the insistence that the sovereignty of the government should be the popular sovereignty of the people. It replaces the administration of things and people with politics and political debate. Popular participation thus demands 'a new democratic political culture'. Democratic political culture was what the ancient Greek city states were made of and what made them into powerhouses of civilisation and humanisation (Ruddock, 1994). It was possible then. It is possible now:

> ...that we encourage development, which helps us to do without aid. An aid dependent policy cannot help us to organise and be ourselves, It simply enslaves us, making us emotionally and psychologically dependent, this makes us irresponsible and prevents us from following new tracks and from being happier. We have therefore rejected, once and for all, any sort of 'dictat' from outside our country, enabling us to create the conditions for a dignity to match our ambition. We reject the survival syndrome. We want to release the pressures and free our country from repression. We want to democratise our society and open our minds to a collective responsibility, so as to dare invent our own new future. (Thomas Sankara, 1991)

BIBLIOGRAPHY

Abdalla, Ismael Sabri, 'The inadequacy and loss of legitimacy of the IMF', Development Dialogue, 2, 1980

Abrams, P D, *Kenya's land resettlement story: How 66,000 African families were settled on 1325 large scale European owned farms*, Nairobi, Challenge, 1979

Abreu, Elsa, *The role of self-help in development of education in Kenya 1900–1973*, Nairobi, Kenya Literature Bureau, 1982

Achebe, Chinua, *A Man of the People*, Oxford, Heinemann Educational Publishers, 1966

African Development Bank, *Fourthline of Credit: East African Development Bank*, Abidjan: AFDB, 1982

Ahmed, Yusuf J, Sammy George K., *Guidelines to environmental impact assessment in developing countries*, London, Hodder and Stoughton, 1985

Akivaga, S K, Kulundu-Bitonye, W, and Opi, M W, *Local authorities in Kenya*, Nairobi, Heinemann, 1985

Allen, Tim and Thomas, Alan, (eds), *Poverty and Development in the 1990s*, Open University Press, UK, 1992

Amin, Samir, *Maldevelopment. Anatomy of Failure*, Zed Books, UNU London, 1990

Amsden, Alice Hoffenberg, *International firms and labour in Kenya 1945–1970*, London, Frank Cass, 1971

Anderson-Brolin, Lillemor *et al.*, *From hospitals to health centres*, Parts I–III, Stockholm, SIDA., 1986

Anker, Richard, and Knowles, Jane C, *Population growth, employment and economic – demographic interactions in Kenya, Bachue-Kenya*, New York, St Martin's Press, 1983

Anjara, Shailendra J; Eken, Sena; Laker, John F, *Payments arrangement and economic-demographic interactions in Kenya: Bachue-Kenya'*. Washington, D.C., IMF (Occasional paper; no.11), 1982

Anyona, A N, 'Investigation into problems emanating from road drainage with suggested methodology for prevention of soil erosion in Muranga and Baring Districts-Post-graduate Diploma Report', Nairobi, University of Nairobi, Depart of Agri. Eng., Mimeo, 1982

Archer, R W, 'Land Pooling for planned urban Development in Perth', Western Australia, metropolitan Research Trust, Canberra, 1976

Aryanayakam, E W, *The Idea of a Rural University*, Sevagram, India: Hindustani Tamili Sangh.

Atbach, Philip, *The knowledge context: Comparative Perspective on the Distribution of knowledge*, State University of New York Press, New York, 1987

Bager, Torben, *Marketing cooperatives and peasants in Kenya*, Uppsala Scandinavian Institute of African Studies, 1980

Barkan, Joel D. (ed.), *Politics and public policy in Kenya and Tanzania.*, New York, Praeger, 1984

Barkan, Joel D, Holmquist, Frank, *Politics and the Peasantry in Kenya – the lessons of Harambee*, University of Nairobi, Institute of Development Studies, 1986

Barnes, Carolyn, Ensminger, Jean and O'Keefe, P, *Wood, energy and households. Perspectives on rural Kenya*, Uppsala, Scandinavian Institute of African studies, 1984

Barnett, A P, 'How intense rainfall affects run-off and soil erosion', in *Agriculture Eng.* November 1938, ppf 103–707, 1958.

Barnett, Donald L and Njama, Karari, *Mau Mau from within. Autobiography and analysis of Kenya's peasant revolt*, 2nd ed., New York, Monthly Review Press, 1970

Bartholomew, Gerald, 'Le pays en debors' (The Country Outside), Port-au-Prince, Haiti, 1990

Barve, Arvind G, *The foreign trade of Kenya*, Nairobi Transafrica/ Simba, 1984

Bassan, Elizabeth, *Survey of U.S. and Kenyan PVOs in Kenya*, Nairobi, USAID, 1983

Batesman, David and Lampkin Nic, 'A shift to organise agriculture, University College of Wales, Aberystwyth, 1985

Bendix, Selina, *Environmental assessment. Approaching maturity*, Ann Arbor, Science Publishers, 1978

Berg-Schlosser, Dirk, *Tradition and change in Kenya. A comparative analysis of seven major ethnic groups*, Paderborn, Germany, Ferdinand Schaningh, 1984

Bermosk, L and Porter, S. *Women's health and Human wholeness*, New York, Appleton-Century-Crofts, 1979

Bernard, Frank E, 'Planning environmental risk in Kenya dry lands' in *Geographical Review*, vol. 75, no.1, pp.58–70

Bienen, Henry, *Kenya. Politics of participation and control*, Princeton, NJ, Princeton University Press, 1974

——, Henry. 'Urbanisation and third world stability' in *World Development*, 1984, vol. 12, no.7, pp.661–691

Bigstern, Arne, *Income distribution and development – theory, evidence and policy*, London, Heinemann, 1983

Bigstern, Arne, *Education and income distribution in Kenya*, Aldershot, Gower, 1984

Bird, Andrew, *The Turkana Rural Development Programme. Some reflections*, Oslo, MDC/NORAD, Mimeo, 1986

Blaikie, Roderic H, *The political economy of soil erosion in developing countries*, London: Longman, 1982

Blum, H, *Planning for Change: Development and Application of Social Change Theory*, New York, Human Sciences Press, 1974

Bogonko, Sorobea N, *Kenya 1945–1963. A study in African national movements*, Nairobi, Kenya Literature Bureau, 1980

Bordenave, Diaz, *Communication and Rural Development*, UNESCO, Geneva, 1977

Bothomani, Isaac B. 'The food crisis in East and central Africa with special reference to Kenya, Malawi, Tanzania and Zambia' in *Journal of African studies,* vol. II, no.4, 1984–1985

Brabin, Loretta, 'Malnutrition among the Kamba of Kenya – problems or response to problem' in *Disasters*, 1985, vol. 9, no.2

Braidotti, Rossi, 'Gender and post-gender: the future of an illusion' in *Gender-Nature-Culture Feminist Research Network. Working Paper no.1*, Odense University, Denmark, 1993

Brandt Report, *North-South: A Programme for Survival*, Pan Books, London, 1980

Brett, E A, *Colonialism underdevelopment in East Africa. The politics of economic change 1919–1939*, London, Heinemann, 1973

Broch-Due, Vigdis, *Women at the backstage of development – the negative impact of project realisation by neglecting the concealed role of Turkana women as producers and providers*, Rome, FAO – Mimeo, 1983

——, Vigdis, *From herds to fish and from fish to food aid. The impact of development on the fishing population along the western Lake Turkana*, Bergen, Norway, University of Bergen. Mimeo, 1986

Brown, Lagale, 'Without Women, No development' in *ATOF – Conference Proceeding*, Birmingham, April, Mimeo, 1984

Brundtland report, 'Our Common Future', report of the World Commission on Environment and Development, Oxford University Press, 1987

Burrows, John, ed., *Kenya into a second decade*, Baltimore, MD, John Hopkins University Press, 1985

Business and Economic Research Co. Ltd, *Study on the production and marketing of women's groups in Kenya. Preliminary impressions*, submitted to SIDA. Draft, Nairobi, BER, Mimeo, 1984a

Business and Economic Research Co. Ltd, *Study on the organisation of women's groups in Kenya*, Preliminary Impressions, submitted to NORAD, Nairobi, BER, Mimeo, 1984b

Business and Economic Research Co. Ltd, *Study on the production and marketing of women's groups products*, Preliminary impressions, submitted to SIDA, Nairobi, BER, Mimeo 1986c

Business and Economic Research Co. Ltd, *Study on integrated approach to women's programmes in Kenya*, Report to DANIDA., Nairobi, BER, Mimeo, 1985

Business and Economic Research Co. Ltd, *Summary of recent recommendations on women's programmes*, Nairobi, BER, Mimeo, 1986

Canter, Leary, *Introduction to environmental impact analysis*, New York, McGraw-Hill, 1977

——, Leary, *Environmental impact of water projects*, Chelsa, Mich., s.n., 1950

Carlsen, John, *Economic and social transformation in rural Kenya*, Uppsala, Scandinavian Institute of African Studies, 1980

Cassen, Robert and associates, *Does Development Aid work*, Oxford, Oxford University Press, 1985

Cernea, M, 'Can Local Participation Help Development'? Finance and Development, IMF December 1984

——, M, 'Putting People First', Sociological variables in Rural Development, Ithaca, New York

Chambers, R, 'The Farmer is a professional', Ceres, April 1980

——, R, Rural Development: 'Putting the Last First', Longman, London, 1984

——, R, 'Short-cut methods of gathering social information for Rural Development Projects', In Cernea, 1985

——, R, *Farmer First: a Practical Paradigm for Third World Agriculture*, Institute of Development Studies, Sussex University, 1988

Chanlett, Emil T., *Environmental Protection*, New York, McGraw-Hill, 1973

Cheema, G Habbir and Rondinelli, Dennis, (eds) *Decentralisation and development – policy implementation in developing countries*, London, Sage, 1983

Cheremisinoff, P N and Moresi, A C, *Environmental assessment and impact statement handbook*, Ann Arbor, Science Publishers, 1977

Chomsky, Noam, 'New World Order? The weak shall inherit Nothing. We are the masters and you shine our shoes' in *The Guardian*, 25 March 1991

Chorafas, D N, *The Knowledge Revolution – Analysis of the international Brain Market and the challenge to Europe*, London, George Allen and Unwin Ltd, 1965

Clapham, Christopher, *Third World politics – an introduction*, London, Croom Helm, 1985

Clark, B D, *Environmental impact assessment – a bibliography with abstracts*, New York, Bowker, 1980

Clayton, Anthony, *Counter-insurgency in Kenya – a study of military operations against Mau Mau*, Nairobi, Transafrica, 1976

Clayton, Anthony and Savage, Donald C, *Government and labour in Kenya 1895–1963*, London, Frank Cass, 1974

Cleaver, Kevin, 'The impact of price and exchange rate policies on agriculture in sub-Saharan Africa', University of Nairobi. Institute for Development Studies. Nairobi, IDS, Mimeo, 1984

Clough, Marshall, 'Kenya after Kenyatta. An introduction', in *Africa Today*, vol. 26, no.3, pp.7–20

Cockar, Saeed, *The Kenya Industrial Court. Origin, development and Practice*, Nairobi, Longman, 1981

Cohen, John M and Hook, Richard M, *District development planning in Kenya. Kenya Rural Planning Project*, Nairobi Ministry of Finance and Planning, Mimeo, 1985

Collier, Paul, and; Lal, Deepak, 'Poverty and growth in Kenya', Washington, DC, IBRD, Staff working paper; no.389, 1980

Collier, Paul, and Lal, Deepak, 'Why poor people get rich: Kenya 1960–1979, in *World Development*, 1984, vol. 12, no.10, pp.1007–1018

Collier, Paul and Lal, Deepak, 'Labour and poverty in Kenya, 1900–1980', Oxford, Oxford University Press, 1986

Cocoyoc Declaration (1874, 1980), 'Text in (1) Development Dialogue, 1974, 2 Uppsala', 1974.2,' Galtung (1980, Appendix)

Conyers, Diana, 'Future direction in development studies – the case of decentralisation', in *World Development*, 1986, vol. 14, no.5, pp.593–603

Cook, H L, 'The nature and controlling variables of the water erosion process', in *Proc. Soil Sci. Soc Amer.* pp.487–494, 1936

Coombs, P H, 'The World Educational Crisis: A Systems Analysis', New York, Oxford University Press, 1968

Coombs, P H, *et al.*, *New Paths to Learning: For Rural Children and Youth*, Essex, Connecticut, International Council of Educational Development, 1973

Coughlin, Peter E, *Converting crisis to boom for Kenyan foundries and metal engineering industries. Technical possibilities versus political and bureaucratic obstacles*, University of Nairobi. Institute for Development Studies, Nairobi, IDS, 1987

Crawford, Eric and Thurbeck, Erik, *Employment, income distribution, poverty alleviation and basic needs in Kenya*, Ithaca, Cornell University, 1978

Currie, Kate, and Ray, Larry, 'State and class in Kenya – notes on the cohesion of the ruling class' in Journal of modern African studies, 1978, vol. 22, no.4, pp.559–593

Dahl, Gudrun; Hjort, Anders, *Having herds. Pastoral herd growth and household economy*, Stockholm, University of Stockholm, 1976

Dale, Reidar *et al*, *Report by a NORAD mission on a rural development programme for Bungoma District in Kenya*, Oslo, MDC/NORAD, Mimeo, 1986

Dalfelt, Arne, 'Turkana Integrated Rural Development Programme', Background paper Oslo, MDC/NORAD, Mimeo, 1986

Damba, J, 'Investigation into causes of gullying and gully control in Kandara Division of Muranga District', Post-graduate Diploma report, Nairobi, University of Nairobi, Department of Agricultural Engineering, Mimeo, 1981

DANIDA, *Kenya rural electrification programme – socio-economic study*, Copenhagen, DANIDA, Mimeo, 1986

DANIDA, NORkD, SIDA, *Report on the programme review of the Women's Bureau in Kenya*, Nairobi, NORAD, Mimeo, 1980

DANIDA, NOBAD, SIDA, *Report on the review of the Women's Programme Bureau in Kenya*, Nairobi, DANIDA, NORAD, SIDA, Mimeo, 1982

David, Dominique, 'Culture and development', *The Courie*, Brussels, May 1993

Diepeveen, Caroline, *Women and Development Means Business*, Wederlandse, den Haag, 1990

De Leon, Jose & Pedersen, Jon, *Research on population and health in developing countries*, Oslo, NUPI, Mimeo, 1985

Diomi de Delupis, Ingrid, *The East African Community and Common Market*, London, Longman, 1970

Dwivedi O P, 1990, 'Satyagrapha for conservation: Awakening the Spirit of Hinduism, Engel and Engel, 1990

Doebele, W A, 'Land Pooling in Seoul and Gwanju Korea with special reference to Land Re-adjustment'. Third Draft, World Bank, Washington, DC, 1976

Dow, Thomas E, & Werner, Linda H, *Modern, transitional and traditional demographic and contraceptive patterns among Kenyan women: 1977–1978*, University of Nairobi, Population studies and Research Institute, Mimeo, 1981

Dow, Thomas E, and Werner, Linda H, 'Prospects for fertility decline in rural Kenya' in *Population and development review*, 1983 vol. 9, pp.77–97

Douglas Ian, *The Urban Environment*, Edward Arnold, 1983

Dublin, Jack and Dublin, Selma M, *Credit Unions in a changing world. The Tanzania-Kenya experience*, Detroit, Wayne State University Press, 1983

Duncan, Alex, & Mosley, Paul, *Development Aid effectiveness: Kenya case study. Study commissioned by the Task Force on Concessional Flows of the World Bank/IMF Development Committee*. Rev draft, 1985

Economic Commission for Africa – (ECA), *Participation in Development*, Addis Ababa – Ethiopia, 1990

EcoSystems, 'Soil erosion in Machakos District, Nairobi, EcoSystems (Survey of Agriculture and land use) 1981, vol. 3, Mimeo

EcoSystems, *Tana delta Ecological impact study – Draft*, 1983

Ellefsen, Einar S, et al, Report on a study of possible Norwegian assistance to health and family planning programmes in Kenya, Oslo, MDC/NRAD, Mimeo

Ellison, W D, 'Soil erosion studies, pt.2. soil detachment hazard by raindrop splash', in *Agric. Eng.* 28, pp.197–201, 1947

Emery, F, Public Policies for Healthy Workplace, Beyond Health Care Conference, Toronto 1984, published as a supplement to the Canadian Proceeding Journal of Public Health, 1985

Englund, Karl, *External Development Aid and the very poor in Kenya*, Nairobi, UNDP, Mimeo, 1977

Ekirapa, A A A, Statement of the 35th Annual General Assembly of the International Press Institute, Vienna, Austria, May 11–14, Vienna: IPI. Mimeo, 1986

Faaland, Karl, 'Norwegian development aid reaching the poor', in *Development policy review,* vol. 2, no.1, pp.1–11

FAO, *Potential Population supporting capacities of lands in Developing World*, FAO: Rome, 1986

Faundez, Antonio, 'Dialogue pour le developpement et le developpement du dialogue', *Adult Education and the Challenges of the Nineties*, Conference Reader, Arenberg Castle, Heverlee, 28 September–1 October, 1986

Forde, C Daryll, 'The Masai – cattle herders on East African plateau', in *Habitat, economy and society – a geographical introduction to ethnology*, London, Methuen, 1963

Forss, Kim, *Planning and evaluation in development evaluations*, Stockholm School of Economics, Economic Research Unit, Stockholm, ERI.

Freire, Paulo and Costigan Margaret, 'You have the Third World inside you', (In conversation with). *Convergence* 16, 4, 1983

Future Group, 'Rapid projections', s.l., Future Group, 1982

Gachen, B M, *A study of the suitability of concrete road drainage chutes on the Ruiru-Githunguri-uplands' roads and some adjoining roads, Post-graduate Diploma report*, Nairobi, University of Nairobi, Depart of Agricultural Engineering – Mimeo, 1985

Gakuru, O N, *Pre-primary education in Kenya*, University of Nairobi, Institute of Development Studies, Nairobi, IDS, Mimeo, 1979

Galaty, John G *et al.* (eds.), *The future of pastoral peoples*, Ottawa, IDRC, 1981

Galeano, Eduardo, 'Open Veins of Latin America', *Monthly Review*, Press, New York, 1973

——, Eduardo, 'Erre comme eux' ('To be like them'), *Le Monde Diplomatique*, October 1991

——, Eduardo, 'Vision of Tomorrow, Channel 4 TV, in conversation with Miguel Bonasso, 1992

Galtung J, O'Brien, P, and Preiswerk R, 'Self-Reliance: A strategy for Development'. Bogle l'Ouverture, London, 1980

Gatara, T and Murungaru, R, 'Family Planning – Part A. Evaluation', Nairobi, National Council for Population and Development, Mimeo, 1980

Gelpi, E, *A future for Life Long Education*, Manchester Monograph (CAHE), 1979

George, H, 'Progress and Poverty, Robert Schalkenback, New York, 1979, Centenary edition

George, Susan, *How the Other Half Dies*, Penguin, Harmondsworth, 1976

——, Susan, *A Fate Worse than Debt*, Zed Books, London, 1988

Gertzel, C J, Goldschmidt and M Rothchild, D, *Government and politics in Kenya – A Nation Building Text*, Nairobi, East African Publishing House, 1969

Ghai, Dharma P and Ghai, Yash P, 'Portrait of a minority – Asian in East Africa. Rev. Ed, Nairobi, Oxford University Press, 1970

Ghai, Dharma and Godfrey, Martin (eds), *Essays on employment in Kenya*, Nairobi, Kenya Literature Bureau, 1979

Ghai, Dharma, Godfrey, Martin and Lisk, Franklyn *Planning for basic needs in Kenya – Performance, policies and prospects*. 3rd ed, Geneva, ILO, 1981

Ghai, Y P and McAuslan, J P W B, *Public law and political change in Kenya – a study of the legal framework of government from colonial times to the present*, Nairobi, Oxford University Press, 1970

Gjos, Tore, 'Report from donors' meeting, *Rural access roads programme and minor roads programme*, Oslo, Public Roads Administration, Mimeo, 1986

Godfrey, Martin, *Kenya to 1990. Prospects for growth*, London, Economic Intelligence Unit, 1986

Goldsmith, E, and Nicholas, H., *The social and environmental effects of large dams*, Camelford: Wadebrige Ecological Centre, 1984, Tom Mboya. The man Kenya wanted to forget'. Nairobi, Heinemann.

Good, R B and Nebauer, N R, 'Erosion control integrates with highway landscape', in *Journal of Soil Conservation Service of NSW*, 1986, vol. 32

Goodland, R and Daly, H, 'Why Northern Income Growth is Not the Solution to Southern Poverty', World Bank, Enviromment Departmentment Working Paper, No. 1993–43, 1993

Goodman, Paul, Compulsory Miseducation, Middlesex, Penguin, 1973

Gordon, David F, *Decolonisation and the state in Kenya*, Boulder, Cob, West view, 1986

Gramsci, Antonio, 'Letter from Prison', *Quartet*, London

Gray, W J, *Commerce in East Africa*, Nairobi, 1980

——, W J, *A guide to business finance in Kenya*, 4th ed, Nairobi, 1984a

——, W J, *A guide to income tax in Kenya*, 4th ed, Nairobi, Longman, 1984b

Green, Reginald Herbold, *The IMF and stabilisation in sub-Saharan Africa. A critical review*, Brighton, Institute of Development Studies (Discussion paper, no.Dp 216), 1986

Greer, Joel and Thorbecke, Erik, *Food poverty and consumption patterns in Kenya*, Geneva, ILO, 1986

Griffin, K, *Under Development in Latin America*, Allen and Unwin, London, 1968

Gulliver, P H, *The family herds. A study of two pastoral tribes in East Africa, the Jie and Turkana*, 3rd ed, London, Routledge & Kegan Paul, 1972

Gutkind, O and Wallerstein, I, *The Political Economy of Contemporary Africa*, Sage, Beverly Hills, London, 1976

Haaland, Ane, Morris, Joseph and Helland Johan, *The Adult Literacy Programme, Diocese of Lodwar, Kenya. An evaluation report prepared for the Norwegian Agency for International Development*, Oslo, MDC/NOPAD, Mimeo, 1985

Hagman, D G, and Misczynski, E J, 'Windfalls for Wipeouts: Land Value Capture and Compensation', US Department of Housing and Urban Development, Washington DC, 1978

Halderman, J M, 'Problems of pastoral development in Eastern Africa', in *Agricultural Administration*, 1985, vol. 18, pp.199–216

Hallak, Jacques, *Investing in the Future: setting Priorities in the Developing World*, IIEP, Paris, 1990

Haq, M, 'Tied credits: quantitative Analysis' in Adler, J., and Kuznets, P, (eds) Capital Movements and Economic Development, London, MacMillan, (314), 1965

Hancock, Graham, *Lords of Poverty: the Freewheeling Lifestyle, Power, Pestige and Corruption of the Multimillion Dollar Aid Business*, Mandarin, London, 1979

Hart, Stewart L, Erik, G A, and Hornick, W F, *Improving import assessment – increasing the relevance and utilisation of scientific and technical information*, s.l., s.n., 1977

Hayek, F A, 'Choice of Currency and Denationalization of Money', Institute of Economic Affairs, London, 1978

Hazlewood, Arthur, *Economic integration. The East African experience*, London, Heinemann, 1975

——, Arthur, *The economy of Kenya. The Kenyatta era*, Oxford, Oxford University Press, 1979

Helland, Johan, *Five essays on the study of pastoralists and the development of pastoralism*, Bergen, Norway, University of Bergen, 1980

Helman, Hall, 'Transportation in the World of the future', New York, Evans, 1974

Henin, Roushdi A, 'Population projections in regional planning', University of Nairobi. Population Studies and Research Institute, Nairobi, PSRI, 1978

——, Roushdi A, *Effects of development on fertility and mortality trends in East Africa. Evidence from Kenya and Tanzania*, University of Nairobi. Population Studies and Research Institute, Nairobi, PSRI, 1979

——, Roushdi A, *Fertility, infertility and sub-fertility in East Africa*, University of Nairobi, Population Studies and Research Institute, Nairobi, PSRI, 1982

——, Roushdi A, and Mott Susan, H, *The impact of current and future population growth rates on the short term social and economic development in Kenya*, University of Nairobi, Population Studies and Research Institute, Nairobi, PSRI, 1979

Henriksen, Georg, *Economic growth and ecological balance, Problems of development in Turkana*, Bergen, Norway, University of Bergen, 1974

Heyer, Judith, Maitha, J K, and Senga, W M (eds.), *Agricultural development in Kenya. An economic assessment*, Nairobi, Oxford University Press, 1976

Heyer, Judith, Roberts, Pepe and Willians, G, (eds.) *Rural development in tropical Africa*, New York, St Martin's Press, 1981

Hogg, Richard, 'Small is also complex, A study of rural development' in Manchester papers on development, vol. 1, no.1, 133,

Holmquist, Frank, 'Self-help the state and peasant leverage in Kenya', in *Africa*, 1984, vol. 54, no.3, pp.7291

Horberry, John and Johnsen, Brian, *Environmental performance of consulting organisations in development aid*, Washington DC, international institute for Environment and Development, 1981

Hosier, Richard, *Energy use in rural Kenya household demand and rural transformation*, Uppsala, Scandinavian institute of African Studies, 1985

House, William J, Killick, Tony, 'Social justice and development policy in Kenya's rural economy', in Ghai, Dharam, Radwan, Samir (eds) *Agrarian policies and rural poverty in Africa*, Geneva, ILO, pp.22–69, 1983

Howard, Sir Ebenezer, 'Garden Cities of Tomorrow', 1902, originally published as 'Tomorrow's Peaceful Path to Reform', Faber and Faber, London, 1898,

Hultberg, Bobby, *Kibwezi rural health scheme. A report to NORAD*, Lodwar, Kenya MDC/NOBAD, Mimeo, 1985

Hunt, Diana, *The impending crisis in Kenya, The case for land reform*, Aldershot, Gower, 1984

Hyden, Goran, *Beyond Ujamaa in Tanzania Underdevelopment and an Uncaptured Peasantry*, Heinemann, London, 1980

——, Goran, 'No shortcuts to progress. African development management in perspective', London, Heinemann, 1980

——, Goran, 'Administration and public policy' in *Barkan*, Joel D (ed.) *Politics and public policy in Kenya and Tanzania*, (Rev. ed.), New York, Praeger, pp.103–124, 1984

——, Goran, Jackson, Robert and Okumu, John (eds.) *Development administration, The Kenyan experience*, Nairobi, Oxford University Press, 1970

IBRD, *Kenya: Growth and structural change*, Washington DC, 1983

IBRD, *Kenya Country Economic Memorandum*, Washington, DC IBRD, (Report no.4689–KE), 1983b

IBRD, *Kenya transport sector memorandum*, Washington D, C, IBRD, (Report no.4610), 1984

IBRD, *Kenya Economic Development and Urbanisation Policy*, Washington DC, IBRD, (Report no.4148–KE), 1985

IBRD, *Kenya-policies and prospects for restoring sustained growth per capita income*, Washington D, C, IBRD, (Report no.6021–KE), 1986a

IBRD, *Kenya Agricultural Sector report*, Washington D, C, Report no.4629–KE), 1986b

IBRD, *Population growth and policies in sub-Saharan Africa*, Washington DC, IBRD, 1986c

IBRD, Project completion report, Rural access roads programme, Washington DC, IBRD, (Report no.6271), 1986d

IBRD, *Report on technical assistance in sub-Saharan Africa*, Washington DC, (Storrar Report), Mimeo, 1983 *Aid for development. The key issues*, Washington, IBRD

IFDA, 'Sharing one earth: responding to the challenge of poverty in Asia', IFDA Dossier, 54–55, 1986

IFDA, 'The Manila Declaration on People's Participation in Development', IFDA Dossier, 78, 1990a

IFDA, 'The African Charter for Popular Participation in Development and Transformation', Arusha, Tanzania, Dossier, 79, 1990b

ILO, *Employment, income and equality. A Strategy for increasing Productive employment in Kenya*, Geneva ILO, 1972

Institute Development, Demographic Survey, University of Nairobi, IDS 1997 Memo

Institute for Development Studies, 'An overall evaluation of the S. R. D. P.' Nairobi, IDS, (IDS Occasional paper, no.12, 1972

Institute of Development Studies, *Second overall evaluation of the special Rural Development Programme (S.R.D.P.)*, Nairobi, IDS, (IDS occasional paper, no.12), 1975

Institute for Development Studies, *Soil and water conservation in Kenya*, Nairobi, IDS, (occasional paper, no.12), 1976

Ishumi, A G M, 'The Place of Education in the Economy' in *International Journal of Educational Development*, 3, 337–349, 1983

Jabara, Cathy L, 'Agricultural pricing policy in Kenya', in *World Development*, 1985, vol. 13, no.5, pp.611–626

Johnsen, Brian and Blake, Robert O, *The environmental and bilateral development aid, Environmental policies, programmes and performance of development assistance for Germany, Netherlands, Sweden, UK and US*, Washington, DC, International institute of Environment and Development, 1980

Jutterstrom, Christina, *Country report Kenya*, 1986

Kameir, El-Wathig and Kursany, Ibrahim, *Corruption as the 'fifth' factor of production in the Sudan'* Uppsala, Scandinavian institute of African Studies, 1985

Kamenetzky, Mario, 'The Economics of the Satisfaction of Needs' in Ekins and Max-Neef, Routledge, 1992

Kantai, Terry, *Women in development, Plan for action, Draft*, Nairobi, MDC/NORAD, Mimeo, 1986

KANU, 'The constitution of Kenya African National Union, Rev. ed, Nairobi, 1974

KANU, *KANU manifesto, Peace, love, unity*, Nairobi, KANU, 1983

KANU, *The KANU code of discipline*, Nairobi, KANU, 1986

Kaplinsky, Raphael (ed.), *Readings on the multinational corporation in Kenya*, Nairobi, Oxford University Press, 1978a

——, Raphael, *Trends on the distribution of income in Kenya 1966–1967*, University of Nairobi, Institute of Development Studies, Nairobi, IDS, Mimeo, 1980

——, Raphael, Capitalist accumulation in the periphery. The Kenya case re-examined, in *Review of African political economy*, no.17, pp.83–105, 1980

Kant, Immanuel, *Groundwork of the Metaphysic of Morals*, translated by Paton, J, New York, Harper & Row, 1964

Karimi, Joseph C, Ochieng Philip, *The Kenyatta Succession*, Nairobi, Transafrica, 1980

Kayongo-Male, D, and Walji, P, *Children at work in Kenya*, Nairobi, Oxford University Press, 1984

Kayongo-Male, Diane, Onyango, Philista, *The sociology of the African family*, London, Longman, 1984

Keller, Edmond J, *Education, man-power and development. The impact of Educational Development in Kenya*, Nairobi Kenya Literature Bureau, 1980

Kenya Colony and Protectorate, *A plan to intensify the development of African agriculture in Kenya*, Nairobi, Colony and Protectorate of Kenya, (Swynnerton plan), 1955

Kenya Central Bureau of Statistics, *Economic Survey*, Nairobi CBS, Annual, various years

Kenya Central Bureau of statistics, *Directory of industries*, Nairobi, CBS, 1974

Kenya Central Bureau of Statistics, *Directory of industries 1977*, Nairobi CBS, 1977

Kenya Central Bureau of Statistics, *Educational trends 1973–1977*, Nairobi, CBS

Kenya Central Bureau of Statistics, *Kenya fertility survey 1977–1978*, First report, 1980, vol. 1, Nairobi, CBS

Kenya Central Bureau of Statistics, *Continuity and change in metropolitan and rural attitudes towards family size and family planning in Kenya between 1966–1967 and 1977–1978*, Nairobi, CBS, 1980b

Kenya, Central Bureau of Statistics, *Report on surveys of industrial production 1973–1976*, Nairobi, CBS, 1980c

Kenya, Central Bureau of Statistics, *The integrated rural surveys 1976–1979, Basic report*, Nairobi, CBS, 1981a

Kenya Central Bureau of Statistics, *Kenya Population census 1979*, 1981b, vol. 1, Nairobi CBS

Kenya Central Bureau of Statistics, *Statistics on education, Development and prospects*, Nairobi, CBS, 1981c

Kenya Central Bureau of Statistics, *Modernisation, birth spacing and marital fertility in Kenya*, Nairobi, CBS, 1981d

Kenya Central Bureau of Statistics, *Population census report*, 1982a, vol. 11, Nairobi CBS

Kenya Central Bureau of Statistics, 'Literacy in Rural Kenya, 1980/81', in *Social Perspectives*, vol. no.1, pp.1–10, 1982b

Kenya Central Bureau of Statistics, *Kenya contraceptive prevalence survey 1984*. First report, Nairobi, CBS, 1984a

Kenya Central Bureau of Statistics, 'Infant feeding practices in Nairobi', Kenya, in *Social perspectives*, 1984b, vol. 8, no.1, pp.l-5

Kenya Central Bureau of Statistics, *Employment and earnings in the modern sector 1981*, Nairobi CBS, Ministry of Finance and planning, 1984c

Kenya Central Bureau of Statistics, *Report of the child nutrition survey 1978/79*, Nairobi, CBS, 1981

Kenya Central Bureau of Statistics UNICEF, *Situation analysis of children and women in Kenya*, Nairobi, CBS/UNICEF, 4 vols, 1984

Kenya: Central Bureau of Statistics, Aids and under-nutrition, Women and Children, BS/UNICEF, 1996

Kenya Government, *African Socialism and its application to Planning in Kenya*, Nairobi, The Government, Sessional Paper no.10, 1965a

Kenya Government, *The policy on trade union organisation in Kenya*, Nairobi, The Government, 1965b

Kenya Government, *Development plan 1966–1970*, Nairobi, The Government, (First development plan), 1966

Kenya Government, *Constitution of Kenya*, Nairobi, The Government, 1969a

Kenya Government, *Development Plan 1970–1974*, Nairobi, The Government, (2nd development plan), 1969

Kenya Government, *Report of the Commission of inquiry 1970–1971*, (Public Service Structure and Remuneration Commission), Nairobi, The Government, (Ndegwa Commission), 1971

Kenya Government, *Sessional paper on employment*, Nairobi, The Government, Sessional paper no.10, 1973

Kenya Government, *Development Plan 1974–1978*, Nairobi, The Government, 2 vols, (3rd development plan), 1974

Kenya Government, *Report of the National Committee on Educational Objectives and Policies*, Nairobi, The Government, 1976

Kenya Government, *Development Plan 1979–1983*, Nairobi, The Government, 1979a

Kenya Government, *Review of statutory boards*, Nairobi, The Government, 1979b

Kenya Government, *Report of the Civil Service Review Committee 1979–1980*, Nairobi, The Government, (Waruhi Committee), 1980

Kenya Government, *Sessional paper on national food policy*, Nairobi, The Government, Sessional Paper no.4, 1981

Kenya Government, *Report and recommendations of the Working Party on Government Expenditure*, Nairobi, Kenya Government, 1982a

Kenya Government, *Sessional paper on development prospects and policies*, Nairobi, The Government, Sessional Paper no.4, 1982

Kenya Government, *Development Plan 1984–1988*, Nairobi, The Government, 5th development plan), 1983a

Kenya Government, *Report of the presidential committee on employment1982/83*, Nairobi, Government, (Wanjigi Committee), 1983b

Kenya Government, *1963–1983 Twenty great years of Independence*, Nairobi, Kenya Government, 1983c

Kenya Government, *Economic Management for renewed growth*, Nairobi Kenya Government, 1986

Kenya Government, UNEP and UNDP, *Environment and Development*, Draft, Nairobi Kenya Government/UNEP Mimeo, 1981

Kenya Government, UNEP, UNDP, *Environment and development*, Draft, Nairobi, Kenya Government/UNDP/UNEP, Mimeo, 1981

Kenya Government, UNFPA, *Kenya, Country programme for population activities, 1986–91'*, Nairobi, Kenya Government/ UNFPA, 1986

Kenya Government, 'Energy Consumption', Nairobi, Ministry of Energy Development, 1996

Kenya Ministry of Agriculture and Livestock Dev, *Soil conservation in Kenya especially in small-scale farming in high potential areas using labour intensive methods*, Nairobi, MAID, 1980

Kenya Ministry of Cooperative Development, DANIDA, *Report of the joint Kenyan/Nordic appraisal mission on possible future support to Kenya's cooperative sector*, Nairobi MOCD/DANIDA, Mimeo, 1985

Kenya Ministry of Culture and Social Services, *Women of Kenya, Review and evaluation of progress. End of a decade*, Nairobi, MCSS, 1985

Kenya Ministry of Education, Science and Technology, *8–4–4 System of Education*, Nairobi, MEST, 1986

Kenya Ministry of Energy and Regional Development, *Turkana District resource survey 1982–84*, Nairobi, EcoSystems, 2 vols, 1985

Kenya, Ministry of Finance and Planning, *Sessional Paper on economic prospect and policies*, Nairobi MFP, Sessional Paper no.4, 1975

Kenya Ministry of Finance and Planning, *Turkana District development plan 1984–88*, Nairobi, MFP, 1984a

Kenya Ministry of Finance and Planning, *Bungoma District development plan 1984–88*, Nairobi, MFP, 1984b

Kenya Ministry of Finance and Planning, *Compendium on development cooperation with Kenya as of 30 June 1984'*, Nairobi, MFP, 1985

Kenya Ministry of Finance and Planning, *Budget rationalisation programme*, Nairobi, MOF, 1986

Kenya Ministry of Labour, *Report on the negotiated wages and other terms and conditions, of employment registered by the Kenya industrial Court in, 1984*, Nairobi, MOL, 1985a

Kenya Ministry of Labour, *Sessional Paper on unemployment*, Nairobi, MOL, Sessional Paper no.2, 1985b

Kenya Ministry of Livestock Development, *National livestock development policy*, Nairobi, MLD, 1980

Kenya Ministry of Works, *Geometric design of rural roads-road design Manual*: Part I', Nairobi MOW, 1979

Kenya National Council for population and Dev, *Population policy guidelines*, Nairobi, NCPD, Sessional Paper no.4, 1984a

Kenya, National Council for Population and Dev, *The 1984 international Population Conference country statement*, Nairobi, NCPD, 1984b

Kenya, Office of the President, *District focus for rural development*, Nairobi, OP, 1984

Kenya, Office of the President, *Project implementation review*, Nairobi, OP, Project status report no.1, 1985a

Kenya, Office of the President, *National training strategy for district focus. District focus for rural development*, Nairobi, OP, 1985b

Kenya, Office of the President, *Project implementation review*, Nairobi, OP, Project status report, no.2, 1986

Kenya, 'The politics of repression' in *Race and Class*, special issue, 1983, vol. 24, no.3, pp.221–326

Khalid, Abdallah, *The Liberation of Kiswahili from European appropriation*, Nairobi East African Literature Bureau, 1977

Khapoya, Vincent B, 'The politics of succession in Africa, Kenya after Kenyatta' in *Africa Today*, 1979, vol. 26, no.3, pp.7–20

Kidd, Ross, 'Popular theatre and popular struggle in Kenya, The story of Dedan Kimathi', in *Race and Class*, 1983, vol. 24, no.3, pp.287–304

Killick, Tony, ed, 'Papers on the Kenyan economy Performance, problems and policies, Nairobi, Heinemann, 1983

——, Tony, 'Economic environment and agricultural development, The importance of macroeconomic policy' in *Food Policy*, 1985, vol. 10, no.1, pp.20–40

Kimokoti, Agnes C, and Burkey, Stan, *Child Welfare Society of Kenya, Review of the Working Party report Aug-Sept, 1985*, Nairobi, University of Nairobi, Parconsult, Mimeo, 1985

King, Kenneth, *The African Artisan Education and the informal Sector in Kenya*, Heinemann Education, London, 1977

King, Oona, The Making something out of nothing, UK Development team visit to Kenya, BBC2 programme transcript, 1998

Kinnock, Glenys, 'Impoverished queen of the Mountain Kingdom' in *The Guardian*, 10 July, 1992

Kinyanjui, Kabiru, *Education and Development in Africa, theories and strategies and practical implications of the university of Nairobi*, Nairobi Evans Brothers, 1980

Kitching, Gavin, *Class and economic change in Kenya, The making of an African petite-bourgeoisie*, New Haven Yale University Press, 1980

——, Gavin, 'Politics, method, and evidence in the Kenya debate', in Bernstein, Heny, Campbell and Boniek, (eds.), *Contradictions of accumulation in Africa*, London, Sage, 1985

Klaus, Hans G and Migot-Adholla, S E, (eds), *The role of public enterprise in development in Eastern Africa*, Nairobi, Institute of Development Studies, 1982

Konczacki, Z A, *Economics of pastoralism. A case study of sub-Saharan Africa*, London, IDS, Mimeo, 1978

Krueger, Anne O, 'Development Aid in the development process, in *Research Observer*, 1986, vol. 1, no.1, pp.57–78

Lamb, Geoff, *Peasant politics, Conflict and development in Muranga*, London, Julian Friedmann, 1974

Langdon, Steven W, 'The state of capitalism in Kenya' in *Review of African Political Economy*, 1977, no.8, pp.90–98,

——, Steven, W, (1981), 'Multinational corporations in the political economy of Kenya', New York, St Martins Press, 1981

Lappe, Frances Moore, Collins, Joseph & Kinley D, *Development Aid as Obstacle*, San Francisco, institute for Food & Development Policy, 1980

Latouche, Serge, 'Standard of Living' in Sachr, 1992

——, Serge, *In the wake of the Affluent Society an exploration of Post-development*, 1993

Law, Dennis L, *Mine-land rehabilitation*, s.l., Van Nostrand Reinhold, 1984

Lee, James A, *The environment, public health and human ecology considerations for economic development*, Baltimore, John Hopkins University Press, 1985

Lele, Uma, *The design of rural development, Lessons from Africa*, 3rd Printing, Baltimore John Hopkins University Press, 1979

Leo, Christopher, *Land and class in Kenya*, Toronto, Canada, University of Toronto Press, 1984

Leonard, David K, (eds), *Rural administration in Kenya, A critical Appraisal*, Nairobi East African Literature Bureau, 1973

Lewis W, A, *Allocating Foreign Aid to promote self-sustained economic growth in Society, for international Development, Motivation and Methods in Development and Foreign Aid*, Washington DC, SID 1964

——, W A, *The evolution of the International Economic Order*, Princeton University Press, 1987a

Leys, Colin, *Underdevelopment in Kenya, The political economy of neocolonialism 1964–1971'*, London, Heinemann, 1975

——, Colin, 'Capital accumulation, class formation and dependency The significance of the Kenyan case' in The Socialist register 1978, London, Merlin Press, 1978

Linear, Marcus, 'Zapping the third world, The disaster of development aid', London, Pluto Press, 1985

Lisk, Franklyn, '"Basic needs activities" and poverty alleviation in Kenya', Geneva, ILO, 1978

Livingstone, Ian, *Youth employment programme in Africa, Kenya*, Addis Ababa, ILO/JASPA, 1985

——, Ian, *Rural development, employment and incomes in Kenya*, Aldershot, Gower, 1986

Loup, Jacques, *Can the Third World Survive?*, Baltimore The John Hopkins University Press, 1984

Luke, Robert S, *The environmental practices of the UNDP and recommendations*, Washington, D, C, international institute for Environment and Development, Mimeo, 1980

Lundquist, Jan, Lohm, U and Falkenmark, M, *Strategies for river basin management. Environmental integration of land and water in a river basin,* Dordrecht, Reidel, 1984

MacCormack, Geoffrey, (1983), 'Problems in the description of African systems of landholding', in *Journal of legal pluralism and unofficial law,* 1983, vol. 12, no.7, pp.1–14, 19

MacWilliam, Scott, 'Rights and the politics of legality in Kenya', in *Manchester papers on development,* 1985, vol. 1, no.1, pp.40–90,

Makokha, Joseph, *The district focus conceptual and management problems,* Nairobi, Africa Press Research Bureau, 1985

Masakha, Fred *et al, Education sector review, Turkana Rural, Development Programme,* 1985, Nairobi Ministry of Planning and National Development MDC/NOPAD, Mimeo, 1985

Max-Neef, Manfred, *From the outside looking in, Experience in Barefoot Economics, Dag Hammarskjold Foundation,* Uppsala, University of Uppsala, 1982

——, Manfred, 'Development and Human needs' in *Ekin and Max Neef,* 1992

Max-Neef, M, Hopenhaya Martin *et al., Human Scale Development, Development Dialogue,* 1989, 1 (also Zed Books, London, 1993)

Max-Neef, M, (Channel 4 TV Programme – transcript), 1990, *Barefoot Economics, Small solutions to enormously large problems,* London

McHale, John and McHale M C, *Basic Human Needs. A framework for Action,* Rutgers Books, New Jersey, 1974

Mazingira institute,' Nairobi, Mazingira institute, 1985

Mbithi, Philip M, *Rural sociology and rural development. Its application in Kenya,* 1974

Nairobi, East African Literature Bureau, 19

Mbithi, Philip M, Barnes, Carolyn, *The spontaneous settlement problem in Kenya,* Nairobi, East African Literature Bureau, 1975

Mbithi Philip M, Ramusson, Rasmus, Self-reliance in Kenya, The case of Harambee, Uppsala, Scandinavian institute of African Studies, 1977

Mboya, Tom, 'Conflict and nationhood, The essentials of freedom in Africa', London, Africa Bureau, 1963

McCabe, Terrence J Hart, Thomas C and Ellis, J E *Road impact evaluation in northern Kenya, A case study in South Turkana, inal report*, s.l., s.n., 1983

McGranahan, D, Pizaro, Eduardo and Richard, Claude, *Measurement and analysis of socio-economic development, An inquiry into international indicators of development and quantitative interrelations of economic and social components of development*, Geneva, UN Research institute for Social Development, 1985

McNicoll, Geoffrey, *Consequences of rapid population growth an overview and assessment'*, New York Population Council, 1984

MDC/NORAD, *Minor urban water supply programme, Kenya, Report of NORAD's Review mission*, Oslo, MDC/NORAD, 1985

MDC/NORAD, *Programme of action on women-related aid to Kenya*, Draft, Nairobi, MDC/NORAD, 1986

Meacher, Michael, 'How to relieve Third World Debt', *The Guardian*, 28 February 1994

Megaham, W F, *Reducing erosional impacts of roads – FAO Conservation guidelines for watershed management*, Rome FAC, 1986

Meilink, Henk A, *The effects of import-substitution the case of Kenya's manufacturing sector*, University of Nairobi, IDS, Nairobi, 1982

Mendis, Padmani, *The Association for the Physically Disabled of Kenya, A project review*, Nairobi, WHO, 1985

Michaelson, Karen L, (ed,) *And the poor get children, Radical perspectives on population dynamics*, New York, Monthly Review Press, 1981

Michelsen institute, Dept. of Social Science & Dev, Kenya Country Study and Norwegian Dev, Aid Review, Oslo, The Chr, Michelsen institute, 1987

Mies, Maria, *Patriarchy and Accumulation on a World Scale – Women and the international Division of Labour*, Zed Books, London, 1986

Migot-Adholla, S E, *Significance of camel pastoralism in Kenya*, University of Nairobi, IDS, Nairobi, 1985

Migot-Adholla, S E, Mkangi, Katama G C, *et al, Study of tourism in Kenya. With emphasis on the attitudes of residents of the Kenya Coast*, University of Nairobi, IDS, Nairobi, 1982

Migot-Adholla, S E, & Nkinyangi, John A (ed.), *Food and nutrition planning in Kenya*, University of Nairobi IDS, Nairobi, 1981

Migot-Adholla, S E & Ogwanda, Okinda, *The evolution of higher education in Kenya, Eastern and Southern African Universities Research Project*, Lusaka, University of Zambia, Mimeo, 1984

Mkangi, George, *The social cost of small families and land reform, A case study of the Wataita of Kenya*, Oxford, Pergamon Press, 1983

Morley, D, Rhode, I, and Wimmiam, G, *Practising Health for All*, Oxford University Press, 1983

Morss, Elliot R, 'Institutional destruction resulting from donor and project proliferation in sub-Saharan countries', in *World Development*, 1984, vol. 12, no.4, pp.465–470, 1984

Mosley, Paul, 'Agricultural performance in Kenya since 1970. Has the World Bank got it right'? in *Development and Change*, 1986, vol. 17, no.3, pp.513–530, 1986

Mosley, W H, Werner, Linda H and Becker, Stanley, *The dynamics of birth spacing and marital fertility in Kenya*, Nairobi Population studies and Research institute, Mimeo, 1981

Mott, Frank L, *Infant mortality in Kenya: evidence from the Kenya Fertility Survey*' Nairobi, PSRI, 1979

Mueller, Susanne D, 'Government and opposition in Kenya, 1966–69 in *Journal of Modern African studies*, 1984, vol. 22, no.3

Muga, Erasto (ed.), *Studies in prostitution (East, West, and South Africa, Zaire and Nevada)*, Nairobi, Kenya Literature Bureau, 1980

Munn, R E, *Environmental impact assessment, Principles and Procedures*, New York, Wiley, 1979

Muthalik-Desai, Priya (ed.), *Economic and political development of Kenya*, Bombay, Himalaya Publishing House, 1979

Mutiso, G C, *Kenya Politics, Policy and Society*, Nairobi, East African Literature Bureau, 1975

Mwangi, W M, *Low income food systems and food safety in Kenya, A case study of Kangemi pen-urban area*, Nairobi, IDS, 1985

Narman, Anders, 'Regional distribution of educational facilities in Kenya, with special reference to secondary school teachers' in *Choros*, no.2, 1984

National Council of Churches of Kenya, *Who controls industry in Kenya? Report of a working party*, Nairobi, East African Publishing House, 1968

Ndegwa, Philip, *The Common Market and development in East Africa*, Nairobi, East African Publishing House, 1965

——, Philip, *Africa's development crisis and related international issues*, Nairobi, Heinemann, 1985

Ndumbu, Abel, 'Seven years of Nyayo, (Moi) in *Africa Report*, 1985, vol. 30, no.6, pp.51–53

Nellis, John R, *The ethnic composition of leading Kenyan government positions*, Uppsala, Scandinavian institute of African Studies, 1976

Nelson, Harold D, (ed,), *Kenya A country study*, 3rd ed., Washington D C, American university, 1983

Ng'ethe, Njuguna, *Income distribution in Kenya. The politics of mystification and possessive individualism*, Nairobi, IDS, Mimeo, 1976

——, Njuguna, Chege, Fred (eds.), *Arid and semi-arid lands pre-investment study Kitui, Embu and Meru*, Nairobi, IDS, Mimeo, 1982

Nieuwenhuijze, Van, C A O, 'Development Begins at Home', Pergamon, Oxford, 1982

——, Van, C A O, Is there non-economic development', In Hilhorst and Klatter, 1985

Njoka, B K, 'Modelling for population and sustainable development in Kenya', in *Modelling for population and sustainable development*, Ed. by A J Gilbert and L C Braat, published by Routledge and The international Social Science Council with the cooperation of UNESCO and The Institute for Environmental Studies, Free University, Amsterdam, 19

Njonjo, Apollo, *Summary of the three reports on Kenyan women's groups*, Nairobi, Ministry of Culture and Social Services, Mimeo, 1986

Njoroge, Lawrence M, *Development administration in the development of Kenyan nationhood*, Montreal, Canada McGill University, 1985

Nkinyangi, John A, *Society and the educational system Public policy and school failure in Kenya*, Nairobi, IDS, 1980

Nkinyangi, John A, and Mbindyo, Joseph, 'The conditions of disabled persons in Kenya, Result of a national survey', Nairobi, IDS, Mimeo, 1982

NORAD, *Mbere Special Rural Development Programme, A report from the joint Kenyan/Norwegian fact finding-mission, Draft*, Oslo, NORAD, 1978

NORAD – Business and Economic Research Co, Ltd, *Kenya – Socio-economic evaluation of the minor urbanwater supply programme*, Oslo, NORAD, 2 vols, (Evaluation report 2, 82) Mimeo, 1982

Nordberg, Erik, *Health, health care and family planning in Kenya. A review indicating problems and needs.* Stockholm, Karolinska institutet, 1986

Northcott, C H, *African labour efficiency survey, Colonial Office*, London, HMSO, 1949

Nyerere, Julius, 'On rural development', Ideas and Actions, 128, 1979

——, Julius, 'No to IMF meddling', Development Dialogue, 2, 1980

——, Julius, 'Who shall inherit the Earth?' *The Guardian*, 16 November, 1992

Nyongo, Anyang, 'The decline of democracy and the rise of authoritarian and factionalist politics in Kenya' in *Horn of Africa*, 1984, vol. 6, no.3, pp.25–34, 1984

Nyoni, Sithembiso, 'Indigenous NGOs: Liberation, Self-reliance and Development', World Development, 15 Supplement, 1987

Nzomo, N D 'entrepreneurship development policy in national development planning, The Kenya case' in *Eastern Africa Economic Review*, 1986, vol. 2, no.1, pp.99–105

O'Keefe, Phil, Raskin, Paul and Bernow, Steve (eds.), *Energy and development in Kenya, Opportunities and constraints*, Uppsalla, Scandinavian institute of African Studies, 1984

Obudho, R, A, (ed.) *Urbanisation and development planning in Kenya*, Nairobi Kenya Literature Bureau, 1981

——, R, A, (1983), *Urbanisation in Kenya. A bottom-up approach to development planning*, Lanham, MD, USA University Press of America, 1983

Ochieng, William R, *A history of Kenya*, Nairobi, Macmillan, 1985

Odingo, Richard S., *The Kenya highlands, Land use and agricultural development*, Nairobi, East African Publishing House, 1971

——, Richard S, *A preliminary report on a trans-disciplinary ecological study on the Kamburu/Gaturu hydro-electrical dam area on the Tana River-Basin in Eastern Kenya*, Nairobi s. n. 2 vols, 1975

OECD, *Methods and procedures in aid evaluation, A compendium of donor practice and experience*, Paris, OECD, 1986

Ogendo, R B, *Industrial geography of Kenya*, Nairobi, East African Publishing House, 1972

Ogendo, Bethwell, A. Ed., *Politics and nationalism in colonial Kenya*, Nairobi, East African publishing House, 1972

Ogot, Bethwell A, (ed), *Politics and Nationalism in Colonial Kenya*, Nairobi, East African Publishing House, 1972

Okot P'Bitek, *Songs of Prisoner*, East African Literature Bureau, 1968

Ominde, Simeon Hongo, *The population of Kenya, Tanzania and Uganda*, Nairobi, Heinemann, 1975

——, Simeon Hongo, *The impact of population growth on social and econimic development*, Nairobi, PSRI, Mimeo, 1983

——, Simeon Hongo, *Population and Development*, Nairobi, Heinemann, 1984

Orendain, Leo E and Barrow, E G C, *Soil conservation along Lodwar-Kakuma Road Project*, Nairobi, University of Nairobi, Mimeo, 1986

Organisation for European Economic Co-operation and Development (OECD), 'A decade of cooperation, Achievements and perspectives 9th Report of the OECD, Paris, 1986

Orvis, Stephen, *Men and women in a household economy evidence from Kisii*, University of Nairobi, IDS, Mimeo, 1985

Oucho, John O, *Population and development the Kenya case*, University of Nairobi, PSRI, Mimeo, 1985

Ouedraogo, Beernard, Ledea, 'Developer sans abimer' ('Development without destruction'), IFDA Dossier 41, 1984

Ouma, Sylvester J, *A history of the cooperative movement in Kenya*, Nairobi, Bookwise, 1980

Overseas Development institute, *Turkana Rehabilitation Project, Interim report'*, London, ODI, 1985

Owino Joseph D, 'Sectoral Study Exploring the Carrying Capacity Assessment, Population growth and self-sufficiency in Kenya using ECCO' in *Modelling for Population and Sustainable Development*, Ed, by A J Gilbert and L C Braat, Routledge and the international Social Science Council, UNESCO, Institute of Environmental Studies, Free University, Amsterdam, 1991.

Oyugi, Walter Ouma, 'Local government in Kenya, A case of institutional decline, Mawhood, Philip (ed.), *Local government in the Third World*, Chichester, John Wiley, pp.107–140, 1983

Pala, A, Awori, T, Krystall, A, (eds.) *The participation of women in Kenya society*, Nairobi, Kenya Literature Bureau, 1983

Palmer, Ingrid, *The impact of male out-migration on women in farming*, West Hartford, Mumarian Press, 1983

Panos institute, *Development Aid and the Third World*, London, Panos institute, 1986

Parsely, L L, *Thurci-Nkubu road evaluation study – study of the traffic flows – transport and road research*, Berkshire, UK, Crawthorne Laboratory, 1986

Patel, I G, 'Aid relationship for the seventies' in Ward, B, Danjou L, and Runnals, J D (eds). The Widening Gap, New York, Columbia University Press, 1965

——, 'Economic Development in Asian Perspective', Tokyo Kinomumiya Bookstore, 1998

Please, Stanley, *From project cycle to policy*, Paper presented to the international Symposium on Effectiveness of Rural Development Cooperation, Amsterdam, Amsterdam, Royal Tropical institute, 1985

Pradervand, Pierre, *Africa on the march, translated as 'Listening to Africa, Developing from – Grassroots*, Praeger, New York, 1989

Pratt, D J and Gwyne, M, D, (eds.), 'Range Land Management and Ecology of East Africa, London, Hodder and Stoughton, 1977

Price Waterhouse Associates, *Executive salary survey 1985/86*, Nairobi, Price Waterhouse, Mimeo, 1986

Rahman, Md, Anisur, *Glimpses of the other Africa*, ILO/WEP, Geneva, 1980

——, Md, Anisur, *People's Self-development: Perspectives on Participatory Action Research*, Zed Books, London, 1993

Raikes, Philip L, *Livestock development and policy in East Africa*, Uppsala, Scandinavian institute of African Studies, 1981

Randall, Vicky, Theobald Robin, *Political change and underdevelopment, A critical introduction to Third World politics*, London, Macmillan, 1985

Ray, Anandrap, *Cost-benefit analysis, Issues and methodologies*, Baltimore, John Hopkins University Press, 1925

Rempel, Henry and House, William J, *The Kenya employment problem, Analysis of the modern sector labour market*, Nairobi, Oxford University Press, 1978

Rempel, Henry, Lobdell, Richard A, 'A model of labour allocation and decision-making in peasant-type households', University of Nairobi, IDS, Nairobi, Mimeo, 1985

Richard, Pablo, 'La theologic de la liberation pour la decennie, ('Liberation theology for the decade of the nineties'). Culture and development, 5, 13/14, Brussels, 1993

Robson, Peter, *Economic integration in Africa*, London, Allen & Unwin, 1968

Rondinelli, Dennis A and Nellis, John, 'Assessing decentralisation policies in developing countries, The case for cautious optimism' in *Developing policy review*, 1986 vol. 4, no.l, pp.3–23

Rosberg, Carl G, jr and Nottingham, John, *The myth of 'Mau Mau', Nationalism in Kenya,* New York, Meridian, 1970

Rosentein-Rodan, P N, 'Notes on theory of the "big push"', Ellis H S (ed.), Economic Development of Latin America, London, MacMillan (160), 1961

Ruster, Bernd and Simma, Brunno, *International protection of environment and related documents'*, Dobbs Ferry, NY, Oceana Publications, 1975

Sachs, Wolfgang, 'The Economist's Prejudice', *Culture and Development*, 2, 5, 1991

——, Wolfgang, 'Development: a guide through the ruins', *The New Interationalist*, 232, June 1992a

——, Wolfgang, 'Where all the World's a Stooge', *The Guardian* (ed), 29 May 1992c

Sandbrook, Richard, *Proletarians and African capitalism. The Kenya case 1960–72*, Cambridge, Cambridge University Press, 1975

Sandbrook, Richard and Cohen, Robin (eds), *The development of an African Working Class, Studies in class formation and action*, London Longman, 1975

Sandford, Stephen, 'Pastoralism under pressure in *ODI review*, no.2, pp.45–68, 1976

——, Stephen, *Management of Pastoral development in the Third World*, Chichester, John Wiley, 1983

Schluter, Michael, *Constraints on Kenya's food and beverage exports*, 19 Nairobi, IDS, Occassional papers, no.43, 1984

Schwab, G, D, *et al.*, *Soil and water conservation engineering*, New York Wiley, 1981

Schwartz, S, *et al*, 'Nomadic past oralism in Kenya – Still a viable production system?' in Agriculture, vol. 24 NO.1, pp.5–21, 19

Scott, James C, *Comparative political corruption*, Englewood Cliffs, USA, Prentice-Hall, 1972

Seideberg, Dana April, *Uhuru and the Kenya indians. The role of a minority in Kenya politics, 1939–1963*, Nairobi, Heritage Bookshop, 1983

Sen, Gita and Crown, Caren, 'Development, Crisis and Alternative Vision', *Third World Perspectives*, Earthscan, London 1988

Senga, W M, House, W J and Manundu, M, 'Assessment of commercial energy supply and demand in Kenya, University of Nairobi, IDS, Nairobi, 1980

Sharpley, Jenifer, *Economic policies and agricultural perfomance. The case of Kenya*, Paris, OECD Development Centre, 1986a

——, Jenifer, *Net Foreign exchange earnings of Kenya's Agricultural sector*, Nairobi, MALD, Mimeo, 1986b

Shiva, Vandana, 'Staying Alive: women, Ecology and Development', Zed Books, London, 1989a

——, Vandana, 'Development, the new colonialism', Development Journal of the Society for International Development, Rome, 1.1 1989b

——, Vandana, 'Science, Nature and Wholeness', Phil shepherd Studios, Schumacher Tapes (transcript), 1992

SIDA, *Swedish support to the agricultural sector of Kenya. Report of Swedish agricultural and livestock mission to Kenya, 15 November–6 December 1982*, Stockholm, SIDA, Mimeo, 1982

Sifuna, Daniel N, 'The vocational curriculum in primary education in Kenya, An evaluation' in *Prospects*, vol. 16, no.1, pp.125–134, 1986

Sindiga, Isaac, 'Land and population problems in Kajiado and Narok, Kenya' in *African Studies Review*, 1984, vol. 27, no.1

Singer, H W, 'External Aid: for plans or projects', Economic Tour, 75, 539–45 (318), 1965

Singh, Makhan, *History of Kenya's trade union movement to 1952*, Nairobi, East African Publishing House, 1986

——, Makhan, *Kenya trade unions, 1952–1956*, Nairobi, Uzima Press, 1980

Sizoo, Edith, *Wearing masks in development: Culture and Development*, Cameroon, 8/9, 1992

Skalnes, Tor and Egeland, Jan (eds), *Human rights in developing countries*, Oslo, Norwegian University Press, 1986

Spencer, John, *KAU – The Kenya African Union*, London, Routledge & Kegan Paul, 1985

Staudt, Kathleen, *Agricultural policy implementation, A case study from Western Kenya*, West Hartford, Kumarian Press, 1985

Stichter, Sharon, *Migrant labour in Kenya, Capitalism and African Response, 1985–1975*, London Longman, 1982

Strayer, Robert W, *Kenya Focus on nationalism*, New Jersey, USA, Prentice Hall, 1975

Sundrum, R M, *Development Economics – A framework for Analysis and Policy*, Chister, Wiley, 1983

Swainson, Nicola, 'The rise of a national bourgeoisie in Kenya', in *Review of African Political Economy*, 1977, no.8, pp.39–55

——, Nicola, *The development of corporate capitalism in Kenya, 1918–1977*, London, Heinemann, 1980

Swartz, D R, *et. al.*, 'Cost-benefit analysis and environmental regulations. Politics, ethics and methods', Washington, DC Conservation Foundation, 1982

Talle, Aud, 'Kvinner og utvikling', Melhuus, M, Klausen, A M, (eds) Sosialantropologens, rolle I bistandsarabeid, Oslo, University of Oslo, pp 45—62

Tamarkin, M, 'The roots of political stability in Kenya' in *African Affairs*, 1978, vol. 77, no.308, pp.297–320

TARDA ADEC, *Tana and Athi Rivers Development Authority*, African Development and Economic Consultant, Kiambere hydroelectric power project pre-construction environmental impact study, vol. 1, Nairobi, TARDA ADEC, 1983

TARDA/Atkins, *Tana and Athi Rivers Development Authority, land and water management and water conservation programme*, Masinga catchment area, vol. 1, Nairobi Atkins, 1984

Tangri, Roger, *Politics in sub-Saharan Africa*, London, James Currey, 1985

Thiongo Ngugi Wa, Women in Cultural works: the fate of Kamariithu People's Theatre in Kenyua, Development Dialogue 1–2, 1982

——, Ngugi Wa, *Decolonising the Mind*, Heinemann, London, 1986

Thomson, J E, 'Ethics of Being a Female Patient and a Female, Care Provider in a Male-Dominated Health-Illness System, in *Issues in Health Care of Women*, 1980, 2, 25–50

——, J E, 'Primary health care nursing for women' in, *Nurses, Nurse Practitioners The Evolution of Primary*, *Care* (eds) Mersey & McGivern (Boston Little, Brown, 1986) pp.173–200

Thornburry W D, *Principles of Geomorphology*, New York, Wiley, 1964

Throup, W D, 'The origins of Mau Mau' in *African Affairs*, 1985, vol. 84 no.33G, pp.399–433, 19

Tibaijuka, Anna Kajumulo, *Kenya: A study of the agricultural sector*, Uppsala Swedish University of Agricultural Science, 1981

Tostensen, Arne, *Between shamba and factory, Preliminary results from a study of oscillatory labour migration in Kenya*, University of Nairobi, IDS, Nairobi, 1986

Traore, Mamadou Balla, 'Le Developpement mirroir et ecran', ('Development mirror and screen'), IFDA Dossier, 80, 1990

UNEP, 'The role of cost-evaluation in environmental quality management', Nairobi, UNEP, 1978

UNEP, *Declaration of environmental policies and procedures relating to Economic Development*, Paris, UNEP, 1979

UNEP, *Environmental decision-making*, Nairobi UNEP, 1984

UNEP, *Development Aid starts thinking environment*, Nairobi, UNEP, 1986

UNEP and CIDIE, *Seventh CIDIE Meeting*, Nairobi UNEP, 1986

UNESCO, Terminology of Adult Education, Paris, 1979, Pour un langage non-sexiste/Guidelines on non-sexist language (bilingual), 1990a,

UNESCO, Office of Conference, Documents and Language (COL), PARIS, The state of the World's Children, Oxford University Press, Oxford 1990b

UNESCO and UNICEF, Basic education for nomads, Nairobi UNICEF, 1978

UNICEF, The State of The World's Children, Oxford University Press, Oxford, 1990

UNICEF/Kenya Medical Research Institute, The Spread of Aids and Life Expectancy, UNICEF/KMRI, memo 1997

United Nations, *World population prospects – estimates and projections as assessed in 1982*, New York, Department of international Economic and Social Affairs' – (Population Studies no.86), 1985

United Nations, *World population prospects – estimates and projections as assessed in 1984*, New York Department of international Economic and Social Affairs, (Population Studies no.87), 1986

United Nations, 'The Nairobi Forward Looking Strategies for the Advancement of Women', UN, Department of Public Information, New York, 1985

UN, International Development, *Critical Policy Issues, Study of the Task Force on Long-term Development Objectives*, UN, New York, 1981

UN, international Development, *UN Report of the international Conference on Population*, UN, New York, 1984

US Congress, 'Preparation of environment impact statement guidelines' in *Council on Environmental Quality US Federal Register*, 1970, vol. 38, no.147, Part III, pp.20550–20555

USDA, 'Forest Service standard specifications for construction of roads and bridges', Washington DC, USDA, 1979

US Department of Agriculture, *Report and recommendations on Organic Farming*, USDA, Washington, DC, 1980

Van Zwanenbedrg, R M A, *The agricultural history of Kenya*, Nairobi, East African Publishing House, 1972

——, R M A, *Colonial capitalism and labour in Kenya 1919–1939*, Nairobi, East African Literature Bureau, 1975

——, R M A and King, Anne, *An economic history of Kenya and Uganda 1800–1970*, Nairobi, East African Literature Bureau, 1975

Vandemoortele, Jan, *Income distribution and poverty in Kenya. A statistical analysis*, University of Nairobi, IDS, Mimeo, 1982

——, Jan, *The wage policy in Kenya past, present and future*, Nairobi, IDS, Mimeo, 1984a

——, Jan, *Wages and wage policies in Kenya between 1964 and 1983*, Nairobi, Kenyan Economic Association, Mimeo, 1984b

——, Jan, *Employment patterns and prospects in Kenya*, Addis Ababa, ILO/JASPA, Mimeo, 1986

Wa-Githumo, Mwangi, *Land and nationalism. The impact of land expropriation and land grievances upon the rise and development of nationalist movements in Kenya, 1885–1939*, Washington, DC, University Press of America, 1981

Wallis, M A H 'Bureaucrats, politicians, and rural communities in Kenya', *Manchester Papers on Development*, 1982, no.6, pp.1–86

Wasserman, Gary, *Politics of decolonisation, Kenyan Europeans and the land issue 1960–1965*, Cambridge, Cambridge University Press, 1976

Watson, CEP, (ed.), 'Evaluation report on the Lake Turkana Fisheries Development Project', Oslo MDC/NORAD, (Evaluation report, 5–85), 1985

Weir, D, and Shapiro, M, *Pesticide and People in a Hungry World*, Institute for Food and Development Policy, San Francisco, 1981

Wenner, C G, *An outline of soil conservation in the Kenya Ministry of Agriculture*, Nairobi, MALD,

Were, Gideon S, (ed.)

'The underprivileged in society, Studies on Kenya', Nairobi, University of Nairobi, 19

Werner, Paul, Deak, Edward J, *Environmental factors in transportation planning*, Lexington, Mass, Heath, 1974

White, J, 'Pledge to Development', London Overseas Development Institute, 1967

Wiggins, Steve, 'The planning and management of integrated rural development in drylands, Early lessons from Kenya's arid and semi-arid lands programmes, in *Public Administration and Development*, 1985, Vol, 5, no.2, pp.91–108, 19

Wilkins, R, and Adams, O, *Healthfulness of Life*, Institute for Research on Public Policy, Montreal, 1983

Wischmer, W H, and Smith, D W, *Predicting rain-fall erosion losses from crop-lands-East of the Rocky Mountains*, Hand-book 282, ARS-USDA, Washington DC, USA, 1965

World Commission on Environment and Development, *Our Common Future*, Oxford University Press, 1987

World Health Organisation, *Health Promotion: a discussion document on the concept and principles*, WHO Regional Office for Europe, Copenhagen, 1984b

Zaoual, Hassan, *The Methodology of the symbolic sites*, Culture and Development, 10/11, 1992

——, Hassan, 'The economy and the symbolic sites of Africa', *Inter-culture*, 1994, 27, vol. 1, Montreal (Canada)

Zolota, X, *Economic Growth and Declining Social Welfare*, Athens, 1980